ISLAM & MUSLIMS IN THE POST-9/11 AMERICA

BY ABDUS SATTAR GHAZALI

Also by Abdus Sattar Ghazali

Islam & the West in the Post-Cold War Era (1999)
(Clash of Civilization or Clash of Interests)

Islam & Modernism (2000)

Hegemony of the Ruling Elite in Pakistan (2000)

Islamic Pakistan: Illusions & Reality (1996)
A political history of Pakistan

Dedicated to my grand children

Sara, Sabah, Imaad, Farhad, Humza, Danial & Hira

About the author

The author is a professional journalist, with Master's degree in Political Science from the Punjab University. Started his journalistic career working in local newspapers in Peshawar, Pakistan. Served as a News Editor in the Daily News, Kuwait from 1969 to 1976.

Joined the English News Department of Kuwait Television as a News Editor in December 1976. Retired in 1998 as the Editor-in-Chief of the Kuwait Television English News. Also worked as the correspondent in Kuwait of the Associated Press of Pakistan (APP) and the Daily Dawn, Karachi, a leading Pakistani newspaper. Also worked briefly as editorial writer in the Daily Dawn, Karachi.

He is the author of Islamic Pakistan: Illusions & Reality (1996), Islam & the West in the Post Cold War Era (1999), Islam and Modernism (2000) and Hegemony of the Ruling Elite in Pakistan (2000).

Contributed a chapter on Civil Rights to "Blessings of Liberty: Individual Rights," published in April 2012 by Perfect Learning, Clive, Iowa. The book is for the K-12 educational market. Contributed to "At Issue: How Does Religion Influence Politics?" published in 2010 by Gale Cengage Learning, Farmington Hill, Michigan.

Contributed a chapter - Why the US image declined in the Muslim World? - to "US Foreign Policy Towards the Muslim World - Focus on Post 9/11 Period," published in 2010 by University Press of America, Inc., Lanham, Maryland.

He has written extensively on the Middle East, South Asia and American Muslims which is published widely by the media in the Middle East, India, Pakistan and the United States.

Currently working as free lance journalist, the Executive Editor of American Muslim Perspective (www.amperspective.com) and the Chief Editor of the Journal of America (www.journalofamerica.net)

Preface

The book deals with the post 9/11 challenges and dilemmas faced by the seven-million strong American Muslim community in the aftermath of the 9/11 ghastly tragedy. It is divided into nine chapters namely: (1) The Civil Rights (2) Islamophobia (3) Campaign against Muslim charities (4) Muslims face inquisition (5) Institutionalized Profiling (6) Stereotyping – Movies, media (7) Hate crimes, discrimination & harassment (8) Attempt to silence genuine Muslim voices and (9) American Muslim response to the Post-9/11 challenges.

The book also includes six appendices: (1) Who are American Muslims? Demographic Data; (2) Muslim Immigration to US; (3) Development of Muslim organizations; (4) American Muslims in Politics; and (5) A decade of civil liberties' erosion.

It was almost four years when the first internet edition of this book was published in March 2008. Since then a lot of major developments have taken place that affected the American Muslim Community. A number of chapters were revised to include the latest developments while new sections were added not to disturb the flow of narration.

The appendix on Muslims in Politics has been expanded to include 2008 and 2010 elections. There is particular emphasize on the bitter campaign against Barrack Obama which directly affected the American Muslim community.

A new appendix has been added about the mis-information agenda of the Gallup Poll and PEW Institute about the demographics of the Muslims in America.

In the last ten years we have seen a steady erosion of the fundamental rights and civil liberties, all in the name of national security. A new appendix is added titled: 2001-2011: A decade of civil liberties' erosion in America.

Three sections of American Muslim Perspective (AMP) reports have been added to provide in-depth information about surveillance of the Muslim community, Islamophobia and revamping of Islam in the image of neocons.

Preface [ii]

This study concentrates on the impact of 9/11 on the American Muslims and how they are responding to the post-9/11 situation when their civil rights have been abridged, their faith is under constant attack and they are virtually treated as second class citizens. It will not be too much to say that after the Japanese attack on the Pearl Harbor, more than 110,000 Japanese Americans on the West Coast were imprisoned in 10 relocation camps in the United States. But after 9/11, the whole country is converted into a virtual detention camp for the Muslims in America by abridging their civil rights.

I hope that the book would help in giving a clear picture about the predicament and quandary of the American Muslim community in the post-9/11 era.

Abdus Sattar Ghazali

Fremont, CA

June, 2012

Islam & Muslims in the Post-9/11 America

Table of Contents

Preface .... Page i

Table of contents .... Page iii

I. Introduction .... Page 1

II. The post 9/11 challenges

Chapter 1: The Civil Rights .... Page 19

Defending civil rights became the single most important challenge before the American Muslims in the post-9/11 America. Arabs and Muslims were the prime targets of the post 9/11 reconfiguration of American laws, policies, and priorities.

Chapter 2: Islamophobia .... Page 33

Campaign against Islam and Muslims - The Christian Right - Venom from the radio talk show hosts - Desecration of the Quran - Controversial cartoons – Impact of Islamophobia - Permission to build new mosques & expansion of mosques denied

Chapter 3: Campaign against Muslim charities .... Page 69

Major charities shut down - Senate Finance Committee's McCarthyite witch hunt of Muslim charities - Holy Land Foundation's prosecution reveals questionable evidence - Government is trying to keep proceedings in the dark - Anti-Terrorist Financing Guidelines revised - No guarantee that a charity is clear even if it follows the Anti-Terrorist Financing Guidelines - Impact on donation collection - Muslim Groups Form National Council of American Muslim Non-Profits

Table of Contents [iv]

Chapter 4: Muslims face inquisition .... Page 111

No freedom of religion – surveillance of mosques – SANE project to spy on mosques - radiation tests of mosques – Muslims forced to spy on fellow Muslims - Muslims repeatedly compelled to condemn terrorism.

Chapter 5: Institutionalized Profiling .... Page 121

Flying While Muslim or Arab - Driving While Arab or Muslim - Interviews of 5,000 Muslims and Arabs - Detentions and Deportations - INS Registration Program

Chapter 6: Stereotyping – Movies, media .... Page 141

Dehumanize a group first before attacking it - Muslims and Arabs have long been negatively portrayed in America - Reel Bad Arabs by Jack Shaheen – Few takes on stereotyping in movies: Children's movies – Stereotyping in News Media - Cartoons, another media of stereotype

Chapter 7: Hate crimes, discrimination & harassment ... Page 155

Hate crimes - Attack on Hijab wearing women – Official Discrimination - Delay in citizenship - Harassment at workplaces - Bank accounts closed - Discrimination against non-citizen Muslims

Chapter 8: Attempt to silence genuine Muslim voices ... Page 175

- Campaign against the major American Muslim civil advocacy organizations such as CAIR and ISNA.
- Alternate compliant groups encouraged: Progressive Muslim Union of North America - American Muslim Group on Policy Planning - Free Muslim Coalition Against Terrorism
 Government encourages so-called moderate Muslims as an alternative voice for American Muslims - Kamal Kawish founder of a newly formed group represents American Muslims at the at the Organization for Security and Cooperation Conference on Anti-Semitism and on Other Forms of Intolerance held in Cordoba, Spain.
- Amid protests by 60 civil advocacy groups and individuals, Zuhdi Jasser, founder of virtually one-man Muslim group is appointed as Commissioner to the US Commission on International Religious Freedom.

Islam & Muslims in the Post 9/11 America

Table of Contents [v]

Chapter 9: Response to the Post-9/11 challenges .... Page 193

Political activism – Muslims and Arabs are asserting their rights; Campaign for Islamic holidays; Activism during the Israeli rampage on Lebanon in July/August 2006.

Participation in the national political process - Elections 2004/2006/2008/2010.

Outreach to other communities - Interfaith outreach – Christian-Muslim dialogue – Jewish-Muslim outreach suffers a setback during the Lebanese crisis.

III. Appendices

1. Who are American Muslims? Demographic Data ...... Page 217

2. Muslim Immigration to US .... Page 221

3. Development of Muslim organizations .... Page 225

4. Hidden agenda of Gallup Poll & PEW Institute .... Page 229

5. American Muslims in Politics .... Page 235

6. Erosion of civil liberties in the Post-9/11 America .... Page 309

© All Rights Reserved

Printed in the USA

Cover design by Talat Mahmood Sheikh

ISBN-13: 978-0615632629

ISBN-10: 0615632629

No part of this book may be reproduced or transmitted in any form or by any means, electronic or mechanical, including photocopying, recording, or by any information storage and retrieval system without the written permission of the author, except where permitted by law.

Islam & Muslims in the Post-9/11 America

A source book

Introduction

More than a decade after 9/11, consequences of this ghastly terrorist attacks continue to unfold on the seven million-strong Muslims in America who became victims of guilt by association. In the Post-9/11 America they were facing a new era where they were not only accountable for their actions but for those who hold false banner in their name. Their civil rights were abridged. Their faith was constantly under attack.

In the pre-9/11 America, Muslims, particularly the new immigrants, were busy in building institutions and enjoyed equal civil rights with the fellow Americans. Barring few exceptions, they were treated fairly by the establishment. Everybody was treated equal before the law. They were elated and optimistic because many of them were deprived the due process and civil liberties in their native countries.

Massive immigration of Muslims from the 1960s had swelled the population of Muslims in America to about seven million now.

Like all minorities, the Muslims were conscious that they have to teach their children in order to preserve their religious tradition. Therefore the newly arrived Muslims concentrated their energies on institution building and took little or no part in the national political process. Even some of them actively opposed participation in the political process. American Muslims, while concentrating all their energies on institution building, are seen active politically in late 1980s.

Introduction [2]

Election year 1998 saw the emergence of various Muslim political groups foremost among them was the American Muslim Political Coordination Committee (AMPCC) which formally endorsed George Bush for Presidency in November 2000 elections. Muslims voted virtually en block for George Bush in 2000 elections. Muslims across their political and denominational spectrum were convinced for the first time that it is within their reach to enter into the American political process and stand on an equal par with other American lawmakers and legislators to shape the political future of the United States.

All this changed on Sept. 11, 2001 with dramatic consequences of the terrorist attacks on the seven-million strong American Muslim community. The American Muslims, who were on their way to what seemed to be a successful integration into the American political process, all of a sudden became suspect. The community no longer dreams of new victories as defending and preserving the existing achievements and assets such as the nearly 2000 mosques, Islamic centers, Islamic schools and charities became an uphill task. The Muslim community not only lost developmental momentum but also its hard earned good will had dissipated. Now it faced hostility and prejudice as never before. The two sources of Muslims' growth in US - immigration and conversion – were arrested. Administration's crusade had put an effective stop to the flow of Muslims into the United States. The strong association between Islam and extremist political violence portrayed in the print and electronic media and some political leaders as well as the Christian right caused unimaginable harm to the image of Islam in America.

Civil liberties curtailed

Defending civil rights became the single most important challenge before the American Muslims in the post-9/11 America. Arabs and Muslims were the prime targets of the post 9/11 reconfiguration of American laws, policies, and priorities. Their constitutional rights to free exercise of religion and assembly, due process and security from unreasonable searches and seizures had been violated. The erosion of civil rights came in the form of various programs and legislations such as the USA Patriot Act, which effectively nullifies Amendments 4, 5, 6, and 8 directly and indirectly amendments 1 and 9 and the INS Special Registration [1] which targeted men from Muslim countries. The fallout impacted the daily life of Muslims at schools, in the workplace, in general public encounters and mistreatment at the hand of federal officials. Many Muslim homes and businesses were raided while profiling-based interrogations and searches became a norm.

Racial profiling by US law enforcement agencies has increased since 9/11 and now affects one in nine Americans, according to an Amnesty International USA (AI-USA) report. State and federal agencies, under the guise of fighting terrorism, have expanded the use of this degrading, discriminatory and dangerous practice. [2]

A report released by the California Senate Office of Research in May 2004 concluded that Arab Americans and the Muslim minority have taken the brunt of the Patriot Act and other federal powers applied in the aftermath of the terrorist attacks. The report – entitled: Patriot Act, Other Post-9/11 Enforcement Powers and The Impact on California's Muslim Communities - said that Muslim communities in California found troubling, if not alarming, was the FBI headquarters directive of February 3, 2003, ordering each of the bureau's 56 regional field offices to base their terrorist investigations on demographic data of Muslim communities. Included in the data for field agents to ascertain were the number of mosques that the FBI could identify in a given area. On Sept. 22, 2004, California Governor Arnold Schwarzenegger signed a bill into law that enhances protections for the faith community by explicitly adding "mosque" to the list of religious institutions covered by California's laws protecting religious institutions.

Immigration laws were being used against Muslims as an anti-terrorism tool. Authorities enforced minor violations by Muslims and Arabs, while ignoring millions of other immigrants who flout the same laws. "The approach is basically to target the Muslim and Arab community with a kind of zero-tolerance immigration policy. No other community in the U.S. is treated to zero-tolerance enforcement," according to David Cole, a Georgetown University law professor. In a high profile terrorist related case, two Imams and son of one of the Imams were arrested in June 2005 in Lodi, CA, but no terrorism charges were filed against them. They were deported to Pakistan for violation of immigration law. [3]

Islam & Muslims in the Post-9/11 America

Muslims were increasingly the target of a "shoot first and ask questions later" policy by the government. In April 2004, two sixteen-year-old Muslim girls - one born in Bangladesh, the other in Guinea - were detained in New York on immigration violations and shipped to a Pennsylvania detention center. The FBI claimed the girls presented "an imminent threat to the security of the United States based upon evidence that they plan to be suicide bombers." After holding the girls for six weeks, the government quietly released the Guinean girl and deported the Bangladeshi girl for visa violation. [4]

Reinforcing Prejudicial Views Against Islam (Islamophobia)

Contributing to the rise of discrimination against Muslims was the continuing anti-Islam and anti-Muslim rhetoric, especially by some evangelical leaders and neoconservatives. Anti-Muslim bias has become an endemic disease. Besides print media, many radio talk show hosts are perpetuating the myth that Islam is a violent faith. The decades old media habit of associating Islam with violence found its eternal 'justification' in the attacks of 9/11. Fox News was dedicated to a full-time anti-Islam campaign. There was also an effective opposition to Islam in America in the political arena. Political and religious leaders also exploited this anti-Islam rhetoric as shown by the remarks of many prominent political leaders. Groups and individuals who had a vested interest in demonizing of Islam and Muslims in the United States have also seized the opportunity to attack Muslims and Islam. [5]

As stereotyping and scapegoating Islam and Muslims and Islam became a popular past time for the US media, many religious and political leaders never missed any opportunity to attack Islam in the name of extremism. In July 2005, Colorado Republican Congressman Tom Tancredo calls for a nuclear attack on Islam's holiest site, Mecca, if there is another terrorist attack on US. A Washington DC radio talk show host repeats "Islam is a terrorist organization" 23 times on his July 25, 2005 program. He also repeatedly claimed that "the problem is not extremism. The problem is Islam."

The election of 2008 witnessed a steeped rise in Islamophobia when an intensive campaign was launched against the Democratic Presidential candidate Barrack Obama. On an Iowa radio station on March 8, 2008,

Congressman Steve King said, "if [Obama] is elected president, then the radical Islamists and their supporters will be dancing in the streets in greater numbers than they did on September 11 because they will declare victory in this War on Terror." In February 2008, a furor has erupted as a photo of Barack Obama in a white turban spread across the Web, drawing accusations of fear-mongering and racism from the Obama campaign. The photo was taken on a 2006 trip Sen. Obama made to Kenya.

In a replay of the 2004 and 2006 elections the desperate Republican Party was playing its typical tactic, Scare America. With little to fall on nearly eight years of President Bush's misrule that landed the nation in the worst economic crisis since the Great Depression, the desperate Republican Party had ratcheted up its campaign with half-truths and fear mongering which has been the hallmark of the Bush Administration. The most blatant use of fear mongering came on the final day of the Republican National Convention when John McCain delivered his GOP nomination acceptance speech and Rudy Giuliani and Mitt Romney hyped the threat of the so-called "Islamic terrorism."

Throughout the 2010 election campaign the American Muslim community and their faith were dehumanized as the Republican Party once again used Islamophobia as a political tool. The anti-Islam and anti-Muslim rhetoric depicting Islam as enemy got steam from the Quran-burning publicity stunts by a minor church in Florida. Two more elements were added to this anti-Muslim hysteria in this election campaign. Controversy over the 51Park project popularly known as Ground Zero mosque and conspiracies that the so-called Sharia law will displace the US constitution.

In August 2010, Republicans amplified their rhetoric to turn the so-called "Ground Zero Mosque" into a campaign issue. The American Society for Muslim Advancement and the Cordoba Initiative received tentative approval in May 2010 for construction of the $100 million Islamic center in lower Manhattan. New York City's Landmarks Preservation Commission voted unanimously August 3, 2010 to allow the demolition of a building on Park Place that would be replaced by a mosque.

Islam-bashing for political gain was a chilling feature of 2010 election campaign and demagogues misled Oklahomans to pass an anti-Muslim ballot measure. The ballot measure 755 - which amends that state constitution - prohibits Okalhoma courts from considering Sharia law when deciding cases. In the current anti-Islam and anti-Muslim environment prevailing in the nation over the Park51 project, known as Ground Zero Mosque in New York, nearly 70 percent of voters in the state cast ballots approving the measure. Tellingly, many legal experts say that there is no need for this law because judges exclusively use state and federal law to guide their decisions.

The Oklahoma anti-Islam measure was one of the best examples of politicians duping the public through fear mongering. It was demonizing the Muslims in order to mobilize votes.

Since the November 2010 Oklahoma 'anti-Sharia' law similar bills were introduced in around 20 states nationwide. The bills were patterned on a template produced by leading Islamophobe David Yerushalmi, a 56-year-old Hasidic Jew, who founded an organization in 2006 with the acronym SANE (the Society of Americans for National Existence) with the aim of banishing Islam from the US. He proposed a law that would make adherence to Islam a felony punishable by 20 years in prison.

During the Republican presidential candidates debate in New Hampshire in June, 2011, Presidential hopeful Newt Gingrich's compared Muslims to Nazis. Another Republican candidate, Herman Cain said he would not be comfortable having a Muslim member in his administration, nor would he appoint one. In July 2011, Herman Cain said in a TV program that communities have a right to ban Islamic mosques.

As the 2012 election neared, some Republican presidential hopefuls and congressional candidates again opted to try to win votes by denigrating Islam and disparaging Muslims. To borrow Wilfredo Amr Ruiz of Huffington Post, taking the lead in the anti-Muslim frenzy was Herman Cain, who has consistently held a hostile discourse on Islam, belittling almost anything or anyone resonating Muslim. For example. Cain is against the construction of an Islamic Center in Murfreesboro, Tenn., unreasonably arguing that it's not religious discrimination for a community to ban a mosque. On this same line, Cain has also affirmed that he wouldn't appoint Muslims to his cabinet and even suggested to impose a loyalty test on any Muslim before allowing him to serve in his administration. In his anti-Muslim rhetoric he claimed that more than half of American Muslims are extremists based on a "trusted adviser" who informed him so. Herman Cain abandoned his White House ambitions in December 2011 after a string of accusations of sexual misconduct.

Rick Santorum, another presidential hopeful, has joined the Islam-bashing team, expressing misleading comments on the question of Sharia taking over the U.S. court system. In a debate Santorum was even more assertive on his opinion on Muslims. When asked if he would support ethnic and religious profiling he replied: "The folks who are most likely to be committing these crimes ... obviously Muslims would be someone you'd look at, absolutely."

Rep. Michele Bachmann, another presidential aspirant said: "not all cultures are equal, not all values are equal, letting it be known that she thought that people of the Muslim faith had an inferior culture to that of the United States and the West."

To the dismay of seven-million strong American Muslim community, another Republican Presidential candidate, Mitt Romney, appointed Dr. Walid Phares, the author of "Future Jihad: Terrorist Strategies Against America," foreign policy adviser to his team. To his credentials, Phares also worked as an official in the Lebanese Forces, a Christian militia, and other militias that reportedly took part in various massacres of Muslims.

The cottage industry of self-styled national security experts

As the cottage industry of self-styled national security experts, pundits, Republican operatives, think tanks, and advocacy groups have spent years in fuelling anti-Muslim bigotry. The anti-Muslim sentiment in America was being generated by a cottage industry of Muslim bashers and Islamophobic groups. Shockingly, more than $42 million from seven foundations over the past decade have helped fan the flames of anti-Muslim hate in America.

Not surprisingly, the self-proclaimed Islamic expert Steven Emerson has collected 3.39 million dollars for his for-profit company in 2008 for researching alleged ties between American Muslims and overseas terrorism. In an investigative report titled "Anti-Muslim crusaders make millions spreading fear," Bob Smietana of The Tennessean pointed out that Emerson is a leading member of a multimillion-dollar industry of self-proclaimed experts who spread hate toward Muslims in books and movies, on websites and through speaking appearances.

Islam & Muslims in the Post-9/11 America

As if the adult media's vitriol wasn't enough, the American Muslims were faced by the alarming publication of a series of 'children's books', containing misleading and inflammatory rhetoric about the Islamic faith. The 10-book series – entitled the "World of Islam," – was published in 2010 by Mason Crest Publishing in collaboration with the Philadelphia-based pro-Israel and pro-war Foreign Policy Research Institute. Anti-Islamic sentiment pervades the entire series, portraying Muslims as inherently violent and deserving suspicion. It encourages young readers to believe Muslims are terrorists, who seek to undermine US society.

Another attempt to demonize Muslims and Islam came in the shape of a children coloring book titled "We Shall Never Forget 9/11: The Kids' Book of Freedom." The 36-page "graphic novel coloring book" published recently by St. Louis, Mo. Publisher Wayne Bell virtually characterizes all Muslims as linked to extremism, terrorism and radicalism, which may lead children reading the book to believe that all Muslims are responsible for the tragedy of 9/11. It could give a message to children that followers of the Islamic faith are their enemies.

Republican head of the congressional Homeland Security Committee Rep. Peter King was also stoking Islamophbia through his controversial hearings. He held four hearings in 2011 on what he calls the "radicalization" of the American Muslim community.

Perhaps Lillian Nakano, a third-generation Japanese American from Hawaii, is right when he says that 1942-style bigotry targets Muslims in the U.S. today. "Muslim Americans became victims of the same kind of stereotyping and scapegoating we faced 63 years ago. They too have become targets of suspicion, hate crimes, vandalism and violence, all in the name of patriotism and national security."

Not surprisingly, January 2010 *Gallup Poll* shows that 53% of Americans have unfavorable views of Islam, more than any other religion, and 43% admit to feeling "at least a little prejudice" toward Muslims. [6] This negative attitude was corroborated in the latest Gallup poll (released on August 2, 2011) which says at least 4 in 10 in every major religious group in the U.S. say Americans are prejudiced toward Muslim Americans, with Jews (66%) saying this. [7]

Introduction [9]

Shockingly, ten years after 9/11, 80 percent of Jews, 59 percent of Catholics, 56 percent of Protestants and 56 percent of Mormons believe that American Muslims are not loyal to their country, according to Gallup (Middle East) poll.

Two polls – conducted by Washington Post-ABC and the Council on American-Islamic Relations (CAIR) – released on March 9, 2006 indicated that almost half of Americans have a negative perception of Islam and that one in four of those surveyed have extreme anti-Muslim views. Not surprisingly a Newsweek poll of July 2007 indicated that thirty-two percent Americans believe that their fellow citizen Muslims are less loyal to the U.S. Although forty percent of those surveyed believe Muslims in the United States are as loyal to the U.S. as they are to Islam but 46 percent of Americans said the U.S. allows too many immigrants to come here from Muslim countries. [8]

The results of these polls were not unexpected as the anti-Islam and anti-Muslim campaign continued unabated since 9/11 by print and electronic media along with politicians, religious leaders as well as the government policies that have reinforced Islamophobia which may be defined as "alienation, discrimination, harassment and violence rooted in misinformed and stereotyped representations of Islam and its adherents.

Muslim charities shut down

To the dismay of the Muslim American community, the government had launched a campaign against Muslim charitable organizations for allegedly providing financial or other material assistance to groups the government designates as "terrorist." A provision of the reauthorized USA Patriot Act gives the government largely unchecked power to designate any group as a terrorist organization. And once a charitable organization is so designated, all of its materials and property may be seized and its assets frozen. The charity is unable to see the government's evidence and thus understand the basis for the charges. Since its assets are frozen, it lacks resources to mount a defense. And it has only limited right of appeal to the courts. So the government can target a charity, seize its assets, shut it down, obtain indictments against its leaders, but then delay a trial almost indefinitely.

Dozens of charitable groups have been investigated since 2001. Several were shut down, without any official finding that they were aiding terrorist organizations. The organizations shut down were not on any government watch list before their assets were frozen. The predictable result is that Muslims have no way of knowing which groups the government suspects of ties to terrorism. Organizations and individuals suspected of supporting terrorism are guilty until proven innocent. The government action has resulted in shutting down five major Muslim charities.

Government crackdown of Muslim charities caused tremendous fear and anxiety among the Muslims, with many fearful that a simple act of charity could lead to federal agents knocking at their door. Since 9/11, millions of dollars in donations were seized and frozen, leaving Muslims with unfulfilled obligations. Some found FBI agents at their doors, asking about specific checks they had written. According to the Illinois Coalition for Immigrant and Refugee Rights, the U.S. government has closed down 25 Muslim charities and frozen $8 million in donations in Illinois alone.

In July 2007, two Muslim charities - the Goodwill Charitable Organization and Al-Mabarrat Charitable Organization - were suspected of having ties to extremist groups in Lebanon. Assets of the two charities were frozen. In February 2006, the Treasury Department froze the assets of KindHearts USA, padlocking the doors of the Toledo-based charity "pending an investigation." On Sept. 21, 2006, US authorities, raided another major Muslim charity, the Michigan-based Life for Relief and Development (LIFE). Federal agents also raided the home of the charity's President and Chief Executive officer, Khalil Jassemm, and the Dearborn office of Muthanna Alhanooti, a former official of the charity.

The federal government has rejected a plea by Muslim groups that wanted a list of pre-approved Islamic charities to which they could donate without being suspected of helping fund terrorism. The case of Dr. Nasar Chaudhry of New York symbolizes the Muslim dilemma. In April 2005, his office and home were raided in a federal investigation for making donations to a Muslim charity in 1996. [9]

However, in a major setback to government campaign against the Muslim charities in the name of security, on October 22, 2007 a District Judge in Dallas, Texas, ordered mistrial in a show case trial of the leading Muslim charity Holy Land Foundation for Relief and Development. After 19 days of deliberations by the Jury, Judge A. Joe Fish declared a mistrial for most former leaders of HLF charged with financing Hamas militants after jurors failed to reach a verdict. One of the defendants, former HLF Chairman Mohammed El-Mezain, was acquitted of most charges.

A juror, William Neal, later told the Associated Press that the panel found little evidence against three of the defendants and was evenly split on charges against charity's former chief executive Shukri Abu Baker and its former chairman Ghassan Elashi, who were seen as the principal leaders of the charity. Neal said the jury was split about 6-6 on counts against Baker and Elashi.

"I thought they were not guilty across the board," said the juror, William Neal, a 33-year-old art director from Dallas. The case "was strung together with macaroni noodles. There was so little evidence," Neil said adding that the government's case had "so many gaps" that he regarded the prosecution as "a waste of time.

On Dec 7, 2011, a federal appeals court upheld the convictions of five leaders of the Holy Land Foundation charity on charges of funneling money and supplies to Hamas, designated a "terrorist" group following a 1995 executive order by President Bill Clinton. The organizers of the Texas-based Holy Land Foundation argued that they were denied a fair trial in 2008 when the government used secret Israeli witnesses to testify against them. The organizers also raised a host of constitutional challenges to the evidence presented against them at trial.

The U.S. Court of Appeals for the 5th Circuit rejected those challenges, concluding that "while no trial is perfect," Holy Land and its leaders were fairly convicted. The court pointed to "voluminous evidence" that the foundation, which was started in the late 1980s, had long-running financial ties to Hamas.

The Holy Land Foundation case was the second show-case trial of Muslims in 2007. In February this year, a federal jury in Chicago acquitted Muhammed Salah and his codefendant Abdelhaleem Ashqar of supporting terrorism financing charges. Muhammed Salah was charged with "terrorism" based upon a confession extracted by torture in an Israeli jail. Salute to the jurors who had the courage and integrity not to fall for the government's much abused "terrorism" rhetoric. This reinforces our belief in the values of fairness, justice and due process.

In short, all the American laws have been twisted and the due-process has been denied in an apparent bid to stifle any future Muslims from ever thinking about equality or competition in what was an accessible American political process before the 9/11. The government initiatives have reshaped public attitudes about racial profiling and created a harsh backlash against the Muslim community. This negative attitude has increased steadily since the September 11 attacks. The most startling survey revealing this rise in antipathy to date was released in December 2004 by Cornell University, which found that 44 percent of Americans surveyed believed that the U.S. government should restrict the civil liberties of Muslim Americans. In June 2006, some New York state legislators attempted to make the profiling of Muslims legal. In November 2011, a Republican presidential hopeful Rick Santorum called for profiling of American Muslims.

Muslim Response

The seven-million-strong American Muslim community has responded to the post 9/11 challenges with political and social activism, media campaigns, outreach and interfaith dialogue. It is now more proactive as it believes that the best way to protect its eroding civil rights is to become more active politically. From coast to coast, Muslim and Arab-American groups are organizing as never before to make known their concerns about civil liberties. They have gone beyond sign-waving demonstrations to hold voter registration drives, meet with politicians and form alliances with other civil rights and religious organizations. Muslims are becoming more organized and vocal in their demands, petitioning school boards to establish prayer rooms in public schools for their children and turning to the courts when they believe their constitutional rights to practice their faith have been violated.

Just one example. On January 16, 2012, Some 400 Washington State Muslims celebrated the 5th annual Muslim Day at the Capitol and meet with dozens of their elected representatives. The event, one of the largest of its kind in the nation, was organized by the Washington state chapter of the Council on American-Islamic Relations (CAIR-WA). The Muslim voters attending the event were representing 33 of the 49 state legislative districts. They spoke with individual legislators, and provided information about recent anti-Muslim incidents and urged their legislators to speak out against Islamophobic rhetoric and hate crimes. [10]

Muslim community played an active role in the 2004 presidential election with dozens of voter registration campaigns, civic education forums and fund raisers. Muslim vote became focus of mainstream media and several presidential candidates addressed their gatherings. Disenchanted by the policies of President George Bush that abridged their civil rights, Muslims on individual as well as organizational level backed the Democratic Presidential candidate, John Kerry, who had pledged to address their grievances.

In the 2006 mid-term elections, Muslims and Arabs voted overwhelmingly for the Democratic Party. A pre-election CAIR poll revealed that 42 percent consider themselves members of the Democratic Party while only 17 per cent are Republican. The exit polls confirmed the findings of the pre-election polls. [11]

Interestingly, Keith Ellison of Minnesota made history to become the first Muslim member of the US Congress. His election campaign was based on making alliances with all groups. Tellingly, he was able to defeat his Republican rival, Alan Fine, who was of Jewish faith as Ellison was able to garner the support of Jewish groups too.

American Muslims overwhelmingly voted for Democratic Presidential candidate Senator Barrak Obama in the 2008 election. In this election,

Muslim Americans changed their party affiliation from Republican to Democratic – a stark change from the strong Muslim support for George Bush in 2000 when they voted for Bush in an en bloc vote. The major shift occurred as many Muslim Americans became subject to wiretapping, mishandling of civil liberties, religious, ethnic, and racial profiling. According to the (AMT) American Muslim Task Force on Civil Rights and Elections, a coalition of Muslim civil advocacy groups, only 2 percent Muslims voted for Republican Presidential candidate John McCain. AMT also indicated that 95 percent of Muslims polled cast a ballot in this year's presidential election—the highest turnout in a U.S. election ever—and 14 percent of those were first-time voters. [12]

Throughout the 2010 election campaign the seven-million strong American Muslim community and their faith were dehumanized as the Republican Party once again used Islamophobia as a political tool. The anti-Islam and anti-Muslim rhetoric depicting Islam as enemy got steam from the Quran-burning publicity stunts by a minor church in Florida. Two more elements were added to this anti-Muslim hysteria in this election campaign. Controversy over the 51Park project popularly known as Ground Zero mosque and conspiracies that Sharia law will displace the US constitution. In August 2010, Republicans amplified their rhetoric to turn the so-called "Ground Zero Mosque" into a campaign issue.

The American Society for Muslim Advancement and the Cordoba Initiative received tentative approval in May 2010 for construction of the $100 million Islamic center in lower Manhattan. New York City's Landmarks Preservation Commission voted unanimously August 3, 2010 to allow the demolition of a building on Park Place that would be replaced by a mosque.

The developer, Sharif el-Gamal, a real estate investor born in New York, has said the center would include meeting rooms, a prayer space, a 500-seat auditorium and a pool. Two mosques, founded in 1970 and 1985, are already within several blocks of the proposed center. They are so busy and crowded that a search was begun for more space.

Motivated by the anti-Islam fervor generated by Park51 Arab and Muslim American organizations and individuals used different methods and tactics were to engage their communities. Leading civil advocacy groups like the Council on Islamic-American Relations (CAIR) and the Muslim Public Affairs

Council (MPAC) were acquainting American Muslims with the voting process. The CAIR released voting guides for 23 states that explain when polls open, how to register to vote, what identification is needed and voters' rights. Leading American Muslim civil advocacy organizations reached out to American Muslims through a series of workshops conducted across the country.

And it was not just in the lead-up to the midterm elections that American Muslims were engaging in the political process. Organizations such as the Council of Islamic Organizations of Greater Chicago helped organize Muslim Action Day in April 2010, when community representatives met legislators at the state capitol to discuss voter issues. In Chicago, with more than 400,000 Muslim population, organizations like Project Mobilize, Mosque Foundation, CIOGC and CAIR-Chicago and have been active in voter registration. In the city's southwest suburbs, in the 10 precincts surrounding one of largest mosques in the country, 20% of the registered voters are Muslim.

"Not in the Name of Islam" ad campaign

In a vigorous response to allegations that the American Muslims have not condemned terrorism enough, The Fiqh Council of North America issued a fatwa, or religious edict, in July 2005 saying that Islam condemns terrorism, religious radicalism and the use of violence. The fatwa was later endorsed by more than 200 American Muslim organizations and groups. It was the first time Muslims in North America had issued an anti-terrorism edict, although they had repeatedly condemned such acts of violence. The fatwa had desired result as it was reported widely by mainstream media. The Council on American-Islamic Relations has, meanwhile, launched "Not in the Name of Islam" ad campaign condemning terrorism. However, many in the community were wondering why only Muslims were compelled to issue an edict or ad against terrorism. Neither Christians nor Jews, or people of other faith feel compelled to issue edits declaring their faith's innocence whenever acts of violence and extremism are carried out by individuals or groups who share their faith.

Besides issuing fatwa and ads, the Muslim organizations have launched interfaith dialogue to remove misconceptions about Islam caused by the growing use of anti-Muslim and anti-Islam rhetoric. There has been tremendous response to Muslim outreach as many individuals, communities and civil right groups responded to their plight. American Civil Rights Union and American Lawyers Guild helped the Muslims called for 'voluntary' FBI interviews.

References

(1) On April 27, 2011, The Department of Homeland Security (DHS) announced the end of the National Security Entry-Exit Registration System (NSEERS). This special registration process is no longer required.

(2) On May 25, 2005, Amnesty International accused the Bush administration of condoning "atrocious" human rights violations, thereby diminishing its moral authority and setting a global example encouraging abuse by other nations. The organization's annual report listed the abuse of detainees at Abu Ghraib prison in Iraq, the detention of prisoners at Guantánamo Bay, Cuba, and the so-called rendition of prisoners to countries known to practice torture as evidence that the United States "thumbs its nose at the rule of law and human rights." Irene Khan, Amnesty's secretary general, labeled the United States detention facility at Guantánamo Bay, where more than 500 prisoners from about 40 countries are being held, as "the gulag of our times." **(New York Times)**

(3) FBI, on June 6, 2005, arrested two Pakistani Americans and two Pakistani nationals in the city of Lodi, CA., for allegedly operating an Al Qaeda cell in the city. One of the men arrested, 22-year-old American citizen, Hamid Hayat, is accused in a FBI criminal complaint of training in an Al Qaeda camp in Pakistan to learn "how to kill Americans" and then lying to FBI agents about it. His father, 47-year-old Umer Hayat, is charged in the complaint with lying about his son's involvement and his own financing of the Al Qaeda camp. Meanwhile, Two Pakistani nationals, Shabbir Ahmed, imam of the Lodi Mosque, and Mohammad Adil Khan, a former

Imam of the mosque, were arrested this morning on immigration violations, according to official sources. Two days later, on June 8, Mohammad Hassan Adil, 19, son of Mohammad Adil Khan was arrested on immigration charges. **(Sacramento Bee)**

(4) On April 9, 2005 two sixteen-year-old Muslim girls - one born in Bangladesh, the other in Guinea - were detained in New York on immigration violations and shipped to a detention center in Leesport, Pennsylvania, the New York Times reported. According to a government document obtained by the paper, the FBI claims the girls present "an imminent threat to the security of the United States based upon evidence that they plan to be suicide bombers." In a statement the Council on American-Islamic Relations said that despite the continuing protests by immigrant and civil rights communities following 9/11, the Federal government's implementation of ethnic and religious profiling and its use of immigration proceedings to circumvent the constitutional protections of the criminal justice system persist. **(New York Times)**

(5) See Chapter II on Islamophobia.

(6) A new poll released by Gallup on January 20, 2010 says 53% of Americans have an unfavorable view of Islam and 43% have at least "a little" bias against Muslims. This is in contrast to a 71% favorable view for Judaism, 91% for Christianity and 58% for Buddhism. In a separate question asking Americans to express their overall view about each of the four religions evaluated, Islam is the most negatively viewed. Nearly one-third of Americans (31%) say their opinion of Islam is "not favorable at all" versus 9% who say their opinion is "very favorable." This stands in contrast to Americans' views of Christianity and Judaism, which are far more likely to be "very favorable" than "not favorable at all," while Buddhism draws almost equally positive and negative opinions at the extremes. Gallup conducted the nationwide U.S. survey between Oct. 31 and Nov. 13, 2009. The findings were based on a new Gallup Center for Muslim Studies report, "Religious Perceptions in America: With an In-Depth Analysis of U.S. Attitudes Toward Muslims and Islam." **[Gallup Polls]**

(7) Sixty percent of U.S. Muslims say they face prejudice from most Americans. However, far fewer Americans of other faiths believe this to be true. U.S. Protestants, Catholics, and Mormons are the least likely (48%, 51%, and 47%, respectively) to say that Americans are prejudiced toward Muslim Americans — the groups also least likely to believe that Muslim Americans are loyal to the U.S. and most likely to believe a terrorist can be profiled. Surprisingly, American Jews agree that there is prejudice toward U.S. Muslims in even higher numbers (66%) than do Muslims themselves. At 48%, Muslim Americans are by far the most likely of major faith groups surveyed to say they have personally experienced racial or religious discrimination in the past year. The next most likely are Mormon Americans, although less than one-third of U.S. Mormons say this. The numbers of U.S. Protestants, Catholics, and Jews who report experiencing discrimination in the past year are far lower, about one in five in each of these groups. Though Jews and Catholics historically have been the most frequent targets of religious discrimination in the U.S., these data suggest that Muslim Americans now perceive themselves to hold this dubious distinction **[Gallup Abu Dhabi – August 2, 2011]**

Islam & Muslims in the Post-9/11 America

(8) Two polls released on March 10, 2006, indicate that almost half of Americans have a negative perception of Islam and that one in four of those surveyed have "extreme" anti-Muslim views. A growing proportion of Americans are expressing unfavorable views of Islam, and a majority now say that Muslims are disproportionately prone to violence, according to a new Washington Post-ABC News poll. The proportion of Americans who believe that Islam helps to stoke violence against non-Muslims has more than doubled since the attacks, from 14 percent in January 2002 to 33 percent today, the poll indicated. Meanwhile, an independent survey by the Council on American-Islamic Relations CAIR), a leading American Muslim civil rights group, showed that some one-fourth (23 to 27 percent) of Americans consistently believe stereotypes such as: "Muslims value life less than other people," and "The Muslim religion teaches violence and hatred." **(American Muslim Perspective Report)**

Americans are largely accepting of their fellow citizens who are Muslims, but remain worried about radicals inside the United States, according to a new NEWSWEEK Poll, the first the magazine has conducted on attitudes toward Islamic Americans. Forty percent of those surveyed believe Muslims in the United States are as loyal to the U.S. as they are to Islam. (Thirty-two percent believe American Muslims are less loyal to the U.S.) But close to half (46 percent) of Americans say this country allows too many immigrants to come here from Muslim countries. A solid majority of Americans (63 percent) believe most Muslims in this country do not condone violence, and 40 percent tend to believe the Qur'an itself does not condone violence (28 percent feel it does). **(Newsweek – July 20, 2007)**

(9) Evening Tribune – April 7, 2005

(10) Washington State Muslims meet lawmakers on MLK Day – AMP Report January 17, 2012

(11) According to the Council on American-Islamic Relations survey of Muslim voters, release on October 24, 2006, 42 percent consider themselves members of the Democratic Party while only 17 per cent are Republican. Another 28 percent do not belong to any party. An informal exit-poll of Muslim voters, conducted by the New Jersey Chapter of the Council on American Islamic Relations (CAIR-NJ), indicated that the vast majority in that state voted for Democrats in the mid-term elections. There are at least 18,000 registered Muslim voters in the state of New Jersey. Seventy-five Muslim voters from Ohio responded to a post-election survey. More than 90 percent of the respondents said they had voted for Democratic Party candidates. **(American Muslim Perspective Report)**

(12) The Newsweek reported a Gallup Center for Muslim Studies survey as saying that U.S. Muslims favored Obama in greater numbers than did Hispanics (67 percent of whom voted for Obama) and nearly matched that of African-Americans, 93 percent of whom voted for Obama. More than two thirds who were polled said the economy was the most important issue affecting their decision on Nov. 4th, while 16 percent said the wars in Iraq and Afghanistan informed their vote—numbers that put Muslims roughly on a par with the general population.

Chapter I - The Civil Rights

Defending civil rights became the single most important challenge before the American Muslims in the post-9/11 America. Arabs and Muslims were the prime targets of the post 9/11 reconfiguration of American laws, policies, and priorities. Their constitutional rights to free exercise of religion and assembly, due process and security from unreasonable searches and seizures had been violated. The erosion of civil rights came in the form of various programs and legislations such as the USA Patriot Act, which effectively nullifies Constitutional Amendments 4, 5, 6, and 8 directly and indirectly amendments 1 and 9 and the INS Special Registration which targeted men from 21 Muslim countries. The fallout impacted the daily life of Muslims at schools, in the workplace, in general public encounters and mistreatment at the hand of federal officials. Many Muslim homes and businesses were raided while profiling-based interrogations and searches became a norm.

On September 11, 2001, Muslim leaders gathered in Washington for a meeting with President George Bush to discuss, among other issues facing the Muslim community, the fulfillment of his election pledge to abrogate the Secret Evidence Act of 1995 that was mainly used against the Muslims. The Bush pledge had come during his election campaign meeting with the Muslim leaders. He had also challenged the use of secret evidence at the second presidential debate. His pledge led to en bloc Muslim vote for Bush in 2000.

However, this all changed on 9/11. The meeting was aborted while more stringent laws were introduced in the aftermath of the terrorist attacks on New York and Washington that significantly curtailed the civil rights of the Muslims. In the nineties the Muslim civil rights were already abridged due to Executive Order of 1994, Secret Evidence clause of the Anti-Terrorism and Effective Death Penalty Act of 1995, and ADC v. Janet Reno decision of the US Supreme Court of February 1999. (1)

The sweeping antiterrorism legislation known as the USA PATRIOT Act was rushed through Congress and signed into law by President Bush on October 26, 2001. The USA PATRIOT Act is the acronym for "Uniting and

Chapter I - The Post-9/11 Challenges: The Civil Rights

Strengthening America by Providing Appropriate Tools Required to Intercept and Obstruct Terrorism Act". The law was passed without meaningful review by a panicked Congress just six weeks after the 9/11 terrorist attacks. The legislation flew through the House 357 to 66 and the Senate 99 to 1 (Senator Russ Feingold, D-Wis.) on Oct. 25, 2001 and signed into law by President Bush the next day. With the rubble of the World Trade Center and the Pentagon still smoking, obviously it was difficult to resist. The act is 342 pages long and includes many sections that do not deal with terrorism, but are provisions aimed at nonviolent, domestic computer crime. Surely, this legislation wasn't written in response to the events of Sept. 11, 2001, but was evidently drafted years before the Bush administration took office and was rushed through Congress one month after the Sept. 11 attacks.

With this law sweeping new powers were given to both domestic law enforcement and international intelligence agencies and eliminated the checks and balances that previously gave courts the opportunity to ensure that these powers were not abused. Most of these checks and balances were put into place after previous misuse of surveillance powers by these agencies, including the revelation in 1974 that the FBI and foreign intelligence agencies had spied on over 10,000 U.S. citizens, including Martin Luther King. The USA Patriot Act gave the government broad new powers to detain non-citizens indefinitely and to conduct searches, seizures, and surveillance with reduced standards of cause and levels of judicial review, among other provisions. Prior to September 11, 2001, many of these provisions would be considered an unthinkable and unconstitutional violation of cherished U.S. ideals of privacy from unwarranted governmental intrusion and of individual rights.

On March 9, 2006, President Bush signed a new version of the USA Patriot Act that permanently extends 14 of 16 expiring provisions of the Patriot Act. Congressman Pete Stark, who voted against the reauthorization of the Act sums up the controversial provisions of the Act: The government can still listen in on your phone conversations without any proof that a terrorist is using the phone and can conduct secret searches of your property. The law will still allow the government to send a letter to your bank, Internet Service Provider, insurance company, or any other business demanding information about you.... A government official can still forbid a business from telling anyone that records have been obtained, although this gag would last for an initial one-year period rather than indefinitely. However, the gag can be renewed.... Finally, the Bush Administration has magnanimously agreed not to look at your library borrowing records, although this agreement makes it easier for them to find out what websites you visit while at the library. (2)

The Patriot Act and other government policies put into place in response to 9/11 terrorist attacks severely impacted the civil rights of the Muslim community in America in a variety of ways. Discrimination against Muslims has been institutionalized through the Patriot Act and other legislations. Muslims in schools, the workplace, airports and encounters with police and other government agencies experienced incidents in which they were singled out because of their religious and ethnic identity.

New laws have also affected donations to the American Muslim charity organizations due to the lack of assurance that donors will be protected if any charity organization later deemed by the government to be a terrorist organization. A fundamental problem is that even those American Muslim charities who follow the government's "best practices" guidelines to the letter do not receive any assurances that they will be safe. With major American Muslim charities - Holy Land Foundation for Relief and Development, Global Relief Foundation, Benevolence International Foundation and Islamic American Relief Agency - shut down by the government over accusations of ties to terrorist groups and several prominent Muslim donors now indicted or detained, American Muslims are scared to do anything that might bring scrutiny from the FBI — and that includes donating to Islamic charities.

The administration while shutting down the Muslim charity organizations, using new powers under the USA Patriot Act, filed no criminal charges against these organizations, nor were they officially designated terrorist supporters. Law enforcement officials simply froze their assets and seized their property "pending an investigation" without producing any evidence, as authorized by the Act. Consequently, the burden of proof has been shifted to the organizations, which must prove their innocence even though, in many cases, the government has not specified wrongdoing. Moreover, they must do this without access to their own documents, computers, records, or other materials that might make their case.

Muslim non-immigrants nationwide were jailed indefinitely over minor visa violations that in the past would have been ignored and about 13,000, who went for INS Special Registration voluntarily, faced deportation. The Justice

Chapter I - The Post-9/11 Challenges: The Civil Rights [22]

Department's inspector general issued a scathing report in April 2003 on the handling of 762 detainees held after Sept. 11 under suspicion of having terrorist ties. It found "significant problems" with the treatment of some and uncovered evidence that family members and lawyers were not told where the men were taken.

The California Senate Report of March 2004 on the impact of the Patriot Act highlighted the plight of the Muslim community in the State of California which has a substantial concentration of the Muslim population. The 82-page report - titled The Patriot Act, Other Post-9/11 Enforcement Powers and The Impact on California's Muslim Communities - pointed out that the Muslim community has taken the brunt of the Patriot Act and other federal powers applied in the aftermath of the 9/11 terrorist attacks. The measures created a fear that gripped the Muslim community in Californian and elsewhere following federal sweeps, round-ups, detentions of innocent Muslims, who had neither terrorist intentions nor any connection to terrorist organizations, said the report, drawn up at the request of Senator Senator Liz Figueroa (D-Fremont). (3)

Congressman Pete Stark spoke for millions of Americans when he said while joining fellow San Francisco Bay Area Representatives George Miller, Barbara Lee, Mike Honda, Lynn Woolsey and Sam Farr in introducing the legislation to repeal provisions of the USA Patriot Act: "Having the honor of representing one of the most culturally diverse districts in the nation, I am keenly aware of the effects of the Patriot Act. Many of my constituents, especially those who are Arab and Muslim Americans, are afraid of losing their rights and being racially profiled and harassed by the government.... Perhaps worst of all Attorney General Ashcroft has wrongly singled out thousands of Americans of Arab, Middle Eastern and South Asian descent for questioning and, in some cases, indefinite detainment."

The bill, titled the "Benjamin Franklin True Patriot Act", was introduced on Sept 24, 2003 in the House by Congressman Dennis J. Kucinich, the only presidential candidate who voted against the PATRIOT Act. The True Patriot Act envisaged repeal of a number of sections of Patriot Act sections, including the sections 441 and 442 related to the detention and deportation of non-citizens without meaningful judicial review. While introducing the True Patriot Act, Kucinich told the House: "Twenty-four months after the Sept. 11th attacks, this nation has undergone a dramatic political change, leading

Islam & Muslims in the Post-9/11 America

to an unprecedented assault on the United States Constitution and the Bill of Rights."

Since its enactment, the PATRIOT Act has come under severe criticism in a variety of quarters. The Act's popularity waned to the point that the House of Representatives, on July 22, 2003, voted with bipartisan support to cut off funds for enforcement of a key section – that allows the FBI to enter and search private premises without showing the occupant a warrant or notifying the occupant that the place was searched, until some indeterminate time in the future. Other bills proposed outright repeal of several sections of the act, including allowing indefinite detention without trial.

There is a growing concern among the masses about the impact of the Patriot Act on their civil rights. As of August 11, 2006, 407 communities had passed resolutions calling for repeal of or otherwise faulting the PATRIOT Act, finding that certain provisions violate civil rights guaranteed by the Constitution. Moreover eight state-wide resolutions were passed in Alaska, California, Colorado, Hawaii, Idaho, Maine, Montana and Vermont. These communities represented approximately 85 million people who opposed sections of the USA PATRIOT Act. (4)

There was also a disturbing legal trend in American law concerning cases that not only specifically targeted Muslims, but ended with admissions of error from prosecutors on the basis of faulty evidence. Brandon Mayfield, a Portland, Oregon, Muslim of Caucasian origin, was wrongly imprisoned as a suspect in the May 2004 terrorist bombings in Madrid. When a sneak-and-peek operation under the Patriot Act discovered a Qu'ran and maps of Spain in Mayfield's house, and his fingerprints were reported on explosives by the Spanish police, Mayfield was arrested. He was freed after two weeks in solitary confinement when the Spanish authorities admitted the fingerprint tests were inconclusive. The FBI subsequently issued Mayfield an apology.

In November 2006, Mayfiled settled his lawsuit against the federal government for $2 million. "Although my family and I can never be made whole for the illegal and unwarranted violations of our privacy, the secret searches of our home and my law office, and the tapping of our phones, the settlement of our financial damages claim allows our case to move forward against the government on its most important issue: that the Patriot Act is unconstitutional," Mayfield said in a statement. As part of the settlement, the federal government issued this apology to Mayfield and his family this week: "The United States of America apologizes to Mr. Brandon Mayfield and his family for the suffering caused by the FBI's misidentification of Mr. Mayfield's fingerprint and the resulting investigation of Mr. Mayfield, including his arrest as a material witness in connection with the 2004 Madrid train bombings and the execution of search warrants and other court orders in the Mayfield family home and in Mr. Mayfield's law office." Mayfield clarified that his financial settlement with the federal government does not preclude him from pursuing his claim that the USA Patriot Act, passed after the Sept. 11, 2001, terrorist attacks and renewed this year, is unconstitutional. Mayfield's attorneys said that they plan to continue their challenge to the federal law. (5)

Other government policies targeting Muslims

But this is not all. In the first twelve months after 9/11, many government policies and initiatives explicitly targeted Arabs and Muslims. These policies and initiatives were not part of the USA PATRIOT Act but implemented through executive orders:

The Attorney General on September 20, 2001 issued an interim rule that allowed immigrants to be detained for an indefinite period of time without being charged in "emergency or other extraordinary circumstances." In the wake of the September 11 attacks, 762 people were held on immigration violations. Justice Department Inspector General Glenn A. Fine issued a series of highly critical reports detailing abuses of the detainees.

The State Department issued a classified cable in October 2001 imposing a twenty-day mandatory hold on all non-immigrant visa applications submitted by men aged eighteen to forty-five from twenty-six countries, most of them Arab or Muslim. All such applicants were to be subjected to special security clearances. Even stricter procedures were put in place in certain countries.

Islam & Muslims in the Post-9/11 America

Chapter I - The Post-9/11 Challenges: The Civil Rights [25]

In November 2001 Attorney General John Ashcroft announces a plan to target some 5,000 young men of Middle Eastern and South Asian heritage who entered the country in the last two years on non-immigrant visas but who are not suspected of any criminal activity for questioning by the federal government. In March 2002 the Attorney General announces second FBI dragnet plan to question an additional 3,000 individuals of Middle Eastern and South Asian heritage. In San Francisco, San Jose, and Oakland, police departments have refused to participate in the interviews because the plan violates state laws or local policies against profiling based on race or national origin.

The Immigration and Naturalization Service (INS is now renamed as US Citizenship & Immigration Services as part of the Department of Homeland Security), in January 2002, launched an initiative to track down and deport non-citizen males from Muslim countries who had been ordered deported by an immigration judge but had never left the U. S. There were an estimated 314,000 so-called "absconders" in the U. S.—the vast majority from Latin America. Although less than two per cent were Middle Eastern, they were the government's target.

In June 2002, Attorney General John Ashcroft announces a plan that required hundreds of thousands of lawful visitors-- including those already in the country-- from mostly Muslim nations to provide fingerprints to authorities upon arrival and register with the Immigration and Naturalization Service after 30 days in the country. Visitors who fail to do either of these things face fines or even deportation. The fingerprinting and tracking proposal was only the latest Bush administration action targeted at Muslims and people of Middle Eastern descent.

In January 2002, the Justice Department announced the Terrorism Information and Prevention System (TIPS) program to recruit millions of United States citizens as domestic informants. The TIPS program, initially introduced in 10 cities, extended its governmental arm to recruit truck drivers, letter carriers, and computer and telephone repair workers to report behavior that could be classified as related to terrorist activities. The TIPS program was abandoned amid fierce criticism in November 2002 when the Homeland Security Act specifically canned it.

Chapter I - The Post-9/11 Challenges: The Civil Rights [26]

The Department of Justice, in June 2002, issued an internal memo to the INS and U. S. Customs requesting that they seek out and search all Yemenis, including American citizens, entering the U. S. As a result, Yemeni Americans were removed from planes and boarding lines, waiting hours for security clearances.

The Justice Department in July 2002 announces the requirement that all non-citizens report changes of address within ten days of moving or risk financial penalties, jail or even deportation. The plan, which relies on a long-neglected 50-year-old law, applies to 10 million people older than 14 who are living in the United States legally as well as 8 to 9 million undocumented immigrants. The Justice Department claims enforcement of the law will allow for a closer tracking system of immigrants.

The Department of Justice, Immigration and Naturalization Service (INS) on 11 September 2002 implemented the Special Registration program, which required that "certain non-immigrant aliens" (visitors) register with the U.S. immigration authorities, be fingerprinted and photographed, respond to questioning, and submit to routine reporting. The Special Registration program was crafted by the office of Attorney General John Ashcroft.

In April 2003 Attorney General John Ashcroft issued a legal opinion that most illegal immigrants can be jailed indefinitely without bond when national security risks exist. The order means such aliens will not be released on bond while their cases are being decided by immigration judges if the government can show national security issues are involved. "Such national security considerations clearly constitute a reasonable foundation for the exercise of my discretion to deny release on bond," Ashcroft said in the 19-page opinion. The opinion was requested by the Homeland Security Department, which now enforces most immigration laws, after the Board of Immigration Appeals upheld a judge's decision to release Haitian asylum-seeker David Joseph on $2,500 bond. Ashcroft's decision applies to all illegal immigrants except Cubans, who by law automatically are permitted to stay in the United States if they reach its shores. Homeland Security sent an especially distressing signal on March 18 2003, when Homeland Secretary, Tom Ridge, announced that asylum seekers from 34 countries will automatically be detained during their proceedings as part of Operation Liberty Shield.

Islam & Muslims in the Post-9/11 America

Chapter I - The Post-9/11 Challenges: The Civil Rights

Stay tuned for more.

Besides the PATRIOT Act and other government policies and initiatives, a number of court decisions also clipped civil rights of the Muslims. In these decisions, the higher courts ruled in favor of double standard in due process, refused to end secret hearings in deportation hearings; strengthened the government's power to strip a person of his citizenship even if he committed the crime after naturalization; and ruled that the government has wide latitude under immigration law to detain non-citizens on the basis of religion, race or national origin, and to hold them indefinitely without explanation. The details if you like:

On April 29 2003, the Supreme Court resurrected a due process double standard, ruling that incarcerating people "without any individualized showing of need was not too much for an alien." By a 5-4 vote, the court for the first time upheld a law authorizing the preventive detention of individuals on a categorical basis. It did so by insisting that the constitutional guarantee of due process means something different for a non-citizen than for a citizen, thus reneging on its own statement 50 years earlier that the due process clause does not "acknowledge any distinction between citizens and resident aliens." The Supreme Court, sixty-seven years ago, reviewed a case involving a confession coerced by torture from a black defendant in Mississippi. The deputy sheriff who presided over the interrogation admitted that the defendant had been whipped, "but not too much for a Negro." The Supreme Court rejected that reasoning and held that the due process prohibition on coerced confessions applies equally to all detainees. (6)

Next month, the US Supreme Court rejected a challenge to the federal government's policy of holding secret immigration hearings of people detained after the Sept. 11, 2001 attacks. The justices, on May 27 2003, declined to review a US appeals court ruling that news media and public access to the deportation proceedings could endanger national security. A federal judge in New Jersey ruled the government's policy violated the First Amendment right of the public and the media to attend the hearings. But a Philadelphia-based appeals court, by a 2-1 vote, upheld the policy on the grounds the press and public possessed no First Amendment right of access to the hearings. (7) During the government's investigation, approximately

Chapter I - The Post-9/11 Challenges: The Civil Rights [28]

766 detainees were designated as 'special interest' cases, 611 of whom had one or more hearings closed. (8)

The US Supreme Court, in February 2004, gave a green light for the government to conduct certain federal court cases in total secrecy. In a case with major implications for public access to the courts, the nation's highest court said it will not examine the circumstances surrounding a habeas corpus appeal filed by an Arab immigrant challenging his detention during the post-9/11 investigation. The proceedings were conducted under a government secrecy request upheld by federal judges. The Bush administration considers the issue so sensitive that its brief to the high court was filed under seal. The government took that unusual action even though the individual at the center of the case--an Algerian living in South Florida-- has been free on a $10,000 bond for two years. (9)

On January 4, 2005, a court ruling further strengthened the US government's power to strip a person of his citizenship even if he committed the crime after naturalization. The 11th US Circuit Court of Appeals allowed the government to strip a Haitian-American restaurant owner of his citizenship even though he was indicted, arrested and convicted after naturalization. The same day the court ruling came, federal agents in Atlanta arrested a prominent Ethiopian human rights abuse suspect, Kelbessa Negewo, 54, and put him in deportation proceedings, for the first time using legal powers granted under a newly-signed intelligence reform law. Immigration lawyers say that the two developments can have far-reaching consequences for thousands of immigrants from Muslim countries who already complain that they have become terror suspects since the Sept 11, 2001 terrorist attacks. (10)

Yet in another decision, on June 14, 2006, Federal judge John Gleeson of United States District Court for the Eastern District of New York ruled that the government has wide latitude under immigration law to detain non-citizens on the basis of religion, race or national origin, and to hold them indefinitely without explanation. The ruling came in a class-action lawsuit by Muslim immigrants detained after 9/11, it dismissed several key claims the detainees had made against the government. This was the first time a federal judge has addressed the issue of discrimination in the treatment of hundreds of Muslim immigrants who were swept up in the weeks after the

Islam & Muslims in the Post-9/11 America

Chapter I - The Post-9/11 Challenges: The Civil Rights [29]

2001 terror attacks and held for months before they were cleared of links to terrorism and deported. (11)

One could multiply examples to prove the point. But it is not necessary and suffice it to say that the government's "anti-terrorism" policies and initiatives launched since the September 11 attacks have had a profoundly negative impact on the Arabs and Muslims in the U. S., largely because they have targeted members of these communities indiscriminately. Starting with the USA Patriot Act, draconian measures and indiscriminate detentions and deportations have destabilized and criminalized Arab and Muslim communities across the United States.

There was a perception in many American Muslims and Arabs that they were being treated as a second class citizen. They feel that their citizenship was becoming less and less meaningful. This was highlighted when thousands of American Lebanese were stranded during the Israeli rampage on Lebanon. On July 24, 2006, Detriot Lebanese-Americans and the American-Arab Anti-Discrimination Committee sued the federal government, Secretary of State Condoleezza Rice and Defense Secretary Donald Rumsfeld for failing to protect U.S. citizens in the war zone of Lebanon. While the evacuation effort by the United States has accelerated considerably in recent days, small European countries acted quicker last week -- in some cases removing a few thousand of their citizens before the United States was able to move 300, according to the lawsuit. "It's sad that we're Americans and got treated like this," said Maha Nasser, of Dearborn Heights who was part of the suit and was vacationing in Lebanon when the attacks started. (12) The lawsuit was later withdrawn when Israeli attacks against Lebanon ended.

The U.S. history is replete with the rollback of individual freedoms in times of national crisis. Many of these rollbacks and their consequences had disturbing results. McCarthyism is one example. Perhaps the most stark example is the ordering of over 110,000 Japanese Americans to detention camps during the World War II. The U.S. Supreme court failed to prevent or correct these national disgraces in a timely manner.

Fred Korematsu, a 22-year old loyal Japanese-American citizen by birth, who violated President Roosevelt's executive order by not going to an internment camp, challenged the constitutionality of the internment of an entire ethnic population class. In the landmark judgment the Supreme Court in 1944 held that Korematsu's constitutional freedoms were not violated and found him guilty. More than 41 years after his internment, in 1983, Korematsu appealed his conviction. Later that year the U.S. District Court Judge Marilyn Patel of San Francisco overturned the conviction, stating that the government's case at the time had been based on false, misleading, and racially biased information. In 1988 Congress passed legislation apologizing for the internments and awarded each survivor $20,000. Korematsu died in March 2005 at the age of 86.

Use of the Patriot Act in criminal cases

The Bush administration, which calls the USA Patriot Act most essential tool in fighting terrorists, was using the law with increasing frequency in many criminal investigations that have little or no connection to terrorism. The government is using its expanded authority under the far-reaching law to investigate suspected drug traffickers, white-collar criminals, blackmailers, child pornographers, money launderers, spies and even corrupt foreign leaders, the New York Times quoted federal officials as saying. Justice Department officials say they were simply using all the tools now available to them to pursue criminals -- terrorists or otherwise. A Justice Department report given to members of Congress in Sept. 2003 cites more than a dozen cases not directly related to terrorism. In those cases, federal authorities have used their expanded power to investigate individuals, initiate wiretaps and other surveillance, or seize millions in tainted assets. For instance, the ability to secure nationwide warrants to obtain e-mail and electronic evidence "has proved invaluable in several sensitive non-terrorism investigations," including the tracking of an unidentified fugitive and an investigation into a computer hacker who stole a company's trade secrets, the report said. (13)

Such use of the law confirms the believe of many that the administration has misled the public, using terrorism as a guise to pursue broader goals. Harvard Professor Gary Orfield got to the heart of the matter when he said: "The loss of civil rights often begins with the reduction of rights in a time of crisis, for a minority that has become the scapegoat for a problem facing the nation. The situation can become particularly explosive in a time of national tragedy or war. But when civil rights for one group of Americans are

Chapter I - The Post-9/11 Challenges: The Civil Rights [31]

threatened and the disappearance of those rights are accepted, it becomes a potential threat to many others." (14)

This resonates very well with what the civil rights groups have been advocating in the post-9/11 era.

References

(1) After the Oklahoma City bombing in 1995, the U.S. Congress passed the Anti-Terrorism and Effective Death Penalty Act that allowed the government to use secret evidence -- evidence that the defendant is unaware of -- to detain and deport immigrants suspected of terrorism. The law has been used almost exclusively against Arab and Muslim immigrants, prompting strong objections from local and national civil rights groups. In Reno v. ADC, the Supreme Court decided (8-1) that under the Illegal Immigration Reform and Immigrant Responsibility Act of 1996 (IIRIRA) an alien unlawfully in this country had no constitutional right to assert selective enforcement as a defense to the deportation action.

(2) California Chronicle – March 7, 2006

(3) California Senate Office of Research - March 2004

(4) The Bill of Rights Defense Committee

(5) Portland Tribune – November 29, 2006

(6) News Day - May 15, 2003

(7) On May 27, 2003,the U.S. Supreme Court rejected a challenge to the federal government's policy of holding secret immigration hearings of people detained after the Sept. 11, 2001, attacks. The justices declined to review a U.S. appeals court ruling that news media and public access to the deportation proceedings could endanger national security. Without any comment, the high court refused to hear an appeal by New Jersey newspapers arguing the government may not keep the proceedings secret without a specific, case-by-case showing that closing the hearing would be necessary. The secret hearings were among the tactics the Bush administration adopted after the hijacked plane attacks on the World Trade Center and the Pentagon. A directive 10 days after the attacks ordered immigration judges to close hearings for detainees whose cases the U.S. Justice Department deemed were of ``special interest" to the government's terrorism investigation. During the government's investigation, approximately 766 detainees were designated as 'special interest' cases, 611 of whom had one or more hearings closed, New York Times quoted department lawyers as saying.

Islam & Muslims in the Post-9/11 America

Chapter I - The Post-9/11 Challenges: The Civil Rights

8) Foreigners (Muslims and Arabs) detained as part of the investigation into the Sept 11, 2001, attacks on the United States were held too long without being charged and subjected to "unduly harsh" conditions of confinement, a US Justice Department audit report said in June 2003. The audit by the department's inspector general found "significant problems" in how authorities handled the 762 foreigners who were detained for immigration violations during the investigation into the hijacked airliner attacks. Some detainees were locked up almost continuously, were moved around in handcuffs and leg irons, subjected to abuse and had their cell lights kept on day and night.

(9) Christian Science Monitor – February 24, 2004

(10) Dawn, Pakistan – January 6, 2006

(11) New York Times – June 15, 2006

(12) The Detroit News – July 25, 2006

(13) The New York Times Sept 28, 2003

(14) One Nation Indivisible, under God, with Liberty and Justice for All: Civil Rights for Arabs, Muslims, and South Asians By Gary Orfield - May 2003

Chapter II - Islamophobia

Islamophobia may be defined as "alienation, discrimination, harassment and violence rooted in misinformed and stereotyped representations of Islam and its adherents."

- A Gallup Poll of January 2010 finds that 53 % of Americans have unfavorable views of Islam, more than any other religion, and 43% admit to feeling "at least a little prejudice" toward Muslims. **[Gallup Polls – January 21, 2010]**

- At least 4 in 10 in every major religious group in the U.S. say Americans are prejudiced toward Muslim Americans, with Jews (66%) saying this, according to the August 2011 Gallup (Middle East) poll. Shockingly, ten years after 9/11, 80 percent of Jews, 59 percent of Catholics, 56 percent of Protestants and 56 percent of Mormons believe that American Muslims are not loyal to their country, the Gallup (Middle East) poll finds. **[Gallup (Middle East) August 2, 2011]**

-- A Newsweek poll of July 2007 indicated that thirty-two percent Americans believe that their fellow citizen Muslims are less loyal to the U.S. Although forty percent of those surveyed believe Muslims in the United States are as loyal to the U.S. as they are to Islam but 46 percent of Americans said the U.S. allows too many immigrants to come here from Muslim countries. **[1A Read more polls]**

Is this surprising? Unfortunately, it's not. Americans' attitudes about Islam and Muslims are fuelled mainly by political statements and media reports that focus almost solely on the negative image of Islam and Muslims. The vilification of Islam and Muslims has been relentless among segments of the media and political classes since 9/11. Politicians, authors and media commentators are busy in demonizing Islam, Muslims and the Muslim world. In the post 9/11 America attacking Islam and Muslims became the

Chapter II - The post 9/11 Challenges – Islamophobia

fashionable sport for the radio, television and print media. Unfortunately, the events of 9/11 were used as an excuse to greatly magnify the hostility toward Muslims and cloak it in pseudo-patriotism. Muslim-bashing has become socially acceptable in the United States. Is Islamophobia, which may be defined as "alienation, discrimination, harassment and violence rooted in misinformed and stereotyped representations of Islam and its adherents," a de facto state policy? **(1B)**

Six days after the 9/11 attacks on the World Trade Center in New York and Pentagon Washington, President George W. Bush, who enjoys political backing of the Christian right, called his war on terror a "crusade," for which he later apologized as a verbal slip. In his first press conference after the alleged London terrorist plot to blow up several aircraft on August 11, 2006, the president said, "this nation is at war with Islamic fascists." **(1C)**

As the alarmed and dismayed American Muslim community protested President's remarks, the White House Press Secretary Tony Snow, adding insult to the injury, said the president will continue to use the phrase. Snow explained that Bush has gradually shifted from general rhetoric about a war on terrorism to the more specific "war with Islamic fascists." With the new description, Bush "tries to identify the ideology that motivates many organized terrorist groups," Snow concluded. **(2)**

Webster's Dictionary defines fascism as a system of government characterized by one party dictatorship that forcibly suppresses opposition. President Bush's remarks linked Islam to the fascist Italian and German regimes of the 1920s. However, Homeland Security Secretary Michael Chertoff explained: "It might not be classic fascism as you had with Mussolini or Hitler. But it is a totalitarian, intolerant imperialism that has a vision that is totally at odds with Western society and our rules of law." **(3)**

When the president uses the term "Islamic fascists" it conveys that fascism is rooted in Islam or fascism that is inspired by Islam. This is the way the Muslims will see it, regardless of what Bush may claim he really means. And his insistence to use "Islamist fascists" leads Muslims to believe that the "crusade" against Islam, was not a verbal slip, but - in the words of Prof. Sam Hamod - a Freudian slip. **(4)**

Islam & Muslims in the Post-9/11 America

Chapter II - The post 9/11 Challenges – Islamophobia

The phrase, Islamist fascists, contrasted sharply with the words used by the British officials, who went out of their way to play down the religion and ethnic background of the terror suspects in the alleged London plot, characterizing them as criminals who did not represent the majority of British Muslim citizens.

Was President Bush's remarks of Islamic Fascist a cynical bid for votes in the election year? This MSNBC report gives some insight: The administration was under pressure to convince the public that controversial security measures, as well as military intervention in Iraq and Afghanistan were the right policies. Bush's approval ratings had been sagging and he had come under fire from conservative critics who have argued that his "war on terror" was too squishy, and losing impact with mainstream America. **(5)**

According to Harris Interactive Poll, President Bush's approval rating was just 34%. President Bush's approval rating was 38% in a Newsweek poll. Harris Poll also indicated that if elections for Congress were held today, 45% of Americans say they would vote for the Democratic candidate and 30% would vote for the Republican. **(6)** According to the Newsweek Poll, right now 53 percent of Americans would like to see the Democrats win control of Congress, compared to just 34 percent who wanted the Republicans to retain control. **(7)** Interestingly, the Democratic Party seized control of Congress in November 2006 elections.

Republican Senator Rick Santorum, who faced a difficult re-election battle against Democrat Bob Casey in November 2006, used "Islamic fascism" repeatedly. "In World War II we fought Nazism and Japanese imperialism," Santorum said in a high-profile speech at the National Press Club on July 20. "Today we are fighting Islamic fascism. They attacked us on Sept. 11, because we are the greatest obstacle in front of them to their openly declared mission of subjecting the entire world to their fanatical rule."

But this is not all. Anti-Islam bigotry remains a popular past time for public officials and personalities:

Chapter II - The post 9/11 Challenges – Islamophobia [36]

Attorney General John Ashcroft once said: "Islam is a religion in which God requires you to send your son to die for him. Christianity is a faith in which God sent his Son to die for you." **(8)**

Republican Colorado Congressman Tom Tancredo advocated nuking Islam's holiest place, Mecca, to get even with another terrorist attacks. He refused to apologize for suggesting the United States could target Muslim holy sites if radical Islamic terrorists set off multiple nuclear attacks in American cities. "It's a tough issue to deal with. Tough things are said. And we should not shy away from saying things that need to be said." **(9)** Tancredo was not the only congressman to suggest nuking the Muslims. Rep. Sam Johnson (R-TX) bragged to a crowd of veterans that he had advised Bush to nuke Syria. "Syria is the problem. Syria is where those weapons of mass destruction are, in my view. You know, I can fly an F-15, put two nukes on 'em and I'll make one pass. We won't have to worry about Syria anymore." **(10)** The two congressmen's remarks probably reflected a general mood of the American public that approves the use of atomic bombs, especially against terrorist targets as indicated by a 2005 Associated Press poll. **(11)**

And this tirade against Islam and Muslims continues. Colorado Rep. Jim Welker, a Republican, sent an e-mail to his constituents titled: "Beware of Islam in America." The text of his e-mail read, in part, "Can a devout Muslim be an American patriot and loyal citizen? Politically, no. Because he must submit to the mullah, who teaches annihilation of Israel and destruction of America, the great Satan." **(12)**

To borrow from Trish Schuh, this state-sponsored smirking has trickled down to spawn a climate of recreational cruelty in the US military. Deputy Undersecretary of Defense, Lt. Gen. William Jerry Boykin propagated hate at the grassroots level in dozens of speeches to church groups, saying that the war on terror was actually spiritual warfare, with the enemy 'Satan' being embodied by Islam. Speaking of God versus Allah he said: "Well, you know what I knew, that my God was bigger than his. I knew that my God was a real God, and his was an idol." **(13)**

Dropping down the chain of command, Marine Corp Lt. Gen. James Mattis said it was "fun to shoot some people." His comment in a gathering of defense contractors in San Diego, California came in reference to fighting

Chapter II - The post 9/11 Challenges – Islamophobia [37]

insurgents in Iraq where he commanded Marines during the battle for Fallujah in spring 2004. "Actually it's quite fun to fight them, you know. It's a hell of a hoot," Mattis said, prompting laughter from some military members in the audience. "It's fun to shoot some people. I'll be right up there with you. I like brawling." Mattis, who also commanded Marine expeditions in Afghanistan, went on to say: "You go into Afghanistan, you got guys who slap women around for five years because they didn't wear a veil....You know, guys like that ain't got no manhood left anyway. So it's a hell of a lot of fun to shoot them." **(14)**

In another hard-line tale for fighting "Islamic terrorists," flyers were posted on a California National Guard military base extolling the World War I General John Pershing as a hero for executing "Muslim terrorists" with bullets dipped in pig's blood, thus excluding them from Paradise. ``Maybe it is time for this segment of history to repeat itself, maybe in Iraq?" stated the flyer that was posted outside a cubicle in the Guard's Civil Support Division. ``The question is, where do we find another Black Jack Pershing?" Initially, the National Guard defended the flyer as ``historically accurate," but later removed it because of concerns raised by some anti-war activists activists. **(15)**

The Christian Right

The Christian Right leaders aligned with the Bush Administration also fanned the flames of fear and hatred. **(16)**

Attacks on Islam from the Christian Right escalated soon after 9/11 when the Rev. Franklin Graham labeled Islam a "very evil and wicked religion." Soon other evangelical leaders weighed in, using the "war on terrorism" as an opportunity to reignite historic Christian-Muslim tensions. Leading rightwing Baptist Jerry Falwell described Muhammad as a "terrorist" — remarks that helped spark deadly riots in India.

Televangelist Pat Robertson who sought the Republican presidential nomination in 1988, calls Prophet Mohammad as fanatic and describes Islam worst than Nazism. In September 2002 he said: "This man [Muhammad] was an absolute wild-eyed fanatic. He was a robber and a brigand." Two months later he adds on his Christian Broadcasting Network:

Chapter II - The post 9/11 Challenges – Islamophobia [38]

"Somehow I wish the Jews in America would wake up, open their eyes and read what is being said about them...This is worse than the Nazis...Adolf Hitler was bad, but what the Muslims want to do to the Jews is worse." Yet in another broadcast in April 2006 he repeated this theme: "we are not listening to what Islam says, just as we did not listen to what Adolf Hitler said in *Mein Kampf*." Robertson claimed that we are ignoring the threats by "not only the radical Muslims but Islam in general," because "it is not politically correct to believe that any religious group would do what they claim they are going to do."

The Rev. Franklin Graham, chosen by George Bush to deliver the prayers at his presidential inauguration, says that the God of Islam is not the same God of Christians. In Nov. 2001 he said: "We're not attacking Islam but Islam has attacked us. The God of Islam is not the same God. He's not the son of God of the Christian or Judeo-Christian faith. It's a different God, and I believe it is a very evil and wicked religion." In August 2002 he went a step further to say that the Quran teaches violence: "I believe the Qur'an teaches violence. It doesn't teach peace, it teaches violence." Franklin Graham reaffirmed his scorn for Islam again on March 15, 2006 when he told an interviewer of the ABC News "Nightline" that he hasn't changed his mind about Islam.

Evangelist Jimmy Swaggart called Mohammed a "sex deviant" and a pervert and demanded that Muslim students in the US be expelled. Jimmy Swaggart says: "I like our President but he's dead wrong when he says Islam or the Quran is a book of love and peace. Mr. President, that has got to be the most asinine, idiotic, ridiculous, utterly ludicrous statement that I've ever heard in my life....You know what we ought to do? We ought to take every single Muslim student in every college in this nation and ship them back to where they came from. And we ought to tell every other Muslim living in this nation, if you say one word, you're gone. You're gone." **(17)**

The record gets worse. Rev. Jerry Vines, former president of Southern Baptist Convention, says "[Muhammad was] a demon-possessed pedophile." **(18)** Rev. Jerry Vines argues: "And I will tell you Allah is not Jehovah, either. Jehovah's not going to turn you into a terrorist that'll try to bomb people and take the lives of thousands and thousands of people." **(19)** Televangelist Benny Hinn believes that the "the Muslim population is going down!...We are on God's side. This is not a war between Arabs and Jews. It's a war between God and the devil." **(20)**

Numerous surveys have found evangelicals in general to have more negative views on Islam than other Americans. This rhetoric is reflected in evangelical books and articles that have been published in the last decade, but particularly since 9/11. A new study by Richard Cimino, editor of Religion Watch newsletter, finds that this discourse sheds as much light on how evangelicals view the challenges of pluralism and relativism in American society as it does about their views on Islam. The study, entitled: "No God In Common: American Evangelical Discourse on Islam After 9/11," through an analysis of popular evangelical books published before and after 9/11, the study finds that most of the post-9/11 literature draws sharper distinctions between Islam and Christianity, as well as asserting that Islam is essentially violent. **(21)**

Yet in another example of Islamophobia, on July 22, 2002, a fundamentalist Christian organization, the American Family Association Center for Law and Policy and three anonymous students file a law suit against the University of North Carolina, Church Hall, because it required new students to read a book – the Quran an Early Revelation by Prof. *Michael A. Sells.* In their complaint, the plaintiffs claimed that UNC indoctrinates students with deceptive claims about the peaceful nature of Islam, violating the separation of church and state. A committee of the state legislature voted to terminate funding for the course. However, the lawsuit fizzled at on Aug.15, U.S. District Court judge Carlton Tilley, Jr., refused to grant a temporary restraining order. Syndicated talk show host Bill O'Reilly fuming against the University of North Carolina's decision said that it is like teaching UNC students Adolf Hitler's Mein Kampf. Freshmen shouldn't study "our enemy's religion," he added.

Rightist syndicated columnist Ann Coulter feeds into this frenzy even further. She suggests: "We should invade their [Muslim] countries, kill their leaders and convert them to Christianity." **(22)** She advocates that the government deport Arabs and Muslims. "Congress could pass a law requiring that all

Chapter II - The post 9/11 Challenges – Islamophobia [40]

aliens from Arabic countries leave. . . .Congress could certainly pass a law requiring all aliens to get approval from the INS before boarding an airplane in the United States." **(23)** Her racist rhetoric labels all Muslims as being terrorists. She urges Muslims who want to avoid deportation to "spy" on fellow citizens: "Not all Muslims may be terrorists, but all terrorists are Muslim. . . There will be two fail-safes: (1) Muslim immigrants who agree to spy on the millions of Americans unaffected by the deportation order can stay; and (2) any Muslim immigrant who gets a U.S. Senator to waive his deportation - by name - gets to stay." **(24)**

And what message the Muslims got from the appointment of a well-known Islamophobist to the government think tank, the U.S. Institute of Peace. In April 2003 President Bush nominated Daniel Pipes, founder of the Anti-Islamist Institute to the board of the Institute. The nomination drew sharp criticism from the Muslim community and fellow Americans. Pipes has been repeatedly criticized in the mainstream American press and by scholars for his agenda-oriented low standards of data collection and unscholarly work. He repeatedly claimed that the majority of Muslims are troublesome, violent, terrorists, or terrorist-supporters. Despite being rejected by Congress amid wide criticism, President Bush made a recess appointment of Pipes to the Peace Institute Board in August 2003.

Islamophobia in 2008 election [24a]

Less than a week after Senator John McCain clinched Republican nomination for November presidential election, Steve King, a leading Republican Congressman launched a bitter racist and Islamophobic attack against Senator Barak Obama, a leading Democratic presidential hopeful.

On an Iowa radio station on March 8, 2008, Congressman Steve King said, "if [Obama] is elected president, then the radical Islamists and their supporters will be dancing in the streets in greater numbers than they did on September 11 because they will declare victory in this War on Terror."

Echoing Cincinnati radio talk show, Bill Cunningham, who warmed up McCain crowd by chanting Barack Hussain Obama, King said: "[Obama's] middle name [Hussain] does matter...because they read a meaning into that

Chapter II - The post 9/11 Challenges – Islamophobia [41]

in the rest of the world...They will be dancing in the streets because of his middle name [and] because of who his father was and because of his posture that says: pull out of the Middle East and pull out of this conflict."

Congressman King, who is the ranking Republican member of the House Judiciary Subcommittee on Immigration, Citizenship, Refugees, Border Security and International Law, reiterated his comments on March 10 in an interview with the Associated Press saying, "[Obama will] certainly be viewed as a savior for them," King told The Associated Press, "That's why you will see them supporting him, encouraging him."

Such bigoted and ignorant comments from a rightwing Republican are not unexpected. They echo outrageous comments that have become commonplace among right-wing commentators and radio talk show hosts. Alarmingly, King's fear promoting comments are part of an increasingly vicious pattern as malicious forms of anti-Muslim and anti-Arab bigotry are becoming more prevalent in mainstream discourse.

Disappointedly, Hillary Clinton, in her negatively campaigning, was also playing the religious bigotry card. When Hillary Clinton lost 11 primaries in a row, and saw her life long dream slipping away, she in effect in words and pictures told the American people, "Barack Obama is a clucking Muslim trigger!" When asked if Barack Obama was a Muslim she said, "I don't know." Hillary Clinton's comment came as her campaign staff sent a picture of Barack Obama dressed like an African Muslim to the Drudge Report. Her negative campaign worked and helped in giving her victory in Texas and Ohio primaries.

Muslim faith used as scare tactic against Obama [24b]

During the 2008 election campaign the right wing launched a smear campaign against Barack Obama with false claims that he is a Muslim. Confusion about Obama's religion was sometimes encouraged during the 2008 campaign.

An Associated Press photograph that circulated on the Internet, and was posted on The Drudge Report, showed Obama dressed in traditional local garments — a white turban and a wraparound white robe — during a visit to Kenya in 2006. The use of the image of Obama in a turban was clearly

Chapter II - The post 9/11 Challenges – Islamophobia

designed to make a visual link between the candidate and Islam, a political tactic that sought to exploit existing anti-Muslim prejudice in our society.

The turban "scandal" was all part of what is being referred to as "the Muslim smear." It included everything from exaggerated enunciations of Obama's middle name to the online whisper campaign that Obama attended a fundamentalist madrassa in Indonesia (a lie) and was sworn in on a Quran while taking oath as Senator (another lie).

What was disturbing about the disgraceful and racist premise behind the entire "Muslim smear," was that being Muslim is de facto a source of shame. This underscores that for many bigoted Americans in the 21st century, calling someone a Muslim is a slur.

Barack Obama has publicly responded to questions regarding his religion on more than one occasion. During a debate of Democratic presidential candidates on January 15, 2008 in Las Vegas, Nevada, moderator Brian Williams asked Obama about the rumor that he's "trying to hide the fact that [he is] a Muslim". Obama responded that "the facts are: I am a Christian. I have been sworn in [to the US Senate] with a Bible." He then said "in the Internet age, there are going to be lies that are spread all over the place. I have been victimized by these lies." [Wikipedia]

In addition to Obama's personal responses, the 2008 Obama presidential campaign responded to the false claims made against him by people opposed to his candidacy by launching a website called "FightTheSmears.com".[Wikipedia]

The Muslim smear campaign brought desired results. Public opinion surveys carried out beginning in 2008 showed that a number of Americans (predominately Republicans), believe that Obama is either a Muslim, is the Antichrist or both. In March 2008, a survey conducted by Pew Research Center found that 10% of respondents believed that he is a Muslim. Those who were more likely to believe he is a Muslim included political conservatives (both Republicans and Democrats), people who had not attended college, people who lived in the Midwest or the South, and people in rural areas. [Wikipedia]

Islam & Muslims in the Post-9/11 America

Chapter II - The post 9/11 Challenges – Islamophobia [43]

A University of Georgia study found that the percentage of Americans who believed that Obama is a Muslim remained constant at approximately 20% in September, October, and November 2008, despite frequent attempts by the media to correct this misperception. [Wikipedia]

Fear-mongering in 2008 presidential election [24c]

In a replay of the 2004 and 2006 elections the desperate Republican Party was playing its typical tactic, Scare America. With little to fall on nearly eight years of President Bush's misrule that landed the nation in the worst economic crisis since the Great Depression, the desperate Republican Party has ratcheted up its campaign with half-truths and fear mongering which has been the hallmark of the Bush Administration.

To borrow Arianna Huffington, fear is a frighteningly effective sales pitch -- one that has worked like a charm for Republicans since the days of the Cold War Red Scares, and especially since 9/11. The most blatant use of fear mongering came on the final day of the Republican National Convention when John McCain delivered his GOP nomination acceptance speech and Rudy Giuliani and Mitt Romney hyped the threat of the so-called "Islamic terrorism."

The Republican presidential nominee Senator John McCain declined to stop using the adjective "Islamic" to describe terrorists and extremist enemies of the United States. Steve Schmidt, a former Bush White House aide who is now a McCain media strategist, told The Washington Times that the use of the word is appropriate and that the candidate will continue to define the enemy that way. Mr. McCain often uses the term "Islamic" to describe terrorist enemies. The two remaining Democrats in the presidential field, Sen. Barack Obama of Illinois and Sen. Hillary Rodham Clinton of New York, generally shun such word usage. Mr. McCain, an ex-Navy fighter pilot and leading hawk on the Iraq war, regularly uses the term "Islamic" in major foreign-policy speeches and in news conferences.

Hate-provoking DVD [24d]

In a pathetic attempt to scare people into voting for John McCain, 28 million copies of a right-wing, terror propaganda DVD produced in Israel -

Chapter II - The post 9/11 Challenges – Islamophobia

"Obsession: Radical Islam's War Against the West" – was mailed and bundled in newspaper deliveries to voters in swing states.

The New York Times in September 2008 inserted 145,000 DVDs in its papers delivered in the following markets: Denver, Miami/Palm Beach, Tampa, Orlando, Detroit, Kansas City, St Louis, Cincinnati, Philadelphia, Pittsburgh, Milwaukee/Madison. These are all in swing states. Next, it was being distributed in many newspapers in the electoral battleground states of Ohio, Michigan, Florida, Pennsylvania and Colorado, in addition to North Carolina.

The Clarion Fund, founded by Israeli-Canadian Rabbi Raphael Shore, paid millions of dollars to get the DVD out. Not surprisingly, the shadowy Clarion Fund has refused to disclose its board of directors or donors.

The noxious propaganda movie, also distributed at the Democratic and Republican parties nomination conventions by Watch Obsession Organization, has been relegated to the university film circuit where right-wing and pro-Israel campus groups have organized screenings.

The arrival of the controversial DVD on the eve of the election was clearly intended to scare voters into supporting McCain, turning them against the candidate whose middle name happens to be "Hussein." "It was intended to be a way of linking Obama to Islam, but it backfired when a lot of people began saying wait, what's going on?" the Newsweek quoted Jen'nan Read, a professor of sociology at Duke University as saying. "It not only mobilized many Muslim-American voters, but brought out other undecided voters in support of Obama rather than McCain."

Islamophobia in 2010 election [24e]

Since 9/11, there has been a steady rise in Islamophobia, however during mid-term election campaign there was an exponential rise of anti-Islam and anti-Muslim bigotry. Many Religious Right leaders and opportunist politicians asserted repeatedly that Islam is not a religion at all but a political cult, that Muslims cannot be good Americans and that mosques are fronts for extremist 'jihadis.' There was a substantial increase in the number of political candidates using Islamophobic tactics in an effort to leverage votes, and use such tactics as a platform to enhance their political visibility.

Islam & Muslims in the Post-9/11 America

Chapter II - The post 9/11 Challenges – Islamophobia [45]

Consequently, Muslims rejected the Republican Party at the polls in 2008 and 2010. According to the American Muslim Taskforce on Civil Rights and Elections, just 2.2 percent of Muslims voted for Sen. John McCain in 2008.

As Stephan Salisbury reported, during the 2010 midterm election campaign, virtually every hard-charging candidate on the far right took a moment to trash a Muslim, a mosque, or Islamic pieties. In the wake of those elections, with 85 new Republican House members and a surging Tea Party movement, the political virtues of anti-Muslim rhetoric as a means of rousing voters and alarming the general electorate have gone largely unchallenged. It has become an article of faith that a successful 2010 candidate on the right should treat Islam with revulsion, drawing a line between America the Beautiful and the destructive impurities of Islamic cultists and radicals.

Throughout the 2010 election campaign the seven-million strong American Muslim community and their faith were dehumanized as the Republican Party once again used Islamophobia as a political tool. The anti-Islam and anti-Muslim rhetoric depicting Islam as enemy got steam from the Quran-burning publicity stunts by a minor church in Florida. Two more elements were added to this anti-Muslim hysteria in this election campaign. Controversy over the 51Park project popularly known as Ground Zero mosque and conspiracies that Sharia law will displace the US constitution.

To borrow Kelley B. Vlahos: In fact, anti-Muslim rage in today's national discourse is populism's low-hanging fruit, and many Republicans hungrily grabbed at it with both fists and were duly rewarded this campaign season. Sure, not every one of the Sarah Palin/Tea Party-endorsed candidates won on Nov. 2, but those who did, won in part because of their willingness to indulge in the Islamophobia coursing through the Republican base today, not despite it. The same Republican base that helped the party torpedo the Democrats last Tuesday, taking back the House, six senate seats, six governorships, and 680 slots in state legislatures.

Never in any U.S. elections before so many campaign ads were aired mongering fear against Islam or Muslims. This year, Republicans have crossed all limits. They are openly bashing Muslims and Islam to get more votes in elections.

Chapter II - The post 9/11 Challenges – Islamophobia [46]

In August 2010, Republicans amplified their rhetoric to turn the so-called "Ground Zero Mosque" into a campaign issue. Republican gubernatorial candidate Rick Lazio voiced concern over the project in early July 2010, calling on N.Y. Attorney General Andrew Cuomo, who was also the Democratic gubernatorial candidate, to investigate the center's funding. Cuomo rejected the call for an investigation and responded to Lazio in a letter, asking, "What are we about, if not religious freedom?"

Leading Republican figures like Newt Gingrich, a former speaker of the House, and former Alaska governor Sarah Palin, the party's 2008 vice-presidential nominee, had been voicing opposition to the Islamic center.

At an iftar dinner for Ramadan held at the White House on Aug. 13, 2010, President Barrack Obama supported the right of Muslims throughout the U.S. – including in lower Manhattan – to build new mosques and community centers, saying, "as a citizen, and as president, I believe that Muslims have the same right to practice their religion as anyone else in this country."

After his remarks were widely interpreted as an endorsement of the New York City Islamic center, he clarified the next day that his comments were meant to address the issue of religious freedom rather than "the wisdom of making the decision to put a mosque" near the ground zero site.

The inflammatory rhetoric surrounding the project has stirred hatred toward Muslims in America. There has been so much fear-mongering and so much misinformation in the debate peddled by bigots and rightwing politicians. The constant vilification of Islam and Muslims over the air on radio talk shows, in newspapers and the Internet was contributing to the rise in anti-Muslim sentiment across the country.

Not surprisingly, a poll on August 29 by the extreme right San Diego, California 760 KFMB AM talk radio station indicated that 70% of those polled are in favor of forced registration for American Muslims in a national database. The same day a poll conducted by Chris Matthews show at the MSNBC revealed that more than half of Republicans polled say they have a negative attitude toward Islam, this compared to only 27% of Democrats.

A PEW Institute poll result released on August 24 corroborated the findings of Chris Mathews show. By more than two-to-one (54% to 21%),

Republicans expressed an unfavorable opinion of Islam and by more than four-to-one (74% to 17%), Republicans say they agree more with those who object to the building of the Ground Zero Mosque. By contrast, more Democrats agree with the center's supporters than its opponents (by 47% to 39%).

According to a new TIME poll, 61% of respondents opposed the construction of the Park51 project, compared with 26% who support it. Yet the survey also revealed that many Americans harbor lingering animosity toward Muslims. Twenty-eight percent of voters do not believe Muslims should be eligible to sit on the U.S. Supreme Court. Nearly one-third of the country thinks adherents of Islam should be barred from running for President — a slightly higher percentage than the 24% who mistakenly believe the current occupant of the Oval Office is himself a Muslim.

Oklahoma anti-Shariah measure [24g]

Islam-bashing for political gain was a chilling feature of this year's election campaign and demagogues misled Oklahomans to pass an anti-Muslim ballot measure. The Oklahoma anti-Islam measure is one of the best examples of politicians duping the public through fear mongering. It is demonizing the Muslims in order to mobilize votes. The voters of Oklahoma were badly misled by demagogues into passing a profoundly un-American measure.

Demagoguery is defined as: "the practice of a leader who obtains power by means of impassioned appeals to the emotions and prejudices of the populace." Oklahoma Rep. Rex Duncan's proposed the anti-Islam ballot measure, known as SQ 755, is a great example of this practice. When it was proposed, Sen. Anthony Sykes, a co-author, dubbed it the "Save Our State," amendment saying, "Sharia law coming to the U.S. is a scary concept."

Muneer Awad, executive director of the Council on American-Islamic Relations in Oklahoma, quickly challenged the amendment, saying it demonizes his faith. In a strongly-worded ruling Chief Judge Vicki Miles-LaGrange of the United States District Court in Oklahoma on November 29, 2010 granted an injunction that bars certification of an anti-Islam state ballot measure (SQ 755) passed in the November 2 election. If it had been certified, SQ 755 would have amended that state's constitution to forbid

Chapter II - The post 9/11 Challenges – Islamophobia [48]

judges from considering Islamic principles or international law when deciding a case.

In a major blow to the anti-Islam and anti-Muslim bigots taking refuge behind the so-called anti-Sharia legislation, a federal appeals court on January 10, 2012 agreed with a lower court that blocked an Oklahoma law. The judge for the 10th U.S. Circuit Court of Appeals in Denver, Colo., agreed with the lower court and upheld the injunction — rejecting an appeal by the state of Oklahoma. "Because the amendment discriminates among religions, it is 'suspect,'" the higher court ruled, "and 'we apply strict scrutiny in adjudging its constitutionality.'"

Muslim-bashing campaign at US campuses

Not surprisingly, other bigots seized this opportunity to create hatred against Islam and Muslims. In a bid to spread fear and hatred under the guise of patriotism and freedom of speech, David Horowitz, a neo-conservative polemicist, launched an Arab/Muslim-bashing campaign at campuses across the nation in October 2007. Borrowing from President Bush's terminology 'Islamo-Fascists,' Horowitz packaged his anti-Arab/anti-Muslim campaign as "Islamo-Fascist Awareness Week."

Horowitz asked students participating in the campaign to disseminate presentations, such as "The Islamic Mein Kampf," (meaning the Quran). In a throwback to McCarthyism, right-wing students were encouraged to issue press releases condemning those who refused to sign for the Islamo-Fascist week. It means either you are with us or with our enemy.

But just who are the "Islamic fascists? According to Horowitz's FrontPage magazine, they include the Muslim Student Association, which has chapters on hundreds of U.S. campuses--and the Council on American Islamic Relations, which advocates for civil rights and tracks hate crimes against Arabs and Muslims.

There was a collection of bigots and crackpots that Horowitz had recruited to speak for the Oct 22-26 2007 Islamophobia week. Islamophobist right wing columnist Ann Coulter was one. Other luminaries included: Rick Santorum, a former US Senator, who has compared homosexuality to incest; Robert Spencer who claims Islam is "the world's most intolerant religion"; and noted

Chapter II - The post 9/11 Challenges – Islamophobia [49]

anti-Arab commentator and Islamophobe Daniel Pipes who once said that "Palestinians are a miserable people...and they deserve to be."

Some other well-known Islamophobist speakers were: Dennis Prager, Sean Hannity and Wafa Sultan. More intellectual takes came from such neoconservative icons of Middle East policy as Michael Ledeen who seeks to apply Machiavellian principles to the modern world.Surely such a notorious lineup of racist, bigoted, Islamophobic, anti-Semitic and Machiavellian speakers did not serve to educate but to promote hatred and spread misinformation and lies.

Venom from the radio talk show hosts

The cult of hatred against Islam and Muslims is manifesting in different sectors of the society. The demonizing of Arabs and Muslims in America began well before the terrible tragedy of September 11, 2001. It can be traced to deliberate mythmaking by the Hollywood movies as enumerated by the Award-winning film authority Jack G. Shaheen in her book Reel Bad Arabs: How Hollywood Vilifies (2001), stereotyping as part of conscious strategy of 'experts' and polemicists on the Middle East, the selling of a foreign policy agenda by the US government officials and groups seeking to affect that agenda, and a public susceptible to images identifying the unwelcome 'other' in its midst. **(25)**

However, what is new after 9/11 is that now demonizing Muslims and Islam is not only more widespread but also considerably more mainstream and respectable.

While print and electronic media continues unabated campaign to smear Islam, radio talk show hosts are busy in spewing out venoms against Islam and Muslims. Event a higher court rules that a letter calling for killing Muslims is protected by the freedom of speech.

Los Angeles radio show host Bill Handel even made fun of the deaths of about 360 Muslim pilgrims during the January 2006 stampede in Mina, Saudi Arabia. Later Handel apologized for his remarks only under pressure from the Muslim civil rights group.

Islam & Muslims in the Post-9/11 America

Chapter II - The post 9/11 Challenges – Islamophobia [50]

Nationally syndicated radio host Michael Savage called for "kill 100 million" Muslims. On his radio show, Savage told listeners that "intelligent people, wealthy people ... are very depressed by the weakness that America is showing to these psychotics in the Muslim world. They say, 'Oh, there's a billion of them.' " Savage continued: "I said, 'So, kill 100 million of them, then there'd be 900 million of them.' **(26)**

The host of a New York morning radio show and the rest of her on-air crew were suspended indefinitely in January 2005 for airing a tasteless song parody that mocked victims of the catastrophic south Asia tsunami. The song included references to "screaming chinks" and orphaned children "sold into child slavery." The chorus began, "So now you're screwed, it's a tsunami, you'd better run ... go find your mommy."

WMAL-AM radio host Geoff Metcalf says: "According to the Quran, believers in Islam are not required to tell infidels, and that's us, the truth. So they apparently have permission to lie when it is appropriate." On his July 25, 2005 program Graham parrots "Islam is a terrorist organization" 23 times. On the same show, he also said repeatedly that "moderate Muslims are those who only want to kill Jews" and that "the problem is not extremism. The problem is Islam." Most callers to the program expressed similar hostility to Muslims and to the faith of Islam. **(27)**

A "Kill Muslims" call got a boost from the Arizona state Supreme Court ruled that a Tucson newspaper could not be held liable for publishing a letter that urged people to kill Muslims to retaliate for the death of American soldiers in Iraq. In a 5-0 ruling, Arizona's highest court found unanimously the Tucson Citizen was protected by the First Amendment to the U.S. Constitution and could not be sued for printing the letter in December 2003. **(28)**

Desecration of the Quran

In May 2005 American Muslims were shocked to know that their Holy book, the Quran has been desecrated by the US interrogators at the US detention center Guantanamo Bay. The revelation by the Newsweek drew worldwide Muslim reaction that compelled the magazine to retract its story about US interrogators flushing the Quran down a toilet at Guantanamo Bay.

Islam & Muslims in the Post-9/11 America

Chapter II - The post 9/11 Challenges – Islamophobia [51]

Secretary of Defense Rumsfeld maintained that the revelation was not true, and demanded that Newsweek explain to the Muslim world "the care that the US military takes" to respect Islamic beliefs. But the desecration had been documented independently elsewhere.

The Denver Post: prisoners were "forced to watch copies of the Koran being flushed down toilets" (January, 2005), Financial Times: "they were beaten and had their Korans thrown into toilets" (Oct 28, 2004), New York Daily News: "They would kick the Koran, throw it into the toilet and generally disrespect it." (Aug. 5, 2004), The Independent UK: "Guards allegedly threw prisoners' Korans into toilets" (Aug 5, 2004), The Observer UK: "copies of the Koran would be trampled on by soldiers and, on one occasion, thrown into a toilet bucket." (March 14, 2004), Washington Post: "American soldiers insulted Islam by sitting on the Koran or dumping their sacred text into a toilet to taunt them." **(29)**

These were but a few of similar media reports over a period of years. The desecration was also confirmed by the Geneva-based International Committee of Red Cross (ICRC). According to an ICRC spokesman the international body confidentially reported in 2002 and 2003 the incidents to U.S. authorities about American personnel at the Guantanamo Bay detention center showing disrespect the Quran. **(30)**

At the same time, detainees told FBI interrogators as early as April 2002 that mistreatment of the Quran was widespread at the Guantanamo military prison. According to the summaries of FBI interviews, obtained by the American Civil Liberties Union as part of an ongoing lawsuit, there were at least a dozen allegations that the Quran was kicked, thrown to the floor or withheld as punishment. One prisoner said in August 2002 that guards had "flushed a Quran in the toilet" and had beaten some detainees. **(31)**

Other instances of Quran's desecration were also recorded.

One online fundraiser sold printed toilet paper with the words "Koran, the Holy Quran" which was then distributed to mosques and the media with a letter claiming the Quran was a "cookbook for terrorists" and incited violence. An American Muslim woman - Azza Basarudin - who ordered a copy of the Quran from Amazon.com was shocked to receive one with the words "F*ck this piece of sh*t" and "Death to all Muslims" scrawled across the inside cover. **(32)**

In Backsburg, Virginia., a bag stuffed with burned Qurans was left in front of an Islamic center, shocking members when they arrived for prayers. The torched copies of the Muslim holy book were inside a plastic shopping bag that was placed at the center's front door sometime before prayers. **(33)**

In Tennessee, a video titled "kill the koran" was posted on MySpace.com showing two men shooting a Quran with a military rifle. The video was later tossed down outside a Chattanooga mosque. The footage first shows a man identified as mully88 holding a paperback Quran outside a Barnes & Noble Booksellers. The next scene, taped in a wooded area, shows mully88 and another man taking turns shooting the Quran with a rifle mully88 identifies as a Colt M-16. The final scene shows a man tossing the bullet-riddled book onto the sidewalk outside the Islamic Center. In his profile on the Web site, mully88 identifies himself as a 33-year-old college-educated Chattanooga resident working as a paramedic and mechanic. He says he would "love to see the white race rule the world" and lists his heroes as "anyone who has killed a Muslim or tried to kill a Muslim." **(34)**

Burning of the Quran stunt [34a]

Desecration of the Quran, Islam's holy book, is another method of bigotry. Anti-Islam and anti-Muslim Pastor Terry Jones of a tiny Florida Church, known as the Dove World Outreach Center, planned to commemorate 9/11 by burning copies of the Holy Quran. He abandoned the Quran burning stunt when US Secretary of Defense phoned him saying that his provocative act would inflame the Muslim world and jeopardize the lives of American troops now deployed in many Muslim countries. The Miami Herald quoted Pentagon spokesman Geoff Morrell as saying that Gates had weighed concerns that making such a call could encourage copycats who want attention, but felt that "if that phone call could save the life of one man or woman in uniform, that call was worth placing."

Pastor of the 50-member Pentecostal church, Jones, made the stunt abandoning announcement at a press conference while standing alongside Imam Muhammad Musri, the president of the Islamic Society of Central Florida. He claimed that his decision to scrap the burning of Muslims' holy book was tied to his understanding that the New York Islamic cultural center project officially named as Park51 but popularly known as the Ground Zero mosque, would be scrapped or relocated.

However, Imam Feisal Abdul Rauf has not agreed to such a deal. Park51 posted a Twitter feed after Jones spoke. It said that "it is untrue that Park51 is being moved. The project is moving ahead as planned." Tellingly, Jones had never invoked the New York mosque controversy as a reason for his planned protest. He cited his belief that "the Quran is evil" because it espouses something other than biblical truth and incites radical, violent behavior among Muslims.

Tellingly, Jones message was not lost to many. Torn pages of the Quran were found on Sept 10 at the front of the Islamic Center of East Lansing, Michigan. Some of the pages appeared to be smeared with feces.

Amid heightened hate speech and fear-mongering mosques in California, Tennessee, New York, Illinois, Wisconsin, Kentucky, Texas, and Florida have faced vocal opposition or have been targeted by hate incidents. In one incident, on the 9/11 eve, vandals spray-painted "9-11" on windows and countertops at the Muslim owned Jaffa Market in Columbus, Ohio. Some cash and a laptop computer were stolen, while several display cases were vandalized.

On Sept 8, back wall of the Hudson Islamic Center in New York was pained with slur "sand n**gers" and an obscenity. In early September, a Phoenix under construction mosque was vandalized. Paint was spilled on the floor and several tall, arched glass windows were broken by what appeared to be gunshots. There was also anti-Muslim graffiti. The same mosque was vandalized in the February.

The presence of mosques and the building of new mosques have become a divisive issue in several communities across the country in recent years. A church may be a church, and a temple a temple, but through the prism of emotion that grips many Americans, almost a decade after 9/11, a mosque can apparently represent a lot of things.

Controversial cartoons

And here is a final take of the anti-Islam tirade.

Again to borrow from Trish Schuh, packaged in western free speech cliches, and marketed as innocent satire, a cheap shot was fired at Islam from Denmark in March 2006. In a "provocation-entrapment" propaganda, the Danish newspaper *Jylland-Posten* published controversial cartoons depicting the Prophet Muhammad as a terrorist/suicide bomber with a ticking bomb for a turban. Many other newspapers across Europe and America have joined the fray as what they disingenuously claim as 'demonstrations of freedom of expression.' Ironically, Jyllands-Posten had refused to run cartoons of Jesus Christ fearing an outcry. Its editor says: "if the cartoon provoked an attack, it would only 'confirm the idiotic positions' of Muslim extremists." Predictably, there were widespread bloody protests throughout the Muslim world. When protests across the Muslim world became louder and some Muslim governments decided to pull off Danish products from their market, Europe appeared to be stunned by such reactions.

President Bush defended the publication of the controversial cartoons as free speech while condemned the protests which had swept the Muslim world. "We reject violence as a way to express discontent with what may be printed in the free press," Bush told reporters after a meeting with Jordan's King Abdullah II on Feb.8, 2006. Major US newspapers – the New York Post, Washington Post, USA Today refrained from joing the fray but the Philadelphia Inquirer, Austin American-Statesman and Rocky Mountain News were few papers which seized upon the free speech privilege.

I could go on giving more and more examples of Islamophobia in the post-9/11 America but conclude by saying that this avalanche of damaging association of Islam with terrorism and violence has increased Americans' prejudice against Islam and Muslims. Numerous opinion polls conducted after 9/11 indicated a steady rise in the sentiments against the Muslims and their faith among the fellow Americans. In February 2002 – less than six months after the terrorist attacks of September 11 – the country was evenly divided in its impression of Islam. Americans today are also more likely to believe that Islam encourages violence, at least in comparison to other religions around the world. Here are some opinion polls that echo the

Chapter II - The post 9/11 Challenges – Islamophobia [55]

climate of hysteria that has been whipped up by the Bush administration and fuelled by the media and political and religious leaders:

Thirty-nine percent of respondents to the USA TODAY/Gallup Poll of August 2006 said they felt at least some prejudice against Muslims. The same percentage favored requiring Muslims, including U.S. citizens, to carry a special ID "as a means of preventing terrorist attacks in the United States." About one-third said U.S. Muslims were sympathetic to al-Qaeda, and 22% said they wouldn't want Muslims as neighbors. 31% said they'd feel more nervous flying if a Muslim man was on the plane; 18% said they'd be more nervous with a Muslim woman. **(35)**

Two polls released on March 9, 2006 indicate that almost half of Americans have a negative perception of Islam and that one in four of those surveyed have extreme anti-Muslim views. The results of the two polls – conducted by Washington Post-ABC and the Council on American-Islamic Relations (CAIR) – were not unexpected as anti-Muslim and anti-Islam campaign continues unabated since 9/11 by print and electronic media along with politicians, religious leaders as well as the government policies that have reinforced Islamophobia which may be defined as "alienation, discrimination, harassment and violence rooted in misinformed and stereotyped representations of Islam and its adherents." The two polls come at a time of increasingly charged atmosphere: the proposed takeover of six US ports operations by a Dubai firm (later abandoned); the wars in Afghanistan and Iraq with little sign of ending; the election of Hamas in the Palestinian territories; and, above all, the riotous protests across the Muslim world against Danish cartoons depicting Prophet Muhammad.

Although Americans believe they are better informed about Islam than they were five years ago, but an April 2006 CBS News poll finds fewer than one in five say their impression of the religion is favorable. Forty-five percent said they have an unfavorable view of Islam, a rise from 36 percent in February. And the public's impression of Islam has diminished even more compared with four years ago. **(36)**

In a shocking revelation to the American Muslims, a December 2004 poll finds nearly half of all Americans believe that the U.S. government should restrict the civil liberties of Muslim-Americans. The Cornell University poll found that 44 percent favored at least some restrictions on the civil liberties of Muslim Americans. The survey also showed that 27 percent of respondents supported requiring all Muslim-Americans to register where they lived with the federal government. Twenty-two percent favored racial profiling to identify potential terrorist threats. And 29 percent thought undercover agents should infiltrate Muslim civic and volunteer organizations to keep tabs on their activities and fund-raising. The poll also found that Republicans and people who described themselves as highly religious were more apt to support curtailing Muslims' civil liberties than Democrats or people who are less religious. Researchers also found that respondents who paid more attention to television news were more likely to fear terrorist attacks and support limiting the rights of Muslim-Americans. **(37)**

The poll result echoes the climate of hysteria that has been whipped up by the Bush administration and fueled by the media.

Since most Americans have little, if any, personal contact with Muslims, their views and opinions are shaped and shaded by what they absorb from the mass media particularly television network news channels. Mainstream movies, magazine periodicals, and newspaper articles also play a central role in fashioning Islamic prejudices and fears. "Our findings highlight that personal religiosity as well as exposure to news media are two important correlates for support of civil liberties," said Dr. James Shanahan, who is one of the authors of the Cornel Report. "We need to explore why these two very important channels of discourse may nurture fear rather than understanding." **(38)**

In this charged atmosphere it was not surprising that in March 2006 a mix of bigotry and political opportunism fuelled opposition to the $6.8 billion sale of the London-based Peninsular & Oriental Steam Navigation Co. to Dubai Ports World. P&O runs shipping terminals in Baltimore, New York, Philadelphia, New Jersey, Miami and New Orleans. Prejudice against Islam and Muslims allowed our politicians to whip a frenzy in rejecting the approval of the Dubai firm to operate American ports.

Exploiting the security concerns, Senator Frank Lautenberg (D-N.J.) went to the extent to announce in a New Jersey public rally: "We wouldn't transfer the title to the devil; we're not going to transfer it to Dubai." During the whole Dubai ports deal debacle, even the Democratic Party leaders engaged in unfounded scare mongering to score political points. The hysteria

Chapter II - The post 9/11 Challenges – Islamophobia [57]

surrounding the Dubai deal issue demonstrates how Islamophobia was used by some politicians to force the cancellation of a normal business deal.

Permission to build new mosques & expansion of mosques denied

The conclusion that flows from this analysis is that the Islamophobia has created an atmosphere of suspicion among the fellow Americans towards the Muslims. One impact of Islamophobia was negative public reaction to the building of new mosques and expansion of the existing ones. In many cases permission to build a new mosque or expansion of the existing mosques was resisted by communities conditioned by the anti-Islam and anti-Muslim rhetoric.

The Islamic Society of Boston was trying to complete a mosque that would be the largest (70,000-square-foot) in this region of the United States. After the city of Boston conveyed a parcel of land to the Islamic Society of Boston (ISB), articles appeared in the Boston Herald in 2003 linking society leaders to Islamic extremists. Boston's Fox TV station followed with broadcasts on the charges, and two local organizations - the David Project, a pro-Israel group, and Citizens for Peace and Tolerance (CPT) - continued to publicize them and pressed for public hearings. CPT claimed that Boston could become a "potential radical Islamic center." The ISB countered that media and local groups, with help from terrorism analyst Steven Emerson, have conspired to halt construction and "incite public sentiment against area Muslims." A local resident also sued the city seeking invalidation of the land sale to the ISB. "It's all part of the unfortunate temper of the times," says John Esposito, a professor at Georgetown University in Washington. "There is such a thing as Islamophobia." **(39)** On May 30, 2007, the two sides in the legal dispute about the construction of a Boston mosque agreed to drop legal actions against each other, a move will allow construction to move forward. The decision came three months after a Suffolk Superior Court judge dismissed a lawsuit by Boston resident James Policastro claiming it was unconstitutional for the city of Boston to sell land at a discount price to developers of an Islamic center. **(40)**

On March 5, 2007, Goldsboro City Council (North Carolina) unanimously voted not allow the construction of a mosque in the northern part of the city. All six councilmen and Mayor Al King agreed with the planning commission's

Chapter II - The post 9/11 Challenges – Islamophobia

recommendation that the building plan was too large for the proposed site off Wayne Memorial Drive and the facility would not provide the required number of parking spaces. Dr. Waheed Akhtar asked City Council last month to rezone his property on the southeast corner of Best Avenue and Wayne Memorial Drive to allow for the construction of a mosque. Akhtar said the building was necessary because he and other Wayne County Muslims have to travel to Greenville or Raleigh to worship. The plans called for a 2,050-square-foot facility that would only be open for a few hours on Fridays and Sundays to prevent traffic congestion along Wayne Memorial Drive. During a public hearing on Feb. 19, 2007, some of those opposed to the mosque did cite traffic concerns, but others simply did not want a mosque in their neighborhood. **(41)**

A South Florida man fighting the opening of a mosque in his suburban neighborhood filed a lawsuit in May 2007 to try and halt construction, a move derided by Arab leaders as anti-Muslim. Rodney Wright claims the relocation of the Islamic Center of South Florida to a new, larger building in his Pompano Beach neighborhood "presents a substantial harm to the well-being, safety and health" of the community. Wright identifies himself as a Christian. The lawsuit claims the leader of the mosque, Imam Hassan Sabri, has repeatedly been associated with others who are tied to terrorist groups including Hamas, al-Qaida and the Palestinian Islamic Jihad, though the connections outlined in the filing appear loose and there is no accusation of direct wrongdoing. Sabri has not been charged with any criminal wrongdoing and neither he nor his mosque have been the target of any publicized investigation. "I'm very much disturbed that in this day and age you'd find people going to such extreme measures to prevent a house of worship from being built in any American city," said Altaf Ali, executive director of the South Florida chapter of the Council on American-Islamic Relations, which is also named as a defendant in the lawsuit. **(42)**

After facing what it saw as anti-Muslim sentiment at a public hearing in March 2006, a Turkish organization dropped its plan to turn a vacant school in South Park, Pennsylvania, into a cultural center. "As a group that promotes peace and dialogue, we have never encountered such negativity in our long history here," the West Penn Cultural Center board said in a statement. The group withdrew its application for a permit to turn the old Broughton Elementary School into a facility where members of the Turkish community could adapt to American culture while maintaining Turkish traditions and language. They also planned to worship in one of the classrooms on Friday afternoons. At the public hearing, some residents said they didn't want the cultural center to renovate the school, claiming Islamic centers and mosques can harbor sleeper cells of terrorists. The group bought the graffiti-covered, boarded up school for $100,000 and planned to make about $300,000 in improvements. In a letter to the editor published by the Pittsburgh Post-Gazette, a resident of South Park demanded that the cultural group openly denounce radical Islam and terrorism if it hopes to be accepted in South Park. **(43)**

The plans for (Michigan) Warren's first mosque were approved in April 2006 after heated discussion by the Planning Commission which once rejected the plan. During the two-hour session when plan was finally approved, one Warren resident was loudly applauded for demanding that the developer prove the Islamic Organization of North America won't have ties to terrorists. **(44)**

Upholding a decision by the borough's Board of Adjustment, a Superior Court Judge in May 2006 denied the Muslim Center of Somerset (NJ) a conditional use variance. The ruling was the latest in a step of obstacles the Center had faced in its quest to run operations out of small house on Southside Avenue. Had the judge approved the request, his decision would have cleared the way for the county's first mosque. The Center acquired the Southside Avenue property in 1998 and had used the facility as a home for its imam -- or spiritual leader -- and as a place for its five daily prayer services. When the borough realized the Center was in violation of parking ordinances, the center applied for variances and site plan approval, which included a proposal for a small expansion. Since then, the Center has been renting space at the Redwood Inn in Bridgewater and the Manville Elks for its services. The board rejected the application in June 2005, but when the Center sued the borough and board, Superior Court Judge Peter Buchsbaum ordered the board to revisit the application, this time considering its beneficial use. But even with conditions in place, the board found the mosque put too much of a burden on the residential neighborhood and denied the application for a second time. **(45)**

A plan to build a mosque in the Houston suburb of Katy was blown up into a neighborhood dispute, with community members warning the place will become a terrorist hotbed and one man threatening to hold pig races on Fridays just to offend the Muslims. One resident had set up a Web site against the mosque project. A committee was formed to buy another property and offer to trade it for the Muslims' land. The Islamic Society of Greater Houston bought the 11-acre site in Katy in September 2006 for $1.1 million. Katy, population 13,000, is 70 percent white and 24 percent Hispanic. **(46)**

In July 2006, the Albanian Associated Fund of Paterson, New Jersey, filed a discrimination lawsuit filed saying that the township officials stalled approving the 4,715-square-foot mosque and 7,957-square-foot school for nearly four years at the planning board level, imposing unusually stringent requirements and several delays. About five years ago, the group bought 11 acres in the township for about $350,000 in an attempt to expand its facilities in safer surroundings. Neighbors have opposed the project, saying it will bring heavy traffic and contribute to existing flooding problems in the area. A federal judge temporarily blocked an attempt to take the property by eminent domain. **(47)**

The Harvard City Council (Michigan) in May 2005 rejected a request to open a Muslim boarding school in the northwest McHenry County town, saying it wasn't compatible with nearby residences. After about 10 minutes of discussion, the council denied the bid by the Ibrahim Education Foundation to convert an old church into a boarding school for Muslim boys. **(48)**

Plans for an Islamic community center and school south of Lodi, California came to a grinding halt in Sept. 2005 when the San Joaquin County Board of Supervisors decided unanimously against a land use permit for the project. Farooqia Islamic Center supporters had filed an application at the county level nearly three years ago, though the vision for the project has been in the making for more than a decade. The project, which included a worship hall and a K-4 school, was approved by the county Planning Commission in July 2005, but was soon appealed by residents living in the agricultural area surrounding the Lower Sacramento Road property. The project had been at the county level since former Imam Mohammad Adil Khan, who lived at a house on the site, applied for a land use permit on Dec. 18, 2003. But in June 2005, the property was put under the microscope in a terror investigation led by the FBI against several members of the Muslim community including Umar Hayat and his son Hamid Hayat. During the investigation, Khan was arrested on an immigration violation and subsequently agreed to be deported to his native Pakistan. **(49)**

Amid controversy, Islamic Society of Sarasota and Bradenton (Florida) has to change the height of the 85-foot minarets for its new $1.5 million mosque. Originally, the mosque's leaders submitted plans to Sarasota County for a 62-foot tall building, including dome, and two 85-feet minarets. But Sarasota County ruled that the building too greatly exceeded the county's height restriction of 35 feet and approved a maximum height of 40 feet. **(50)**

There was some good news too. In some cases, the Muslims were able to get permission for their mosque projects.

Hernando (Florida) County's lone mosque received approval in May 2007 for a significant expansion. The Barclay Avenue mosque plans to expand to more than seven times its current size, creating a single-story building with space for offices, community events and 3, 790 square feet of assembly space for prayer. The five-member Hernando County Planning and Zoning Commission unanimously recommended approval to revise a special use permit that will allow the expansion of the mosque. Neighbors complained about the noise and traffic from the mosque. Afterward, several criticized the commissioners for not giving them enough time to air their concerns. **(51)**

The Bridgeview Village Board (Michigan) in April 2006 approved expansion of a mosque on the village's southwest side after a group of homeowners dropped their opposition. The mosque proposal had languished for months before the village's Zoning Board of Appeals while residents and officials considered traffic and other quality-of-life issues surrounding expansion of the Mosque Foundation of Bridgeview's worship center. Earlier the Plan Commission was deadlocked 3-3 on the project. **(52)**

In June 2006, Franklin Township (New Jersey) officials approved the first official mosque in Somerset County in a ranch home that has quietly served as a house of worship for local Muslims for the past several years. "We're absolutely thrilled," said Ibrahim Conteh, one of the imams at the Da'awatu Islamia of Somerset mosque. "We've been fighting for this for quite some time." Conteh, a native of Freetown in Sierra Leone, lives in the neighborhood. **(53)**

In May 2005, the Islamic Center of America in Detroit formally opened its $12 million complex to provide its 3,000 members with more room to worship and have community activities. The Islamic Center -- which is among the largest mosques in the country -- is a 120,000-square-foot complex that includes the mosque, the Muslim American Youth Academy, an auditorium and library. There are about 500,000 Arab-Americans in Metro Detroit. About 30,000 Dearborn residents -- about one-third of the city's population -- are of Arab descent. The Islamic Center's existing mosque in Detroit began as the Islamic Center of Detroit in 1963. Coupled with the American National Museum and Cultural Center and mosque, Dearborn will now be the country's hub of Arab American culture and religion. The Dearborn Arab Community Center for Economic and Social Services also opened the $12.8 million museum this month. **(54)** In the pre-9/11 era, there was an extensive growth of mosques and Islamic centers that has now been arrested.

Park51 project or the Ground Zero Mosque controversy [55]

In August 2010, anti-Islam and anti-Muslim bigotry was sparked by the opposition to the planned Park51 project popularly known as the Ground Zero Mosque in Manhattan, New York. The American Society for Muslim Advancement and the Cordoba Initiative received tentative approval in May 2010 for construction of the $100 million Islamic center in lower Manhattan. New York City's Landmarks Preservation Commission voted unanimously August 3, 2010 to allow the demolition of a building on Park Place that would be replaced by a mosque.

Islam & Muslims in the Post-9/11 America

The developer, Sharif el-Gamal, a real estate investor born in New York, has said the center would include meeting rooms, a prayer space, a 500-seat auditorium and a pool. Two mosques, founded in 1970 and 1985, are already within several blocks of the proposed center. They are so busy and crowded that a search was begun for more space.

Republican gubernatorial candidate Rick Lazio voiced concern over the project in early July 2010, calling on N.Y. Attorney General Andrew Cuomo, who was also the Democratic gubernatorial candidate, to investigate the center's funding. Cuomo rejected the call for an investigation and responded to Lazio in a letter, asking, "What are we about, if not religious freedom?"

Other New York Republicans who have voiced opposition include Michael Faulkner, a congressional candidate in New York's 15th district, who argued against the center on Chris Matthew's television program, Hardball, and Dan Maloney, a candidate in New York's 4th district who gave a speech at a rally hosted by the organization Stop Islamization of America.

Republican George Pataki, the former governor of New York, argued against the construction on Fox News and MSNBC. The New York Observer reported that nine-term Repub;ican Congressman Peter King and Senate candidate Gary Berntsen voiced concerns about the Islamic center in a shared conference call.

Politicians elsewhere in the country have also joined the debate. Leading Republican figures like Newt Gingrich, a former speaker of the House, and former Alaska governor Sarah Palin, the party's 2008 vice-presidential nominee, had been voicing opposition to the Islamic center.

"Nazis don't have the right to put up a sign next to the Holocaust Museum in Washington," Mr. Gingrich said on the Fox News program "Fox and Friends." "We would never accept the Japanese putting up a site next to Pearl Harbor. There's no reason for us to accept a mosque next to the World Trade Center."

Sarah Palin tweeted, "Peace-seeking Muslims, pls understand, Ground Zero mosque is UNNECESSARY provocation; it stabs hearts. Pls reject it in interest of healing." Sen. Joe Lieberman (I-Conn.) said developers should "put the brakes" on the planned mosque.

Chapter II - The post 9/11 Challenges – Islamophobia [64]

Interestingly, not all New York politicians were opposed to the Islamic center, however. In addition to Cuomo, New York City Mayor Michael Bloomberg supported the center's construction. He called Lazio's proposed investigation into the center's finances "un-American." Democratic Massachusetts Gov. Deval Patrick also backed the Islamic center.

Obama backs [56]

At an iftar dinner for Ramadan held at the White House on Aug. 13, 2010, President Barack Obama supported the right of Muslims throughout the U.S. – including in lower Manhattan – to build new mosques and community centers, saying, "as a citizen, and as president, I believe that Muslims have the same right to practice their religion as anyone else in this country."

After his remarks were widely interpreted as an endorsement of the New York City Islamic center, he clarified the next day that his comments were meant to address the issue of religious freedom rather than "the wisdom of making the decision to put a mosque" near the ground zero site.

Representative Peter King, a New York Republican, said Obama should have urged leaders to compromise and find a new location for the mosque. The symbolism of having it near Ground Zero is wrong, he said. "If the president is going to get involved, one way I would suggest is to have the leaders, the developers, the builders and the Muslim community meet with people who feel aggrieved, who do feel anguish, and arrive at a common site," King said on CNN's "State of the Union."

Inflammatory rhetoric surrounding the project stirred hatred [57]

The inflammatory rhetoric surrounding the project has stirred hatred toward Muslims in America. There has been so much fear-mongering and so much misinformation in the debate peddled by bigots and rightwing politicians. The constant vilification of Islam and Muslims over the air on radio talk shows, in newspapers and the Internet was contributing to the rise in anti-Muslim sentiment across the country.

The hate speech and fear-mongering has resulted in hate crimes against Muslims and their prayer centers. At least three anti-Muslim acts were reported in one day, on August 24. In New York, taxi driver Ahmed H. Sharif was stabbed after the passenger asked the driver "Are you Muslim?" When

Chapter II - The post 9/11 Challenges – Islamophobia [65]

the driver said yes, the man slashed him with a knife on the throat, arm and face. The same night a drunk man barged into a Queens (New York) mosque and shouted anti-Muslim slurs at the congregation during the nightly Tarawee prayers. He then proceeded to urinate on the prayer rugs. Anti-Muslim acts are not limited to New York. Several thousand miles away in Madera, California, a mosque was vandalized with a sign reading 'Wake up America, the enemy is here.' Tellingly, earlier last month, a mock pig inscribed with "No Mosque in NYC" was left at a California Islamic center. It was also inscribed with "Remember 9-11" and "MO HAM MED the Pig."

Amid growing anti-Muslim sentiment--stirred up by a raging debate over the Ground Zero mosque, at least two more incidents were reported till August 31. In New York State's tiny town, Carlton, five teenagers harassed worshippers at the town mosque. The teenagers were charged with disrupting religious services at the mosque after they honked their car horns and yelled obscenities during one prayer service, and fired a weapon outside of another. In the Nashville suburb of Murfreesboro (Tennessee) a fire was reported at the site of a planned Islamic center and mosque. More alarmingly, gunshots were fired when the community members arrived to inspect the site.

All these hate incidents came in an atmosphere of near anti-Muslim hysteria that was generated by the feverish discourse and manufactured controversy over the Ground Zero mosque. It was generating anti-Muslim and anti-Islam public sentiments.

Not surprisingly, a poll on August 29 by the extreme right San Diego, California 760 KFMB AM talk radio station indicated that 70% of those polled are in favor of forced registration for American Muslims in a national database. The same day a poll conducted by Chris Matthews show at the MSNBC revealed that more than half of Republicans polled say they have a negative attitude toward Islam, this compared to only 27% of Democrats.

A PEW Institute poll result released on August 24 corroborated the findings of Chris Mathews show. By more than two-to-one (54% to 21%), Republicans expressed an unfavorable opinion of Islam and by more than four-to-one (74% to 17%), Republicans say they agree more with those who object to the building of the Ground Zero Mosque. By contrast, more Democrats agree with the center's supporters than its opponents (by 47% to 39%).

Islam & Muslims in the Post-9/11 America

Chapter II - The post 9/11 Challenges – Islamophobia [66]

According to a new TIME poll, 61% of respondents opposed the construction of the Park51 project, compared with 26% who support it. Yet the survey also revealed that many Americans harbor lingering animosity toward Muslims. Twenty-eight percent of voters do not believe Muslims should be eligible to sit on the U.S. Supreme Court. Nearly one-third of the country thinks adherents of Islam should be barred from running for President — a slightly higher percentage than the 24% who mistakenly believe the current occupant of the Oval Office is himself a Muslim.

References

(1A) Thirty-nine percent Americans say they felt at least some prejudice against Muslims. The same percentage favored requiring Muslims, including U.S. citizens, to carry a special ID "as a means of preventing terrorist attacks in the United States." (TODAY/Gallup Poll - July 2006)
The proportion of Americans who believe that Islam helps to stoke violence against non-Muslims has more than doubled since the attacks, from 14 percent in January 2002 to 33 percent today. (The Washington Post-ABC News Poll – March 2006) Some one-fourth (23 to 27 percent) of Americans consistently believe stereotypes such as: "Muslims value life less than other people," and "The Muslim religion teaches violence and hatred." only six percent of Americans have a positive first impression of Islam and Muslims. (CAIR Poll – March 2006)
(1B) The term Islamophobia – often described as prejudice against, hatred or irrational fear of Islam or Muslims - dates back to the early 1990s, but it came into common usage after the September 11, 2001 attacks in the United States. It was defined in the 1997 by the Runnymede Trust Commission on British Muslims and Islamophobia as the "dread or hatred of Islam and therefore, to the fear and dislike of all Muslims." The 2001 Stockholm International Forum on Combating Intolerance recognized Islamophobia as a form of racism alongside xenophobia and anti-Semitism. Stephen Sheehi in his book - Islamophobia: The Ideological Campaign Against Muslims – (published in February 2011) argues that Islamophobia is "an ideological formation created by a culture that deploys particular tropes, analyses and beliefs, as facts upon which governmental policies and social practices are framed." He believes that Islamophobia is an ideological phenomenon which exists to promote political and economic goals, both domestically and abroad.
(1C) This was more propaganda than a plot as later detailed emerged. The plot that later proved almost a hoax as the main actor of the plot, a British Pakistani – who allegedly took orders from Al-Qaeda's No.3 in Afghanistan – was found innocent. Other reports said that the UK police had been following up the alleged plot for months and waited for an appropriate time to announce it as both President Bush and British Prime Minister Tony Blair faced political problems. Their popularity was down because of war in Iraq and Lebanon. One immediate outcome of the dramatic announcement of the alleged plot was the removal from the headlines the bloody fiasco of Israeli aggression in Lebanon.
(2) Atlanta Journal-Constitution – August 12, 2006

(3) MSNBC's Hardball – August 11, 2006

(4) Professor Sam Hamod is an expert on the Middle East and Islam; he is a former advisor to the U.S. State Department and Ex-Director of The Islamic Center in Washington, DC Look.

Islam & Muslims in the Post-9/11 America

(5) MSNBC – August 11, 2006
(6) The Wall Street Journal - August 12, 2006

(7) Ref Newsweek - May 14, 2006
(8) The comment was broadcast by syndicated columnist Cal Thomas in November, 2002, who says he heard it from Ashcroft himself. Fox News
(9) Rocky Mountain News - July 19, 2005
(10) Fox News – July 15, 2006
(11) Ref. In 2005, for the first time since the atomic devastation of Japan, an Associated Press poll found that half of all Americans would approve the use of atomic bombs, especially against terrorist targets. A mushroom cloud of anti-Muslim hate, with a sickly "humorous" spin, has been winning American 'hearts and minds' into acceptance of the Bush administration's nuclear attack against the "axis of evil" terror sponsor- Islamic Republic of Iran.
(12) Loveland Daily Reporter-Herald - March 17, 2006
(13) Islamophobia, a Restrospective – Racism and Religious Desecration as US Policy, Counter Punch – May 6, 2006
(14) AP/CNN Feb. 4, 2005
(15) Mercury News July 11, 2005
(16) In the 2004 re-election of President Bush, the Christian Right played a key role. It was hailed as a victory for religious conservatives, especially the president's fellow evangelicals.
(17) November 10, 2002
(18) June 2002
(19) June 2002
(20) July 2002
(21) Religion Watch – Dec. 14, 2005
(22) "This is War" by Ann Coulter - September 14, 2001
(23) "Where is Janet Reno when we need her" by Ann Coulter - Septebmer 20, 2001
(24) "Future Widows of America: Write Your Congressman" by Ann Coulter - September 27, 2001.
(24a) AMP Report - American Muslims overwhelmingly voted Democratic in 2008
(24b) Ibid.
(24c) Ibid.
(24d) Ibid.
(24e) AMP Report - American Muslims in 2010 election
(24g) Ibid.
(25) The aftermath of September 11, 2001: The targeting of Arabs and Muslims in America by Susan M. Akram Arab Studies Quarterly, Spring-Summer 2002
(26) Media Matters- April 17, 2006
(27) Washington Post - August 23, 2005
(28) Reuters – July 1, 2005
(29) March 26, 2003
(30) Associated Press - May 19, 2005
(31) Washington Post - May 25, 2005
(32) Woman says she received desecrated Quran through Amazon.com – Associated Press May 18, 2005
(33) Newsday - June 16, 2005
(34) Times Free Press – July 11, 2006
(34a) AMP Report

Islam & Muslims in the Post-9/11 America

Chapter II - The post 9/11 Challenges – Islamophobia

(35) USA Today - August 9, 2006
(36) CSB News April 14, 2006
(37) MSNBC – Dec. 17, 2004
(38) Islamophobia by Steven Malik Shelton – Media Monitors - February 9, 2005

(39) Christian Science Monitor/Reuters- Jan. 5, 2006)

(40) South Coast Today - May 30, 2007)

(41) Goldsboro News Argus - March 5, 2007)

(42) Associated Press - May 1, 2007)

(43) Pittsburgh Post-Gazette – March 15, 2006)

(44) Detroit Free Press - April 12, 2006)

(45) New Jersey Reporter - May 25, 2006)

(46) Associated Press – Dec. 7, 2006)

(47) The Herald News New Jersey – Dec. 10, 2006

(48) Chicago Tribune - May 6, 2005)

(49) Lodi News News-Sentinel – September 28, 2005)

(50) Bradenton Herald - Dec. 31, 2005)

(51) St. Petersburg Times - May 14, 2007)

(52) Chicago Tribune - April 7, 2006)

(53) Star-Ledger - June 11, 2006)

(54) The Detroit News - May 12, 2005

(55) AMP Report - American Muslims in 2010 election

(56) Ibid.

(57) Ibid.

Chapter III

It's guilty until proven innocent for American Muslim charities

In the name of "anti-terror financing campaign," the government has launched a systematic campaign against the Muslim American charities. In the post 9/11 era, Muslim American charities and donors lived in constant fear of frozen funds, indictments and even closure, regardless of whether they have done anything wrong. The government's campaign has had its desired effect: to scare Muslim Americans to donate freely to their charities thus abandoning one of the premier tenets of Islam -- giving to those in need and donate freely to their own charities.

The government denies these charges, saying it is merely trying to cut off funding to a wide variety of so-called charitable organizations that funnel money to groups that practice terrorist tactics. The Treasury Department cites President Bush's pledge to ensure "that Arab Americans and American Muslims feel comfortable maintaining their tradition of charitable giving".

However, facts belie this assertion. Dozens of charitable groups have been investigated since 2001. Several have been shut down, without any official finding that they were aiding terrorist organizations. The organizations shut down were not on any government watch list before their assets were frozen. The predictable result is that Muslims have no way of knowing which groups the government suspects of ties to terrorism.

Organizations and individuals suspected of supporting terrorism are guilty until proven innocent.

The USA Patriot Act gives the government largely unchecked powers to designate any group as a terrorist organization. Once a charitable organization is so designated all of its materials and property may be seized and its assets frozen. The charity is unable to see the government's evidence and thus understand the basis for the charges. Since its assets

Chapter III - Campaign against Muslim charities [70]

are frozen, it lacks resources to mount a defense. And it has only limited right of appeal to the courts. So the government can target a charity, seize its assets, shut it down, obtain indictments against its leaders, but then delay a trial almost indefinitely.

The community has been in a great deal of limbo, because there is no standard established for what would constitute material support of terrorism. Money that used to go to large national or international organizations is going instead to smaller, local projects. The government investigations have also been focusing more closely on local mosques and imams. As a result, donors were concerned that any involvement will bring you under scrutiny. People have also stopped giving to local organizations, because they don't want to be viewed as supporting anti-American sentiment in the US. (1)

In 2002, members from several Arab and Muslim American groups requested that the US Treasury Department assist US-based Islamic charities in building trust with donors while ensuring the government that their financial activities were clear of wrongdoing. In response, the Department developed a set of "voluntary best practice guidelines" that advise charitable organizations on how to establish proper transparency and vetting of potential foreign aid recipients.

Treasury Department says that the department's Office of Foreign Assets Control maintains a "one-stop shopping" list of banned entities, known as the Specially Designated Nationals List, on its Web site, http://www.treasury.gov/ofac . The department has declined to produce a list of approved charities in the Middle East "for two reasons: No. 1, any charity that we deemed clean, we could not guarantee that it would always remain so. And No. 2, it would put the government in the position of playing favorites." (2)

On Dec. 15, 2005, the U.S. Department of Treasury released new guidelines, which replace ones Treasury issued three years ago. The new guidelines in many parts closely resembled the original rules and the new guidelines did not go far enough to assuage the worries of Muslim charities. The guidelines were further revised on Sept. 29, 2006. But nonprofit groups say revised government guidelines still are too onerous and vague.

Chapter III - Campaign against Muslim charities [71]

The Illinois General Assembly passed bipartisan resolutions, in May 2006, calling on the federal government to create a list of Muslim charitable organizations to which one can safely donate. These were the first resolutions of its kind. It was natural that such an effort would begin in Illinois because it is home to a sizable and well-organized Muslim population, as well as some of the most prominent charities shut down after the attacks. "Americans giving charity to Muslim charities need assurance that the charitable contributions they make in good faith to charities in good standing will indeed go to humanitarian purposes and will not give rise to potential retroactive criminal or immigration prosecution," read the advisory resolutions, which passed by voice vote.

"It's an issue of fairness and what's right," said John Millner, a Republican from Carol Stream who sponsored the Illinois House measure. The resolutions also cited legislation known as the REAL ID bill--passed in the 2005 spring by Congress and signed by the president--that threatens to deport immigrants who make a donation to a charity that was in good standing at the time but is later linked to terrorism.

Since 9/11, millions of dollars in donations have been seized and frozen. Some donors have found FBI agents at their doors, asking about specific checks they have written.

Consequently, Muslim charities reported a precipitous decline in contributions. Contributions that do arrive come increasingly in cash from anonymous givers. And donors who happen to be Muslim are increasingly turning to the large household names like Oxfam and Save the Children, which may conduct programs in predominantly Muslim areas abroad.

Another impact has been that a number of charities that support Muslim causes have been forced to shut down. This applies not only to the few that have been formally named as wrongdoers, but also to smaller groups that are not in a position to pay for defense lawyers if fingered by the government.

Campaign against Muslim charities

Soon after the terrorist attacks of Sept. 11, 2001, the U.S. government shut down three major U.S.-based charities - Holy Land Foundation for Relief and Development, Global Relief Foundation and Benevolence International

Chapter III - Campaign against Muslim charities [72]

Foundation - for allegedly funneling support to terrorists and it has designated more than 40 charities internationally as terrorist financiers. In August 2006, the Treasury Department barred U.S. citizens from contributing to two more groups: the Philippine and Indonesian branches of the Saudi Arabia-based International Islamic Relief Organization.

Under the USA Patriot Act, the U.S. government is authorized to close down a charity while an investigation is going on. The government is under no obligation to reveal the evidence used to justify the seizure of assets and the designation of the charity as an entity supporting terrorists and put it on the list of banned groups issued by the Treasury Department.

The administration while shutting down the Muslim charity organizations, using new powers under the USA Patriot Act, filed no criminal charges against these organizations, nor were they officially designated terrorist supporters.

Law enforcement officials simply froze their assets and seized their property "pending an investigation" without producing any evidence, as authorized by the Act. Consequently, the burden of proof has shifted to the organizations, which must prove their innocence even though, in many cases, the government has not specified wrongdoing. Moreover, they must do this without access to their own documents, computers, records, or other materials that might make their case.

The organization can file an appeal, but as was noted by the OMBWatch - in its report titled Muslim Charities and the War on Terror - appealing Treasury actions to the federal courts is relatively useless, as the court's scope of review is very limited.

Since Sept. 11, 2001, at least six major American Muslim charities have been shuttered in this fashion. The government still doesn't have a single terrorism conviction against any of the employees or board members of any of those charities. Similarly, the government has never been able to document a bona fide trail showing how money from the charity got into the hands of actual terrorists.

The five year campaign against the Muslim charities leads to the belief that under former attorney general John Ashcroft, American Muslim charities

Chapter III - Campaign against Muslim charities [73]

were closed as part of the charade to make the American people believe that the government was disrupting terrorist financing and under Alberto Gonzales, the message was that Muslim Americans would be punished if they want to help Palestinians. Either way the assault on the charities was not about the safety and security of the American people but about politics. (3)

Major charities shut down: Since 9/11, the Bush administration has shut down a number of Muslim charity organizations including the following major charities:

Holy Land Foundation for Relief and Development (HLF)

On Dec. 4, 2001, the FBI raided the Texas office of the Holy Land Foundation for Relief and Development. Interestingly, the same day during a public appearance with Israeli Prime Minister Ariel Sharon, President Bush said HLF was diverting funds to Hamas -- which he described as "one of the deadliest terror organizations in the world today" -- and providing funds to families of suicide bombers. HLF denied the charge, saying it only provided humanitarian relief, with a focus on Palestinian refugees and victims of the wars in Bosnia, Kosovo, and Turkey.

In shutting down HLF, the FBI seized more than $5 million, along with all documents and property, which included satellite offices in three states. FBI agents and local police guarded the offices while all property was removed. Two weeks after being shut down, Ghassan Elashi, HLF's founder and co-chair, and three of his brothers were arrested on a 33-count indictment, which charged that they used an Internet services company to make investments for Hamas leader Mousa Abu Marzook. On October 13, 2006, Ghassan Elashi, was sentenced to nearly seven years in prison for financial ties with Abu Marzook and for making illegal computer exports to countries that back terrorism.

On July 27, 2004, the Holy Land Foundation for Relief and Development and seven of its directors and fundraisers were charged with supporting the militant Palestinian group Hamas and with money laundering and

Chapter III - Campaign against Muslim charities

conspiracy. The 42-count indictment, returned by a federal grand jury in Dallas, alleges that the Holy Land Foundation for Relief and Development provided more than $12.4 million to individuals and organizations linked to Hamas from 1995 to 2001.

The indictment names the foundation along with its president, Shukri Abu Baker; chairman, Ghassan Elashi; executive director, Haitham Maghawri; and four others. The charges include conspiracy, providing material support to a foreign terrorist organization, tax evasion and money laundering. The indictment accused Abu Baker, el-Mezain and Elashi of creating Holy Land in 1988 to provide financial and material support to Hamas.

The HLF trial

The Holy Land Foundation for Relief (HLF) went on trial on July 24, 2007 in Dallas, Texas. The same day, as the HLF prosecution presented its case to the jury, the federal agents were raiding two other Muslim charities in Dearborn, Michigan. The Holy Land was being tried on suspicion of aiding terrorism by helping the Palestinian militant group Hamas while the two Michigan charities - the Goodwill Charitable Organization and Al-Mabarrat Charitable Organization - were suspected of having ties to extremist groups in Lebanon. Just like the Holy Land, assets of the two Michigan charities have been frozen.

The Holy Land, founded in 1989 was one of the largest Muslim charities in the nation before it was shut down under executive orders in December 2001. The government says Hamas' support organization in the United States, known as the "Palestinian Committee," organized the "Occupied Land Fund" in 1988. The name was later changed to the Holy Land Foundation. First based in California, the foundation moved to Richardson, Texas in 1992.

The Bush administration froze the Holy Land Foundation's assets charging it with funneling money to Hamas, an allegation strongly refuted by the Holy Land officials. According to its mission statement, the Foundation is a humanitarian organization that works to find "solutions to human suffering," primarily focusing on providing urgent nutritional and medical care to the destitute and displaced Palestinian refugees in Jordan, Palestine, and Lebanon.

Chapter III - Campaign against Muslim charities [75]

The defendants named in a 42-count indictment in 2004 are Holy Land Foundation; Shukri Abu Baker, the charity's president; Ghassan Elashi, its chairman; Abdulrahman Odeh; Mohammad El-Mezain; and Mufid Abdulqader. Two other men named in the indictment remain fugitives.

The five men on trial aren't accused of being terrorists. Rather, they are charged with funneling $36 million to individuals and groups tied to Hamas, including $12.4 million sent after Clinton's designation.

Acknowledging that the Holy Land Foundation did not directly carry out terrorist attacks, prosecutors say that the charity acted as the "social wing" of Hamas, "much like a social welfare agency," providing money and assistance to such places as schools, clinics and worship centers "to win the hearts and minds of the Palestinian population and solidify loyalty to Hamas." "In order for Hamas to achieve its ultimate ... goal of annihilating Israel, it had to win the broad support of the Palestinian population. The [foundation] set out to do just that," the government's brief said.

This case is shrouded in secrecy and heavily dependent on testimony from Israeli agents. Prosecution witnesses to testify include a retired Israeli Army colonel.

Though defense attorneys already have government clearances that allow them to review the material, under the federal Classified Information Procedures Act they have been prohibited from sharing it with their clients. And unless the act's rules are declared unconstitutional in the case, defense attorneys argue, the defendants will have no way of proving that the statements attributed to them were misconstrued or never made.

Unindicted co-conspirators

The indictment also lists about 300 individuals and groups as unindicted co-conspirators — among them long-established and U.S.-based organizations engaged in traditional lobbying efforts.

The government's co-conspirator's list includes the largest Muslim civil right group, the Council on American-Islamic Relations (CAIR); the nation's largest Muslim educational source, the Islamic Society of North America (ISNA), and the North American Islamic Trust, the country's largest holding

Chapter III - Campaign against Muslim charities [76]

company of deeds to about 300 mosques, Islamic centers and schools in the U.S.

Newsweek quoted an un-named senior law-enforcement official as saying that the listing of ISNA, CAIR and other groups as "unindicted co-conspirators" was largely a tactical move by the government. By listing the groups, the official said, it makes it easier for prosecutors to introduce documents, tapes and other evidence mentioning them and which relate to what the government charges is a wide-ranging conspiracy to raise money in the United States in support of Hamas. (4)

Typically, prosecutors identify a person or a group as an unindicted co-conspirator so that their statements, or those of people involved in the listed organizations, about the defendants can be used in court without them being considered hearsay, which is not permitted in trial.

The document gave scant details, but prosecutors described CAIR as a present or past member of "the U.S. Muslim Brotherhood's Palestine Committee and/or its organizations." The government listed the Islamic Society of North America and the North American Islamic Trust as "entities who are and/or were members of the U.S. Muslim Brotherhood."

While the Holy Land was charged in the case, which was filed in 2004, none of the other groups was. However, the co-conspirator designation could be a blow to the credibility of the national Islamic organizations, which often work hand-in-hand with government officials engaged in outreach to the Muslim community.

The practice of publicly naming unindicted co-conspirators is frowned on by some in the legal community, chiefly because there is no trial or other mechanism for those named to challenge their designation. Justice Department guidelines discourage the public identification of unindicted co-conspirators by the government.

"In all public filings and proceedings, federal prosecutors should remain sensitive to the privacy and reputation interests of uncharged third-parties," the Justice Department's manual for prosecutors says. When co-conspirator lists have to be filed in court, prosecutors should seek to file them under seal, the guidelines say.

Chapter III - Campaign against Muslim charities [77]

In practice, the lists are often made public. A list of co-conspirators was released in connection with the federal trial in 2005 of a former college professor, Dr. Sami Al-Arian, on terrorism support charges.

However, when Enron executives went on trial in 2006, the list of alleged co-conspirators was kept under seal.

Commenting on the unindicted list, Adam Braun, a former federal prosecutor told the Los Angeles Times said: "It seems like the government is painting with a pretty broad brush." He said office policy was to avoid "sullying someone's reputation unnecessarily" — generally limiting use of named co-conspirators unless there is proof of wrongdoing.

Surely, the prosecution is using McCarthyite tactics by implicating mainstream Muslim groups to silence genuine Muslim voices while providing ammunition to the anti-Muslim organizations. This is a brutal attempt to marginalize and disenfranchise mainstream Muslim groups.

The three trials

The court, because of the complexities of the investigation, decided to break the HLF proceedings into three trials, with the one beginning on July 24, 2007 being the most expansive and the one directly related to the Holy Land Foundation.

In July 2004, during the trial of the export violations portion of the indictment, all five Elashi brothers (Basman Elashi, Bayan Elashi, Ghassan Elashi, Hazim Elashi and Ihsan Elashi), and Infocom Corporation, were convicted on charges they conspired to violate the Export Administration Regulations and the Libyan Sanctions Regulations.

During the second trial on the remaining charges in the indictment, in April 2005, the jury found that Bayan Elashi, Ghassan Elashi, Basman Elashi and Infocom Corporation conspired together and sent money to co-defendant Mousa Abu Marzook, an investor in Infocom and a self-admitted leader of the Islamic Resistance Movement, a/k/a Hamas.

Brothers Hazim and Ihsan Elashi were sentenced in January 2006 to 66 months imprisonment and 72 months imprisonment, respectively.

Chapter III - Campaign against Muslim charities [78]

In a series of hearings conducted in October 2006 in federal court in Dallas, United States District Judge sentenced Bayan Elashi, Ghassan Elashi, Basman Elashi, and Texas-based Infocom Corporation. Basman Elashi, age 50, was sentenced to 80 months imprisonment. Ghassan Elashi, age 52, was also sentenced to 80 months imprisonment. Bayan Elashi, age 51, was sentenced to 84 months imprisonment and Infocom Corporation was sentenced to two years probation (the corporation is defunct).

In July 2007 trial, Ghassan Elashi was now facing another trial for his role in helping run the Holy Land Foundation for Relief and Development which the government has accused of funneling millions to the Palestinian militant group Hamas.

Mistrial declared for 5 defendants in HLF case

After 19 days of deliberations by the Jury, on October 22, 2007, U.S. District Judge A. Joe Fish declared a mistrial for most former leaders of HLF charged with financing Hamas militants after jurors failed to reach a verdict.

One of the defendants, former HLF Chairman Mohammed El-Mezain, was acquitted of most charges.

The outcome came about an hour after a confusing scene in the courtroom, in which three former leaders of the group were initially found not guilty. But then when jurors were polled, three of them said those verdicts were read incorrectly.

Judge A. Joe Fish sent them back to resolve the differences. After about an hour of renewed deliberations, Fish said he received a note from jury saying 11 of 12 feel further discussion would not lead to a unanimous decision.

A juror, William Neal, later told the Associated Press that the panel found little evidence against three of the defendants and was evenly split on charges against charity's former chief executive

Shukri Abu Baker and its former chairman Ghassan Elashi, who were seen as the principal leaders of the charity. Neal said the jury was split about 6-6 on counts against Baker and Elashi.

Islam & Muslims in the Post-9/11 America

Chapter III - Campaign against Muslim charities [79]

"I thought they were not guilty across the board," said the juror, William Neal, a 33-year-old art director from Dallas. The case "was strung together with macaroni noodles. There was so little evidence," Neil said adding that the government's case had "so many gaps" that he regarded the prosecution as "a waste of time."

Appeal of Holy Land Foundation leaders rejected

On Dec 7, 2011, a federal appeals court upheld the convictions of five leaders of the Holy Land Foundation charity on charges of funneling money and supplies to Hamas, designated a "terrorist" group following a 1995 executive order by President Bill Clinton.

The organizers of the Texas-based Holy Land Foundation argued that they were denied a fair trial in 2008 when the government used secret Israeli witnesses to testify against them. The organizers also raised a host of constitutional challenges to the evidence presented against them at trial.

The U.S. Court of Appeals for the 5th Circuit rejected those challenges, concluding that "while no trial is perfect," Holy Land and its leaders were fairly convicted. The court pointed to "voluminous evidence" that the foundation, which was started in the late 1980s, had long-running financial ties to Hamas.

On appeal, the leaders argued that the trial judge should not have allowed two Israeli witnesses to testify without revealing their real names. Pseudonyms prevented their lawyers from examining the witnesses' credentials and backgrounds, they contended. "The Confrontation Clause of the U.S. Constitution basically didn't apply to these experts," said Gregory Westfall, a lawyer for defendant Abdulrahman Odeh. He said his client would likely file an appeal and predicted that the case would eventually reach the Supreme Court. Westfall described the prosecution as an unfortunate event in U.S. history. The foundation provided food and relief supplies to the Palestinian people, who were in great need, he said.
[Reuters – 12-7-2011]

On October 19, 2010, attorneys submitted a 149-page brief. It provided convincing evidence of wrongful convictions. Appellate issues raised include:

Chapter III - Campaign against Muslim charities [80]

(1) Names of two prosecutorial witnesses were withheld from defense attorneys, including its key one. Doing so violated Fifth Amendment due process rights and the Sixth Amendment's right of a defendant to confront accusers.

(2) The district court allowed prejudicial hearsay evidence. One source admitted sending money to Hamas. He also defrauded his employer of $610,000 in a scam unrelated to HLF. Moreover, he cheated on his taxes and lied to the FBI. As part of a plea bargain, he agreed to lie again under oath - against innocent HLF principles.

(3) The court allowed irrelevant prejudicial evidence to be presented. It included alleged Hamas suicide bombing exhibits, killing Israeli collaborators, a video showing demonstrators stomping on and burning the American flag, and more. All of it was unrelated to the case.

(4) Irrelevant prejudicial testimonies were also allowed, including erroneous legal and religious opinions.

(5) At the same time, the court denied defense attorneys the right to review government recorded, intercepted, or otherwise gotten statements, based on Foreign Intelligence Surveillance Act (FISA) authority.

Muslim charity principals denied justice

Stephen Lendman, commenting on the judgment under the title "Muslim charity principals denied justice," Wrote:

"FISA, in fact, is classic police state tyranny. It violates Fourth Amendment protections against unreasonable searches and seizures. It also requires warrants to be judicially sanctioned, based on clear probable cause. However, using undisclosed (likely manufactured) secret evidence, FISA permits unrestricted warrantless spying, data mining, and intercept of domestic and foreign Internet, telephone, and other communications, based on alleged national security threats. As a result, it permits illegal searches, seizures, and privacy invasions. Anyone now for real or concocted reasons may be charged, convicted and imprisoned for alleged crimes they never conceived, planned or committed.

Chapter III - Campaign against Muslim charities [81]

"Based on Sixth Amendment issues, the National Association of Criminal Defense Lawyers (NACDL) submitted an amicus brief for HLF defendants. In part, it states:

"If the Confrontation Clause means anything, it is that a criminal defendant must be allowed to know his accusers (to) have a fair opportunity to cross-examine them. Yet an expert witness whose testimony was critical to proving the government's case was allowed to testify anonymously...."

"The witness called "Avi" had no relevance to the case. An alleged Hamas/Palestinian Islamic charities (zakat committees) expert, he belonged to Israel intelligence or security. "The total secrecy of Avi's identity is unprecedented: no reported cases have ever approved fully anonymous expert testimony like" his. As a result, the right of defense attorneys to cross-examine Avi was "completely impaired."

"However, Judge Solis wrongfully claimed revealing his identity, and another anonymous witness called "Major Lior," would harm national security. Moreover, with no evidentiary hearing, prosecutors said doing so would place them in harm's way. By allowing their testimony to stand, the appeals court "mark(ed) a significant departure from existing case law."

As a result, justice demands overturning HLF defendants' convictions because:

"Sixth Amendment protections require revealing the true identify of expert witnesses to defense attorneys; and Confrontation Clause rights forbid secret witness testimonies, "no matter the circumstances."

"Based on Fifth Amendment due process violations and material support issues, Georgetown University Law Professor David Cole and attorney J Craig Jett of Burleson, Pate & Gibson submitted his own amicus brief.

Twenty organizations provided amicus support

"Twenty organizations provided amicus support as interested parties, including: American Friends Service Committee, Atlantic Philanthropies, The Carter Center, Christian Peacemaker Teams, The Constitutional Project, The Nathan Cummings Foundation, The Fund for Constitutional

Chapter III - Campaign against Muslim charities [82]

Government, Global Greengrants Fund, Grantmakers Without Borders, Grassroots International, The Humanitarian Law Project, Islamic Relief USA, Milt Lauenstein, Operation USA, The Peace Appeal Foundation, The Rockefeller Brothers Fund, The Samuel Rubin Foundation, Rutherford Institute, Tikva Grassroots Empowerment Fund, and The Urgent Action Fund for Women's Human Rights.

"In part, the brief addresses whether anyone "can be convicted for violating a prohibition on 'knowingly' providing 'material support' to designated 'foreign terrorist organizations' without proof that he or she knowingly" did it.

"Defendants, in fact, were convicted on multiple counts even though the district judge's jury instructions relied on an erroneous and dangerously expansive interpretation of the material-support statute.

"As a result, legitimate charitable work henceforth will be jeopardized based on unsubstantiated charges.

"In fact, five recipient West Bank charities receiving HLF funds weren't designated foreign terrorist organizations (FTOs). Yet district court instructions told jurors they could find defendants guilty without proof of FTO connections.

"Even prosecutors didn't advance that argument. As a result, failing to reverse these wrongful convictions will have a chilling effect on legitimate charitable work. None henceforth will know if they'll be free from criminal investigation, prosecution, or conviction.

"Amici maintain that the judge's jury charge violates fundamental due process principles requiring fair notice of what conduct is prohibited, as well as proof of individual culpability. Moreover, the jury charge conflicts with (requiring) proof that defendants knew that they were supporting a designated organization." **[OpEdNews 12-11-2011]**

Global Relief Foundation (GRF)

Ten days after closing HLF, the FBI raided the Global Relief Foundation's headquarters in Chicago, freezing all of its assets "pending an investigation" and taking computers, filing cabinets, furniture, pictures, and more. On the

Chapter III - Campaign against Muslim charities [83]

same day, the Immigration and Naturalization Service arrested GRF's director, Rabih Haddad, and raided his home.

The INS (now renamed as US Citizenship and Immigration Services) cited visa violations as the reason for Haddad's imprisonment and potential deportation. In the past, these violations would have resulted in small fines or other minor punishment. Yet for the next 14 months, Haddad was transferred from one jail to the next, without notice to his family. Haddad's deportation trials were held in secret, were not listed on the courthouse docket, and were closed to the press and Haddad's family. Eventually, Haddad sued to open his deportation hearings, and won.

However, the government pressed forward without ever accusing Haddad of a serious crime -- just visa violations -- or linking him directly to terrorism. Nineteen months after the day of his arrest, Haddad was deported, again without notice to his family. Two weeks later, on July 28, 2003, Haddad's wife and four children (ages 5-13) flew to Kuwait after being deported by the INS. The story of Rabih Haddad and his family is not unique, as scores of Muslims have been deported since 9/11 on minor visa violations, without open trials, or any factual evidence associating them with terrorism.

How Al Qaeda was linked to Global Relief through false reporting?

In April 2004, USA Today admitted that its star correspondent Jack Kelley linked the Global Relief Foundation, one of the Muslim charity that was shut down in December 2001, with Al Qaeda. Among Kelley's fictitious story of January 2002 reported that the CIA and U.S. Special Forces searching caves and safe houses in Afghanistan had found documents linking two Chicago-based Islamic charities to al Qaeda. One of those charities was Global Relief Foundation (GRF), which was co-founded by Rabih Haddad, an imam who was arrested in Ann Arbor shortly after 9/11 for a visa violation. Haddad was detained for 19 months before his deportation in 2003. The USA Today reported that soon after Kelley's story ran, GRF attorney Roger Simmons contacted the paper challenging the reporter's claims. USA Today told Simmons "that the newspaper would neither correct nor retract the story." (5)

Chapter III - Campaign against Muslim charities [84]

Benevolence International Foundation (BIF)

On the same day as the GRF was raided, the FBI raided Benevolence International Foundation, another Muslim charity based in Illinois that describes its mission as providing humanitarian relief services worldwide. In 2002, Enaam Arnauout, BIF's chief executive officer, was indicted on racketeering charges for misleading donors and using funds to provide material support to terrorist organizations, including al Qaeda. In February, Arnauout pled guilty to a lesser fraud charge -- using charitable donations to fund fighters in Chechnya and Bosnia. In August he was sentenced to 11 years in prison. Prosecutors had sought a 20-year sentence, but Judge Suzanne B. Conlon said they had "failed to connect the dots" to prove the al-Qaeda ties. Arnaout had contact with al-Qaeda leader Osama bin Laden during the Afghan war against the Soviet Union during the 1980s, but the FBI could not establish subsequent contact.

Safa Trust

In March 2002, Customs agents raided Safa Trust -- a Herdon, Va., group founded by major Republican decision makers and Bush associates -- and the headquarters of what the Washington Post **(Oct. 7, 2002)** called some of the nation's "most respected Muslim leaders," including the Institute for Islamic Thought and the Graduate School of Islamic and Social Sciences. The government did not reveal the reasons for its actions, but "sources familiar with the investigation said the agents were looking for evidence of money laundering and tax evasion as well as possible ties to a worldwide private financial empire that Western governments have long suspected of funding terrorist activities," according to the Post. (6)

During the raids, federal agents fanned out to more than 15 sites in Falls Church, in Leesburg and in Fairfax County, including Herndon. They spent 12 hours alone at IIIT -- an Islamic think tank set up in Herndon in the early 1980s -- where they seized about 25 computers and documents that included financial records, mailing lists and staff lists.

Chapter III - Campaign against Muslim charities [85]

In May 2002, these organizations sued in U.S. District Court in Alexandria, Va., alleging a government "fishing expedition." In August the government filed an affidavit claiming the charities gave $3.7 million to BMI Inc., an investment company the government said may have passed money on to terrorists.

On January 13, 2005, BMI founder Soliman Biheiri was sentenced to 13 months in prison for lying to investigators about his dealings with Mousa Abu Marzook, a former northern Virginia resident who has been deported and was now a top officer in the political wing of Hamas. Defense lawyer David Schertler said there is no evidence that Marzook received any money from Biheiri after Marzook was designated a terrorist. Biheiri said during the hearing that he rejects any associations with terrorism. "How did I know that three years later Abu Marzook would be a member of Hamas?" Biheiri asked, reflecting on the fact that most of his dealings with Marzook came before Marzook ever joined Hamas. (7)

However, after more than four years, till October 2006, no charges were filed against the principals of the Herndon-based cluster of companies and charities that are at the center of the investigation. Federal prosecutors have strongly defended the raids, saying during a 2004 court hearing that they would file charges against some or all of the Herndon-based network, possibly under racketeering statutes once used to target the Mafia.

Washington Post, in a report entitled, "Muslim anger burns over lingering probe of charities," said: More than four years ago, federal agents swarmed into homes and businesses in Herndon and elsewhere in Northern Virginia, carting away 500 boxes of documents they believed contained evidence of an international terrorism financing network. The raids, which targeted some of the most established Islamic organizations in the United States, caused an immediate firestorm in the Muslim community. But no charges have been filed against the principals of the Herndon-based cluster of companies and charities that are at the center of the investigation, and Muslims say the raids were no more than a fishing expedition. (8)

Al-Haramain Islamic Foundation

In February 2004, the U.S. Treasury's Office of Foreign Assets Control seized the assets of the US branch of the Saudi charity, Al-Haramain Islamic

Foundation, while investigating whether the charity was involved in terrorism. Seven months later, in September, Treasury officials designated Al-Haramain a global terrorist organization, accusing it of sending money to fighters in Chechnya. On February 17, 2005, a federal grand jury in Eugene, Oregon returned a three-count indictment against the Al-Haramain and two of its officers on charges of conspiring to defraud the U.S. government. The indictment charged that defendants Pirouz Sedaghaty, also known as Pete Seda and Abu Yunus, and Soliman Al-Buthe conspired with the U.S. branch of the Al-Haramain to defraud the U.S. government by obtaining $150,000 in funds intended for distribution in Chechnya, and concealing their intent by filing a false tax return and failing to acknowledge they were transporting funds out of the United States.

In September 2005, a federal judge in Eugene, Oregon, dismissed criminal charges against the Al-Haramain Islamic Foundation but prosecutors said new charges are possible. Federal prosecutors had asked in August that the charges be dropped, saying the case would be a waste of time because all that remains of the organization is its corporate shell. However, the two men – an Iranian Perouz Sedaghaty and a Saudi named Soliman Al-Buthe - who ran the Ashland branch of Al-Haramain were considered international fugitives.

At the hearing Marc Blackman, the attorney representing the Al-Haramain, asked U.S. Magistrate Thomas Coffin to reject the government's motion to dismiss the charges. He argued that the case should either proceed to trial with the current indictment or be dismissed with prejudice, which would prevent the government from reviving it.

The Al-Haramain Foundation filed a lawsuit on February 28 2006 asserting that the Bush administration had circumvented the US Constitution by authorizing warrantless wiretaps. They asserted that the President lacked the authority to authorize wiretaps that circumvented the Foreign Intelligence Surveillance Act. Three individuals whose conversations were intercepted, Suliman al-Buthe, Wendell Belew and Asim Ghafoor, learned of the eavesdropping when U.S. officials accidentally delivered transcripts to them.

Islamic American Relief Agency (IARA)

In the crackdown on Muslim charities, on Oct. 13, 2004 , US authorities froze the assets of the Islamic American Relief Agency (IARA) of Columbia,

Chapter III - Campaign against Muslim charities [87]

Missouri, and accused five of its officials of helping finance Osama bin Laden and the Palestinian organization Hamas. The agents also searched home of its director. Earlier in the day, the U.S. Treasury Department designated the IARA and five of its international officers as financial sponsors of terrorists. The designation freezes IARA's assets and accounts and makes it a crime to contribute to the group.

U.S. Rep Kenny Hulshof, R-Columbia, in a news release aimed to reassure anyone who might have donated to Islamic American Relief Agency, said: "Treasury officials point out that people who have given donations to IARA in good faith, prior to Wednesday, need not worry about the legality of their donation."

"The government has not presented one shred of evidence linking IARA to funding for terror, but by seizing their funds and interviewing their donors, they have effectively destroyed the charity and created a chilling effect in the Muslim community in Columbia," its attorney, Shereef Akeel argued. He suggested the government may have confused IARA, founded two decades ago as the Islamic African Relief Agency (the name changed during the Bosnia conflict when demands for aid moved beyond an African focus), with a Sudan-based charity called the Islamic African Relief Agency, which the government claims has links to terrorists. (In these times - May 27, 2005)

On Dec. 30, 2004, IARA filed a suit in the U.S. District for the District of Columbia challenging the constitutionality of Treasury's action, asking for a preliminary injunction against the designation and seizure of its assets. In January 2005, Treasury wrote to Akeel saying the designation of IARA was not a case of mistaken identity with the African group. The court denied the injunction request in February, and on Sept. 15, 2005 granted the government's motion to dismiss.

KindHearts USA

On Feb. 19, 2006 the Treasury Department froze the assets of KindHearts USA, padlocking the doors of the Toledo-based charity "pending an investigation." The Treasury Department claimed the group has connections to Hamas, but KindHearts officials vigorously denied the allegations.

Islam & Muslims in the Post-9/11 America

Chapter III - Campaign against Muslim charities [88]

The Treasury Department announcement stated, "KindHearts officials and fund-raisers have coordinated with Hamas leaders and made contributions to Hamas affiliated organizations." Hamas has been designated as a terrorist organization by the U.S. government. Stuart Levey, Treasury Under Secretary for Terrorism and Financial Intelligence, said, "KindHearts is the progeny of Holy Land Foundation (HLF) and Global Relief Foundation (GRF)," groups that were shut down by Treasury in 2001. The announcement says "former GRF official Khaled Smaili established KindHearts from his residence in January 2002... KindHearts leaders and fundraisers once held leadership or other positions with HLF and GRF."

KindHearts, a humanitarian aid organization, raised $5.1 million in 2004 and has branches in Lebanon, the Gaza Strip and Pakistan. The Treasury Department alleges it gave more than $250,000 to the Sanabil Association for Relief and Development, which was designated as a terrorist organization in August 2003. KinderHearts board chair Dr. Hatem Elhady told the Toledo Blade, however, that it contracted with Sanabil to provide aid in refugee camps before the designation was made, and the amount was no more than $115,000. He said: "We did not just give money. We gave it for specific projects, and we saw the results, and we have the receipts."

The Treasury Department also cites a KindHearts "connection" to a former employee of HLF who was indicted by a federal grand jury in Texas for providing material support to Hamas. Mohammed El-Mezain had been retained to raise funds for the organization, but Smaili said the contract was voided as soon as KindHearts learned about the indictment.

Jihad Smaili, an attorney and KindHearts board member, rejected the Treasury Department's allegations: "I know the government has listened to every conversation that we've made and traced every wire sent from KindHearts USA to Lebanon or Palestine. They know exactly what's going on and that we have not done anything wrong." Smaili noted that by using its authority under Executive Order 13224, the Treasury Department does not have to prove its allegations in court. There is no deadline for the Treasury Department to complete its investigation, making it likely that the organization will go out of business even if it is ultimately cleared.

A statement from KindHearts said that over $1 million was frozen, most of which had been earmarked for earthquake victims in Pakistan and for a new office in Indonesia.

The statement also pointed out that KindHearts was among the Muslim organizations investigated by the Senate Finance Committee, which found no wrongdoing.

Kids in Need of Development, Education and Relief (KinderUSA)

In January 2005, the board of Dallas charity, Kids in Need of Development, Education and Relief (KinderUSA), made an unusual request to its 6,800 donors: Please don't send gifts. The Islamic charity, which delivered food and aid to children in war zones, had just received a federal grand jury subpoena asking its officials to turn over all meeting minutes, tax returns, and other documents. It feared that the government could freeze its assets or seize its list of donors at any moment.

In a statement, KinderUSA said the government probe has taken the form of unwarranted and obtrusive surveillance by the FBI, wiretapping, attempts to bribe and subvert our employees (which has caused them to resign in fear), spreading of malicious disinformation about the organization, and the possible invasion of our office space.

"In the current environment, we cannot in good faith continue to solicit donations when there are no safeguards in place to guarantee that the federal government will not seize these funds and divert them from their intended, legitimate destination. We have approached the government seeking an explanation to help us understand the basis of this investigation and are currently awaiting a response.

"We feel it is in the best interests of the beneficiaries, donors and the foundation to enter into a period of evaluation and review of our options during the calendar year of 2005," KinderUSA concluded.

After four months with no word from the FBI about whether KinderUSA was being investigated, the board resumed fund-raising. However, it was difficult to bring back its donors. Board Chairperson Dr. Laila Al-Marayati said "Our donors are afraid. They don't know what to do." KinderUSA had gained a reputation among Islamic charities for good governance and transparency and posts audited financials on its Web site. But such measures did little to prevent a formal inquiry. (9)

Chapter III - Campaign against Muslim charities [90]

Life for Relief and Development raided

On Sept. 21, 2006, US authorities, raided another major Muslim charity in the United States, the Michigan-based Life for Relief and Development (LIFE). Federal agents also raided the home of the charity's President and Chief Executive officer, Khalil Jassemm, and the Dearborn office of Muthanna Alhanooti, a former official of the charity who has ties to an Islamic party in Iraq. Its officials say the charity has distributed more than $50 million to more than 13 million people since its founding in 1992. Most recently, the group distributed $2.2 million in medicine in August 2006 to Lebanese people affected by the conflict between Hizballah and Israel.

The charity operated in a number of countries, including Pakistan, Iraq, Palestinian territories, Lebanon, Afghanistan and parts of Africa. It was founded by a group of Iraqi-Americans who said they were concerned about the condition of Iraqis after the Gulf War in 1991. The charity's head of legal services, Ihsan Alkhatib, said the agents are investigating whether the charity conducted business in Iraq before the 2003 war in violation of legal sanctions against the country.

LIFE is one of the very few American organizations licensed by the U.S. Treasury Department to do humanitarian relief in Iraq during the embargo period. It is the only American humanitarian organization that is working throughout Iraq. Many other U.S. charities have partnered with LIFE to deliver medicines and other humanitarian aid to the central part of Iraq. It also runs schools for orphans in Afghanistan as well as medical clinics in poor neighborhoods in Iraq.

The charity is registered with the United States Agency for International Development (USAID), which is a U.S. government agency under the State Department. It is also a member of the American Council for Voluntary International Action (InterAction), which is the largest alliance of American international NGOs, and a member of the Michigan Non-Profit Association. It is also certified by the Combined Federal Campaign (CFC), which promotes philanthropy among all federal employees. In addition, it is in Consultative Status with the Economic and Social Council of the United Nations.

The charity has established partnerships with many of the largest American and international NGOs including AmeriCares, Veterans For Peace,

Chapter III - Campaign against Muslim charities [91]

American Friend's Service Committee (AFSC), Brother's Brother Foundation, Care International, Wheelchair Foundation, United Nations Development (UNDP) and United Nations Children's' Fund (UNICEF).

LIFE President Dr. Khalil Jassemm had participated in an outreach effort by the U.S. State Department speaking about successful Arab and Muslim integration in the U.S. He believed that LIFE presents a positive image of America to the Muslim world. However, "the pattern of ongoing investigations, raids and closure can only curtail our country's efforts to combat the negative image of America abroad, especially during the time when we need win hearts and minds in the Muslim and Arab world," he argued. (10)

Agents raid two Muslim charities in Michigan

On July 24, 2007, as the trial of the Holy Land Foundation began in Dallas, Texas, federal agents raided two Muslim charities - the Goodwill Charitable Organization and Al-Mabarrat Charitable Organization - in Dearborn, Michigan.

In a news release, the U.S. Treasury Department said that the Goodwill Charitable Organization is a Hizballah front group that solicits money from Hizballah members who live in the United States. "We will not allow organizations that support terrorism to raise money in the United States," said Stuart Levey, the Treasury Department's undersecretary for terrorism and financial intelligence.

The other charity that was raided, Al-Mabarrat Charitable Organization, often held fund-raisers in metro Detroit and enjoyed support from many in the area. Federal officials maintained that its founder, Hussein Fadlallah, is the spiritual leader of Hizballah and a terrorist. But the Treasury Department did not designate Al-Mabarrat as a terrorist group, which means it technically can still operate, though agents hauled away its documents and computers, making it difficult to function.

The Treasury Department, however, placed the Goodwill Charitable Organization and its parent group, the Iran-based Martyrs Foundation, on its list of terrorist groups. The move freezes the groups' assets and prohibits any person in the United States from conducting transactions with them.

Islam & Muslims in the Post-9/11 America

Chapter III - Campaign against Muslim charities [92]

According to the Treasury Department, the Martyrs Foundation also backs Hamas and the Palestinian Islamic Jihad, two other groups the U.S. government considers to be terrorist outfits.

Interestingly many politicians, including Congressman John Dingell, a Dearborn Democrat, donated money to Al Mabarrat. According to tax records, Goodwill Charitable received $167,628 in contributions in 2005 and $202,500 in 2004. Al-Mabarrat raised $954,027 in 2004. **(11)**

Muslim charity's account closed

Since 9/11, the American Muslim community has also noticed disturbing trends within the national banking community where law-abiding American Muslims are seemingly and summarily being denied service based solely on their name, religion or ethnicity.

In March, 2005, a Chicago bank closed the account of a Bridgeview mosque because the mosque donated $10,000 to the Islamic American Relief Agency that is now under federal scrutiny for allegedly helping terrorists. The mosque made its donations in August and September 2004, before the U.S. government froze the charity's assets and raided its Missouri offices in October. At that time, the Treasury Department alleged the organization was involved in helping terrorist activities.

In November 2005, the Herndon, Virginia-based Foundation for Appropriate and Immediate Temporary Help (FAITH) received a letter informing them that its Wachovia accounts would be closed effective January 2006 despite its good standing as a customer. However, the bank officials failed to sufficiently explain the decision, instead wrote that the decision was in line with "the Bank's contract with FAITH which provides that the Bank can close any customer's account at any time..."

The FAITH is a social service organization that provides emergency aid and crisis counseling to Northern Virginia residents of all faiths. Current anti-terror financing legislation requires financial institutions to report suspicious activity to the Treasury Department. FAITH Treasurer Margaret Farchtchi told the *Washington Post* that a recent donation to the charity may have sparked suspicion. In April 2005, the charity received $150,000, intended as an endowment, from M. Yaqub Mirza, a Northern Virginia resident. Although

Chapter III - Campaign against Muslim charities [93]

Mirza's home and offices were raided by federal officers in 2002, he has not been officially charged with any crime. Farchtchi said that the "origin and purpose of the money could have been easily explained if bank officials had asked" (12)

In response to the closure of the group's accounts without warning or explanation, CAIR and the MAS Freedom Foundation had planned a campaign against Wachovia that was to include protests and boycotts. However, Wachovia contacted FAITH and CAIR directly to inform them that the case was being re-examined.

In "terror war" all names are not equal

A major Washington-based government watchdog group, OMB Watch, has charged that Muslim charities are being shut down for supposedly backing terrorist causes, while giant firms like Halliburton are receiving the full protection of U.S. law for allegedly breaking government sanctions against doing business with Iran -- a country designated as a sponsor of terrorism. "There is unequal enforcement of anti-terrorist financing laws," the OMB Watch said in a report on the plight of Muslim charities in April 2006.

Even though little is known about the evidence the Treasury's Office of Foreign Assets Control (OFAC) relied on to freeze and seize assets of Muslim charities, it appears there is much stronger evidence against Halliburton... What legal distinction is OFAC making? If U.S. charities formed Cayman Island subsidiaries, could they avoid the USA PATRIOT Act, IEEPA, and Executive Order restrictions on dealings with groups or countries linked to terrorism?

To support its claim that the government is applying the law unevenly and targeting Muslim-American groups, OMB Watch cites the government's "velvet glove" treatment of the Halliburton Corporation, a giant defense contractor once headed by Vice President Dick Cheney.

Halliburton has been under investigation by the Treasury Department, which oversees the terror-financing campaign, and the Department of Justice since 2001 for doing business with Iran, which is listed as a sponsor of terrorism.

But, says OMB Watch, rather than seizing and freezing assets "pending an investigation", Treasury's Office of Foreign Assets Control (OFAC) and the

Chapter III - Campaign against Muslim charities [94]

Justice Department sent an inquiry to Halliburton requesting "information with regard to compliance".

Halliburton sent a written response explaining why it felt it was in compliance with the law. Halliburton's defense seemed to rest on the fact that its dealings with Iran were done through a Cayman Islands subsidiary, not its U.S.-based entity.

Over two years later, in January 2004, OFAC sent a follow-up letter requesting additional information, to which Halliburton responded that March. In July of that year, the U.S. attorney for the Southern District of Texas sent a grand jury subpoena requesting documents and the case was referred to the Justice Department.

On Sep. 22, 2005, the Progressive Caucus in the House of Representatives wrote to President George W. Bush, asking that Halliburton be suspended from hurricane relief contracts for a host of reasons, including "dealing with nations that sponsor terrorism". The White House took no action and Halliburton received no-bid contracts valued currently at 61.3 million dollars, and growing, to provide clean-up, rebuilding and logistical assistance to victims of Hurricanes Katrina and Rita. (13)

Senate Finance Committee's McCarthyite witch hunt of Muslim charities

In December 2003, the Senate Finance Committee launched an enquiry against 24 Muslim charities and groups. The Senate Committee asked the Internal Revenue Service to turn over confidential tax and financial records, including donor lists, of 24 Muslim charities and foundations as part of a widening congressional investigation into alleged ties between tax-exempt organizations and terrorist groups.

Government officials, investigations by federal agencies and the Congress and other reports have identified the crucial role that charities and foundations play in terror financing," Committee chairman Charles Grassley, an Iowa Republican, and the panel's senior Democrat, Montana Senator Max Baucus, wrote in a 22 December, 2003 letter to the IRS.

"We have a responsibility to carry out oversight to ensure charities, foundations and other groups are abiding by the laws and regulations, to examine their source of funds, and to ensure government agencies, including the IRS, are policing them and enforcing the law efficiently and effectively," the letter added.

The Washington Post pointed out that the request "marks a rare and unusually broad use of the Finance Committee's power to obtain private financial records held by the government."

Muslim leaders and attorneys for charities protested saying that the government's investigation has tarnished their reputations and chilled financial support for groups that provide humanitarian support in the Middle East and elsewhere. According to the Council on American-Islamic Relations (CAIR), the Senate Finance Committee's investigative net has been cast so wide that it seems to target all American Muslims as terrorism suspects. Its indiscriminate scope smacks of a McCarthyite witch hunt and creates the impression that the presumption of innocence no longer applies to Muslims. "The Muslim community would view this as another fishing expedition solely targeting Muslims in America," Ibrahim Hooper, spokesman for CAIR said. "Are they now going to start a witch hunt of all the donors of these now closed relief organizations, so that Muslims feel they're going to be targeted once more based on their charitable giving?" he questioned.

In November 2005, the U.S. Senate committee concluded its work with no plans to issue a report, forward any findings to law enforcement agents, hold hearings or propose new legislation. "We did not find anything alarming enough that required additional follow-up beyond what law enforcement is already doing," Senator Charles Grassley, the Iowa Republican who heads the committee, said in a statement. "If something in the future does cause new concern, we will continue the investigation." (14) However, three weeks later, Senator Grassley issued a new statement saying its lack of action does not mean the groups had been "cleared." The committee, the statement said, "will continue to gather information and examine the operations of the charities." (15)

List of Muslim groups probed by the senate finance committee

Al Haramain Foundation
Alavi Foundation
Benevolence International Foundation

Global Relief Foundation
Help the Needy
Holy Land Foundation for Relief and Development
Human Appeal International
Institute of Islamic and Arabic Sciences in America
International Islamic Relief Organization
Islamic American Relief Agency
Islamic Assembly of North America
Islamic Association for Palestine
Islamic Circle of North America
Islamic Foundation of America
Islamic Society of North America
Kind Hearts
Muslim Arab Youth Association
Muslim Student Association
Muslim World League
Rabita Trust
SAAR Foundation
Solidarity International
United Association for Studies and Research
World Assembly of Muslim Youth

4 – It's guilty until proven innocent for American Muslim charities

Common law says, you are innocent until proved guilty. However, in the case of Muslim charities, they are guilty until proved innocent. The emerging national trend also goes to the very foundation of America's legal system: transparency. If one side makes an argument to a judge, the other side gets to be there to disagree. But not in the cases of Muslim charities.

While the Treasury Department has allowed U.S.-based groups an opportunity to submit information on their behalf after assets have been frozen "pending an investigation," the groups cannot respond effectively, because they are put in the position of having to prove a negative (i.e. that they do not support terrorism) without knowing what secret information Treasury is using against them.

This new standard of "guilty until proven innocent" is reflected in the actions of the Senate Finance Committee. In November 2005, the Senate Finance Committee concluded a high-profile investigation into U.S. Muslim organizations and terrorism financing, saying it discovered nothing alarming enough to warrant new laws or other measures. The inquiry, which took nearly two years to conduct, used financial records given to the Internal Revenue Service, including donor lists of two dozen Muslim charities. Yet despite a lack of any alarming evidence of terror financing, Grassley's committee issued a statement on Dec. 6, 2005 saying that "the fact that the committee has taken no public action based on the review of these documents does not mean that these groups have been 'cleared' by the committee," and that they will "continue to gather information and examine the operations of the charities." Perpetual suspicion seems to be the order of the day. (16)

Under a provision of the newly reauthorized U.S.A. Patriot Act, the government has largely unchecked power to designate any group as a terrorist organization. When that happens, a group's property may be seized and its assets frozen. The charity is unable to see the government's evidence and thus understand the basis for the charges. And it has only a limited right of appeal. So, the government can target a charity, obtain indictments against its leaders, then delay a trial indefinitely.

Holy Land Foundation's prosecution reveals questionable evidence

Criminal prosecution of the Holy Land Foundation, shut down in December 2001, provided a glimpse into the government's use of evidence to justify seizure and freezing of charitable assets in the name of the war of terrorism. Pre-trial filings show sanctions have been imposed against charities and their officials for contacting organizations that are *not* designated by the government as supporters of terrorism. The case also appears to depend on questionable foreign intelligence information and faulty translations.

Chapter III - Campaign against Muslim charities [98]

The Holy Land Foundation brought a formal complaint with the Justice Department inspector general and requested an investigation, saying that the F.B.I. used as the crux of its case a "distorted" and erroneous translation of sensitive Israeli intelligence material. The Holy Land said it hired an independent translating service in Oregon, which cited 67 discrepancies or errors in translation in a four-page F.B.I. document used in the case.

John Boyd, a lawyer for the foundation, maintained that the courts relied on secret evidence, including the challenged F.B.I. memorandum, and that Holy Land was never allowed to present a full defense. "The government's case rests on highly questionable evidence, and my hope is that someone in a position of authority is finally going to take a look at what happened here," Boyd said.

According to Los Angeles Times, the Justice Department's criminal case against officials of the Holy Land Foundation relies more heavily than previously known on Israeli intelligence. Federal prosecutors, accusing charity officials of aiding terrorists, have disclosed receiving 21 binders of documents from the Israeli government, according to records originally sealed by the court. The binders contain an estimated 8,000 pages that, in sheer volume, dwarf earlier shared intelligence — including Israeli military and police reports, translated interrogation transcripts and financial analyses.

Previous intelligence from Israel was a factor in 2001 when the White House, with great fanfare, froze assets of the Holy Land Foundation for Relief and Development, based in Richardson, Texas.

The paper pointed out that the case figures to hinge on the government's ability to prove, largely with Israeli-provided information, that the defendants knowingly supported groups tied to Hamas. Israel's prominent investigative role appears to be unprecedented in post-Sept. 11 terrorism cases.

Defense lawyers already have argued that allegations against Holy Land are influenced by political pressure from Tel Aviv. Bush's presidential order closing down the charity came on the eve of a White House visit by then-Israeli Prime Minister Ariel Sharon.

Chapter III - Campaign against Muslim charities [99]

Contents of the evidence binders provided by Israel have not been disclosed, but court records make clear that they are considered sensitive. During one hearing, for example, prosecutors revealed that the Israeli government retained control over what specific intelligence materials the U.S. could use publicly. And Justice Department lawyers traveled to Israel to negotiate what could be disclosed in court, prosecutors acknowledged.

Court records available to the public show that Israeli intelligence is central to a claim that the charity specifically earmarked money for the families of suicide bombers. That allegation was based on records seized in an Israeli raid on Holy Land's Jerusalem offices a decade ago. (17)

Substantial discrepancies

According to a February 25, 2007 report by the Los Angeles Times, Holy Land Foundation defense attorneys cited substantial discrepancies between an FBI official summary and a word for word transcript of a wiretapped conversation involving Holy Land officials in 1996. The summary, used as evidence by the government, ascribes numerous hateful anti-Semitic statements to charity officials that are not found in the recorded conversation.

The LA Times said that when the Bush administration shut down the nation's largest Muslim charity five years ago, officials of the Dallas-based foundation denied allegations it was linked to terrorists and insisted that a number of accusations were fabricated by the government. Now, attorneys for the Holy Land Foundation for Relief and Development say the government's own documents provide evidence of that claim.

The LA Times (18) reported:

"In recent court filings, defense lawyers disclosed striking discrepancies between an official summary and the verbatim transcripts of an FBI-wiretapped conversation in 1996 involving Holy Land officials. The summary attributes inflammatory, anti-Semitic comments to Holy Land officials that are not found in a 13-page transcript of the recorded conversation. It

Chapter III - Campaign against Muslim charities [100]

recently was turned over to the defense by the government in an exchange of evidence.

"Citing the unexplained discrepancies, defense lawyers have asked U.S. District Judge A. Joe Fish in Dallas to declassify thousands of hours of FBI surveillance recordings, so that full transcripts would replace government summaries as evidence. In December, the judge denied a defense request to declassify the documents so they could be examined by defendants in the case.

"The recently declassified summary of surveillance on April 15, 1996, asserts that during a conversation wiretapped by the FBI, Holy Land's former executive director Shukri Abu Baker told two associates there was no need to worry about the foundation being unfairly targeted because U.S. courts were not under the control of the American Israel Public Affairs Committee or its sponsor, "the government of the demons of Israel."

The summary portrays Baker as raging against "the Jews of the world" and as claiming that Jews have no allegiance to anything but "their pockets and to preserving the illegal Zionist state of Israel."

Additional anti-Semitic comments the FBI summary attributed to Baker or Ghassan Elashi, Holy Land's former board chairman, included:

- "Their [Jews'] only purpose here in the U.S. is to purchase as many politicians as possible and to warp the way the American Christians feel and think not just about the Christian religion but mainly about the Palestinian people ... and to rob as much money as possible from American taxpayers for the illegitimate excuse of protecting and preserving the chosen people of God."

- "Even Jesus Christ had called the Jews and their high priests ... the sons of snakes and scorpions."

- "I am confident that in the end justice, and not the Jews, will prevail. I believe that there is still justice in America."

Chapter III - Campaign against Muslim charities [101]

None of those quotes was contained in a 13-page transcript of the conversation, defense lawyers said in their motion to expand access to classified evidence.

The LA Times pointed out that because the court records are heavily redacted, it could not be determined who provided the summaries of the FBI wiretaps.

Other alleged discrepancies also have dogged the case, the paper said. Holy Land lawyers challenged the accuracy of an FBI memo, for example, that quoted a foundation office manager as telling Israeli authorities that charitable funds were "channeled to Hamas." But defense lawyers told the court the translation from Arabic to Hebrew to English distorted the official's original statement, and that he should have been quoted as saying, "We have no connection to Hamas."

Government is trying to keep proceedings in the dark

Meanwhile a veil of secrecy prevails in the court proceedings in the trial of charities. The story of the Al-Haramain Islamic Foundation attorney, Terence L. Kindlon, is perhaps the best example of how the government is trying to keep the court proceedings in the dark.

Kindlon got security clearance to look at classified documents in the case, but watched as government lawyers repeatedly brought matters to the judge privately. "Despite my elevated status as a trustworthy, secure guy, I was defending a case in which there were, I think, 19 (private) communications of which I know absolutely nothing," Kindlon told the Oregonian. (19)

The Al-Haramain Foundation, against whom criminal charges were dismissed in Sept. 2005, filed a lawsuit in February 2006 asserting that the Bush administration had circumvented the US Constitution by authorizing warrant-less wiretaps. The lawsuit accuses federal officials of illegally intercepting telephone calls between Soliman al-Buthe, a director of Al-Haramain, and two of the charity's American lawyers, Wendell Belew and Asim Ghafoor, in 2004

Chapter III - Campaign against Muslim charities [102]

After filing the suit, attorneys filed under seal a classified document that they said supports the allegations. Government officials have acknowledged that a classified document was inadvertently turned over to Al-Haramain lawyers while the Treasury Department was in the process of designating the charity as providing support for terrorists.

Neither government lawyers nor lawyers for Al-Haramain specifically described the document. The government filed a 19-page response opposing the unsealing of the classified document. The government filed another response, but for the judge's eyes only.

Something remarkable and disturbing is happening in this case and in others across the country, Al-Haramain lawyers wrote in a court brief filed in April 2006. The government "is attempting to draw a veil of secrecy over judicial proceedings."

"Unless a party can see and respond to evidence submitted against it, the court's impartiality is jeopardized," Al-Haramain lawyers wrote. Private "contacts that limit a party's ability to participate in hearings or refute the government's evidence violate the spirit of due process."

However, the District Judge Thomas J. McAvoy allowed the government to respond privately, then rejected Kindlon's motion and classified his reasoning.

No guarantee that a charity is clear even if it follows the Anti-Terrorist Financing Guidelines

In 2002, several Arab and Muslim American groups requested the US Treasury Department to assist US-based Islamic charities in building trust with donors while ensuring the government that their financial activities were clear of wrongdoing. In response, the Department developed a set of voluntary best practice guidelines that advise charitable organizations on how to establish proper transparency and vetting of potential foreign aid recipients.

However, the problem is that while most of the guidelines involve basic, common sense accounting standards, the section called "Anti-Terrorist Financing Procedures" contains some parameters that are too far-reaching and logistically impractical.

Islam & Muslims in the Post-9/11 America

Chapter III - Campaign against Muslim charities [103]

Among other things, these guidelines say charities should take steps to ensure that no individual employees of any foreign recipient organizations or subcontractors of those organizations support terrorism in any way. It also recommends a thorough investigation of any financial institutions used by the organizations in order to determine whether they could be "shell banks" involved in money laundering activities.

In short Muslim charities:

Must be on guard on several fronts. They must make sure they do not accept funds from anyone identified as a suspected terrorist, which they say can be difficult when many donations come as $10 or $20 bills given by anonymous donors at religious services.

Must also ensure that none of their employees or board members are affiliated in any way with thousands of individuals or groups designated as terrorist by the U.S. government.

Once they raise money, charities must make certain none goes to a project or person linked to terrorists or banned groups.

Severe restrictions

According to Dr Riad Abd al-Karim, co-founder of Kids in Need of Development, Education and Relief (KINDER USA) certain aspects of the guidelines are beyond the scope of what many charities are able to do and called them "ridiculous and burdensome". During times of humanitarian crisis, conducting background checks of every individual who could possibly be involved with foreign relief organizations is irrational. The Red Cross does not keep a list of everyone they give a band aid to after a tornado," he argues.

Attracting charities to help rebuild Lebanon in the aftermath of Israeli rampage of July/August 2006 highlighted the problem faced by the Muslim charities in the post-9/11 America. While various US groups and organization were busy in easily raising millions of dollars for Israel, Muslim and Arab groups faced serious difficulties in raising money for the reconstruction of Lebanon devastated by the Israeli attacks on mainly civilian targets such as residential buildings, bridges, industries and infrastructure.

Islam & Muslims in the Post-9/11 America

Chapter III - Campaign against Muslim charities [104]

The Illinois-based Zakat Fund pledged to raise $250,000 for Lebanon, but it was able to collect about $140,000 because many Muslims and Arabs feared that writing a donation check could bring FBI agents to their doors. Only about $40,000 came from Chicago donors despite the Charity Without Fear resolutions passed by the Illinois Legislature. The donors were particularly cautious because their donations may not land in the hands of Hizbullah which the U.S. government considers a terrorist organization. (20)

Umar Moghul, a partner in the law firm of Ahmed & Moghul LLP, in Manhasset, N.Y., says it was beyond the capacity of most donors, and even many foundations, to comply with guidelines. Compliance requires, for example, detailed information about the names and legal status of groups and staff members overseas that administer the American contributions. Moghul said: "You have to question just how practical it is to obtain this information while people are dying you're waiting to get certified copies of passports." For Muslim charities a donor can't really donate with absolute confidence in the current environment." (21)

New regulations have also affected donations to the American Muslim charity organizations due to the lack of assurance that donors will be protected if any charity organization later deemed by the government to be a terrorist organization. A fundamental problem is that even those American Muslim charities who follow the government's "best practices" guidelines to the letter do not receive any assurances that they will be safe.

The Council on Foundations in Washington, which represents more than 2,000 philanthropic groups in humanitarian work around the world, called on the Treasury Department to reconsider its antiterrorism financing guidelines issued in 2002. Calling the guidelines "unrealistic, impractical, costly, and potentially dangerous," the council said they discourage organizations from efforts to relieve suffering at a time of great need.

Anti-Terrorist Financing Guidelines revised

On Sept. 29, 2006, the U.S. Department of the Treasury released the third version since 2002 of its Anti-Terrorist Financing Guidelines: Voluntary Best Practices for U.S.-Based Charities. The new Guidelines come after Treasury requested public comments on the Dec. 2005 revision of the original

Guidelines. Nonprofit groups say revised government guidelines still are too onerous and vague. The OMB Watch, in an analysis of the new guidelines said that in an annex to the latest version, Treasury provides an unconvincing explanation of its perception that abuse of charities by terrorists is a substantial problem. "Treasury also uses the latest version to place greater emphasis on the voluntary nature of the guidelines. However, the fundamental problems that lead the nonprofit sector to call for withdrawal of the Guidelines remain unchanged."

Although the guidelines are voluntary, the Treasury Department has taken a passive aggressive approach in promoting their usage, hinting that any charity unable or unwilling to fully comply with them could be subject to closure under Executive Order 13224.

Even when the Muslim charities abide by the guidelines, the government said there are no guarantees that you'll be cleared. "Even if you comply with all of these, there is no guarantee you won't get in trouble," says Ihsan Alkhatib, a lawyer working with Life for Relief & Development, a Muslim charity in Southfield, Michigan.

Many American Muslim advocacy groups have argued that a line must be drawn between policing charities and interfering with an individual's right to practice his or her religion. The California-based organizations, American Muslim Voice and Muslim Public Affairs Council, have argued that the ability to contribute to charity is both an American right and, for Muslims, a religious commandment.

Impact on donation collection

Government crackdown of Muslim charities has caused tremendous fear and anxiety among Muslims, with many fearful that a simple act of charity could lead to federal agents knocking at their door. Since 9/11, millions of dollars in donations have been seized and frozen, leaving Muslims with unfulfilled obligations. Some have found FBI agents at their doors, asking about specific checks they have written. According to the Illinois Coalition for Immigrant and Refugee Rights, the U.S. government has closed down 25 Muslim charities and frozen $8 million in donations in Illinois alone.

The case of Dr. Nasar Chaudhry of New York symbolizes the Muslim dilemma. In April 2005, the Internal Revenue Service's Criminal

Chapter III - Campaign against Muslim charities [106]

Investigation Division raided the home and office of Pakistani-American Dr Nasar Chaudhry. for making donations to a Muslim charity in 1996. Dr Chaudhry of Hornell, New York state, was contacted in 1996 by a former medical school peer for making donation to his Florida-based charity to aid needy Pakistani children. He decided to give Zakat to the charity. Dr Chaudhry said if the charity misused the funds, how would he be responsible for that? (22)

In January 2005, Kinder USA suspended its operation as it was targeted for federal investigation. "In the current environment, we cannot in good faith continue to solicit donations when there are no safeguards in place to guarantee that the federal government will not seize these funds and divert them from their intended, legitimate destination," Kinder USA said. The charity later resumed its operation but found difficult to bring back its donors.

On the impact of government campaign against the Muslim charities, Washington Post reported on October 30, 2006, many US Muslims are donating less and less to Islamic charities, fearing that they might be placed on FBI watch lists and accused of channeling money to organizations designated as terrorist by the State Department. The Washington Post substantiated its story with three examples:

1. Ahmad Chebbani, the owner of Omnex Accounting and Tax Service Corporation and the president of the American Arab Chamber of Commerce for eight years until June 2006, used to donate $50,000 annually to charity, basically to Muslim organizations. Now he changed the target to avoid unwanted attention from federal powers, giving money to secular institutions like the Arab American National Museum.

2. In the past, Najah Bazzy, who established the Zaman International charity in Dearborn, used to raise up to $10,000 in cash donations for the poor and needy. By the end of `Eid Al-Fitr last week, which marks the end of the holy fasting month of Ramadan, donations amounted to less than $4,000. When she called people to donate, they hung up, fearing that their phones might have been tapped by authorities. Nobody wants to write a check for any amount, and they look at her in horror when she offers a receipt.

3. The Islamic Center of America Dearborn, Michigan, has not managed to raise funds to cover the $15 million spent on building the center because of the clampdown on charity. , The center - the largest in the U.S. - is indebted by $6 million.

US Muslim charity in Dearborn, Michigan, home to the largest Muslim and Arab concentrations in the US, is down by almost half.

Amaney Jamal, a Princeton University professor who completed a survey of the Dearborn, Michigan, Arab-American community, said the uncertainty is one of the most distressing problems Muslims feel these days. "If someone says to me, `Do you want to support an orphan for US$30 a month?' I say, `Sure, that's a noble cause.' And then later someone comes and knocks on my door and says, `Her father was a suicide bomber.'" Hence, charity giving to the Arab world has become a big no-no. One result has been an increase in non-traceable cash donations to local mosques or religious institutions. (23)

The "Cat Stevens affair" is another example. Yusuf Islam, a popular singer in the 1970s, when he was known as Cat Stevens, was barred in Sept. 2004 from entering the United States because he allegedly supported terrorist groups through donations he made to Muslim charities. The case against Yusuf Islam, whom most Muslims regard as a moderate voice, has had a chilling effect on local Muslims. If it could happen to the man who wrote "Peace Train," it could happen to anyone. "If they have a problem with this guy, there is not an imam in the whole of America that the U.S. administration would not have a problem with," said Asad Zaman, treasurer of the Muslim American Society's Minnesota chapter. "We do not perceive that the administration is trying to help. We think they're trying to put a cap on Muslim charity." (24)

Despite difficulties, the Muslim organizations were among the first to respond to the relief efforts for the hurricane Katrina victims. Islamic Relief transferred $1 million to an interfaith fund to feed 25,000 persons. In Sept. 2005, a coalition of major American Islamic groups meeting at the annual convention of the Islamic Society of North America (ISNA) in Chicago announced a pledge to raise $10 million in humanitarian relief for the victims of Hurricane Katrina. However, they were disappointed to see that not a single Muslim organization was included in the list of charities accepting donations.

Muslim Groups Form National Council of American Muslim Non-Profits

In March 2005, the Treasury Department endorsed and guided the creation of a National Council of American Muslim Non-Profits, as a self-policing organization working for transparency, accountability and the safe delivery of charitable funds to the proper recipients. The Council, spearheaded by the Muslim Public Affairs Council and the Islamic Society of North America, was established during a meeting of twenty national American Muslim organizations in Chicago.

The Council envisaged generating a collective bargaining power in a bid to bolster the community's ability for advocacy, and encourage the government to engage with the American Muslim community with full transparency. By creating a structure to allow for a community-based certification process, the Council planned to empower the community by instituting a culture of responsibility and self-governance.

Assistant Secretary of the Treasury Department for Terrorist Financing Juan Zarate, who sat in on the working session, expressed his Department's support for the Council. "The creation of the national council is also a testament to the community taking ownership of this corrosive and difficult issue," said Zarate. "At stake in the project to preserve the sanctity of charity is not only the confidence of the Muslim American donor community but also the compassionate voice and view of America in the Muslim world. The work of the members of the council -- which will now begin in earnest -- will shape how charities are protected, how Muslim American's dollars are spent at home and abroad, and how America is viewed in the Muslim world."

Timothy Keefer from the Homeland Security Department told the Supplemental Human Dimension meeting in Vienna on July 15, 2005: "The Treasury Department has also encouraged and helped facilitate the creation of the National Council of American Muslim Non-Profits by the Islamic charitable community in the United States. The Council is comprised of a diverse group of representatives from the Muslim-American community who

Chapter III - Campaign against Muslim charities [109]

are joining forces to organize, protect and promote charitable giving against the backdrop of demonstrated terrorist abuse."

However, the National Council of American Muslim Non-Profits could not help in protecting the Muslim charities and the initiative suffered a major set back when one of its steering committee member, KindHearts, was shut down in February 2006.

The OMB Watch has pin pointed the following top ten concerns about the negative overall impact of U.S. anti-terrorism policy on the Muslim charities:

1. Drastic sanctions in anti-terrorist financing laws are being used to shut down entire organizations, resulting in loss of badly needed humanitarian assistance around the world and creating a climate of fear in the nonprofit sector.
2. Despite sweeping post-9/11 investigative powers, authorities have failed to produce significant evidence of terror financing by U.S.-based charities.
3. Questionable evidence has been used to shut down the largest U.S.-based Muslim charities.
4. Anti-terrorist financing policies deny charities fundamental due process.
5. There are no safe harbor procedures to protect charities acting in good faith or to eliminate the risk of giving to Muslim charities or charitable programs working with Muslim populations.
6. Government action has created the perception of ethnic profiling and negatively impacted Muslim giving.
7. Organizations and individuals suspected of supporting terrorism are guilty until proven innocent.
8. Charitable funds have been withheld from people in need of assistance and diverted to help pay judgments in unrelated lawsuits, violating the intentions of innocent Muslim donors.
9. There is unequal enforcement of anti-terrorist financing laws. Treatment of Muslim charities hurts, not helps, the war on terrorism. (25)

For 10 years before 9/11, American Muslim groups were working to make the Muslim relief organizations more professional, and to raise funds for more effective long-term projects. Now people are reverting to giving cash to individuals they know who are traveling to a specific country, to offer to the

Chapter III - Campaign against Muslim charities [110]

needy. They also prefer to give cash donations to their mosques and Islamic centers. That surely undermines the beneficial growth of Muslim nonprofit institutions.

References

(1) ACLU Report: The Fallout of "anti-terrorism" policies on Muslim charities – Dec. 8, 2004
(2) Muslim charities say fear is damming flow of money, Washington Post - August 9, 2006
(3) The Crime of Being a Muslim Charity By Laila al-Marayati and Basil Abdelkarim
(4) Newsweek – August 8, 2007
(5) Fiction hits home: USA Today admits false reporting against Muslim charity - Metro Times – April 28, 2004
(6) Washington Post, May 3, 2002
(7) AP report, January 14, 2005
(8) Washington Post - Oct. 11, 2006
(9) OMB – Sept. 25, 2005
(10) Muslim charities are assets not liabilities By Khalil Jassemm - The Arab American News, October 26, 2006
(11) Detroit Free Press - July 25 & 26, 2007
(12) Wachovia Bank Action Riles Muslim Activists - The Washington Post, May 6, 2006
(13) Inter Press Service - April 20, 2006
(14) Indianapolis Star – Nov. 15, 2005
(15) Indianapolis Star – December 8, 2005)
(16) OBM Report Feb. 2006
(17) Questions arise over case against Islamic charity - Los Angeles Times – June 18, 2006
(18) Los Angeles Times - February 25, 2007
(19) The Oregonian - April 25, 2006
(20) Hizbullah: Dilemma for the American Muslim charities By Abdus Sattar Ghazali – American Muslim Perspective - Sept. 4, 2006
(21) American Muslims curb donations to Islamic charities fearing scrutiny - New York Times - April 16, 2003
(22) Evening Tribune – April 7, 2005
(23) Muslim charities in the US facing a climate of fear AMP Report - Oct. 17, 2004
(24) Muslim charities in the US facing a climate of fear AMP Report - Oct. 17, 2004
(25) OMB Watch Report: U.S. Anti-Terrorism Policies Hurt Muslim Charities – March 2006

Chapter IV - Inquisition of Muslims in America

January 16th is officially observed "Religious Freedom Day." It commemorates the day when Thomas Jefferson and other patriots met in Fredericksburg to draft the Virginia Statute for Religious Freedom. This is the first legislation in history to guarantee religious liberty for every citizen which later served as the model for the First Amendment in the U.S. Bill of Rights. Recognizing the importance of faith to our people, our founding fathers guaranteed religious freedom in the constitution.

The Virginia Statute for Religious Freedom passed on January 16, 1786 is considered as one of Thomas Jefferson's three greatest accomplishments, along with writing the Declaration of Independence and founding the University of Virginia. This is an obscure day as we don't see any enthusiastic commemoration events on this day with the exception of Fredericksburg, the birthplace of the Virginia Statute for Religious Freedom. In this historic town, the day is celebrated traditionally with a colorful Religious Freedom march.

But in the post-9/11 America, the Muslim community has little to celebrate on this day because it was under siege. Its mosques were under surveillance and its charities were being scrutinized or shut down. American Muslims attending an Islamic conference abroad were detained and fingerprinted like criminals when they return home. Its religious leaders (Imams) were kicked off from a US Airways Minneapolis-to-Phoenix flight and briefly detained on suspicion of terrorism.

In February 2003, FBI Director Robert Mueller's top aides directed chiefs of the bureau's 56 field offices to develop "demographic" profiles of their localities-including tallying the number of mosques. According to the Newsweek (Feb. 3, 2003), when FBI executive assistant director Wilson Lowery Jr. briefed congressional staffers on the project, and explained that mosque tallies would be used to help set investigative goals, "there were a lot of eyebrows that went up," said one of those present. The approach

Chapter IV - Inquisition of Muslims in America

raised concerns that the FBI was engaging in a new form of religious "profiling."

In a letter to Attorney General John Ashcroft, Congressmen John Conyers Jr. (D-Mich.) Jerrold Nadler (D-N.Y.) and Senator Russell D. Feingold (D-Wisc.) wrote: "We write to ask you to immediately terminate the Justice Department's new policy directing the fifty-six FBI field offices to count the number of mosques and Muslims, as well as other community groups and religious organizations, in their areas. We cannot sanction the targeting of Muslim populations and mosques, or any other community group or institution, to gather intelligence without any suspicion or cause that a specific individual or group of individuals, or a particular mosque or religious organization, is engaging in terrorist activities. We urge you to follow the constitutionally prescribed channels of investigation to ensure that the rights of American citizens are not violated..."

The FBI abandoned its plans to count the mosques but later the FBI agents who requested a meeting with the leadership of the Islamic Society of Frederick, Md., "mentioned casually" they would be asking for a list of the society's members. This sent red flags up for the Islamic Society, who immediately informed media outlets, interfaith partners and civil rights groups. Local FBI officials then said they would not press for the list local agents had requested.

On June 13, 2007, an anti-Muslim group known with the acronym SANE - the Society of Americans for National Existence - unveiled its so-called "Mapping Shari'a in America Project" devoted to spying on 2,300 Islamic institutions in the United States. "The project will collect information about America's 2,300-plus mosques and associated day schools, provide information to both law enforcement officials and the public, and test the proposition that Shari'a (read Islam) amounts to a criminal conspiracy to overthrow the U.S. government," the SANE project said. While launching its "Mapping Sharia Project," the SANE claimed that hundreds of Islamic centers in the United States have become a hot-bed of extremist activity and promote violence, terrorism and hatred against America. **(1)**

Islam & Muslims in the Post-9/11 America

Chapter IV - Inquisition of Muslims in America [113]

The SANE project seems an extension of Center for Religious Freedom's anti-Muslim project entitled "Saudi publications on hate ideology invade American mosques." The Center for Religious Freedom is an affiliate of the rightist think tank Hudson Institute which includes necon Richard Perle among its supporters. The ultimate objective of the SANE is banishing Islam from the US by making "adherence to Islam" punishable by 20 years in prison. **(2)**

In December 2005, the Muslim community was stunned to know that the U.S. government had been monitoring for suspicious radiation levels outside more than 100 predominantly Muslim-related sites in the greater Washington, D.C., area, as well as various sites in other cities. The monitoring has been taking place since the Sept. 11, 2001 terrorist attacks.

Under the program, agents with the FBI and U.S. Department of Energy targeted a range of private Muslim institutions without court approval or warrants. Federal officials said they set up the program in Detroit and five other cities to thwart a nuclear attack from Islamic extremists, according to a U.S. News and World Report article that was confirmed by the U.S. Justice Department. **(3)**

The US News and World Report also reported that the monitoring was conducted at more than 100 Muslim sites in the Washington, D.C., area -- including Maryland and Virginia suburbs -- and at least five other cities when threat levels had risen: Chicago, Detroit, Las Vegas, New York, and Seattle. At its peak, three vehicles in Washington monitored 120 sites a day, nearly all of them Muslim targets identified by the FBI. Targets included mosques, homes, and businesses. **(4)**

Muslims urged to spy on fellow Muslims

At the same time, the Bush administration had launched an operation seeking Muslim informants to spy on fellow Muslims. A Wall Street Journal report of July 11, 2006 gives an insight into the covert operation. The WSJ report titled, "A Muslim's Choice: Turn U.S Informant or Risk Losing Visa," detailed the case of Yassine Ouassif whose green card was taken away from him when he crossed the border from Canada in November 2005. Ouassif was then sent home to San Francisco and told to contact a counterterrorism agent at the FBI. The agent made him an offer: become an informant and regularly report to the FBI on what his Muslim friends in San Francisco were saying and doing. In exchange he would get back his green card." According to Ouassif, if he refused, the agent threatened to deport him back to Morocco.

The WSJ said that Ouassif's story provides a window into a largely covert front of the war on terror: the FBI's aggressive pursuit of Muslim informants. Since the terror attacks of Sept. 11, 2001, the bureau has had the difficult task of penetrating a culture that few agents know anything about. It has responded with a forceful effort to conscript eyes and ears within Muslim communities. The paper said that some of the recruitment is public. FBI agents plead for community assistance in meetings at mosques and other Muslim conclaves. Agents also are under pressure to develop confidential sources. **(5)**

On May 19, 2006, the New York Times reported testimony of a Muslim informer that confirmed what many Muslims have believed since the Sept. 11 attacks: that law enforcement agencies have worked to infiltrate their community during terrorism investigations. A young police detective testified at the Herald Square bombing plot trial that he was recruited from the Police Academy 13 months after 9/11 to work deep undercover in the Muslim community to investigate Islamic extremists. The detective, a Muslim who came to America from Bangladesh when he was 7, testified that he was a 23-year-old college graduate when he was plucked from the academy in October 2002. He took an apartment in Bay Ridge, Brooklyn, where, he testified, his assignment was to be a "walking camera" among Muslims there. He said he had no regular contact with the department other than through his handler, to whom he reported by e-mail at first.

During two years of living in Bay Ridge, he was involved in "numerous" investigations, he testified, and was at times shadowed by a field team to ensure his safety. The detective was the final witness at the four-week trial

Chapter IV - Inquisition of Muslims in America [115]

of Shahawar Matin Siraj, 23, a Pakistani immigrant who is charged with plotting to blow up the Herald Square subway station in 2004.

The New York Times said that the Police Intelligence Division's program to post detectives overseas has been widely publicized. But this detective's testimony in federal court in Brooklyn provided the closest look yet at how the division is using undercover investigators to penetrate mosques, bookstores and other places where Muslims gather in the city. **(6)**

In another high profile terror trial of two Pakistani Americans a Muslim informer was paid $ 250,000 to infiltrate the large Muslim community in Lodi, California. In the trial of Hamid Hayat, 23 and his father Umer Hayat, 48, in February 2006, defense attorney Washma Mojaddidi told the court that the government case was founded on cultural ignorance that confused a wedding party for a terrorist gathering and depended heavily on the testimony of an informer who was paid $250,000 by the FBI to infiltrate the Muslim community in Lodi.

Lodi trial was one of the show case trials that was heralded, during the debate over the renewal of the USA Patriot Act, as an important milestone in the fight against terrorism. "I was very impressed by the use of intelligence and the follow-up," President Bush said at the time of the high profile arrest of the Hayats. "And that's what the American people need to know, that when we find any hint about any possible wrongdoing or a possible cell, that we'll follow up," the president added. **(7)**

An operative of the FBI, Darren Griffin, known as the Trainer was a part-time employee for three years at KindHearts, the Toledo-based Muslim charity shut down by the government in February 2006. During the three years Darren Griffin worked a $7-an-hour, part-time job at KindHearts, his co-workers knew him as Bilal and considered him to be a faithful Muslim and an American patriot who served in the U.S. military in Iraq. His work led to the arrests of three men on terrorism charges in February 2006. KindHearts' attorney and a board member Jihad Smaili said he believes investigators planted Griffin inside KindHearts in an effort to link the charity with terrorists.

Chapter IV - Inquisition of Muslims in America

A U.S. Treasury undersecretary already has labeled KindHearts the offspring of both Global Relief and Holy Land Foundation, the two charities shut down in December 2001. **(8)**

The FBI paid almost $56,000 to two confidential informants who were key to the case against seven men accused of being involved in a terrorist plot to blow up the Sears Tower and other targets. According to a document filed by federal prosecutors, the FBI paid one unnamed informant $10,500 and an additional $8,815 in expenses. They also paid a second informant $17,000 with another $19,570 for expenses. U.S. officials also granted the second informant a "significant public benefit" -- immigration parole so he could remain in the country. The seven men, part of a religious group headquartered in the Liberty City area of Miami-Dade County, are facing various charges in connection with attacks they allegedly planned. Much of the case hinges on the two informants, one of whom knew the men and participated in the investigation after alerting authorities. The second man posed as an al-Qaida operative at the FBI's direction, according to prosecutors. Secret recordings made by the informants are also central to the case. **(9)**

Muslims are repeatedly compelled to condemn terrorism

While the Islamic centers and mosques became targets of security agencies and anti-Muslim groups in the aftermath of 9/11, the Arab and Muslim Americans were compelled, time and again, to apologize for acts they did not commit, to condemn acts they never condoned and to openly profess loyalties that, for most U.S. citizens, is merely assumed. Within hours of the Sept. 11, 2001, attacks on the Pentagon and World Trade Center, every major Muslim group in the nation signed a joint statement vehemently denouncing the terrorist act. Since then American Muslims have been condemning every act of terrorism. But their denouncing is ignored and the most frequent criticism that's tossed at the American Muslim community is, 'You never denounce terrorism.' Whenever there is an act of terrorism, American Muslims and Arabs come under pressure to again and again denounce terrorism which is often ignored or played down by media.

Islam & Muslims in the Post-9/11 America

Chapter IV - Inquisition of Muslims in America [117]

Responding to ceaseless urgings by columnists, religious personalities and other American public figures for Arabs and Muslims to condemn terrorism and repudiate individuals and groups connected with terrorist acts, a leading Muslim civil rights group, the Council on American-Islamic Relations (CAIR) in 2004 and 2005 launched an online petition and advertisement campaigns denouncing terrorism.

In May 2004, after the beheading of an American civilian, Nicholas Berg, in Iraq, CAIR launched an online petition drive designed to disassociate the faith of Islam from the violent acts of a few Muslims. The "Not in the Name of Islam" petition states:

"We, the undersigned Muslims, wish to state clearly that those who commit acts of terror, murder and cruelty in the name of Islam are not only destroying innocent lives, but are also betraying the values of the faith they claim to represent. No injustice done to Muslims can ever justify the massacre of innocent people, and no act of terror will ever serve the cause of Islam. We repudiate and dissociate ourselves from any Muslim group or individual who commits such brutal and un-Islamic acts. We refuse to allow our faith to be held hostage by the criminal actions of a tiny minority acting outside the teachings of both the Quran and the Prophet Muhammad, peace be upon him."

The CAIR also published a full-page advertisement in the Los Angeles Times titled "No to terrorism, No to bigotry." The ad read: "Over the last few weeks, Americans of all faiths have been horrified by images of violence in the Middle East. The Iraqi prisoner abuse scandal does not represent America or Christianity. The Israeli missile that killed innocent Palestinian children in Gaza does not represent Judaism. And the beheading of an innocent American man, Nicholas Berg, does not represent Islam. "Islam, Christianity and Judaism share the basic values necessary to create a world in which tolerance and peace prevail. We have an opportunity to build bridges between our faiths and to challenge those who attempt to divide humanity along religious and ethnic lines. American Muslims condemn all acts of terrorism and are as outraged as their fellow Americans by atrocities committed in the name of God and their faith...." **(10)**

Fourteen months later, in July 2005, after the London bombings, CAIR launched a national TV advertisement campaign repudiating terrorism in the name of Islam. The 30-second spot featured two American Muslims, a man

Chapter IV - Inquisition of Muslims in America

and a woman, denouncing violence in the name of Islam and vowing to "not to allow our faith to be hijacked by criminals." The spots were distributed nationwide as public-service announcements, meaning stations could choose to air them or not. Later research showed they were seen by as many as 5 million people. The spot ran 105 times for four days on 13 cable channels in Tampa, including CNN, Fox Sports Net and the Weather Channel. Members of the Tampa CAIR chapter donated the money to get the ads on as paid commercials in prime time in the local market, at a cost of more than $10,000. **(11)**

Pundits of the militant Right found in the London attacks (July 7, 2005) another opportunity to equate Islam with terrorism, to question the sincerity of the Muslim rejection of terrorism, and to incite the public against Islam and Muslims. Given the loud and extensive condemnation of terrorism by Muslims, particularly in North America and Europe, the militant-Right cry has shifted from "why Muslim leaders do not speak out against terrorism?" to "are Muslim leaders sincere in their condemnation of terrorism, or are they doing it to deflect anger and prevent a backlash?" **(12)**

Clearly, Muslims were genuinely appalled by the brutality of the terrorist acts, and some were going the extra mile to make sure their condemnation is made loud enough, and is repeated enough, so that they can be heard by the deafest of their critics. A Fatwa, or religious edict, issued by the Religious Council of North America, and supported by major Muslim organizations, was the latest effort in this regard. **(13)**

The Fiqh Council of North America issued a fatwa - endorsed by all major American Muslim organizations - says that Islam condemns terrorism, religious radicalism and the use of violence. "Targeting civilians' life and property through suicide bombings or any other method of attack is forbidden, and those who commit these barbaric acts are criminals, not martyrs....All acts of terrorism targeting the civilians are *haram*, forbidden in Islam. It is *haram*, forbidden, for a Muslim to cooperate or associate with any individual or group that is involved in any act of terrorism or violence."

The fatwa also says it is the "civic and religious duty of Muslims to cooperate with law enforcement authorities to protect the lives of civilians." The fatwa was prompted by a similar ruling from the Muslim Council of Britain, following the July 2005 terrorist attacks in London.

The fatwa against terrorism and "Not in the Name of Islam" campaign condemning terrorism is a sad commentary about America. Neither Christians nor Jews feel compelled to take out newspaper ads declaring their faith's innocence whenever acts of violence and extremism are carried out by individuals or groups who share their religion. And that's simply because we are enlightened enough as a nation to know that you can't condemn Christianity just because a few Christians committed the Oklahoma City bombing terrorism.

Chapter IV - Inquisition of Muslims in America

References

(1) US Newswire – June 13, 2007

(2) In February 2007, SANE issued a policy paper that in part stated: "Whereas, adherence to Islam as a Muslim is prima facie evidence of an act in support of the overthrow of the US. Government through the abrogation, destruction, or violation of the US Constitution and the imposition of Shari'a on the American People. . .It shall be a felony punishable by 20 years in prison to knowingly act in furtherance of, or to support the, adherence to Islam."

(3) Detroit Free Press - December 24, 2005

(4) Associated Press – December 24, 2005

(5) How the Bush administration recruits Muslim informers? AMP Report – August 8, 2006]

(6) Ibid.

(7) Ibid.

(8) The Plain Dealer – March 2, 2006)

(9) South Florida Sun-Sentinel – July 26, 2006)

(10) May 13, 2004 - CAIR Bulletin

(11) Orange County Register – July 14, 2005

(12) Beyond the Condemnation of Terrorism by Louay M. Safi

(13) Ibid.

Chapter V - Profiling Institutionalized

Racial profiling is any use of race, religion, ethnicity, or national origin by law enforcement agents as a means of deciding who should be investigated. Official profiling of Muslims and Arabs began with the Attorney General Ashcroft's announcement in November 2001 to target about 5,000 young men of Middle Eastern and South Asian heritage who entered the country in the last two years on non-immigrant visas but who were not suspected of any criminal activity for questioning by the federal government.

Race, ethnicity and religion have become proxies for suspected terrorist activity since September 11, 2001. The Bush Administration claimed that its anti-terrorism efforts do not amount to racial profiling, but singling out for questioning and detention Muslims and Arabs and selective application of the immigration laws to the nationals of Arab and Muslim countries, were practices that spoke louder than words.

Post 9/11 legislative activity sanctioned racial profiling. In 2002 Congress passed and the president Bush signed, a customs service reauthorization bill that expanded legal immunity for Customs officers engaged in unconstitutional searches. The legislation was approved despite evidence from the General Accounting Office that the Customs Service has a history of racial profiling. In order to avoid the U.S. Constitution's Fourth Amendment protections from "unreasonable searches and seizures," airport searches now fall under the rubric of "administrative searches."

Amid mounting incidents of profiling, Senator Feingold and 12 other Senators in February 2004 introduced the End Racial Profiling Act of 2004 bill that was referred to the Committee on the Judiciary. The bill said: In the wake of the September 11, 2001, terrorist attacks, many Arabs, Muslims, Central and South Asians, and Sikhs, as well as other immigrants and Americans of foreign descent, were treated with generalized suspicion and

Chapter V - Profiling institutionalized [122]

subjected to searches and seizures based upon religion and national origin, without trustworthy information linking specific individuals to criminal conduct. The bill also pointed out that such profiling has failed to produce tangible benefits, yet has created a fear and mistrust of law enforcement agencies in these communities.

New York was probably the only state where an attempt was made to make profiling of Muslims legal when identical bills were presented in the NY Assembly and Senate on June 8, 2006. The proposed legislation would have authorized law enforcement officials to "consider race and ethnicity as one of many factors that could be used in identifying persons who can be initially stopped, questioned, frisked and/or searched." The bill had the support of politicians from both sides of the aisle. Assemblyman Dov Hikind, a Democrat and a twelve-term legislator, while introducing the bill argued that the Supreme Court set precedent in Grutter v. Bollinger, maintaining that factors such as race and ethnicity can be considered in making governmental decisions provided that such consideration serves a compelling governmental interest. (1)

"Flying While Muslim or Arab"

Since 9/11, the Muslims and Arabs have been resigned to some extra checks while traveling by air but they were shocked to hear a prominent congressman and at least three Republican office-seekers publicly calling for ethnic profiling. It actually became a Republican campaign issue in November 2006 elections.

House Homeland Security Committee Chairman Peter King endorsed requiring people of "Middle Eastern and South Asian" descent to undergo additional security checks because of their ethnicity and religion. Seizing on the incident of the alleged London plot to blow up U.S.-bound airliners in August 2006, the Republican Congressman said that, "if the threat is coming from a particular group, I can understand why it would make sense to single them out for further questioning." He said that airport screeners shouldn't be hampered by "political correctness." Peter King's prejudice against the American Muslims was nothing new. In 2004 he said that 85 percent of the mosques in the United States have extremist leadership. (2)

Islam & Muslims in the Post-9/11 America

Mark Flanagan, a congressional candidate from the 13th District of Florida proposed that passengers who appear to be Arab or Muslim would be pulled out of security lines for additional screening. He said: "It is a fact that over the past 34 years, starting with the Munich Olympics, the majority of terrorist attacks have been carried out by Muslims." (3) Joining the fray, Paul Nelson, a Republican running in the third district of Wisconsin, also endorsed the idea. Asked on a radio show how screeners would spot a Muslim male, Nelson said, "If he comes in wearing a turban and his name is Muhammad, that's a good start." (4) The Republican gubernatorial candidate in New York, John Faso joining the chorus of profiling said that law enforcement officials should be able to question a Muslim man without fear of being slapped by an ACLU lawsuit. "Looking for Muslims for participation in Muslim jihad is not playing the odds. It is following an ironclad tautology." (5)

Adding fuel to the fire, Bill O'Reilly at Fox News argued repeatedly for profiling of Muslims at airports. In his view detaining all Muslims between the ages of 16 and 45 for questioning "isn't racial profiling," but "criminal profiling." (6)

Not surprisingly, the panic caused by the alleged London plot – that later proved no more than a hoax (7)– prompted a flurry of incidents not only in US but also on the trans-Atlantic flights.

Three incidents of profiling happened in one day on August 17, 2006:

- A terminal at the Tri-State Airport in West Virginia was shut down for nine hours after an airport security screener grew suspicious of two bottles of liquid inside the carry-on bag of Rima Qayyum, a Pakistani woman, traveling to Detroit by U.S. Airways. Chemical tests of the bottles' contents turned up no explosives. Adding insult to injury, U.S. Airways refused to allow her to board a flight the next day, despite being completely cleared by the Federal Bureau of Investigation.

- A Pakistani national, Azar Iqbal, traveling from Manchester to Atlanta with his family on Delta airlines was separated from his wife and children, held for questioning by US immigration officials, and deported to the UK.

Chapter V - Profiling institutionalized [124]

- A Canadian Muslim doctor, Dr. Ahmed Farooq, and his two colleagues were kicked off a United Airlines flight from Denver to Winnipeg (Canada) after a passenger identified them as a terrorist threat because he was offering prayers.

Earlier on August 10, a British Muslim airline pilot, Amar Ashraf, was hauled off a Continental Airlines' flight from Manchester, UK to Newark, NJ, just before take-off. He was returning to his job as a pilot for one of Continental's partner airlines in the U.S.

Yet in another incident, on August 15, a group of about 200 American Muslims were detained for hours at New York's Kennedy Airport when they came back to the United States from trips abroad. The passengers of Arab, Muslim or South Asian backgrounds were plucked from the baggage area, held six hours without food or water by Customs and Border Protection agents and questioned some about their views of Iraq.

Obviously, many Americans were jittery after the alleged London plot. A poll conducted by the Quinnipiac University Polling Institute between August 17-23 found that most Americans support the screening of people who look "Middle Eastern" at airports and train stations. Surely, the by-product to the fear and hysteria generated by the administration and the media was not surprising. (8)

Unfortunately, discrimination against Arabs and Muslims at U.S. airports did not begin after 9/11. The phenomenon of "flying while Arab" has been part of the profiling landscape since the late 1980's. In particular, the bombing of Pan Am flight 103 over Lockerbie, Scotland in 1988, caused many Americans to link the threat of airline-related terrorism with Arabs. According to the Civil Rights Organization (civilrights.org) by the mid-1990's, the popular association of Arabs and Muslims with terrorist activities caused the American public to immediately suspect Arab and/or Muslim involvement whenever an unnatural disaster of significant proportions occurred. In the wake of the Oklahoma City bombing in 1995, law enforcement officials immediately posted bulletins looking for Arabs and/or Muslims, and authorities detained a Jordanian. That terrorist attack, of

Chapter V - Profiling institutionalized [125]

course, turned out to be the work of an Anglo-American, Timothy McVeigh. (9)

Similarly, the 1996 crash of TWA flight 800 off Long Island was initially attributed to Arabs by many, but ultimately attributed to equipment malfunction. After that crash, large numbers of Arab Americans, Muslims, and other Middle Eastern-looking airline passengers were subjected to harsh questioning, demeaning treatment, and searches of their personal possessions. Some were told that they were receiving special treatment because they "fit a profile." (10)

Discriminatory screening and abusive treatment of Arabs and Muslims by airport personnel continued well into the 1990's. The FAA attempted to address these abuses in 1998 through its implementation of the Computer Assisted Passenger Screening (CAPS) system, which standardized the criteria for deciding which passengers to scrutinize closely. While the elements of CAPS have not been made public, the government insists that the CAPS system does not rely on race or ethnicity in determining who should be subjected to heightened scrutiny at airports. (11)

In August 2006, the Transportation Security Administration's new behavioral profiling system Screening of Passengers by Observation Techniques (SPOT) went on-line in many major airports in the U.S. SPOT will allow TSA and law enforcement to focus on persons who look Middle Eastern or "Muslim," while justifying it through a subjective psychological impression. (12)

Since September 11, 2001, the "flying while Muslim or Arab" phenomenon has returned with a vengeance. Passengers perceived to be Arab or Muslim have experienced abuse or humiliation, have been subjected to especially intrusive security screening procedures, and have even been ordered off planes for no reason other than that they appeared to be Arab or Muslim and were therefore perceived to be terrorist threats. (13)

The most notorious example of this treatment involved Secret Service Agent Walid Shatter, an Arab American who was flying to Texas on Christmas Day 2001 to join President Bush's security detail. Agent Shatter was removed from his flight when a flight attendant spotted a book on Middle Eastern history on his seat and airline officials refused to believe that his credentials and badge were authentic. There is no question that Agent Shatter would not have been treated in this manner had he not been an Arab American. The same can be said of scores of Arabs, South Asians and Muslims who experienced discrimination at airports and on airplanes post-September. (14)

There was a spate of profiling incidents in 2001 and 2002

Soon after the 9/11 attacks, there was a spate of profiling incidents. Let's illustrate this with some most important cases.

- On January 1, 2002, an Arab American passenger en route to Washington, D.C. passed through security checks, submitted his boarding pass, and stood in line at the jet way during boarding. Two police officers approached him and escorted him back to the airport. When he asked why this had happened, the officers informed the passenger that the airplane's pilot had requested that he be "checked out" because he had an "Arabic name." Three FBI agents then appeared and questioned the passenger about his identity. (15)

- Two Arab Americans, Michael Dasrath and Edgardo Cureg, were unceremoniously and unapologetically forced off of Continental Flight #1218 on New Year's Eve in 2001, after a fellow passenger stated that the "brown men are behaving suspiciously." (16)

- On October 28, 2001, three Arab American women were prevented from boarding their flight to New York City from Minneapolis because airline personnel had overheard them quietly praying before the flight and became concerned on hearing one of the women say the word "Allah." (17)

- A Muslim businessman was singled out for extra interrogation before boarding a flight from Los Angeles to Tampa on Oct. 10, 2001. When he inquired about why he was receiving this extraordinary attention, he was told by the airline employee that "[m]ay be you were acting suspiciously or maybe (because of)] the way you look." (18)

- On November 7, 2001, a 22-year-old Muslim American woman was asked to remove her head scarf - which many Muslim women wear for religious reasons - after passing through an airport metal detector without setting it off. After a manual detector was passed along her body, again revealing nothing, she was asked to remove her head scarf and was escorted to a private room where female airport security personnel conducted a full body search and ran their fingers through her hair. (19)

If you are not convinced, here are few more takes:

- On November 19, 2006, six Imams (Muslim religious leaders) were taken off a US Airways flight in Minneapolis and detained for several hours after some passengers and crew members complained of behavior they deemed suspicious. Before boarding the flight, three of the six men went to a corner at the gate to perform obligatory prayers, one of the five pillars of Islam and a constitutionally protected right. The flight's captain decided to remove the Imams after the passenger passed him a note pointing out "suspicious Arabic men." The six imams, who were returning after attending a Minneapolis conference of the North American Imams Federation, were handcuffed by the police and led off the flight. Among the group was NAIF President Omar Shahin - an American citizen and Imam in Arizona for the last 30 years - later told the media that he and his five colleagues, including a blind man, were made to line up 10 feet apart in the airport terminal before hundreds of others passengers waiting for other flights. They were then handcuffed and led to separate rooms where they were detained for nearly three hours. (20)

- On January 31, 2006, Mohammed Khan and his father, Fazal Khan, had boarded their flight from Los Angeles to Oakland and were waiting for the plane to take off. Both men wore traditional South Asian tunics and white skullcaps, and both had long beards. After the flight was delayed an hour on the runway, a customer service representative boarded the plane and told the Khans that they would have to leave the aircraft to discuss something inside the terminal. There, the representative informed the men that they could not remain on the flight because their presence made the flight attendant uncomfortable. She found them seats on a different flight that departed two hours later. The circumstances make it abundantly clear that no security rationale existed for the Khans' removal. The airline even left the

Chapter V - Profiling institutionalized [128]

men's checked luggage on board the original flight, which took off shortly after the Khans were removed. (21)

- On December 11, 2004, Dr. Salam Al-Marayati the executive director of the Muslim Public Affairs Council, was interrogated at Los Angeles airport by security agents when he returned after vacation in Mexico. Writing in the Los Angeles Times, Al Marayati said: One officer asked whether we had committed any criminal act in the past or had done anything that would warrant an investigation. Of course the answer was no. Another officer wanted to know which charities we donated to and whether those organizations send money overseas. (22)

Clearly, it has become commonplace for security personnel to exercise their discretion in a manner that distinguishes Muslims and Arabs from the rest of the air traveling public. This treatment is based on the unfair assumption that Arabs and Muslims share a general propensity for terrorist activity and is directly analogous to the treatment of Blacks and other minorities on America's highways and streets. (23)

In the aftermath of 9/11, Arab-Americans have a greater fear of racial profiling and immigration enforcement than of falling victim to hate crimes, according to a national study financed by the Justice Department. The study also concluded that local police officers and federal agents were straining under the pressure to fight terrorism, and that new federal policies in this effort were poorly defined and inconsistently applied. The two-year study, released in June 2006 by the Vera Institute of Justice, explored the changed relationship between Arab-Americans and law enforcement in the years since the 2001 terrorist attacks. The Vera Institute is a nonprofit policy research center based in New York. About 100 Arab-Americans and 111 law enforcement personnel, both FBI agents and police officers, participated in the study, which was conducted from 2003 to 2005. Both Arab-American community leaders and law enforcement officials interviewed in the study said that cooperation between both groups had suffered from a lack of trust. (24)

"Driving While Arab or Muslim"

"Driving while Arab or Muslim" has joined the profiling lexicon alongside "driving while Black" and "driving while brown" since 9/11. Arabs, Muslims, South Asians, and Sikhs are now subjected to traffic stops and searches based in whole or in part on their race, ethnicity, or religion due to law enforcement perceptions that they are likely participants in terrorist activity. For example:

- On Sept. 5, 2006, a federal judge in Bay City, Michigan, threw out all charges against three Texas men who were arrested in August 2006 while driving at the Mackinac Bridge. State prosecutors slapped them with terrorism charges for buying hundreds of cell phones, but soon dropped them. The prosecutors then charged them with conspiring to traffic in counterfeit goods and carrying out an unlawful activity involving a financial transaction. Magistrate Judge Charles Binder dismissed the federal charges saying there was no terror plot. The Texas men -- brothers Adham Othman, 21, of Dallas and Louai Othman, 23, and their cousin Awad Muhareb, 18, - were of Palestinian descent. Surely, they were the victims of racial profiling - "Driving while Arab" - and there will forever be a stigma attached to them. (25)

- On October 4, 2001, in Gwinnett, Georgia, an Arab American motorist was pulled over by a patrol car following an illegal U-turn. The police officer approached the car with gun drawn. He ordered the motorist out of his car, searched him, threatened him, and called him a "bin Laden supporter." (26)

- On December 5, 2001, in Burbank, Illinois, a veiled Muslim woman was stopped by a police officer for driving with suspended plates. After she showed the officer her license and registration, as requested, the officer asked her when Ramadan would be over. She was arrested for driving with suspended plates, was pushed by the officer as she got in the patrol car, and was asked inappropriate questions about her hair by the officer. The woman was released later that day. (27)

- On October 8, 2001, in Alexandria, Virginia, two police officers stopped an Arab American motorist and his two Arab American passengers, questioned them about the verse of the Koran hanging from the car's rear view mirror, and inquired about documents and photocopies in the backseat. After asking for and receiving the motorist's and passengers' identification cards, the police officer returned to his car and drove off without explanation. He returned 10 minutes later, explaining that he had had to take another call. (28)

Some other instances of profiling

A group of 36 American Muslims were searched, fingerprinted and photographed at the Lewiston Bridge crossing near Niagara Falls, New York on return from an Islamic conference in Toronto in December 2004. A spokeswoman for Homeland Security's Customs and Border Protection confirmed that agents stopped anyone who said they attended the three-day conference, titled "Reviving the Islamic Spirit," based on information that such gatherings can be a means for terrorists to promote their cause. "We have ongoing credible information that conferences such as the one that these individuals just left in Toronto may be used by terrorist organizations to promote terrorist activities, which includes traveling and fund raising," another US official said. Several of the Muslim citizens held at the border for up to six hours said that when they objected strenuously to being fingerprinted, they were informed by Customs and Border Protection representatives that "you have no rights" and that they would be held until they agreed to the fingerprinting procedure. (29)

- The agents of the New Jersey Office of Counter-Terrorism were barred from filing reports to the State Police database after the discovery of more than 100 entries that seemed to target suspects only because they were practicing Muslims or were active in the Muslim community. The State Police action sparked a dispute that became so intense that the acting Gov. Richard Codey's office had to intervene by summoning Attorney General Peter Harvey, State Police Superintendent Rick Fuentes and Counter-Terrorism Director Sydney Caspersen to a Statehouse meeting to broker a peace. (30)

- Five Muslim men attending the Sept. 19 (2005) Giants football game against the New Orleans Saints were detained and questioned for about a half hour by the FBI after they were observed praying at the stadium. The men were allowed to return to the stadium, but in different seats, and were escorted to their cars when they left. (31)

- In August 2005 an increasing number of calls for legal advice from Iranian Americans sent up red flags for a coalition of civil rights organizations monitoring the treatment of Muslims and natives of two dozen countries in North Africa, the Middle East and South Asia. Iranians were increasingly seeking legal aid after being questioned by the FBI, put on government watch lists and losing their jobs or security clearances. "Over the past year or so there are increasing numbers of Iranian Americans who are being discriminated against across the board," Dalia Hashad of ACLU told a news conference in San Francisco. (32)

Interviews of 5,000 Muslims and Arabs

Official profiling of Muslims and Arabs began with the Attorney General Ashcroft's announcement in November 2001 to target about 5,000 young men of Middle Eastern and South Asian heritage who entered the country in the last two years on non-immigrant visas but who were not suspected of any criminal activity for questioning by the federal government.

In planning these interviews - which were expected to number 5000 in late 2001 and an additional 3000 in early 2002 - the federal government sought the support of state and local governments and law enforcement agencies. In a stunning reversal, many of these state and local offices balked at assisting federal authorities, arguing that to single out Arab men for questioning amounted to racial profiling. (33)

Nevertheless, the interviews were carried out as planned. Ninety percent of those sought for questioning appeared and were interrogated about their political and religious beliefs and those of their families; whether they sympathized with the September 11 hijackers; whether they had any scientific or weapons training; and where they had traveled. It is not believed that any person interviewed provided any useful information to law enforcement authorities, although Attorney General Ashcroft claimed that the interviews "generated a significant number of leads . . . into the September 11 attacks . . .fostered new trust between law enforcement' and the Arab and Muslim communities, and helped to disrupt potential terrorist activities." (34)

Islam & Muslims in the Post-9/11 America

Chapter V - Profiling institutionalized [132]

Just five months before the November 2004 presidential election, the FBI began a third round of interviews of members of the Arab and Muslim communities in July. The FBI and the Department of Justice had described the move as an ongoing effort to "establish contacts with community organizations and leaders in their territories", but for many in the Arab/Muslim community that outreach effort has triggered painful memories of the post-9/11 security dragnet that landed hundreds of Arab and Muslim suspects in police detention, most of whom were later exonerated of any terrorist-related activities. Civil rights groups received numerous complaints about coercive or intimidating tactics used by FBI agents. The new interviews provoked heavy scrutiny from the American Civil Liberties Union (ACLU), which had offered to provide free legal representation to those contacted by the FBI for information.

The FBI interviews came at a time when the Arab American community was also dealing with a controversial decision by the US Census Bureau to provide the Department of Homeland Security with new statistics on the Arab American population. The data, which included detailed information on the number of Arabs who live in certain zip codes, was tabulated in August 2002 and December 2003 at the request of the Customs and Border Protection (CBP), a division of the Homeland Security Department. The report documented US cities with more than 1000 Arab Americans residents, along with a second listing for zip code demographics on individuals with Egyptian, Syrian, Jordanian, Palestinian, Moroccan, Iraqi and Lebanese heritage. Two other categories were "Arab/Arabic" and " Other Arab". Census Bureau officials have said they were legally obligated to provide the information, while CBP officials said they wanted the statistics in order to post Arabic signs in certain airports.

Detentions and Deportations

A particularly disturbing form of terrorism profiling has been the federal government's use of race as a basis for the detention without due process and its subsequent use of the anti-terrorism investigation as a vehicle for the disproportionate application of U.S. immigration laws against detainees who were found to be innocent of any terrorist activity. In the wake of 9/11, the United States detained hundreds - perhaps thousands - of Arabs, South Asians and Muslims on suspicion of terrorist activity. Almost none of these individuals were ultimately found to have been in any way involved in terrorism. Yet many continued to be held without being formally charged with any crime or immigration violation. (35)

The US government acknowledged at one point that the number of detainees was in the range of 1200, although it refused to give out specific information about how many persons were detained and why. This information has been sought by various civil rights groups under the Freedom of Information Act, a request that was upheld in November 2002 by a federal district court ordering release of names and other information on detainees. (36)

Unfortunately, a divided 2-1 decision in the U.S. Court of Appeals for the D.C. Circuit in June, 2003, reversed that ruling and upheld the withholding of all information. The plaintiffs filed for review by the Supreme Court, but that petition was denied on January 12, 2004.

Many of those who were ultimately charged with immigration violations were held to be deportable based on relatively trivial offenses. One Palestinian man was detained and charged for failing to notify INS of a change of address; and a Pakistani was detained and charged with helping some illegal immigrants find housing. During some of the often unexplained detentions, law enforcement officials interrogated the detainees rudely and even abusively, limited their access to families and lawyers severely, threw them into jails where guards and other prisoners taunted and in at least one case badly beat them, kept them behind bars long after abandoning any claim that they were terrorists. (37)

The story of Ali al Maqtari, a French teacher from Yemen, provides a chilling example of what many Arabs and Muslims have faced since 9/11. Mr. al Maqtari was married on June 1, 2001 to an American citizen and was therefore himself eligible for citizenship. On September 15, 2001, Mr. al Maqtari and his wife drove up to the Fort Campbell, Kentucky, U.S. army base so that she could report for duty as a new recruit. Federal agents descended on them, separated them and questioned Mr. al Maqtari for 12 hours. The federal agents falsely accused Mr. al Maqtari of violating the immigration laws, abusing his wife, and conspiring with terrorists from Russia; claimed to have evidence against him which proved not to exist; and threatened him with beatings. Even after polygraph tests showed that he was telling the truth, and even after INS and FBI officials indicated he would be freed, Mr. al Maqtari was held for an additional seven weeks, during which time he was housed with hardened criminals in two separate jails, taunted by guards, and limited to one phone call per week. Mr. al Maqtari's experience supports the conclusion of Amnesty International that "a significant number of detainees continue to be deprived of certain basic rights guaranteed under international law," according to the LCCREF.

The government detained at least 70 men, all but one a Muslim, as material witnesses and abused their civil rights in a largely secret operation launched by the Justice Department after the Sept. 11 attacks, according to a Human Rights Watch and the ACLU report released in June 2005. The civil rights groups said that in many cases the detainees were not told why they were arrested and did not get immediate access to lawyers, and that the Justice Department often would not confirm whether they were being held. Federal law allows the government to temporarily detain people who are suspected of having knowledge of a crime to ensure they testify. But the report accused the government of operating in "a Kafkaesque world of indefinite detention" for many people who were never linked to terrorism. Of the 70 men identified in the report, 42 were released without any charges filed. Seven were charged with terrorism-related offenses. At least 13 received apologies from the government for being wrongfully detained. "Muslim men were arrested for little more than attending the same mosque as a Sept. 11 hijacker or owning a box-cutter," the report pointed out. (38)

Alien Registration Program

In the post-9/11 America, immigrants from predominantly Muslim countries were victimized by U.S. legislation that unjustly targetted them as a group. Harsh immigration and anti-terrorism laws and policies had a devastating effect on many Muslim communities leaving a legacy of fear and disillusionment, especially among young people.

Most forms of profiling, such as "driving while Black," feature the exercise of law enforcement discretion based on certain assumptions about the propensity of a particular group toward certain criminal behavior. This discretion was exercised on a case-by-case basis at the point of contact. That is, the officer observes and decides to take action against a person who the officer believes, based on the assumptions under which he operates, is likely to engage in criminal activity. (39)

But profiling can also occur at a more general level, when a law enforcement institution makes the determination that an entire group of people is so dangerous that all persons in that group should automatically receive heightened attention. In such cases, profiling is not a function of the exercise of law enforcement discretion, but represents the absence of law enforcement discretion. (40)

An example of this type of profiling was the Alien Registration Program, which went into effect in late 2002. The program enforced a requirement that foreign visitors to the United States register with the Immigration and Naturalization Service (INS) – which is now renamed as U.S. Citizenship and Immigration Services - and keep law enforcement apprised of their whereabouts. The Justice Department claimed that the registration program will eventually cover visitors from all foreign countries, but the first individuals subjected to the requirements were visitors from five Arab or Muslim countries - Iran, Iraq, Syria, Sudan, Libya - and those from North Korea - who were required to register by December 16, 2002. Pakistan, Indonesia, and Saudi Arabia were later added to the original list and, overall, the program was extended to cover 25 countries. Registrants were required to re-register annually. The program was cancelled in December 2003. (41)

A California Senate report on the impact of INS Registration said: Rather than developing evidence against individual suspects gathered through policing intelligence methods, in the one activity that affected Muslim immigrants most acutely, the federal government seemingly abandoned investigations of terrorism directly altogether. It did so by imposing severe sanctions on any male visa-holder of a certain age from a Muslim country whose compliance of immigration regulations fell short of the letter of the law. Widespread instances of arrests, detentions and deportations and threatened deportations resulted. No suspected connection to terrorism formed the criteria for sanctions. (42)

Chapter V - Profiling institutionalized [136]

The CA report entitled "the Patriot Act, other post-9/11 enforcement powers and the impact on California's Muslim communities," also said: Muslim communities reacted with anger, fear and confusion. The breadth of concern is shown by a letter sent to the Secretary of Homeland Security, Tom Ridge, and signed by 77 civil rights, immigration and Muslim community groups – seven from California. The letter states in part: "We urge your Department to revisit the overarching assumptions of post 9/11 detentions – that immigration law should be a tool for the blanket detention of individuals who are not connected to terrorism and cannot be charged criminally."

When the program was announced, Justice Department officials defended it on the grounds that the requirements were merely administrative measures that would assist the anti-terrorism struggle by helping authorities keep track of visitors to the United States - not as a vehicle for prosecuting or investigating these individuals for activity unrelated to terrorism. These representations proved false. Almost immediately after the registration requirements went into effect, the government began to detain registrants found to have been guilty of immigration violations, not terrorism. According to reports, 500-1000 registrants were detained in the Los Angeles/Orange County area alone when they attempted to meet the initial December 10 (2002) registration deadline. (43)

Some 83,000 Muslim men registered with the program, officially called the National Security Entry Exit Registration System (NSEERS0, from its inception in September 2002 to its termination in April 2003.

Out of those 83,000, more than 13,000 were taken to detention centers or deported. Not one of them was ever charged with a terrorism-related crime.

According to an unofficial tally:

_ Number of foreign visitors from 25 predominantly Muslim nations (and North Korea) who were ordered to register with the government: 83,310.

_ Number of those from 83,310 who were ordered into deportation proceedings: 13,740

_ Number who were publicly charged with terrorism, although officials say a few have terrorism connections: 0 (44)

Islam & Muslims in the Post-9/11 America

Many of the detainees had committed only minor immigration infractions, had experienced delays or difficulties in adjusting their status to citizen or legal permanent resident, and/or had been living in the United States legally for years, often with spouses and families. In one such case, a Moroccan man living in the Washington, D.C., area with an application for legal permanent residency pending was handcuffed, placed in leg irons, and held in a county jail overnight. He now faces deportation, even though he was not found to be connected at all to terrorism. (45)

Most of the detainees were released, but problems lingered with the registration program in general. Some registrants reported being subjected to verbal abuse and taunting by government officials. Officials at one Florida registration site mockingly offered ham sandwiches to hungry registrants who had been held for hours and interrogated about their immigration status and suggested that the registrants wash their hands in "camel's milk" before being fingerprinted. (46)

The experience of Ejaz Haider, an editor at one of Pakistan's most respected English-language news magazines and a visiting research fellow at the Brookings Institution, demonstrates the twisting of INS registration programs into vehicles for the unfair treatment of Muslims under the guise of counter-terrorism. Pursuant to INS regulations, Mr. Haider registered in the United States upon his arrival and was told to report for an interview within 40 days. Mr. Haider subsequently checked with both the State Department and INS and was told that in fact that he did not have to report for the interview. (47)

On January 28, 2003, however, Mr. Haider was accosted by two INS agents in front of the Brookings Institution, taken into custody, fingerprinted, photographed, and told that he would spend the night in jail. Only the intervention of Mr. Haider's colleagues at Brookings and the Pakistani Foreign Minister caused his release and saved him further hardship. (48)

The mixed advice provided by the U.S. officials to Mr. Haider was yet another layer of unfairness to the process. Writing in Washington Post, Mr. Haider said: "I did not know I was in violation of the INS policy. Brookings did not know I was in violation. My friends in the State Department did not know I was in violation. And if - even after following the policy closely and calling INS for information - we could not understand the law, what hope can there be for the cabdriver or the restaurant worker who doesn't have the leisure to discover the letter and intent of INS policies." (49)

The registration program not only became another pretext for the disproportionate targeting of Muslims and Arabs but there is also no evidence that the program had been useful to the anti-terrorism struggle. In fact, as The Washington Post had pointed out, "The bait and switch, which punishes and humiliates those who tried to follow the rules, can only undermine the purpose of the registration program." (50)

Special registration was not a program mandated by Congress. It was crafted by members of the executive branch of government. Attorney General Ashcroft amended the Code of Federal Regulations (CFR) declaring willful failure to register and provide full and truthful disclosure of information a failure to maintain nonimmigrant status, a deportable offense.25 He also amended the CFR by declaring that failure to register upon departure from the United States is an unlawful activity, making one presumed to be inadmissible to the United States because one "can reasonably be seen as attempting to reenter for purpose of engaging in an unlawful activity."(51)

Ashcroft thereby made noncompliance with the special registration program a bar to immigration, although only Congress has the right to establish such categories of inadmissibility. Special registration may also deny Arabs and Muslims the right to benefit from any future amnesty or legalization program.

David Cole, Law Professor at Georgetown University believes that the nation is experiencing the largest example of ethnic profiling after the Sept. 11 attacks since World War II, when the U.S. government interned Japanese-Americans. "Our government says we will sacrifice foreign nationals' rights, Arabs and Muslims most notably, for Americans' security."

As a matter of fact, the racial profiling by US law enforcement agencies has increased since 9/11 and now affects one in nine Americans, according to an Amnesty International USA (AI-USA) report of 2004. State and federal agencies, under the guise of fighting terrorism, have expanded the use of this degrading, discriminatory and dangerous practice, the AI-USA pointed out.

Chapter V - Profiling institutionalized [139]

References

(1) From website of Assemblyman Dov Hikind
http://assembly.state.ny.us/mem/?ad=048&sh=story&story=19484
(2) Profiling of Muslims: Latest Republican campaign issue By Abdus Sattar Ghazali, Al-Jazeerah.net, August 24, 2006
(3) Ibid.
(4) Ibid.
(5) Ibid.
(6) The O'Reilly Factor August 16 , 2006
(7) Ghazali, Op. Cit.
(8) Reuters August 29, 2006
(9) Civil Rights Report by Leadership Conference on Civil Rights Education Fund (LCCREF), Feb. 26, 2003
(10) Ibid.
(11) Ibid.
(12) South Florida Sun-Sentinel, August 28, 2006
(13) Civil Rights Report, Op. Cit.
(14) Ibid.
(15) American Arab Anti-Discrimination Committee, Report on Hate Crimes and Discrimination Against Arab Americans (2003)
(16) Ibid.
(17) Ibid.
(18) Ibid.
(19) Ibid.
(20) New York Times/ Minneapolis Star Tribune reports on six imams removed from flight - Sept. 21, 2006
(21) CAIR Bulletin – March 16, 2006
(22) Los Angeles Times - December 11, 2004
(23) Civil Rights Report Op. Cit.
(24) New York Times – June 26, 2006
(25) Detroit Free Press – Sept. 5, 2006
(26) ADC Report, Op. Cit.
(27) Ibid.
(28) Ibid.
(29) CAIR Bulletin – Dec. 29, 2004
(30) Star-Ledger - September 26, 2005
(31) Newsday – Nov. 22, 2005
(32) Mercury News - August 3, 2005
(33) See Fox Butterfield, "Police Are Split on Questioning of Mideast Men," The New York Times, November 22, 2001; Jodi Wilgoren, "University of Michigan Won't Cooperate in Federal Canvas," The New York Times, December 1, 2001. See also Michael Janofsky, "Cities Urge Restraint in Fight Against Terror," The New York Times, December 23, 2002

Chapter V - Profiling institutionalized [140]

(noting the passage in many jurisdictions of resolutions urging the federal government to respect the civil rights of local citizens when fighting terrorism).
(34) ADC Report, Op. Cit.

(35) Civil Rights Report, Op. Cit.

(36) Center for National Security Studies v. Department of Justice, 215 F.Supp.2d 94 (D.D.C. 2002).

(37) Civil Rights Report, Op. Cit.

(38) USA TODAY- June 26, 2005

(39) Civil Rights Report, Op. Cit.

(40) Ibid.

(41) Ibid.

(42) CA Senate Report – March 2004
(43) James Nash, "INS Frees Some Detainees; No Apology for Middle Easterners' Arrests," Los Angeles Daily News, December 20, 2002. The Los Angeles area has a large Iranian population.)

(44) From a Chicago Tribune study, Immigration Crackdown Shatters Muslims' Lives, Nov. 11, 2003

(45) Dan Eggen and Nurith Aizenman, "Registration Stirs Panic, Worry: Some Muslim Foreign Nations Risk Arrest to Meet INS Deadline," The Washington Post, January 10, 2003)
(46) Civil Rights Report, Op. Cit.

(47) Ibid.

(48) George Lardner, Jr., "Brookings Scholar is Detained by INS; Registration Rule Snags Pakistani Editor," The Washington Post, January 30, 2003.
(49) Ejaz Haider, "Wrong Message to the Muslim World," The Washington Post, February 5, 2003.

(50) Editorial, "The Wrong Way," The Washington Post, December 29, 2002.

(51) 8 Code of Federal Regulations 264.1 (f) (9), (Washington D.C.: USGPO).

Chapter VI - Stereotyping Muslims & Arabs

As the "war on terror" entered into its sixth year, a new racial stereotype was emerging in America. Brown-skinned men with beards and women with head scarves were seen as "Muslims" -- regardless of their actual faith or nationality. At the same time Muslims are the object of a series of stereotypes, caricatures and fears which are not based in a reality and are independent of a person's experience with Muslims.

Dehumanize a group first before attacking it

Dehumanize a group first before attacking it. Violent, catastrophic confrontations seldom occur unless the contending parties have dehumanized one another. Once this de-humanization occurs, opponents are seen as having no legitimate rights and any atrocities are considered justifiable. Thus the law was passed in the US congress regarding airport "profiling" which is really stereotyping and racism. (1) The idea is that you can identify "risky" people based on the countries they traveled to in the past – Arab and Muslim Americans - and search them more thoroughly than the "normal" people. Yes, your impression of a line at the airport for Arabs and Muslims and a line for others.

The Fox network 2006 Emmy award winning series entitled '24' is perhaps the best example of de-humanizing Muslim and Arab Americans and promoting their racist stereotyping in the post 9/11 America. The controversial propaganda series won an acclaim from the self proclaimed scholar and Islamophobist Daniel Pipes who congratulated Fox for "not caving in to Islamists" in its decision to go ahead with airing the show.

The drama featured an upper-middle class Muslim family operating as a sleeper terrorist cell. A young man is seen helping his parents mastermind a plot to kill as many Americans by launching an attack on a commuter train. The drama showed the mother poisoning her son's non-Muslim girlfriend

Chapter VI - Stereotyping Muslims & Arabs [142]

because she poses a threat to their plans. The US secretary of state is also seen taken hostage by the "Muslim terrorists." It climaxes with the defense secretary shown on an Internet video tape.

The implication of the episode is that one can never be certain that the Muslim or Arab family next door are not terrorists. Episodes like '24' perpetuate the stereotype that all Muslims are terrorists. How television influences viewers' perception of Muslims and Arabs is shown by a public opinion survey conducted by Cornell University in 2004. The survey showed a correlation between television news-viewing habits, a respondent's fear level and attitudes toward restrictions on civil liberties for all Americans. Respondents who paid a lot of attention to television news were more likely to favor restrictions on civil liberties, such as greater power for the government to monitor the Internet. Respondents who paid less attention to television news were less likely to support such measures.

No doubt when average Americans don't have any personal interaction with Muslims, whether it be at work or at school, they base their perception of Islam and Muslims from what they see on TV.

Jack Shaheen who catalogs Arab and Muslim images in the U.S. media, is worried that "24" represents a new trend, where even the Muslim or Arab next door is a potential threat. Shaheen says, "To present a truly balanced image, why don't Fox and other networks create some Arab or Muslim characters who aren't building bombs? Maybe they're just an everyday family, like the Cosbys." (2)

The Council on American-Islamic Relations (CAIR) challenged the Fox network when it first aired the show. Fox agreed to remove some of the stereotypical scenes, and to broadcast CAIR public service announcements featuring American Muslims of European, African-American, Hispanic, and Native American heritage. Each person in the spots states how he/she and his/her family have served America and ends by saying, "I am an American Muslim."

Islam & Muslims in the Post-9/11 America

In another gesture to the Muslims and Arabs the show was interrupted to present a short statement by the actor Kiefer Sutherland: "I'm Kiefer Sutherland. I play counter-terrorist Jack Bauer on Fox's *24*. While terrorism is obviously one of the most critical challenges facing our nation and the world, it's important to recognize that the American Muslim community stands firmly beside their fellow Americans in denouncing and resisting terrorism in every form."

Kingdom of Heaven

Kingdom of Heaven is another example when the film director Ridley Scott tried to address the sensitivities of Muslims and Arabs about the historical movie story.

To assuage any Muslim and Arab concerns ahead of the Kingdom of Heaven release in May 2005, its director Ridley Scott and the studio behind the film, 20th Century Fox, arranged private screenings for Muslim and Arab organizations. Film Director Ridley Scott wrote in a letter to the American-Arab Anti Discrimination Committee (ADC), "while the primary focus of the film is one man's personal journey of faith, I have also given much care to addressing the very sensitive nature of the larger political and religious issues of the Crusades."

'Kingdom of Heaven' is an epic-scale historical drama inspired by the events of the third Crusade of the 12th century and is based on real characters, including Balian of Ibelin, a Crusader knight, and Salah El Din (Saladin), the renowned Muslim leader. The movie, a 20th Century Fox production with a $130 million budget, was shot in Morocco with hundreds of extras, horses and elaborate costumes. The script, written by William Monahan, follows the story of Balian who rises to knighthood and embarks on a life-changing journey to find peace and a better world.

The ADC praised the portrayal of Arabs and Muslims in the move. Its Communications Director Laila Al-Qatami said, "Scott's 'Kingdom of Heaven' presents a more complex and human representation of Muslim characters than is evident in most Hollywood films. "We definitely welcome 20th

Century Fox and Ridley Scott's efforts to provide a fair and multifaceted portrayal of cultural and religious realities during the Crusades." (3)

Another major Muslim civil rights organization, the Council on American-Islamic Relations (CAIR) pointed out that initial fears that the film offered stereotypical portrayals of Muslims were unfounded. "Our overall impression is that 'Kingdom of Heaven' is a balanced and positive depiction of Islamic culture during the Crusades. Muslims are shown as dignified and proud people whose lives are based on ethics and morality." (4)

No doubt, stereotypes about Islam and Muslims, which were once used to rally the Crusaders, persist to this day. These misperceptions are not mere footnotes in history but they continue to have a negative impact, sometimes influencing the US policies when dealing with Muslims both at home and abroad.

The word "crusade" itself remains a loaded term. In September 2001, President George Bush stoked resentment among Muslims when he described his campaign against terrorism as a crusade. Bush said later through a spokesman that he regretted using the word "crusade," which invokes images of religious wars against Muslims.

The West Wing

Yet in another recent incidence of stereotyping, the NBC series "The West Wing" showed storylines revolving around actual Middle Eastern countries, including negative portrayals of Saudi Arabia and Iran (May 1, 2002), the Sudan (Dec. 3, 2003) and Syria (Oct. 27, 2004). This happened despite a protest by the the American-Arab Anti-Discrimination Committee.

In 1999, when the series first began Hala Maksoud, the ADC President, expressed "profound shock and dismay" over the first two episodes in which "the Republic of Syria had, for no apparent reason, shot down an unarmed American Air Force jet killing over 50 Americans." In a letter to NBC, Maksoud pointed out: "This storyline constitutes a slander and calumny against the Syrian nation and the Syrian people, who have never been

Islam & Muslims in the Post-9/11 America

Chapter VI - Stereotyping Muslims & Arabs [145]

involved in any way in such an incident....By creating a fictional story that blames a real and actually existing nation, government and people for such a heinous crime, NBC has slandered an entire nation in the most unfair manner possible...Moreover, this slander against Syria deliberately promotes fear and hatred of Syria, Syrians and Arabs in general. Why was Syria chosen as the villain in this instance? What would have prevented NBC from concocting a fictional nation to play this role? Why are we not surprised that, as usual, the villains in this fantastic scenario are Arabs? How would NBC, the producers, or the rest of American society react if Israel, not Syria, were accused of such a fictional crime?" (http://www.adc.org/action/1999/7oct99.htm)

In response to this criticism, from the third season, the creators of The West Wing did indeed create an ongoing storyline involving a fictional Middle Eastern country named Qumar, Qumar was portrayed as a country that abused its women and actively supported terrorism, and the President eventually approved a covert assassination of the Qumari leader (May 22,2002).

Muslims and Arabs have long been negatively portrayed in America

Muslims and Arabs have long been negatively portrayed in America. This negative stereotype is evident in songs, jokes, comic books, novels, Halloween masks, advertising, wrestling, television, cinema, and many other forms of American popular culture. It can be found even in media that are supposedly factual, such as school textbooks. In the post 9/11 America the stereotyping of Muslims and Arabs became even more negative. From political leaders to media and "experts on Islam" manipulate and mock American patriotism while using Muslims like magnets to attract fears and hatreds.

Not only Hollywood movies, television shows, and popular fiction have long dwelled on stereotypical portrayals of Arabs and Muslims, but similar typecasting, framing patterns and clichés are used in the news. The events of 9-11 affected the news about Islam and Muslims in terms of volume,

Islam & Muslims in the Post-9/11 America

Chapter VI - Stereotyping Muslims & Arabs [146]

themes, stereotypical references, frames, and viewpoints in several negative ways.

Long before the advent of radio and television, Walter Lippmann (1889-1974), observed that what people knew about the world around them was mostly the result of second-hand knowledge received through the press. If anything has changed, Americans in the late 20th and early 21st century have been less involved in community life than earlier generations and are therefore more susceptible to the news media's influence on "the pictures in our head" about events, developments, and people in their own communities. Moreover, people's perceptions about fellow-Americans around the country and people around the world are equally, and perhaps even more so, affected by the information provided by the mass media. (5)

The demonizing of Arabs and Muslims in America began well before the terrible tragedy of September 11, 2001. Popular fiction and Hollywood motion pictures have perpetuated the stereotype of Muslims and Arabs as villains and terrorists for many years. The news in the United States, too, has long displayed anti-Muslim and anti-Arab bias.

When a powerful bomb destroyed the Alfred P. Murrah Federal Building in Oklahoma City on April 19, 1995, news organizations were quick to identify Middle Easterners as suspects and reported that the FBI was specifically looking for two men with dark hair and beards. Within hours, Arab and Muslim Americans became the targets of physical and verbal assaults. As it turned out, an American with European ancestors, Timothy McVeigh, committed what was said at the time to be the most deadly terrorist deed on American soil.

Reel Bad Arabs by Jack Shaheen

Stereotyping can be traced to deliberate mythmaking by film and media as documented by the Award-winning film authority Jack G. Shaheen in her book Reel Bad Arabs: How Hollywood Vilifies (2001). This is a groundbreaking book that dissects a slanderous history dating from cinema's earliest days to contemporary Hollywood blockbusters that feature

Islam & Muslims in the Post-9/11 America

Chapter VI - Stereotyping Muslims & Arabs [147]

machine-gun wielding and bomb-blowing "evil" Arabs. Noting that only Native Americans have been more relentlessly smeared on the silver screen, Shaheen pointed out that "Arab" has remained Hollywood's shameless shorthand for "bad guy," long after the movie industry has shifted its portrayal of other minority groups. In this comprehensive study of nearly one thousand films, arranged alphabetically in such chapters as "Villains," "Sheikhs," "Cameos," and "Cliffhangers," Shaheen documents the tendency to portray Muslim Arabs as Public Enemy #1-brutal, heartless, uncivilized Others bent on terrorizing civilized Westerners.

Professor Jack Shaheen concluded that the "vast majority [of Hollywood films]...portray Arabs by distorting at every turn what most Arab men, women and children are really like" . Shaheen found that Islam in particular is targeted by "imagemakers (who) regularly link the Islamic faith with male supremacy, holy war, and acts of terror, depicting Arab Muslims as hostile alien intruders and as lecherous, oily sheikhs intent on using nuclear weapons."

Reel Bad Arabs begins with a quote from media analyst Sydney Harris: "The popular caricature of the average Arab is as mythical as the old portrait of the Jew. He is robed and turbaned, sinister and dangerous, engaged mainly in hijacking airplanes and blowing up public buildings. It seems that the human race cannot discriminate between a tiny minority of persons who may be objectionable and the ethnic strain from which they spring. If the Italians have the Mafia, all Italians are suspect; if the Jews have financiers, all Jews are part of an international conspiracy; if the Arabs have fanatics, all Arabs are violent. In the world today, more than ever, barriers of this kind must be broken, for we are all more alike than we are different."

Shaheen suggests that selective news coverage of "a minority of a minority of Arabs, the radical fringe" creates conditions that further these damaging stereotypes in the public mind. "The seemingly indelible Arab-as-villain image wrongly conveys the message that the vast majority of the 265 million peace-loving Arabs are 'bad guys'." He argues that ever since the late 1940s, "when the state of Israel was founded on Palestinian land," this

Islam & Muslims in the Post-9/11 America

Chapter VI - Stereotyping Muslims & Arabs [148]

image has intensified with selective news reports on wars, hijackings, hostage-taking and oil embargos that paint Arab people in a negative manner.

Stereotyping of Arab people in U.S. films has become a major issue after 9/11. In an article published by Pacific News Service Jack Shaheen wrote that Hollywood widens slur targets to Arab and Muslim Americans since Sept. 11. (6)

"Our country's leadership has gone out of its way to distinguish between Islam and terrorism in the aftermath of Sept. 11. Yet, Hollywood has ignored that distinction completely," he said while adding that major television networks -- including NBC, Fox, ABC and CBS -- have not only gone to great lengths to vilify Arab Muslims since then, but have introduced a very dangerous new equation: Arab Americans and Muslim Americans equals terrorist.

"Hollywood has chosen to focus on a few stock caricatures and repeat these images over and over again. These images project American Arabs, American Muslims, Arabs and Muslims as members of a lunatic fringe. We come to think all "those people" are this way. We are never allowed to see, for example, Arabs and Muslims who do what normal people do -- go out on picnics, go to work, love their children.

He argues that showing only vilifying images of any group, incessantly, and after a while -- 100 years in the case of the Arab stereotype -- it becomes "natural" not to like certain people. It is a sin of omission -- we omit the humanity -- and of commission -- we show only hateful images that make a stereotype that injures the innocent.

Shaheen pointed out that one reason these images and stereotypes continue is politics. The Arab-Israeli conflict has played a paramount role in shaping these images. Many of the movies I write about in my book "Reel Bad Arabs" were shot in Israel, with the cooperation of the Israeli government. It is naïve to overlook this. Another reason is that there is no American Arab or American Muslim presence in Hollywood moviemaking.

Islam & Muslims in the Post-9/11 America

Chapter VI - Stereotyping Muslims & Arabs [149]

Deconstructing Hollywood

In Deconstructing Hollywood: Negative Stereotyping in Film, Kim Deep points out that cinema pigeonholes Arabs in three main ways: the Arab as being wealthy, the Arab as terrorist, and the Arab as "the other" - one who is heathen, evil, and uncivilized. Popular western cinema also stereotypes the Islamic religion and portrays followers of Islamic faith as religious fundamentalists. (7) Dr. Mazin Qumsiyeh calls this the three B syndrome: Arabs in the media are portrayed as either bombers, belly dancers, or billionaires. (8)

According to Scott J. Simon of Northeastern University, Boston, the characterization of the Middle East and the Arab culture began during the silent movie era of the 1925. Rudolph Valentino's roles in *The Sheik* (1921) and *Son of the Sheik* (1926) set the stage for the exploration and negative portrayal of Arabs in Hollywood films. Both *The Sheik* and *Son of the Sheik* represented Arab characters as thieves, charlatans, murderers, and brutes (Michalak 29). Numerous other films that graced the silver screen during the twenties seemed to hold the same low standard of Arabs. *The Song of Love* (1923) tells the story of a power-hungry Algerian chief who schemes to overthrow French colonial rule and make himself the king of all of North Africa; *A Cafe in Cairo* (1924) is about an Arab desert bandit who kills a British man and his wife but saves their daughter so that they may be wed; and *The Desert Bride* (1928) portrays an Arab named Kassim Ben Ali as the leader of a group of "Arab nationalists" who capture and torture a French officer and his lover. All of these movies portray the Arab as the villain and are sure to conclude with the victory of the good Western symbol: the Algerian chief in *The Song of Love* is killed by French troops; the girl who is to marry the desert bandit in *A Cafe in Cairo* is rescued by an Englishman, and *The Desert Bride* concludes with the escape of Ben Ali's two captives and the death of Ben Ali. Throughout the 20th century, little has changed regarding the stereotypes of Arabs in Hollywood. In recent years Arabs were still being characterized as villainous, deranged, and murderous. (9)

Islam & Muslims in the Post-9/11 America

Chapter VI - Stereotyping Muslims & Arabs [150]

Many movies imply that the Islamic faith is closely tied with terrorists. In Network (1977), Arabs are seen as barbaric religious fanatics. Rules of Engagement (2000) was criticized because it portrayed Arabs as a senseless, extremist mob attacking the U.S. Embassy. Another film, The Siege (1998), tied Islamic practices, such as washing before prayers and the call to prayer, with violence. Thus, The Siege reinforces the idea that the Islam is closely associated with terrorism.

The image of the Arab terrorist is appallingly prevalent within the medium of film. These terrorist images lead to harassment, physical attacks, violence and distorted perceptions of Arab people. Arabs are seen as to be continually at war with Western concepts of politics, social economy and order. Frequently however, the Arab population is seen as the 'other' - an uncivilized, boorish people, who are loud, crude and irrational. In the Mummy (1999), one Arab character is described as a "smelly little friend" and a "stinky fellow," this shows that many films depict Arabs to be a people opposite to how the West perceives itself.

Here are few more take on stereotyping in movies:

In the 1997 movies "G. I. Jane" and "Operation Condor" viewers chant as a hero blows away Arabs marauding attackers. Demi Moore plays a Navy SEAL officer in the hit G. I. Jane gaining her stripes and feminist zeal, while killing Arabs. In "Operation Condor" starring Jackie Chan, we have Arabs as villains and a money grubbing inn-keeper (no good Arabs). Another scene shows Arabs praying and then cuts to an auction where Chan's women companions are being auctioned.

Operation Condor was a campaign of counter-terrorism and intelligence operations implemented by authoritarian right-wing governments that dominated the Southern Cone in Latin America from the 1950s to 1980s, heavily relying on numerous assassinations. It is not surprising then that Disney and Operation Condor received a "Dishonor Award" at the 2005 national convention of the American Arab Anti-discrimination Committee

Islam & Muslims in the Post-9/11 America

(ADC) which has been at the forefront in combating stereotypes and negative portrayal of Arabs in the media. (10)

In the 1994 feature film, Crimson Jihad, the character played by Arnold Schwarzenegger works for a super-secret government agency fighting terrorism. He and his wife are captured by Muslim extremists and taken to an island where the terrorists have nuclear warheads. In this scene, Aziz, the leader of "Crimson Jihad," who is nicknamed "Sand Spider" by the U.S. agents, is making a videotaped threat to the U.S. government. The film reinforces stereotypes that Arab and Muslim people are vengeful, hate the U.S., are terrorists, are intimidating and abusive, and are compliant to authority.

Movies, such as Into the Night (1985), associate Arabs with power and wealth, often through organized crime, such as smuggling operations. Other examples include Rollover (1981), where Arabs are seen as an evil force trying to bring ruin to the American economy, and the now famous The Sheik (1921), in which Rudolph Valentino plays a licentious sheik who captures a British woman and leads her to his wealthy residence in the desert. (11) The popular James Bond movie series, which is heralded on the official website as "one of the longest running and most successful film franchises in history," uses the stereotype of the wealthy, dangerous Arab in many of its films. In Octopussy (1983), the villain, Prince Kamal Khan, is described on the website as "an exiled Afghan prince with a penchant for fine food, jewels and atomic weaponry," who "teams with a power-crazed communist general in an attempt to unleash nuclear holocaust in Western Europe." Thus, the stereotype of the wealthy Arab is invariably tied to that of the Arab as terrorist. (12)

Children's movies: Stereotyping is not confirmed to general feature films. Even children's movies are not exempt from this negative portrayal of Arabs. The Disney movie Aladdin (1992) is one example of the idea of the Arab as "the Other". The original lyrics from the beginning number (before they were banned due to pressure from various Arab-American groups) were as follows:

Islam & Muslims in the Post-9/11 America

Chapter VI - Stereotyping Muslims & Arabs [152]

"Oh, I come from a land
From a far away place
Where the caravan camels roam.
Where they cut off your ear
If they don't like your face
It's barbaric, but hey, it's home!"

Although many popular movies are made for entertainment purposes, films, being a powerful and popular form of mass communication, invariably transmit social and political messages. By portraying Arabs and Muslims in a negative fashion, the Western film industry only serves to further the ideology of Western expansionism that has prevailed since the Middle Ages.

The former congressman, Paul Findley laments that Hollywood, where most movies and many documentaries are produced, the image of Muslim 'terrorism' keeps re-appearing. In early 2000, Paramount Pictures profited greatly from Rules of Engagement, a movie that maligned Muslims generally and Yemenis in particular and grossed over $43 million. The most misleading and inflammatory part of the film was a voice recording played during an imaginary US court-martial trial of the Marine who ordered the counterattack. In the recording, the leader of the Yemeni mob exhorted his Muslim followers to "kill Americans," a call that he said came directly from Allah. (13)

News Media: The fictional world of Hollywood does not stop with films; even the news media uses the same stereotypes and images. News media play a role in cultivating this new racial image, consciously or not. The image of Muslims and Arabs is closely associated with conflict -- the wars in Iraq, Afghanistan and Israel. The news cycle's barrage of images, from Guantanamo and Abu Ghraib to Iraq and Afghanistan, "gets transformed into an archetypal image of a terrorist," said Professor Jess Ghannam, chief of medical psychology at University of California, San Francisco. "That gets internalized very quickly into the 'Muslim/Arab' stereotype." This happens regardless of whether people know or meet individual Muslims, says Ghannam, affirming assertions made by several other scholars. (14)

Islam & Muslims in the Post-9/11 America

Chapter VI - Stereotyping Muslims & Arabs [153]

Cartoons, another media to stereotype: Cartoons are another media to stereotype the Arabs and Muslims.

In 2006, during the controversy over Dubai ports deal, a series of cartoons appeared in the US media ridiculing the Arabs, Muslims and linked with terrorism. A series of cartoons were used to demonize Arabs and Muslims and ridicule their faith. This surely helped in mobilizing the public opinion against the abortive deal. Caption of one cartoon said: Just because you own the oil doesn't mean you have the run of this place. Another cartoon says: UAE Port deal = Arabs = Terrorists. "Dubai is anti-democratic. Its nationals were involved in 9/11...Its money supports terrorists..." (15)

In 2003, a series of advertisements appeared on College campus newspapers by a group calling itself "CampusTruth.org". The ads from these groups were overtly racist and inflammatory. All ads juxtapose two pictures and a caption. In one advertisement, the picture on the left wa of an Israeli athlete with the caption on top: Israeli school children hero. The picture on the right was of a gun toting Palestinian militant and you guessed it: Palestinian school children's hero. Underneath it says: "There are two sides to each story but only one truth." (16)

The ads are produced by professional propagandists who are used to walking the fine line of libel and thus they certainly had their lawyers go over it. The results are ads that promote racism without being challengeable on the fine point of racism. One ad juxtaposes pictures about the World Trade Center attacks and uses: that says that "Israelis mourn" while "Palestinians celebrate." The absence of words like "all" or "the" obviously protects the advertisers from charges of overt racism. (17) Stereotyping is a psychological assault on one's identity that has resulted in an increased number of Muslims suffering from anxiety, depression and traumatic stress. The phenomena has had other profound effects. Sixty percent of respondents to a national poll released in August 2006 by the Quinnipiac University Polling Institute in Connecticut said that authorities should single out people who look "Middle Eastern" for security screening at locations such as airports and train stations. Another national study released in July

2006, by economics researchers at the University of Illinois, found that the earnings of Muslim and ethnically Arab men working in the United States dropped about 10 percent in the years after the Sept. 11, 2001, terrorist attacks.

References

(1) In 2002 Congress passed and the president Bush signed, a customs service reauthorization bill that expanded legal immunity for Customs officers engaged in unconstitutional searches. The legislation was approved despite evidence from the General Accounting Office that the Customs Service has a history of racial profiling. In order to avoid the U.S. Constitution's Fourth Amendment protections from "unreasonable searches and seizures," airport searches now fall under the rubric of "administrative searches."
(2) Muslims: Making Enemies - Newsweek - Jan. 31 2005 issue
(3) ADC statement dated April 29, 2005
(4) CAIR statement dated April 24, 2005
(5) Muslim Americans in the News before and after 9-11 by Brigitte L. Nacos and Oscar Torres-Reyna of Columbia University
(6) February 28, 2002
(7) Deconstructing Hollywood: Negative Stereotyping in Film by Kim Deep - The Peak - February 18, 2002
(8) Arab And Muslim Bashing As A Political Tool by Dr. Mazin Qumsiyeh
(9) Arabs in Hollywood: An Undeserved Image by Scott J. Simon
(10) Dr. Mazin Qumsiyeh, Op. Cit
(11) Kim Deep, Op. Cit.
(12) Ibid.
(13) Silent No More: Confronting America's False Images of Islam by Paul Findley - P-80
(14) Typecasting Muslims as a race - San Francisco Chronicle, Sept. 3, 2006
(15) In March 2006 a mix of bigotry and political opportunism fuelled opposition to the $6.8 billion sale of the London-based Peninsular & Oriental Steam Navigation Co. to Dubai Ports World. P&O runs shipping terminals in Baltimore, New York, Philadelphia, New Jersey, Miami and New Orleans. Prejudice against Islam and Muslims allowed our politicians to whip a frenzy in rejecting the approval of the Dubai firm to operate American ports. Exploiting the security concerns, Senator Frank Lautenberg (D-N.J.) went to the extent to announce in a New Jersey public rally: "We wouldn't transfer the title to the devil; we're not going to transfer it to Dubai." During the whole Dubai ports deal debacle, even the Democratic Party leaders engaged in unfounded scare mongering to score political points.
(16) Dr. Mazin Qumsiyeh Op. Cit.
(17) Ibid.

Islam & Muslims in the Post-9/11 America

Chapter VII - Hate crimes and discrimination

Muslim Americans have experienced a large volume of negative reprisals from sectors of the American public in the form of violent hate crimes, defamatory speech, attacks on hijab-wearing Muslim women and discrimination and harassment at work place. There is an increase in law enforcement discrimination against American Muslims which was causing delay in citizenship process for Arab-sounding immigrants. There is discrimination against non-citizen Muslims. American Muslims were shocked to find their bank accounts closed for no other reason but because of their faith.

Six years after the 9/11 terrorist attacks, these incidents still occur although with less frequency and fear still reins within the community. Surely this was the logical consequence of the U.S. government's sweeping actions against the Muslim community and the media's sensational coverage of them for encouraging anti-Arab and anti-Muslim sentiments. The continuing attacks on Muslims and Arabs may also be attributed to the ongoing right-wing campaign to demonize Muslims and Islam which is having an impact on those in the society vulnerable to the siren song of hatred and prejudice.

1- Hate Crimes

Muslims fear that the war on terror has lead to policies which can perpetuate hate crimes and discrimination.

In the aftermath of the 9/11 terrorist attacks, American Muslims and Arabs and those perceived to be Arab or Muslim, such as Sikhs and South Asians, became victims of a severe wave of backlash violence. The hate crimes included murder, beatings, arson, attacks on mosques, shootings, vehicular assaults and verbal threats. This violence was directed at people solely

Chapter VII - Hate crimes and discrimination [156]

because they shared or were perceived as sharing the national background or religion of the hijackers and al-Qaeda members deemed responsible for the 9/11 attacks. Those involved in such hate crimes were motivated by evangelists, some politicians and anti-Muslim elements in the media.

In November 2002, the FBI reported that hate crimes and other acts of vengeance skyrocketed nationwide against Muslims and other immigrants from the Middle East after the Sept. 11 terrorist attacks. The FBI found that while attacks against Muslims had previously been the least common hate crime against a religious group--just 28 in 2000--the number of incidents surged to 481 in 2001, an increase of 1,600%. The huge rise was presumably as a result of the heinous incidents that occurred on Sept. 11 of 2001. Most incidents targeting Muslims and others of Middle Eastern background ranged from assaults to intimidation. There also were three cases of murder or manslaughter and 35 arson fires. **(1)**

Amid mounting reports of hate crimes, the US Senate in May 2003 unanimously adopted a resolution condemning violence against Muslims and other minorities.

The resolution, presented by a Democrat Senator Dick Durbin, named Arab Americans, Muslim Americans, South-Asian Americans and Sikh Americans as the minorities targeted for hate crimes. "Now, more than ever, we simply cannot allow prejudice to divide our nation," Senator Durban said after the vote. The senator noted that in the aftermath of 9-11 and the war in Iraq, bias-motivated crimes, including violent physical assaults against Arab Americans, Muslim Americans, Sikh Americans, and South-Asian Americans increased.

According to the 2007 annual report by the Council on American-Islamic Relations' (CAIR) there was an almost 25 percent increase in the number of anti-Muslim bias incidents from 2005 to 2006. The CAIR report - the only annual study of its kind **(2)** - outlines 2,467 incidents and experiences of anti-Muslim violence, discrimination and harassment in 2006, the highest number of civil rights cases ever recorded in the Washington-based group's report. According to the report that total is a 25.1 percent increase over the preceding year's total of 1,972 cases. One of the most significant increases is in the category dealing with government agencies, which rose sharply from 19.22 percent of total reports in 2005 to 36.32 percent in 2006. This increase was due primarily to the number of cases related to immigration issues such as citizenship and naturalization delays. **(3)**

CAIR also received 167 reports of anti-Muslim hate crime complaints, a 9.2 percent increase from the 153 complaints received in 2005. Nine states and the District of Columbia accounted for almost 81 percent of all civil rights complaints to CAIR in 2006. They include (in descending order): California (29 percent), Illinois (13 percent), District of Columbia (7 percent), Florida (7 percent), Texas (6 percent), New York (5 percent), Virginia (4 percent), Michigan (3 percent), New Jersey (3 percent) and Ohio (3 percent). **(4)**

The report pointed out that American citizens have also been victims of overzealous governmental actions in regard to border crossings and terrorism 'watch lists'. According to *The New York Times, in response to American Muslim citizens desire to see* an efficient system, many Americans "...want increased Congressional oversight of the terrorist watch list system insure that the [government] is not abusing the basic civil rights of United States citizens at the borders."

Anti-Muslim hate crimes soared by an astounding 50% in 2010, skyrocketing over 2009 levels in a year marked by the vicious rhetoric of Islam-bashing politicians and activists, especially over the so-called "Ground Zero Mosque" in New York City. Although the national statistics compiled by the FBI each year are known to dramatically understate the real level of reported and unreported hate crimes, they do offer telling indications of some trends. The latest statistics, showing a jump from 107 anti-Muslim hate crimes in 2009 to 160 in 2010, seem to reflect a clear rise in anti-Muslim rhetoric from groups like Stop Islamization of America. Much of that rhetoric was aimed at stopping an Islamic center in lower Manhattan. **[Huffington Post - November 14, 2011]**

Chapter VII - Hate crimes and discrimination [158]

In 2006, several key polls indicated that the level of Islamophobia continues to rise today in American society, the CAIR report said. An August 2006 USA Today/Gallup poll showed that 39 percent of Americans felt at least some prejudice against Muslims. The same percentage favored requiring Muslims, including American citizens, to carry a special ID "as a means of preventing terrorist attacks in the United States." Most surprising was the fact that 22 percent of those polled for the USA Today/Gallup poll said they would not want American Muslims as neighbors.

A similar poll by the Washington Post and ABC News, in March 2006, also found that one in four Americans "admitted to harboring prejudice toward Muslims." That survey indicated that 46 percent of Americans have a negative view of Islam, a seven percent jump since the months following the 9/11 terror attacks. The Post-ABC poll also showed that the number of Americans who believe that Islam promotes violence has more than doubled since 2002. [Read more in Chapter II on Islamophobia]

While there are known hate crimes that are a cause of great concern, Muslims were more concerned with the many unreported incidents, especially those affecting children on school campuses. American Muslim children do not have the same access to hate crime victim assistance mechanisms or even educational materials and presentations as other potential victims of hate crimes. When they do report harassment, they become vulnerable to retaliation and further harassment because of their Muslim identity. Many youth have reported feeling isolated at school by some classmates as well as teachers. Muslims fear that the war on terror has lead to policies which can perpetuate hate crimes.

Resolution introduced in the House to counter anti-Muslim sentiment

Not surprisingly, on May 26, 2011, the Detroit Democrats John Conyers and Hansen Clarke introduced a resolution in the House of Representative resolution urging federal investigators to avoid unconstitutional profiling. It also called on the government to target rhetorical attacks and violence against Muslim, Arab, Sikh and South Asian American communities.

Islam & Muslims in the Post-9/11

"Communities should be protected from the threat of violence and suspicion that, for example, was at the heart of last January's thwarted attack against the Islamic Center of America in Dearborn," Conyers and Clarke said in a joint statement. "They should also be able to rely on law enforcement's fundamental integrity and respect for First Amendments protected rights. Ultimately, the American Muslim community should be able to rely on the federal government to lead the effort in fostering an open climate of understanding and cooperation. Only through a balanced examination of the challenges facing the nation will we establish a strong policy framework for protecting security, while respecting the Constitution and the interests of affected communities." The resolution came in the wake of complaints from several Metro Detroit Muslim Americans who said they were harassed, searched, groped or jailed without reason when crossing into Michigan from Canada. The complaints prompted a probe by the Department of Homeland Security's office of Civil Rights and Civil Liberties. The resolution, supported by many representatives, was referred to the Committee on the Judiciary. **[AMP Report – May 27, 2011]**

2. Attack and discrimination against the Hijab wearing Muslim women

About 100 people from various faiths gathered on Nov. 13, 2006, in Fremont, CA to observe "Hijab Day," prompted by the murder of a hijab wearing woman in the city. Alia Ansari, 37, an Afghan mother of six, was shot and killed in Fremont on Oct. 19, 2006. She was walking with her 3-year-old daughter to pick up her other children from school. The shocked Muslim community believed her traditional headscarf, or hijab, made the Afghanistan native a target.

Hijab Day was aimed to highlight the plight Hijab wearing Muslim women who have become a frequent target of discrimination and hate crime in the post-9/11 America, since Hijab is considered by many an Islamic symbol. The CAIR 2007 study reported 143 hate crimes and discrimination cases related to hijab wearing in 2006.

For media and some rightwing politicians, House Speaker Nancy Pelosi's donning of scarf during her April 2007 visit to Syria was an appropriate opportunity to launch an assault on the scarf as an Islamic symbol. News

Chapter VII - Hate crimes and discrimination [160]

reports in the Associated Press and the *New York Post*, and an editorial in *Investor's Business Daily*, quoted Republican presidential candidate Mitt Romney criticizing Nancy Pelosi by saying that "being seen in a head scarf and so forth is sending the wrong signal to the people of Syria and to the people of the Middle East," without noting that Secretary of State Condoleezza Rice and first lady Laura Bush have both done the same when visiting the Middle East. Neither the AP report nor the *Post* article made it clear in the text that Pelosi wore the scarf during a visit to the tomb of John the Baptist inside the Umayyad mosque in Damascus and not in her meeting with Syrian President Bashar Al-Assad. Romney's quote could be read to suggest that Pelosi wore the scarf during that meeting. **(5)**

Here are some examples of official discrimination:

In June 2007, two cases of discrimination were reported because of hijab wearing. A Georgia Muslim woman seeking to contest a speeding ticket was barred from a courtroom in that state because she wears an Islamic headscarf, or hijab. The woman was prevented from entering the Valdosta, Ga., courtroom of Municipal Court Judge Vernita Lee Bender by uniformed officers who reportedly demanded that she remove her scarf. According to the woman, the officers barred her entry despite being told that she wears the scarf for religious reasons and after she offered to let a female officer perform a body search. One of the officers stated that the denial of entry to the
courtroom was due to "homeland security" and that allowing her to enter would show "disrespect" to the judge. The officers reportedly summoned the clerk of court who told the Muslim woman that she could schedule a future court date. After being told that she would be unable to enter the court at any future date while wearing her scarf, the Muslim woman felt compelled to agree to a plea of nolo contendere and was fined $168. **(6)**

In another case, a supervisor in the lunchroom of Seaside High School in Seaside, Calif., demanded that 13-year-old Muslim student, Issra Omer, remove her scarf, despite being told that it was worn for religious reasons. The student, who was visiting the school to take part in a summer algebra

Chapter VII - Hate crimes and discrimination [161]

program, said she broke down in tears after the supervisor allegedly shouted, "You have to take it off now," in front of more than 100 other students in the lunchroom. Despite the shouted demands of the school official, the girl refused to remove her scarf. **(7)**

The CAIR 2007 study enlists two sample cases of hijab wearing discrimination in 2006. On April 13, a female Muslim employee at a Jiffy Lube store in Virginia was told that she could not wear her headscarf due to a "no hats" policy. Following CAIR's intervention, company officials agreed to allow the headscarf and apologized to the Muslim employee for the denial of her constitutionally protected religious accommodation. On June 1, a 10-year-old female Muslim student at a Jacksonville, Florida elementary school was discriminated against by her teacher for merely wearing a headscarf. The cello instructor reportedly asked mocking questions, such as asking her why she wore that "nun thing." The teacher also refused to let her play in a school concert.

Another demonstrative case (2004) is that of a Palestinian American Muslim named Carol Douglas. When attempting to get passports at a US Consulate in Jerusalem, her pictures were repeatedly denied, even when she met the requirement of "showing the face to the hairline and ears" while wearing hijab. **(8)**

Fortunately there are also positive legal decisions happening in the United States.

In Oklahoma, the school district attempted to restrict a 12 year old student, Nashala Hearn, from wearing hijab. The U.S. Justice department backed her side in the legal battle. In May 2004, the Department of Justice announced the settlement of a lawsuit alleging that the Muskogee, Oklahoma Public School District had violated the constitutional rights of a sixth-grade Muslim girl when it barred her from wearing a Muslim headscarf, or hijab. Under the consent agreement signed by the parties, the school district allowed the girl to wear the headscarf and revise its student dress code policy to accommodate exceptions for bona fide religious reasons. **(9)**

Islam & Muslims in the Post-9/11

In Alabama, the driver's license photo rule was changed to allow hijab. In January 2004, the Council on American-Islamic Relations (CAIR) called for a review of a new Alabama Department of Public Safety (DPS) policy banning all head coverings in license photographs. CAIR sought the review after receiving reports from Muslim women in Alabama who were prevented from obtaining or renewing licenses because they refused to take off their religiously-mandated scarves. **(10)**

More Muslim women defy stares and prejudice by wearing head scarves

While it remains arguable for many if the hijab donning is obligatory in Islam, in America, hijab has become a symbol of religious freedom in spite of verbal and physical abuse. It is a way for Muslim women to express what they believe, and generally the courts were supporting this right.

While some women stopped wearing headscarves in the aftermath of the Sept. 11, 2001, attacks, there has been a noticeable increase overall in recent years. A survey by the Pew Research Center found that 43 percent of Muslim women in the United States usually wear hijab or head coverings in public, with an additional 8 percent wearing them sometimes.

A generation ago, hijabis, or those who wear hijab, were a distinct minority among Muslims in metro Detroit. In 1990, only seven seniors at the Dearborn school wore hijab in their class photos. That's less than 5 percent of the female students in the senior class of a public school with a student body that's at least 85 percent of Arab descent. In the class of 2006, 78 are wearing hijab - 40 percent of the women in the class.

The usual outfit for women's volleyball teams is sleeveless shirts and snug shorts, but the 2006 captain of the volleyball team at Fordson wore long pants and a hijab while playing on the courts. In 2006 also, public pools in Washtenaw County began allowing Muslim women to cover their entire bodies while swimming. The policy change came after Jumanah Saadeh of Ann Arbor, then 13, was kicked out of a pool for swimming with long pants, a full-sleeve shirt, and her Islamic head scarf. In Dearborn, there are now hijab-wearing cheerleaders. **(11)**

Islam & Muslims in the Post-9/11

Chapter VII - Hate crimes and discrimination [163]

Wearing hijab in America can be an expression of religious freedom, while wearing it elsewhere can be construed as religious rebellion. In other parts of the world, hijab is seen as a form of resistance to society; it has become a battleground for secular and religious points of view. Hijab is represented by the so-called Muslim women liberators as a dress forced on women by men, in order to marginalize them.

3. Rising law enforcement discrimination against American Muslims

There is a steady increase in civil rights violation occurrences at the government agencies. Of the 2,467 total reports processed by CAIR in 2006, the most common places of occurrence for civil rights violations were the following (in descending order): government agencies, workplace, mosques/community organizations, schools and prison, according to the CAIR 2007 report on the Civil Rights of Muslims in USA. **(12)**

Although government agency complaints constituted 19 percent of complaints for two years in a row (2004 and 2005), there was a significant increase to 36 percent of complaints in 2006.

The CAIR 2006 Report enlisted 379 occurrences of civil rights violations in government agencies which amounted to 19.22 percent of the total complaints. **(13)**

In view of sharp increase in civil rights violations at the government agencies, the CAIR called its 2005 Report: "Unequal Protection: The Status of Muslim Civil Rights in the United States 2005," The report detailed a sharp increase in law enforcement discrimination against American Muslims in 2004. The main conclusions of the 2005 report were that in 2004 the reported cases to CAIR of harassment, violence and discriminatory treatment increased nearly 50% from 2003 to 1,522 incidents. CAIR Legal Director Arsalan Iftikhar, explained: "By far the greatest increase over last year, in both real and proportional terms, occurred in the areas of unreasonable arrests, detentions, searches/seizures, and interrogations. In 2003, complaints concerning law enforcement agencies accounted for only

Chapter VII - Hate crimes and discrimination [164]

seven percent of all reported incidents. In 2004, however, these reports rose to almost 26 percent of all cases." **(14)**

4. Delay in citizenship process for Arab-sounding immigrants

There were 729 complaints related to Legal and Immigration issues during 2006. These issues primarily involved government agencies and citizenship/naturalization delays.

The depth of the citizenship delay problem was highlighted by the Center for Human Rights and Global Justice (CHR&GJ) at the New York University School of Law. The NYU report states: The U.S. government is illegally delaying the naturalization applications of thousands of immigrants by profiling individuals it perceives to be Muslim and subjecting them to indefinite security checks. The 63-page report, titled *Americans on Hold: Profiling, Citizenship, and the " War on Terror*," documents the impact of expanded security checks on the lives of those experiencing citizenship delays, often for years on end. **(15)**

CAIR has joined with several national human rights organizations to help litigate these citizenship delay cases to ensure that the legal rights of all people are protected. The CAIR 2007 Report release was marked with an announcement by the CAIR Chicago office of the resolution of a citizenship delay case that has been pending for the past five years. Despite successfully passing his citizenship exam in 2002 and taking part in repeated interviews, CAIR-Chicago's client had his naturalization delayed pending a background check.

According to immigrant advocates hundreds - if not thousands - of men with Arabic-sounding or Muslim names were experiencing endless delays in what should be the pro forma final step of the citizenship application process. "I understand the burden that the government has in wanting to make sure that all security checks go through," said Dev Viswanath, a Queens attorney who said he has two clients who have waited years for their swearing-in ceremonies. "But having to wait two or three years ... is just ridiculous." In April 2006, the American-Arab Anti-Discrimination Committee launched a

Chapter VII - Hate crimes and discrimination [165]

national legal campaign to get the government to resolve hundreds of cases. More than 40 lawyers filed lawsuits in federal courts, requesting that a judge step in and force U.S. Citizenship and Immigration Services to complete the stalled naturalization cases. In response, CIS decided it will stop interviewing people whose FBI background checks have not cleared. **(16)**

Ali Ali, Iraqi immigrant of Dearborn, was unable to become a U.S. citizen, despite passing all the citizenship tests and requirements and waiting for almost a year. His problem was shared by other Arab and Muslim men in metro Detroit and across the United States. Under federal law, immigrants who have taken citizenship interviews are supposed to be notified within 120 days on whether their U.S. citizenship request has been approved. Ali had his interview in May 2005, but after more than one year he still hasn't heard from the U.S. Citizenship and Immigration Service. **(17)**

In another case, it took immigration authorities nearly three years to determine that commercial jet pilot Mazin Shalabi was not a security threat. Each time Mazin Shalabi settled into the cockpit of an American Eagle jet, he was entrusted with the lives of all passengers on board. As a Jordanian citizen and a pilot for the regional affiliate of the world's largest airline, Shalabi was vetted regularly by the Federal Aviation Administration, the FBI and other federal agencies. But when Mr. Shalabi applied for U.S. citizenship, it took immigration authorities nearly three years to determine that he was not a threat. **(18)**

In May 2006, ten Chicago area Muslim men filed a class-action lawsuit against the federal government alleging their quest to become U.S. citizens is being delayed because of their Islamic faith and male gender. The Syrian, Moroccan, Jordanian, Pakistani and Egyptian natives have no criminal records, but they have been waiting one to four years for the government to make a decision on their applications. Some of their wives applied at the same time and have since received their U.S. citizenship. The plaintiffs, including the Council on American Islamic Relations' Chicago office, agree the government must conduct background checks on all potential citizens.

But they say Muslim men, more than any other group, have their cases delayed too often with no explanation. **(19)**

In October 2005, Muslim American Society's Freedom Foundation announced a national campaign to speed up immigration process for Muslims because of delay in issuing Green Cards and processing of their citizenship applications. It is dubbed as "Project BFAIR: Better Fair American Immigration Rules" The MAS Freedom Foundation said that despite approval, many Muslims have waited years to receive their green card or citizenship. Project BFAIR envisaged to (1) Collect a nationwide database - at mosques, public events and online - of American Muslims affected by unreasonable delays in receiving their green cards and citizenship. (2) Legally challenge all unwarranted or unnecessary detention of Muslims at airports. (3) Convene a legal team to prepare to legally challenge and sue the government on behalf unfair immigration practices directed at Muslims concerning the lengthy time it takes for Muslims to receive their green cards and/or citizenship after they have been approved.

5. Discrimination and harassment at work place

According to the U.S. Equal Employment Opportunity Commission report, charges of discrimination against Muslims — or those perceived to be Muslim, such as South Asians — has doubled nationwide from 1,100 to 2,168 since Sept. 11, 2001, given a similar time span. The most common types of employment discrimination against Muslims include name-calling, job termination and denial of religious wear or other accommodations for religious practices. Among all ethnic groups, Arab Americans and South Asians fared the worst in employment hiring in the Bay Area, according to the Berkeley-based Discrimination Research Center. **(20)**

In July 2005, CAIR reported that nearly four years after the terrorist attacks, Muslim, South Asian and Arab-American employees continue to report discrimination on the job. Compared with the first two years after the Sept. 11 attacks, the number of employees saying they've been discriminated

Chapter VII - Hate crimes and discrimination [167]

against as a form of backlash because of the attacks has declined. But charges continue to come in, indicating that Arab-American and other workers still feel discriminated against. People were being called 'terrorist' at work, things of that sort. People were also called Osama bin Laden, told they are going to mosque to learn how to build a bomb. Nearly 280 claims of discrimination in the workplace were received by CAIR in 2004, and the workplace was the second-most-common location for an alleged incident. The first was government agencies. **(21)** The number of assault and other discriminatory complaints filed with the CAIR jumped from 1,019 in 2003 to 1,972 in 2005. **(22)**

In certain discrimination cases, victims were awarded compensation by court. A jury in Oakland, CA, in June 2006, awarded $50 million in punitive damages and $11 million in compensatory damages to two FedEx drivers who said a manager subjected them to a hostile work environment because of their ethnicity. The two drivers, who are independent contractors for FedEx Ground, claimed that over a two-year period, a manager directed ethnic slurs, such as "terrorists" and "camel jockeys," at them because they are Lebanese-Americans. In the lawsuit, they alleged that they complained to management but the company failed to take steps to prevent harassment. **(23)**

In April 2006, an El Paso jury decided that Samantha Carrington, a California woman of Iranian descent, arrested in El Paso three years ago after Southwest Airlines employees accused her of assaulting a flight attendant and interfering with a flight should receive $27.5 million in damages for false imprisonment and malicious prosecution. The jurors agreed that Samantha Carrington was wrongfully arrested on Oct. 7, 2003, when a flight to Houston from Los Angeles made a scheduled stop in El Paso. In the evidence it came out that one of the flight attendants stated that Ms. Carrington reminded her of a terrorist. The jury found the airline caused Carrington to be maliciously prosecuted and falsely imprisoned. **(24)**

Yet in another case of harassment, in March 2006, the U.S. Equal Employment Opportunity Commission (EEOC) announced a $360,000 settlement of a workplace discrimination lawsuit against Lithia Subaru of Oregon City on behalf of two former car salesmen, one of whom was subjected to a hostile work environment because of his national origin (Iranian) and religion (Islam), forcing him to quit. The EEOC's suit alleged that a new management team subjected the Iranian charging party to a daily barrage of slurs, including "terrorist" and "camel jockey" as well as commenting that he went to Al-Qaeda training camps. The charging party was also physically harassed, including being intentionally tripped by a co-worker, resulting in a broken nose and a knee injury. **(25)**

In another case of harassment, the University of Colorado paid a psychiatrist $1.54 million to settle his claim that he was wrongly fired. The settlement with Dr. Gordon Neligh includes a $300,000 he won from a federal jury after filing a civil suit, along with back pay, missed future pay and other components. Neligh filed the lawsuit after the CU Health Sciences Center in Denver declined to renew his annual contract in 1998. He claimed it was retaliation because he stood up for his administrative assistant, a Muslim woman, when she was harassed by her peers. **(26)**

A former sales manager for Nicolet Biomedical - now Viasys NeuroCare - won a $1.56 million damage award in a race discrimination case, and got his job back along with a raise. A seven-member U.S. District Court jury in Madison (Wisconsin) sided with Sami Elestwani, a native of Lebanon, who claimed he lost his job because he is an Arab and a Muslim. Elestwani was a key account manager for Nicolet Biomedical, handling some of the Fitchburg company's larger clients. He said his supervisor told him in 2002 to take a demotion because his high profile with Nicolet was "not good for the company in light of 9/ 11." Elestwani was fired when he reported the remarks to the company's human resources department. **(27)**

An Egyptian-born radiologist initially suspected of having terrorist ties in the wake of Sept. 11, 2001 and later cleared was awarded $2.45 million by a federal jury in Pittsburgh, PA, that decided his right to privacy was violated.

Chapter VII - Hate crimes and discrimination [169]

Dr. Basem Moustafa Hussein, 40, won the award from his former landlord in Neshannock Township outside New Castle, where he was living in 2001. The jury said his building manager at The Meadows Apartments, Sherri Lynn Wilson, was liable along with her company for violating his privacy when she walked into his unit on Sept. 11 and saw, among other items, a compact disc jacket that showed a jetliner flying through two buildings next to a fireball. Wilson called state police, leading to a federal investigation that ended a few days later when the FBI concluded Hussein had nothing to do with terrorism. **(28)**

A Muslim woman fired at a Columbia store in Maryland shortly after the terrorist attacks of Sept. 11, 2001 won a settlement from the company that terminated her employment. Shabana Ahmed, a Columbia resident, received $16,000 in an agreement reached with School & Pre-School Supply Center Inc., of Baltimore County, the owner of Learning How, in Columbia. In November 2001, Ahmed filed a complaint with the Maryland Commission on Human Relations alleging religious discrimination in the company's decision to fire her the month before. The $16,000 represents the amount of salary the company would have paid Ahmed prior to the time she found new employment after being fired. **(29)**

Discrimination can take many forms. After spending years fighting a former employer who thought his name wasn't good enough, Mamdouh El-Hakem was vindicated by the 9th U.S. Circuit Court of Appeals in July 2005 with a modest amount of money -- and an opinion that reaffirmed the value of his name. In a ruling that bolstered plaintiff arguments that discrimination can take many forms, the 9th Circuit said that Gregg Young, the CEO of BJY Inc. should not have insisted on calling El-Hakem "Manny." Or, for that matter, "Hank." "Young intended to discriminate against El-Hakem's Arabic name in favor of a non-Arabic name," Judge Johnnie Rawlinson wrote for a three-judge panel, "first by altering Mamdouh to 'Manny' and then by changing Hakem to 'Hank.'" **(30)**

Discrimination cases involving Muslims in the workplace, at school and in airports increased markedly after Sept. 11 but are most commonly brought by American-born Muslims because immigrants are reluctant to take legal action, the New York Times quoted lawyers and civil rights advocates as saying. A fear of retaliation by employers or more extreme outcomes, like deportation, drives many Muslim immigrants to stay quiet. The cases, some of which have been settled by the Equal Employment Opportunity Commission, cover a spectrum of harassment and discrimination claims. Children have been barred from boarding airplanes because their names resembled those on a terrorist watch list; longtime female employees were suddenly told, after 9/11, to remove their hijabs. **(31)**

Interestingly, discrimination was not confined to work place, but Muslims experienced it in leasing apartments. In February 2005, Channel 3 News (Vermont) reported: There are signs it's less of a landlord's market-- as more and more vacant apartments become available in Vermont. They're ready to rent, but not to everyone. A year-long study at the Fair Housing Project tested landlords in Vermont according to the Fair Housing Project survey. The group found nearly 50% illegally discriminated against Muslim immigrants. **(32)**

Interestingly, the civil rights complaints involving the workplace declined significantly from 25.41 percent in 2005 to 15.57 percent in 2006, as recorded by the CAIR 2007 report.

6. Bank accounts closed

American Muslims were shocked to find their bank accounts closed for no other reason but because of their faith. Increasing numbers of banks across the country were closing accounts of what they deem "high risk" customers in part because of confusing regulations put in place as part of the Patriot Act, the News Day reported quoting a national banking official in Union City, New Jersey. The issue came to the fore in New Jersey when the Islamic Education Center protested the closing of its account at Hudson United Bank after almost 13 years. The bank did not say why it took the action, and cited laws that allow financial institutions to shut down accounts at any time without giving a reason for the closure. John Byrne, director of the American Bankers Association's Center for Regulatory Compliance, said more banks are taking an aggressive posture toward account closures because of a lack of consistency in the interpretation and enforcement of regulations instituted after the Sept. 11 terrorist attacks. The number of suspicious-activity reports filed by banks rose from 81,197 in 1997 to 288,343 in 2003, the newspaper reported. Civil rights groups have said that Muslim account holders have been targeted for unreasonable requests for private information such as financial statements, proof of residency and proof of identity. **(33)**

In April 2006, Bank of America Corp. in Boston agreed to resolve allegations by Arab and Muslim groups that the former Fleet Bank discriminated against 15 customers with Arabic names by closing their accounts in 2002 and 2003 over suspicions of terrorism or money laundering. Although a state investigation found no evidence of discrimination, Bank of America agreed to take steps including paying the state $50,000 to create a brochure and video on consumer finance geared toward Arab-American and Muslim communities. **(34)**

Western Union blocks funds over name "Muhammad"

In the post-9/11 America, Muslims were facing difficulties in legally transferring funds. In January 2003, Western Union blocked funds over name "Muhammad" and African-American Muslim in New York were asked to state country of birth. The Council on American-Islamic Relations (CAIR) reported that a Muslim by that name recently attempted to send $80 to relatives in Connecticut from a Western Union site in Brooklyn, N.Y. After returning home, the African-American customer said he received a call from Western Union's main office demanding that, because of his name, he must provide photo identification and state his country of birth, otherwise the funds would not be delivered. When the customer protested that policy and requested a refund, he was told that the funds would not be returned unless he met the company's demands. **(35)**

A year ago, Western Union had to apologize for freezing the funds of a Muslim family apparently based on religious and ethnic profiling. In that incident, an African-American Muslim was informed that the money his family sent him from Virginia was not in Western Union records. When his mother called to see what had happened to the funds she transferred, she

Chapter VII - Hate crimes and discrimination [172]

discovered that the money was frozen until her son provided further documentation of his American citizenship. **(36)**

The Bush administration has been quietly tracking people suspected of bankrolling terrorism through a secret program that gives the government access to a massive data base of international financial transactions. Treasury Department officials said they used broad subpoenas to collect the financial records from an international system known as Swift. Under the program, U.S. counterterrorism analysts could query Swift's financial data base looking for information on activities by suspected terrorists as part of specific terrorism investigations. The program involved both the CIA and the Treasury Department. Swift, or the Society for Worldwide Interbank Financial Telecommunication, is a cooperative based in Belgium that handles financial message traffic from 7,800 financial institutions in more than 200 countries. **(37)**

7. Discrimination against non-citizen Muslims

In the aftermath of 9/11, immigrants from Muslim countries have found themselves living in a newly suspicious America. Many of their businesses and mosques were closely monitored by federal agents, thousands of men have been deported and some have simply been swept away - "rendered" in the language of the C.I.A. - to be interrogated or jailed overseas. A New York Judge ruled that U.S. has broad powers to detain non-citizens indefinitely Federal judge John Gleeson of United States District Court for the Eastern District of New York ruled in June 2006 that the government has wide latitude under immigration law to detain non-citizens on the basis of religion, race or national origin, and to hold them indefinitely without explanation. The ruling came in a class-action lawsuit by Muslim immigrants detained after 9/11, and it dismissed several key claims the detainees had made against the government. This is the first time a federal judge has addressed the issue of discrimination in the treatment of hundreds of Muslim immigrants who were swept up in the weeks after the 2001 terror attacks and held for months before they were cleared of links to terrorism and deported. The roundups drew intense criticism, not only from immigrant

Chapter VII - Hate crimes and discrimination [173]

rights advocates, but also from the inspector general of the Justice Department, who issued reports saying that the government had made little or no effort to distinguish between genuine suspects and Muslim immigrants with minor visa violations. Lawyers in the suit said parts of the ruling could potentially be used far more broadly, to detain any non-citizen in the United States for any reason. "This decision is a green light to racial profiling and prolonged detention of non-citizens at the whim of the president," said Rachel Meeropol, a lawyer for the Center for Constitutional Rights, which represented the detainees. "The decision is profoundly disturbing because it legitimizes the fact that the Bush administration rounded up and imprisoned our clients because of their religion and race." **(38)**

Highlighting the plight of new immigrants, the New York Times reported that in the wake of 9/11, Muslim immigrants from Pakistan, Egypt and other countries have found themselves living in a newly suspicious America. Many of their businesses and mosques have been closely monitored by federal agents, thousands of men have been deported and some have simply been swept away - "rendered" in the language of the C.I.A. - to be interrogated or jailed overseas. But Muslim immigrants are not alone in experiencing the change. It is now touching the lives of some American converts: men and women raised in this country, whose only tie to the Middle East or Southeast Asia is one of faith. **(39)**

References

(1) Los Angeles Times – November 26, 2002
(2) Ref CAIR began documenting anti-Muslim incidents following the 1995 attack on the Murrah Federal Building in Oklahoma City.
(3) CAIR Report on the Status of Muslim Civil Rights in America 2007
(4) Ibid.
(5) Media quoted criticism of Pelosi for wearing headscarf in Middle East without noting that Rice, Laura Bush have also done so – Media Matters - April 5, 2007
(6) CAIR Bulletin – June 28, 2007
(7) CAIR Bulletin – June 21, 2007
(8) http://www.islamonline.net/English/In_Depth/hijab_campaign/articles/15.shtml
(9) The Department of Justice press release May 19, 2004
(10) CAIR bulletin – February 20, 2004
(11) Free Detroit Press – June 12, 2007

Islam & Muslims in the Post-9/11

Chapter VII - Hate crimes and discrimination [174]

(12) Op Cite. CAIR Report 2007
(13) Ibid.
(14) CAIR Report on the Status of Muslim Civil Rights 2005
(15) The Center for Human Rights and Global Justice Report released on April 25, 2007
(16) Daily News - May 28, 2006
(17) Detroit Free Press - April 25, 2006
(18) The Dallas Morning News - March 14, 2006
(19) Sun Times - May 4 2006
(20) The Argus – September 19, 2005
(21) USA TODAY – July 5, 2005
(22) CAIR Report on the Status of Muslim Civil Rights 2006
(23) The Oakland Tribune – June 13, 2006
(24) El Paso Times - April 11, 2006)
(25) CAIR bulletin - March 9, 2006
(26) AMP Report - Jan 27, 2005
(27) Wisconsin State Journal - June 29, 2005
(28) Pittsburgh Post-Gazette - September 23, 2005
(29) Howard County Times, Maryland - Oct. 27, 2005
(30) The Recorder– July 26, 2005
(31) New York Times - April 30, 2005
(32) Channel 3 News - February 8, 2005
(33) News Day - Feb 27, 2005
(34) Boston Globe - April 12, 2006
(35) CAIR Bulletin – Jan. 15, 2003
(36) CAIR Bulletin – Jan. 15, 2003
(37) MSNBC - June 23, 2006
(38) New York Times - June 15, 2006
(39) The New York Times - April 30, 2005

Chapter VIII

Attempt to silence genuine Muslim voices and encourage 'moderates'

In the post-9/11 America, the Muslim community witnessed a systematic campaign defame and dislodge established prominent Muslim civil rights advocacy groups. The object was to silence genuine Muslim voices. At the same time, attempts were made to establish and prop-up compliant Muslim groups.

In a new assault on the leading American Muslim organizations, the Washington Times on June 12, 2007 published a long tirade against the Council on American-Islamic Relations (CAIR), the most visible public American Muslim group that has a distinguished record of social and political activism since its establishment in 1994.

The Washington Times story was titled "CAIR membership falls 90% since 9/11" but the punch of the story is that CAIR cannot claim to be the voice of American Muslims since its membership has been reduced sharply.

It is not difficult to understand why formal membership of American Muslim institutions and organizations such as CAIR has declined after 9/11. In the words of Dr. Hatem Bazian, Professor at the Near East and Ethnic Studies Department, University of California, Berkeley, "Similar to the COINTELPRO against the African Americans during the 1960s, the Arab, Muslim and South East Asian communities are currently facing a new FBI counter intelligence program."

The seven-million strong community was under siege with constant pressure on its institutions through legal process. Harassment through the legal system was used as one of the COINTELPRO methods in 1960s. Since 9/11, the community has been affected by the high profile arrests, raids or search warrants against the Muslim and Arab individuals, groups and

Chapter VIII - Attempt to silence genuine Muslim voices

organizations. With the high profile arrests of Muslims in "terrorist" cases and closure of prominent Muslim charities, American Muslims are discouraged or frightened (which is the main objective of such arrests) to support their institutions such as Islamic centers, mosques, charities and civil right organizations and groups. Now people prefer to give cash donations to mosques instead of writing a check to avoid any paper trail that may lead to an unexpected FBI knock at their door.

The case of Dr. Nasar Chaudhry of New York symbolizes the Muslim dilemma. In April 2005, the Internal Revenue Service's Criminal Investigation Division raided the home and office of Pakistani-American Dr Nasar Chaudhry, for making donations to a Muslim charity in 1996. Dr Chaudhry of Hornell, New York state, was contacted in 1996 by a former medical school peer for making donation to his Florida-based charity to aid needy Pakistani children. He decided to give Zakat to the charity. Dr Chaudhry said if the charity misused the funds, how would he be responsible for that? (1)

In this hostile atmosphere it may not be surprising that the CAIR lost some of its formal membership but it does not mean that its support has diminished in the community. I remember attending a CAIR fund raiser in the fall of 2000 in the Chandni Restaurant of Newark, CA, when the organization was only six year old with few chapters. It was a $5 dinner. The ornate Chandni hall was full to capacity. If I remember correctly, the dinner raised about $300,000 in donations. Now after 13 years the organization has grown into a major American Muslim group with more than 30 chapters in America and Canada.

The increase in CAIR's grassroots support in the American Muslim community is clearly demonstrated by the opening of 25 chapters and offices since 2001, all of which are funded exclusively through local donations. Each year, CAIR fundraising banquets in Washington, D.C., and nationwide are sold-out events of up to 2000 people.

The Washington Times report was based on the CAIR tax returns which it filed with the Internal Revenue Service. The IRS provided the tax returns at the request of Washington Times which refreshes the memories of the December 2003, Senate Finance Committee enquiry against 24 Muslim

Chapter VIII - Attempt to silence genuine Muslim voices [177]

charities and groups. The Senate Committee asked the Internal Revenue Service to turn over confidential tax and financial records, including donor lists, of 24 Muslim charities and foundations as part of a widening congressional investigation into alleged ties between tax-exempt organizations and terrorist groups.

However, after almost two years, in November 2005, the U.S. Senate committee concluded its work with no plans to issue a report, forward any findings to law enforcement agents, hold hearings or propose new legislation. "We did not find anything alarming enough that required additional follow-up beyond what law enforcement is already doing," Senator Charles Grassley, the Iowa Republican who heads the committee, said in a statement. **(2)**

The Washington Times report reproduced many of the accusations against CAIR which had been recycled and disseminated again and again by agenda-driven individuals and groups who seek to marginalize and disenfranchise the American Muslim community and its leaders.

The Washington Times quoted Mr. Zuhdi Jasser, director of a little known group, American Islamic Forum for Democracy, as claiming that the sharp decline in membership calls into question whether the organization speaks for American Muslims, as the group has claimed.

The Washington Time assault on CAIR came amid an offensive against CAIR and the Muslim Public Affairs Council (MPAC) launched by the self-proclaimed terrorism expert Steven Emerson whose apparent goal was to banish Muslim Americans from American civil life.

No doubt there was a deliberate attempt by certain groups and individuals to defame and discredit prominent Muslim groups such as CAIR, Islamic Society of North America (ISNA), Islamic Circle of North America (ICNA) and the Muslim Public Affairs Council (MPAC) in a bid to suppress genuine voice of American Muslims.

It appears that CAIR's visibility in advocating American Muslim civil rights has alarmed many interested parties. In a bid to suppress CAIR's voice an Anti-CAIR (www.anti-cair-net.org) website has been launched to spew venom against CAIR. Some other interested people have established

Chapter VIII - Attempt to silence genuine Muslim voices [178]

namesake groups - like California Association for Institutional Research (CAIR) and Colorado Alliance for Immigration Reform (CAIR) - to confuse the people.

No doubt, the smear campaigns against the established American Muslim organizations such as CAIR, ICNA, ISNA and MPAC were aimed at marginalizing Muslims in America by silencing the most prominent and respected American Muslim voices.

These vicious campaigns against the mainstream Muslim groups were disseminated by agenda-driven individuals such as Steve Emerson and Daniel Pipes and groups in a bid to marginalize and disenfranchise the American Muslim community which was under siege since 9/11.

Alternate compliant groups: While defamation campaign continues against major American organizations, certain marginal groups were propped up by interested individuals and organizations to replace the mainstream American Muslim organizations. In recent years, attempts have been made to divide the community and establish alternate compliant American Muslim groups in the name of moderate voices.

Progressive Muslim Union of North America

In November 2004, Progressive Muslim Union of North America (PMUNA) was launched with great funfair to become a voice of "moderate" American Muslims. It was formed by some professed moderates who embraced the simple proposition that "you are a Muslim if you say you are a Muslim -- for whatever reason or set of reasons -- and that no one is entitled to question or undermine this identity." Ironically, the PMUA drew bitter criticism from both the staunch advocates of moderate Islam, who did not find them moderate at all, and also the mainstream Muslims and scholars who saw them as publicity monger perverted Muslims who may prove a Trojan horse, by design or default, for the Rand Report - titled "Civil Democratic Islam: Partners, Resources, and Strategies" – that called for revamping of Islam by, among other things, encouraging moderate Muslims to counter what it described as fundamentalist and traditionalist Muslims. **(3)**

Chapter VIII - Attempt to silence genuine Muslim voices [179]

An analysis of the PMUNA statement of principles gives some insight into the mindset of its founders. The PMUNA tries to create a big tent to embrace Muslims of all shades, leanings and schools of thought when it defined a Muslim as is anyone who identifies herself or himself as "Muslim," including those whose identification is based on social commitments and cultural heritage. It also calls for critical inquiry and dynamic engagement with Islamic scripture (read Quran which Rand Report describes as legend). The PMUNA also supports the political separation of religious institutions and state functions, and the strict neutrality of the state on matters of religion. This provision may put them in the category of secular Muslims rather than modernists. **(4)**

The MPU had a bumpy start as many invited to join its advisory board either declined the request or were dropped because of their support to Bush administration's policies in Iraq. Among those who were dropped from the advisory board are Seeme and Malik Hassan, founders of Muslims For Bush website. Their son Mohammad Ali Hassan wrote an article entitled: The Muslim World's Savior (referring to Mr. Bush), that included this sentence: "I believe Bush is bringing liberation not war." Another person not included in the board is Fareed Zakariyya who wrote in Newsweek (August 5th, 2002) that the invasion of Iraq is "the single best path to reform the Arab world." Nawaal al-Sadawl, an Egyptian writer, was also dropped. She has campaigned for the enforcement of the hijab (head scarf) ban in French public schools. **(5)**

Farid Esack, a South African theologian who teaches at St. Xavier University in Cincinnati, stunned the PMUNA organizers by refusing an invitation to join the board. He didn't want to work with those who, although they might defend gender equity and homosexual rights, also support Bush's "expansionist" policies. In a critique of the PMUNA, he pointed out that the PMUNA's emphasis on diversity and pluralism rather than justice and liberation shows its ideological lines clearly. "There is of course another dimension – virtually the entire list that you have put together consists of the mighty, wealthy and/or famous. Is this really what progressive Islam is about?" **(6)**

Not surprisingly, the PMU was given wide coverage in the mainstream media. The New York Times on Nov. 16, 2004 reported the launch of the Progressive Muslim Union under the headline: A little late, but a stand

Chapter VIII - Attempt to silence genuine Muslim voices [180]

against hate. Before the formal launching of the PMUNA, Washington Post on Oct. 16, 2004 carried a long story entitled: For U.S. Muslims, a push from the progressive wing; broader rights backed for women and gays. On Oct. 7, 2004, USA Today reported: Progressive Muslim members plan to form the Progressive Muslim Union of North America as an alternative U.S. voice of Islam.

The PMUNA was launched at a time attack on Islam became a past time for many, particularly the Christian right. Just two recent examples: (1) After the terrorist attacks on Sept. 11, 2001, Franklin Graham called Islam "an evil and wicked religion." In an interview with The Los Angles Times on Nov. 27, 2004, he was asked if he still thought of Islam in the same way. "I haven't changed my mind," he said. (2) Bruce Tefft, a founder of the CIA's counter-terrorism center and now an advisor to the New York Police Department's intelligence and counter-terrorism divisions, told a seminar in Canada in Nov., 2004: Islamic terrorism is based on Islam as revealed through the Qu'ran and that while there may be moderate Muslims, Islam itself is immoderate.

The PMUNA apparently came as a response to this pressure on the American Muslim community. The PMUNA founders in their formal launching statement emphasized: "PMUNA will defend the Muslim community from the calumnies of those who seek to insult and degrade Islam and/or the Muslim community, in particular the relentless campaign of defamation from some evangelical preachers, like Jerry Falwell and Pat Robertson, or from supporters of the extreme right in Israel, like Daniel Pipes." A prompt response from Pipes was not unexpected. He described the PMUNA founders as "the worst Islamist and leftist extremists in the United States."

Pseudo event

In his famous book entitled "The Image: A Guide to Pseudo-Events in America," well-known American historian Daniel Boorstin coined the term *pseudo-event* to describe events fabricated for the mass media. Much of the news consists of pseudo-events manufactured by the various arms of the public relations industry. Boorstin writes that the common prefix pseudo comes from the Greek word meaning false or intended to deceive. The characteristics of pseudo-events are that they are not spontaneous but

Islam & Muslims in the Post-9/11

Chapter VIII - Attempt to silence genuine Muslim voices [181]

come about because someone has planned them to create a desirable effect in the media.

The Progressive Muslim Union of North America, in March 2005, tried to corner the major American Muslim organizations by sponsoring a pseudo event of Friday prayer in New York led by a woman - Dr. Amina Wadud, professor of Islamic studies at Virginia Commonwealth University - who says that she has problem with the Quran. The circus of holding this prayer at a Church amid focus of TV cameras and presence of mainstream media showed the motives and designs of the perpetrators of this stunt and their backers.

This was a pseudo-event as it illustrates all the essential features of pseudo-events as described by Mr. Boorstin: (1) It is not spontaneous, but comes about because someone has planned, planted, or incited it. (2) It is planted primarily for the immediate purpose of being reported or reproduced. Its success is measured by how widely it is reported. The pseudo event of Friday prayer in the New York Church was well publicized in advance and it was given wide publicity afterwards.

Just before the stunt, one of PMUNA's co-founders demanded that the Muslim Public Affairs Council (MPAC), the Council on American-Islamic Relations (CAIR) the Islamic Society of North America (ISNA), KARAMAH, the American Sufi Muslim Association, Women in Islam and Azizah Magazine should take a position on this non-issue. Interestingly one of the directors of PMUNA himself refused to take a position. Convincingly this reflected on the integrity of the PMUNA people. **(7)**

In my view it will neither strengthen nor weaken his/her belief in Islam if a Muslim accepts or rejects the idea that a woman could lead Friday prayer. That is why I called it a non-issue or pseudo event which was aimed at diverting the attention from pressing issues facing the seven-million strong American Muslim community.

It is not an uncommon knowledge that the status of woman in Islam is now being used by many "independent" think tanks and neo-Orientalists to defame Islam and promote western political objectives. I know there is a problem related to women in Muslim society, but it is not dissimilar than other societies. However, it exists not because of Islam as the neo-

Chapter VIII - Attempt to silence genuine Muslim voices [182]

Orientalists and the embedded intellectuals want us to believe. It is just like the issue of lack of democracy in the Muslim world which is also attributed to Islam.

One latest example of using of the feminine paradigm against Muslims is Afghanistan. The 2001 war in Afghanistan was sold to the American public by means of the Burqa. Even at one point a congressional aid was calling around Muslim organizations in Washington, if they can borrow a Burqa to wear at a press conference and show the oppression in Afghanistan. Now there is no story about Burqa anymore although the Afghan women are still wearing the Burqa.

American Muslim Group on Policy Planning launched

To give a helping hand in the daunting task of countering the anti-American sentiments in the Muslim world due to Bush administration's policies, some 'moderate' Muslims established the American Muslim Group on Policy Planning (AMGPP) on December 13, 2004. The AMGPP formation conference at the Brookings Saban Center for Middle East Policy was co-sponsored by Dr. Muqtedar Khan, one of the Board members of the Progressive Muslim Union of North America and attended by Ahmed Nassef, the PMUNA Executive Director."

Dr. Muqtedar Khan's article titled, "American Muslims push for role in policy planning", gives some insight into the objectives of the newly formed group of 'moderate' Muslims: "The AMGPP is willing to play a very active role in helping improve the U.S. image and to counter the tide of extremism and anti-Americanism in the Muslim world. The group is eager to take a leadership role on issues of public diplomacy and outreach on behalf of the State Department and also act as a spokesperson for American policies, concerns and interests........ One of the questions constantly raised after Sept. 11, 2001 is: "Where are the moderate Muslims?" So far many of them have been working as individuals or as part of mainstream American Muslim organizations that are already overwhelmed with the challenge of rising Islamophobia in the U.S. Now with the constitution of the American Muslim Group for Policy Planning, moderate Muslims in America have a name and an address. They are here, they are now organized and willing to provide their input for policy making and their assistance in policy implementation. The ball is now in the government's court; hopefully they will respond and help build a partnership with American Muslims." (8)

Interestingly, very little is heard about the AMGPP after its foundation. However, it is seen at the US-Islamic Forum held annually in Doha, Qatar, as representative of the 'moderate' American Muslims. The Doha conference is co-sponsored by the Brookings Saban Center, which is named after its founder, the Israeli Media-mogul Haim Saban.

PMUNA becomes dysfunctional

The Progressive Muslim Union of North America (PMUNA) suffered a major setback when three of its four founding members resigned from the PMUNA Board of Directors on August 24, 2005 saying that "the PMUNA is not a forum that will allow us to successfully pursue the agenda we envisioned at its founding." The three founding members, who resigned in an open letter, were: Omid Safi, Hussein Ibish and Sarah Eltantawi. Ahmed Nassef, Executive Director of the PMUNA and Editor-in-Chief of the controversial website Muslimwakeup.com, is the fourth founding member. **(9)**

One of its board member, Dr. Muqtedar Khan, quit the PMUNA board on July 1, 2005 saying that he found the environment with Progressive Muslims Union extremely oppressive, abusive and hateful. In an open resignation letter Dr. Khan said: "I have found both PMUNA and MWU (Muslimwakeup.com) extremely intolerant of difference and disagreement. This is the only Muslim group where people who believe in the teachings of the Quran are ridiculed and those who express ambivalence about it even about the existence of God are celebrated." **(10)**

Finally the Progressive Muslim Union of North America became dysfunctional when its chairperson Pamela Taylor and executive director Zuriani "Ani" Zonneveld resigned from the board in December 2006.

Islam & Muslims in the Post-9/11

Chapter VIII - Attempt to silence genuine Muslim voices [184]

Free Muslim Coalition Against Terrorism

Another fringe new group propped up by the establishment and media is the Free Muslim Coalition Against Terrorism. It was formed in May 2004 by Kamal Nawash, a lawyer and Palestinian immigrant. He has appeared on CNN, Aljazeerah, Fox News Channel shows including like O'Reilly Factor, as well as on Al-Arabiya.

Kamal Nawish ran for Virginia State Assembly in November 2003 as a Republican candidate. One can well understand his political ambitions and hidden agenda of his organization. Just one example, how it is working against the American Muslim groups. In January 2005 the Executive Director of Free Muslims Against Terrorism, wrote an e mail to Enver Masud of an Islamic website, Wisdom Foundation www.twf.org, saying: We are very disappointed in your site and it should be taken down.. I will recommend to our extremist watch committee that we place your site on our list of extremist sites or sites that support terrorism.

Kamal Nawash says American Muslims have not engaged enough in fighting terrorism and denouncing 'radical Islamist ideology'. He also says that investigations of many Islamic organizations after the September 11th attacks were justified and many of them deserved to be closed. "I think one good thing that happened is that September 11th weakened many of the traditional Muslim organizations and many of the Muslim charities. They have become either much weaker or just closed down altogether," said in an interview with the Voice of America, Sept. 10, 2006.

In June of 2005, the work of the *Free Muslims* Coalition Against Terrorism was recognized by the U.S. government when the White House appointed Kamal Nawish to represent the United States of America and more than six million American Muslims at the Organization for Security and Cooperation Conference on Anti-Semitism and on Other Forms of Intolerance held in Cordoba, Spain.

Chapter VIII - Attempt to silence genuine Muslim voices [185]

In March of 2006, Nawish, as the president of the Free Muslims Coalition, was invited to Jerusalem to advance an alternative approach to solving the Palestinian/Israeli conflict.

In search of a 'moderate' Muslim

This discussion leads us to the basic question, who is a moderate or progressive Muslim? Moderation is a quality of being moderate and avoiding extremes. American Heritage dictionary defines a moderate "one who holds or champions moderate views or opinions, especially in politics or religion." However, these days apparently the title of "moderate Muslim" is only reserved for those who do not question the U.S. foreign policy in the Muslim world (particularly towards Israel) and openly abandon Islam's beliefs and malign its scripture.

In September 2006, the American Jewish Congress honored another resident of California, Tashbih Sayyed, Editor of Pakistan Today, and four other 'moderate' Muslims for what it sees as their friendly attitudes toward Israel. **(11)**

Sayyed was honored along with Satanic Verses-famed author Salman Rushdie, who received the AJC's highest honor, the Stephen Wise Humanitarian Award. The three other Muslims honored by the AJC were: Salim Mansur, Nonie Darwish and Wafa Sultan. The honoring ceremony was billed as "Profiles in Courage: Voices of Muslim Reformers in the Modern World."

Gary Ratner, executive director of the Congress' Western region office in Los Angeles, pointed out that his group believes support for Israel's right to exist as a Jewish state is central to the definition of a moderate.

The definition Mr. Ranter implies that a moderate Muslim should support:

>   Israel's occupation of the Palestinian land.

>   Israel's occupation of the Syrian Golan Heights.

>   Israel's killing of unarmed Palestinian men, women and children.

Islam & Muslims in the Post-9/11

Chapter VIII - Attempt to silence genuine Muslim voices [186]

Israel's right to imprison some 10,000 Palestinians.

Israel's right to imprison elected government of the Palestinians.

Israel's attack on civilian targets in Lebanon killing hundreds of innocent men, women and children.

Israel's sole right to have nuclear weapons in the Middle East.

Israel's right to defy all the UN Security Council resolutions while Arab and Muslim states should comply.

Apparently another factor in AJC's choice of honorees was that at least three of them have renounced their faith. Salman Rushdie is a self-described atheist while Wafa Sultan and Nonie Darwish say they left their faith years ago.

If you are not convinced, here are some more takes on the credentials of the six honorees:

The less said the better about the Indian-born British author Salman Rushdie. Contrary to the basic Islamic belief that the Quran is a revealed book, Rushdie subscribes to the Rand Corporation criteria for a moderate Muslim that he/she believes that the Quran is a historical document. While honoring Rusdhdie, the AJC said "Mr Rushdie is among the great minds of today that can help us learn how to understand and combat terrorism."

Egypt-born Nonie Darwish is the founder of Arabs for Israel and author of Now They Call Me an Infidel. She blames Arabs and Palestinians for all the strife and killings in the Middle East.

Syria-born Wafa Sultan is a resident of California who came into prominence for her bitter attack Islam in her TV on Al Jazeera in February 2006. She believes that the Muslims are the ones who began the so-called clash of civilizations.

Pakistan-born Tashbih Sayyed is editor of 'Pakistan Today' weekly that is supported by a number of Jewish groups because Muslims declined to give ads when he published pro-Israeli and anti-Palestinian articles. Sayyed says

Islam & Muslims in the Post-9/11

Chapter VIII - Attempt to silence genuine Muslim voices [187]

it is debatable that Islam was spread by the sword and Prophet Muhammad's actions were divinely inspired.

India-born Salim Mansur is one of the leading members of Canadians Against Suicide Bombing (CASB). Mansur, a political science professor at the University of Western Ontario, Canada, argues that the Muslim world must stop blaming the West for all its own ailments, including poverty, illiteracy, injustice or extremism.

Now the question is why the AJC wants to honor such Muslims whose only qualification is criticism of the Islamic faith and of course, support for Israel. The reason is obvious. The Jewish groups have been trying to promote alternative Muslim leaders in America who are friendly to Israel though they may enjoy little following among the Muslims. In this drive they are helped by the mainstream media.

Another attempt to undermine mainstream American Muslim advocacy groups

The latest effort to undermine well established and vocal American Muslim civil advocacy organizations while promoting fringe compliant Muslim groups came in March 2012 in the shape of the appointment of Dr. Zuhdi Jasser, founder president of a fringe organization, the American Islamic Forum for Democracy (AIFD) as a commissioner of the U.S. Commission on International Religious Freedom which advises the president, Congress and State Department on religious rights abuses internationally.

Dr. Zuhdi Jasser has amassed a reputation as a prominent Islamophobia-enabler and ally of anti-Muslim organizations and individuals, well known for their attempts to diminish civil and religious liberties of American Muslims or make the practice of Islam a punishable offense.

Mother Jones quoted Jasser as saying that his group has received a one-time, unsolicited donation of $10,000 from the Clarion Fund, which is associated with Aish HaTorah, a right-wing Israeli group described by Jeffrey Goldberg of The Atlantic as "just about the most fundamentalist movement in Judaism today."

Chapter VIII - Attempt to silence genuine Muslim voices [188]

In 2008 Jasser narrated an anti-Islam and anti-Muslims film bankrolled by the Clarion Fund called *The Third Jihad*, that was shown to thousands of NYPD officers as part of their counterterrorism training, which the police department later apologized for.

Not surprisingly, Zuhdi Jasser lauded New York City police surveillance program that targeted Muslims and helped lead the opposition to construction of the Park51 Islamic and cultural center in Manhattan, known as the Ground Zero mosque. He also supports the profiling of Muslims based solely on their religion, and calls for increasing the illegal surveillance of Muslims in their places of worship, businesses and universities.

Like anti-Islam and anti-Muslim Islamophobic groups, Jasser is critical of major prominent American Muslim organizations such as the Council on American-Islamic Relations (CAIR), the Muslim American Society (MAS), Islamic Society of North America (ISNA), the Islamic Circle of North America (ICNA), the Muslim American Society (MAS), Muslim Students' Association (MSA) and the Muslim Public Affairs Council (MPAC). He is also critical of the North American Islamic Trust (NAIT), a non-profit 501-(C)3 organization that holds the deed to over 300 properties for mosques and Islamic schools.

In April 2012, a broad national coalition of more than 60 civil advocacy organizations and individuals have sent a joint letter to Senators Inouye, McConnell and Durbin expressing "deep concern" at the controversial appointment of Zuhdi Jasser to the United States Commission on International Religious Freedom (USCIRF). The coalition asked that Jasser's appointment by Senate Minority Leader Mitch McConnell (R-KY) be rescinded because he has been a vocal opponent of religious freedom for American Muslims.

The coalition noted that Jasser's organization, the American Islamic Forum for Democracy, "applauded" an amendment to Oklahoma's constitution that both a federal district court and the U.S. Court of Appeals 10th Circuit have held is in violation of the Establishment Clause of the First Amendment by clearly favoring all other religions over Islam. That amendment specifically targeted Islam for official censure.

The letter also cited Jasser's opposition to the constitutionally-protected construction of a Muslim community center in lower Manhattan, his support

Islam & Muslims in the Post-9/11

Chapter VIII - Attempt to silence genuine Muslim voices [189]

for the New York Police Department's blanket surveillance of Muslims based on religion rather than evidence or suspicion of wrongdoing and his ties to virulently anti-Muslim groups and individual Islamophobes.

The joint letter also pointed out: "The USCIRF promotes the freedom of religion and belief and it seeks to combat religious extremism, intolerance and repression throughout the world. In contrast with these laudable goals, Dr. Jasser believes '...operationally, Islam is not peaceful.' His consistent support for measures that threaten and diminish religious freedoms within the United States demonstrates his deplorable lack of understanding of and commitment to religious freedom and undermines the USCIRF's express purpose."

Ironically, Zuhdi Jasser was not the only problematic new appointee. The Speaker of the House John Boehner appointed McCormick Professor of Jurisprudence, Robert George, who sits on the board of the Bradley Foundation. The Bradley Foundation is well known for supporting anti-Muslim organizations.

Why the USCIRF has appointed controversial commissioners, the reason one can see is the anti-Islam bias of the Commission reauthorized on Dec. 16, 2011 by the Congress through 2018, just hours before it was scheduled to go out of existence?

According to Michelle Boorstein (Washington Post 2-17-2011) some past commissioners, staff and former staff of the USCIRF is rife, behind-the-scenes, with ideology and tribalism, with commissioners focusing on pet projects that are often based on their own religious background. In particular, they say an anti-Muslim bias runs through the commission's work.

Writing under the headline, "Agency that monitors religious freedom abroad accused of bias," Boorstein wrote, the commission was hit this fall with an Equal Employment Opportunity Commission complaint filed by a former policy analyst, Safiya Ghori-Ahmad, who alleges that her contract was canceled because of her Muslim faith and her affiliation with a Muslim advocacy group. Boorstein went on to say:

"The commission's six researchers signed a letter unsuccessfully urging their bosses to keep Ghori-Ahmad because of what they described as her

Chapter VIII - Attempt to silence genuine Muslim voices [190]

strong résumé and the need for an analyst to cover the key region of South Asia. One researcher, Bridget Kustin, quit in protest, saying in her resignation letter that she would not "remain part of an organization that would be willing to engage in such discrimination."

"Rumors about infighting and ineffectiveness have swirled for years around the commission, which was created by Congress in 1998 as part of the International Religious Freedom Act. The legislation, which was signed into law by President Bill Clinton, was championed primarily by Christian groups, along with people of Jewish, Bahai and other faiths, to get the government to pay more attention to religious persecution overseas and be an advocate for religious freedom in its foreign policy."

The commission's nine members, who are appointed by the president and congressional leaders of both parties, include two Catholics, two evangelical Protestants, one Southern Baptist, one Orthodox Christian, one Jew and one Muslim, with one vacancy.

Boorstein pointed out that from the start, critics say, the commission has disproportionately focused its efforts on the persecution of Christians, while too often ignoring other religious communities and downplaying their claims of persecution. "It was predetermined who the bad guys are and who the good guys are," said Khaled Abou El Fadl, a Muslim who served as a commissioner from 2003 to 2007 and teaches human rights at UCLA. "There is a very pronounced view of the world, and it is that victims of religious discrimination are invariably Christian. It was rather suffocating."

On December 14, 2011, Patrick Goodenough of the Cybercast News Service (CNSNews) writing under the title – "Claims That U.S. Religious Freedom Commission Has Been Too Focused on Christians Don't Stack Up" – also pointed out that critics have alleged an anti-Islam bias, and some say Christians have been overrepresented among the nine unpaid commissioners.

Of the present and former commissioners over the lifetime of the USCIRF, as far as CNSNews.com can ascertain 14 are Christian (six Roman Catholic, seven Protestant – Baptist, Methodist, Lutheran, evangelical – and one Orthodox), five Muslim, three Jewish, one Mormon, one Hindu, one Buddhist and one Baha'i.

Islam & Muslims in the Post-9/11

Not surprisingly, rejecting the USCIRF's 2012 annual report Turkey said on April 5, 2012: "The report, which is prepared by politicians representing some interest groups, contradicts the findings of U.S. State Department's annual reports so far." In a written statement the Turkish Foreign Ministry also criticized the report for failing to address incidents in Europe based on Islamophobia, with many mosques having been attacked and religious leaders being appointed by the state. The statement thus said that "the report [had been] prepared for political reasons."

Chapter VIII - Attempt to silence genuine Muslim voices

References

(1) Evening Tribune – April 7, 2005

(2) Indianapolis Star – November 15, 2005

(3) Agenda of the Progressive Muslim Union of North America – AMP Comment - December 13, 2004

(4) Ibid.

(5) Ibid.

(6) Ibid.

(7) Pragmatic Muslims of North America – AMP comment - April 15, 2005

(8) American Muslims push for role in policy planning by Dr. Muqtedar Khan- http://www.ijtihad.org/AMGPP.htm

(9) Progressive Muslim Union: Three founding members of resign - AMP Report – August 26, 2005

(10) Ibid.

(11) In search of a moderate Muslim By Abdus Sattar Ghazali - Al-Jazeerah, September 22, 2006

(12) The Politics of Freedom of Religion, AMP Comment, April 13, 2012

Chapter IX

The Muslim Response

The seven-million-strong American Muslim community has responded to the post 9/11 challenges with political and social activism, media campaigns, outreach and interfaith dialogue. It is now more proactive as it believes that the best way to protect its eroding civil rights is to become more active politically. From coast to coast, Muslim and Arab-American groups are organizing as never before to make known their concerns about civil liberties. They have gone beyond sign-waving demonstrations to hold voter registration drives, meet with politicians and form alliances with other civil rights and religious organizations. Muslims are becoming more organized and vocal in their demands, petitioning school boards to establish prayer rooms in public schools for their children and turning to the courts when they believe their constitutional rights to practice their faith have been violated.

9/11 legacy stoked political aspirations of US Muslims

The 9/11 attacks have a lasting effect on the lives of American Muslims and led to two significant changes: More are attending mosques and activities in Islamic centers and they want to become more involved in American politics to change policies they oppose. Fallout from the attacks made them realize they are a vulnerable community, according to Dr. Ihsan Bagby, lead researcher of the study "A Portrait of Detroit Mosques," released in April 2004. **(1)**

The study provides a penetrating look at the American Muslim community and its member's views on policy issues, politics and religion. The study participants came from 42 countries. About one-third of the respondents were the second generation immigrants. Bagby, professor of Islamic studies at the University of Kentucky, said the study focused on the Detroit area but identified trends typical of the broader Islamic community. Other Islamic experts agree that his findings do reflect trends among pious Muslims across the country. "I think this is an absolutely accurate study," said Yvonne Haddad, an expert on Islam in America and a professor at the Center for Muslim-Christian Understanding at Georgetown University. "This

Chapter IX - The Post-9/11 Challenges: The Muslim Response [194]

is exactly what I have been observing in Los Angeles, near Washington and in other parts of the country. "As a result of 9/11, many women who never put on a scarf are now covering their hair. Many women are starting Qoran study groups. This is a response to the incredible anti-Muslim campaign in the United States."

As their sense of identity has grown stronger, American Muslims have become more concerned with participating in U.S. politics to influence government policies. Ninety-three percent of those surveyed said they believed Muslims should be involved in politics. About 68 percent of those eligible to vote were registered to do so. Their primary reason for becoming more active is the change in U.S. policies that violate their civil rights.

According to the study, more than 85 percent of Detroit-area mosques have experienced an increase in attendance in the last five years and 67 percent have seen growth of 10 percent or more. Fifty-four percent of the Muslims surveyed said they attend mosque prayers every week, and 48 percent of those said they regularly attend other activities held at the mosque, such as social events or religious study sessions.

One of the most significant findings concerns Muslims' views on the primary purpose of a mosque. Thirty-nine percent said the mosque was a center for activities, while 32 percent said it was primarily a place for prayer. The view of a mosque as more than a place for prayer has led Muslims to feel more interconnected in the U.S.

Principals at Islamic schools across the country said there is an increasing demand among Muslims for an Islamic education. "There is a growing desire for Islamic schools, especially now that Islamic schools are academically competitive," said Audrey Zahra Williams, principal of the Toledo Islamic Academy in Ohio. "In the 1980s, people laughed when I suggested establishing an Islamic school."

There are also increasing signs that the younger generation of Muslims could be more religious than their parents from the proliferation of Muslim Students Associations in high schools and colleges to the kind of Islam the youth prefer to practice. The average mosque participant is 34 years old, married with children, has at least a bachelor's degree and makes about $75,000 a year.

Chapter IX - The Post-9/11 Challenges: The Muslim Response

Political activism

Encouraged by the 2000 Muslim bloc vote, the American Muslim organizations charted an ambitious plan to launch a massive registration campaign to register Muslim voters and contest at least 200 seats in 2002 mid term elections. However, after the 9/11 tragic attacks the Muslim community found itself besieged by profiling, official discrimination, negative media campaign and hate crimes. Consequently, the number of Muslim candidates in November 2002 elections was much smaller as compared to the 2000 elections. In 2000, 152 candidates for various public offices were elected out of about 700 candidates. In 2002, ten candidates out of about 70 elected to various public offices which include one State Senator and three State Assemblymen and one judge of the Superior Court.

Muslim community played an active role in the 2004 presidential election and the 2006 mid-term elections with dozens of voter registration campaigns, civic education forums and fund raisers. Muslim vote became focus of mainstream media and several presidential candidates addressed their gatherings. Disenchanted by the policies of President George Bush that abridged their civil rights, Muslims on individual as well as organizational level backed the 2004 Democratic Presidential candidate, John Kerry, who had pledged to address their grievances.

2004 election

Civil rights remained the most significant issue for the Muslims who this time voted overwhelmingly for Senator John Kerry. An exit poll, on Nov. 4, 2004, by the Council on American-Islamic Relations (CAIR) indicated that more than 90 percent of Muslim voters were casting their ballots for John Kerry. In a democratic system vote is the best instrument to express one's opinion. And Muslims joined millions of citizens to express their opinion about the Bush administration policies. **(2)**

As the American Muslim community grows, it is becoming increasingly aware of its social and political potential. American Muslims have distinct views on issues such as abortion, prayer in public schools, welfare reform,

Chapter IX - The Post-9/11 Challenges: The Muslim Response [196]

immigration, and civil rights. They seek to promote family values, prevent crime, combat drug abuse, and encourage other worthwhile social goals but it will not be an exaggeration to say that abridgement of civil rights was the single issue that galvanized the Muslim and Arab community. A barrage of post 9/11 discriminatory policies impacted them. This is not to say that the Muslims and Arabs were not concerned with other election issues. But obviously all communities are motivated by the issues that affect them most. A Democratic Presidential hopeful, Dennis Kucinich best reflected their sentiments when he said during a visit to a Florida Mosque: "The defining issue for Muslims is the restriction of civil liberties."

However, in this election, the American Muslim and Arab organizations played important role in motivating the voters who from the very beginning of the campaign were focused mainly on the civil rights issue because they were affected by the biased policies of the Bush administration in the aftermath of 9/11.

The civil rights issue even overshadowed the Middle East problem and the Muslims and Arabs supported Senator Kerry despite their reservations about his support toward Israel. Besides becoming the most important election issue, the abridgment of the civil rights proved an important factor in motivating the American Muslims and Arabs for political activism. American Muslims have increased their participation in political and social activities since 9/11, according to a poll released on Sept. 10, 2003 by the Council of American-Islamic Relations. The poll said that roughly half of American Muslims surveyed say they have increased their social (58

percent), political (45 percent), inter-faith (52 percent) and public relations activities (59 percent) since the 9/11 terror attacks.

2006 election

In the 2006 elections, Muslims and Arabs voted overwhelmingly for the Democratic Party. **(3)** A pre-election CAIR poll revealed that 42 percent consider themselves members of the Democratic Party while only 17 per

Chapter IX - The Post-9/11 Challenges: The Muslim Response [197]

cent are Republican. The exit polls confirmed the findings of the pre-election polls. **(4)**

The seven-million-strong American Muslim community got a big political push when the Minnesota Democrat Keith Ellison was elected as the nation's first Muslim member to the US Congress in November 7, 2006 elections. Ellison's election was accompanied by a massive turnout of the American Muslim voters to make their voices heard. "Tonight, we made history," Mr Ellison said in a victory speech to supporters. "We won a key election, but we did much more than that. We showed that a candidate can run a 100% positive campaign and prevail, even against tough opposition." **(5)**

Throughout his campaign Ellison, a criminal defense attorney who converted to Islam as a college student, focused on issues that resonate in his electoral District in Minneapolis. Ellison won 56 percent of the vote, defeating Republican Alan Fine and the Independence Party's Tammy Lee, both of whom garnered 21 percent of the vote. Before Ellison's election to the House, Larry Shaw, a Democrat State Senator of North Carolina, was the highest Muslim elected official in the United States. Larry Shaw, a corporate executive, was re-elected to the State senate on November 7, 2006.

The midterm elections witnessed an intensive voter registration and get-out-to-vote campaigns by the American Muslim groups. Consequently, in key elections throughout the country, candidates were beginning to realize the impact of the Muslim electorate which is the result of the increasing interaction of Muslim communities with elected officials and candidates.

The Muslim community demonstrated its importance in this election particularly in the states where it has large concentration of population. In states like Virginia which has substantial concentration of Muslim population, the Muslim vote became the critical vote in tipping the balance on control of the US Senate. In Virginia Incumbent senator George Allen was defeated by his Democratic opponent, Jim Webb, giving Democrats control of the Senate with 51-members.

Chapter IX - The Post-9/11 Challenges: The Muslim Response [198]

There are approximately 60,000 Muslim voters in Virginia, with 85% of them living in Northern Virginia. According to the Muslim American Society Center for Electoral Empowerment Director (MASCEE) Mukit Hossain, it is

estimated that 47,700 Muslims voted for Jim Webb, which positively contributed to his narrow victory over Senator George Allen. The MASCEE also helped support a larger Muslim voter turnout in Virginia by recruiting 230 volunteers for some 200 election sites.

The Muslim groups had launched a vote registration campaign and also get-out-to-vote campaign. They particularly targeted 12 states with a high concentration of Muslim population: California, 20 percent; Illinois, 8.9 percent; New York, 8.6 percent; Texas, 7 percent; New Jersey, 6.8 percent; Michigan, 6.7 percent; Florida, 6.4 percent; Virginia, 6.3 percent; Maryland, 3.1 percent; Ohio, 3 percent; Pennsylvania, 2.9 percent; and Minnesota, 2.8 percent.

The Muslim American Society, which had set up voter registration booths in mosques across the country, has added 30,000 new voters to the rolls just weeks before the election.

In Illinois, another state with a heavy concentration of Muslims, the Council of Islamic Organizations of Greater Chicago had been working to register more of the area's approximately 400,000 Muslims to vote.

2008 Election [5a]

According to the American Muslim Task Force on Civil Rights and Elections, a coalition of Muslim civil advocacy groups, American Muslims overwhelmingly voted for Democratic Presidential candidate Senator Barrak Obama in the 2008 election.

On November 6, 2008, the American Muslim Task Force released a poll of over 600 Muslims from more than 10 states, including Florida and Pennsylvania, and it revealed that 89 percent of respondents voted for Obama, while only 2 percent voted for McCain. It also indicated that 95 percent of Muslims polled cast a ballot in this year's presidential election—the highest turnout in a U.S. election ever—and 14 percent of those were first-time voters.

Chapter IX - The Post-9/11 Challenges: The Muslim Response [199]

The Newsweek reported a Gallup Center for Muslim Studies survey as saying that U.S. Muslims favored Obama in greater numbers than did Hispanics (67 percent of whom voted for Obama) and nearly matched that of African-Americans, 93 percent of whom voted for Obama. More than two thirds who were polled said the economy was the most important issue affecting their decision on Nov. 4th, while 16 percent said the wars in Iraq and Afghanistan informed their vote—numbers that put Muslims roughly on a par with the general population.

In this election, Muslim Americans changed their party affiliation from Republican to Democratic – a stark change from the strong Muslim support for George Bush in 2000 when they voted for Bush in an en bloc vote. The major shift occurred as many Muslim Americans became subject to wiretapping, mishandling of civil liberties, religious, ethnic, and racial profiling.

According to the Newsweek, in 2008, many more Muslims were drawn into the Democratic party by Obama himself since Muslims across the country were captivated by the senator's promise of unity and hope. On the Muslim-Americans for Obama Web site (Mafo2008.com), their mission statement includes the following: "That we support Barack Obama because, among other reasons, he rejects the politics of fear, challenging our nation to embrace its collective identity, where each American has a stake in the success and well-being of every American."

But many Muslims kept their presidential preference a secret in the months leading up to Super Tuesday, fearing that an endorsement from them might in fact work against Obama, the Newsweek said addin: After all, this was an election year in which the word "Muslim" was used as shorthand to connote anti-American leanings and a hidden love of terrorism.

Extensive campaigns to motivate the Muslim voters

The seven million-strong American Muslim community had a rough time during the 2008 election campaign with smear against Islam, bigotry and stereotyping. Tellingly, despite the messages of inclusiveness and tolerance from both major parties, neither campaign has been overly anxious to court the Muslim vote. To their disappointment, neither presidential candidate has visited a mosque, yet both have made multiple visits to churches and synagogues.

Chapter IX - The Post-9/11 Challenges: The Muslim Response [200]

This is the reason that no major American Muslim organization - such as AMT, CAIR and MPAC -has formally endorsed Obama although they remain heavily tilted towards him because of their grievances against the Bush's anti-Muslim policies. However, the Muslim organizations have launched extensive campaigns to motivate the Muslim voters to go out and vote.

The American-Arab Anti-Discrimination Committee (ADC) has dedicated major resources to protect the Arab and Muslim American votes through the ADC Voter Protection Unit (ADC VPU). The ADC VPU is a special unit composed of a full-time lobbyist, three attorneys in Washington, DC, and one attorney in Dearborn, Michigan. This unit of professionals is dedicated to protecting the Arab and Muslim American communities from voter intimidation and other attempts at chilling the communities' right to vote.

The Arab American Institute has launched the Yalla Vote campaign, "Our Voice. Our Future. Yalla Vote '08." It is organizing Arab Americans across the country to motivate the Arab voters. More than 50 Arab American organizations from around the country have signed on to Yalla Vote '08 campaign.

The American Muslim Taskforce had designated Friday, Oct. 31st as 'National Muslim Voter Education Day USA' and Nov 1-2 as 'National Voter Mobilization Weekend.' The American Muslim Voice has urged the Muslims to participate in the national political process to make their voice effective. The Council on American-Islamic Relations (CAIR) called on American Muslim voters to turn out in large numbers at the polls on November 4th as a positive response to Islamophobic bias and stereotyping in political campaigns.

In October 2008, the Muslim Public Affairs Council held seven election town hall forums in Ohio and Pennsylvania in an effort to educate Muslim American voters on key issues and provide an opportunity for interaction with candidates for local, state and federal offices.

2010 election [5b]

Since 9/11, there has been a steady rise in Islamophobia, however during mid-term election campaign there was an exponential rise of anti-Islam and anti-Muslim bigotry. Many Religious Right leaders and opportunist politicians asserted repeatedly that Islam is not a religion at all but a political cult, that

Muslims cannot be good Americans and that mosques are fronts for extremist 'jihadis.' There was a substantial increase in the number of political candidates using Islamophobic tactics in an effort to leverage votes, and use such tactics as a platform to enhance their political visibility.

Consequently, Muslims rejected the Republican Party at the polls in 2008 and 2010. According to the American Muslim Taskforce on Civil Rights and Elections, just 2.2 percent of Muslims voted for Sen. John McCain in 2008.

As Stephan Salisbury reported, during the 2010 midterm election campaign, virtually every hard-charging candidate on the far right took a moment to trash a Muslim, a mosque, or Islamic pieties. In the wake of those elections, with 85 new Republican House members and a surging Tea Party movement, the political virtues of anti-Muslim rhetoric as a means of rousing voters and alarming the general electorate have gone largely unchallenged. It has become an article of faith that a successful 2010 candidate on the right should treat Islam with revulsion, drawing a line between America the Beautiful and the destructive impurities of Islamic cultists and radicals.

Throughout the 2010 election campaign the seven-million strong American Muslim community and their faith were dehumanized as the Republican Party once again used Islamophobia as a political tool. The anti-Islam and anti-Muslim rhetoric depicting Islam as enemy got steam from the Quran-burning publicity stunts by a minor church in Florida. Two more elements were added to this anti-Muslim hysteria in this election campaign. Controversy over the 51Park project popularly known as Ground Zero mosque and conspiracies that Sharia law will displace the US constitution.

To borrow Kelley B. Vlahos: In fact, anti-Muslim rage in today's national discourse is populism's low-hanging fruit, and many Republicans hungrily grabbed at it with both fists and were duly rewarded this campaign season. Sure, not every one of the Sarah Palin/Tea Party-endorsed candidates won on Nov. 2, but those who did, won in part because of their willingness to indulge in the Islamophobia coursing through the Republican base today, not despite it. The same Republican base that helped the party torpedo the Democrats last Tuesday, taking back the House, six senate seats, six governorships, and 680 slots in state legislatures.

Chapter IX - The Post-9/11 Challenges: The Muslim Response [202]

Never in any U.S. elections before so many campaign ads were aired mongering fear against Islam or Muslims. This year, Republicans have crossed all limits. They are openly bashing Muslims and Islam to get more votes in elections. In August 2010, Republicans amplified their rhetoric to turn the so-called "Ground Zero Mosque" into a campaign issue.

The inflammatory rhetoric surrounding the project has stirred hatred toward Muslims in America. There has been so much fear-mongering and so much misinformation in the debate peddled by bigots and rightwing politicians. The constant vilification of Islam and Muslims over the air on radio talk shows, in newspapers and the Internet was contributing to the rise in anti-Muslim sentiment across the country.

Not surprisingly, a poll on August 29 by the extreme right San Diego, California 760 KFMB AM talk radio station indicated that 70% of those polled are in favor of forced registration for American Muslims in a national database. The same day a poll conducted by Chris Matthews show at the MSNBC revealed that more than half of Republicans polled say they have a negative attitude toward Islam, this compared to only 27% of Democrats.

Park51 controversy leads to political engagement

Motivated by the anti-Islam fervor generated by Park51 Arab and Muslim American organizations and individuals used different methods and tactics were to engage their communities.

Leading civil advocacy groups like the Council on Islamic-American Relations (CAIR) and the Muslim Public Affairs Council (MPAC) were acquainting American Muslims with the voting process. The CAIR released voting guides for 23 states that explain when polls open, how to register to vote, what identification is needed and voters' rights.

Leading American Muslim civil advocacy organizations reached out to American Muslims through a series of workshops conducted across the country.

And it's not just in the lead-up to the midterm elections that American Muslims were engaging in the political process. Organizations such as the Council of Islamic Organizations of Greater Chicago helped organize Muslim

Action Day in April 2010, when community representatives met legislators at the state capitol to discuss voter issues.

Project Mobilize Chicago

In Chicago, with more than 400,000 Muslim population, organizations like Project Mobilize, Mosque Foundation, CIOGC and CAIR-Chicago and have been active in voter registration. In the city's southwest suburbs, in the 10 precincts surrounding one of largest mosques in the country, 20% of the registered voters are Muslim.

Project Mobilize is a nonprofit organization with the mission of developing the political potential of the Muslim community in Chicago's southwest suburbs. Launched in 2009, it is the first professional political action organization that focuses on the grass-roots political empowerment and engagement of American Muslims through local politics.

Election Day saw the Muslim community in full force doing everything in their civic repertoire from canvassing the houses of people who have yet to vote to making phone calls to registered voters to standing outside polling sites with postcards listing Muslim endorsements of candidates.

The twist this year came in the form of colorful, clearly printed endorsement postcards listing 6 candidates who committed themselves to working on behalf of their Muslim constituents should they be elected to office. Project Mobilize mailed over 1500 of these postcards ahead of Election Day to Muslim voters throughout the Stickney, Palos, Lyons, and Worth townships. On Election Day, almost 20 volunteers spread their efforts across 8 polling sites to make sure Muslim voters had these postcards in hand when they cast their votes.

The Muslim community came out in record numbers to vote during an election season many other communities decided to sit out. The hallmark example of this comes from precinct 44 in Bridgeview, IL. The Muslim community makes up almost 80 percent of the registered voters in this precinct alone and therefore serves as a trend indicator for the Muslim American electorate. Exit polls from precinct 44 revealed that the candidates specific to those voters – candidates Project M endorsed – won in that precinct.

Chapter IX - The Post-9/11 Challenges: The Muslim Response [204]

Reema Ahmad, the Director of the Project Mobilize, says that the goal of her group is fielding Muslim American candidates for office. "This is really the next logical step towards us fulfilling our political aspirations. It's about developing that potential, ensuring that people who have aspirations to hold public office know how to get into those positions and garner the support they need," Ahmad said.

Civic participation

Another positive outcome of the post-9/11 period was an increase in the civic participation of Arabs and Muslims and their organizations. Mosques and Muslim organizations were forced to come out of the isolation in which they lived and build bridges with other sectors of American society. Amaney Jamal, a Princeton University political scientist, observes that although civic engagement has been increasing, there has been a shift in focus from influencing Middle East policy to strengthening domestic institutions. **(6)**

Muslim donors gave approximately $200,000 to Virginia candidates, up from $40,000 in 2002, according to Mukit Hossain, director of the Virginia Muslim Political Action Committee. **(7)**

There was a substantial increase in the attendance at Muslim-oriented political events. More than 600 people attended the Virginia Muslim Civic Picnic in summer 2006, an event held for state candidates that has grown since it began in 2001. About 1,300 people attended a candidates' night a few weeks before the 2006 election at Falls Church mosque Dar Al Hijrah, in Virginia. **(8)**

Muslim groups have also been involved in various social programs such as food drives and providing help to homeless Americans. The Council on American-Islamic Relations (CAIR) has launched an annual summer-long "Muslims Care" campaign, to encourage volunteerism in the nation's Muslim community. The "Muslim Care" campaign includes collection of food and blood donations. In July 2007, the CAIR New York called on local mosques to host food drives and collect canned goods for City Harvest, a non-profit food rescue program to feed more than 260,000 hungry New Yorkers. Other Muslim organizations and groups also have similar programs.

Chapter IX - The Post-9/11 Challenges: The Muslim Response [205]

During Katrina disaster in August 2005, American Muslims organizations and mosques joined the massive national relief efforts to help the victims of Katrina hurricane. At the call of Muslim organizations mosques nationwide collected donations for the hurricane disaster relief following the congregational of Friday prayers. The funds collected were sent to the American Red Cross or other relief groups offering assistance to the victims of Hurricane Katrina. Muslim groups formed the Muslim Hurricane Relief Task Force (MHRTF) coordinate the aid effort. The Task Force pledged $10 million for victims of Katrina. The MHRTF members include (in alphabetical order) Council on American-Islamic Relations (CAIR), Islamic Circle of North American (ICNA), Islamic Relief, ISNA, Kind Hearts, Life for Relief and Development, Muslim Alliance in North America (MANA), Muslim American Society (MAS), Muslim Public Affairs Council (MPAC), and Muslim Ummah of North American (MUNA).

Outreach to other faiths, civil rights and ethnic groups

Another Muslim community response was more outreach to non-Muslim communities and organizations and more interfaith dialogues and activities—providing non-Muslims with a better understanding of Islam, greater levels of Muslim civic participation, more critical thinking, and greater cohesion among the congregation of Muslims. At the same time, non-Muslim civil society institutions — especially civil rights, legal, religious, immigrant, and ethnic — opened their doors to Arabs and Muslims by sponsoring public educational forums. The most common topics of these forums were civil rights, Islam, federal laws and policies and their impacts such as the USA Patriot Act and special registration, women in Islam, and the war in Iraq. American Muslim groups and organizations received positive response to their intensive efforts to outreach other civil rights, ethnic and religious groups, organizations and movements.

Incidentally, increased racial profiling and more widespread public acceptance of it brought together ethnic minorities and immigrants in a shift in the civil rights movement. At the 2003 Amnesty International USA hearings in Chicago on racial profiling witnesses included not just those typically perceived to be victims, such as African-Americans, but also recent immigrants from far-flung parts of the world. Sitting in the pews were African-

Chapter IX - The Post-9/11 Challenges: The Muslim Response [206]

Americans, Southeast Asians, Koreans, Arab-Americans, Pakistanis, Indians, Haitians and Latinos--groups that organizers say were unlikely to assemble in one place a few years ago. They were people who might ordinarily think they have little in common, other than the persecution they experienced due to the Patriot Act and other measures.

To express support to the Muslim community's eroding civil rights, about 30 civil rights, ethnic and religious groups were present, in Fremont on Oct. 24, 2004 at the formal launching of American Muslim Voice, a new civil rights group that is dedicated to building bridges with other communities in order to protect and defend civil rights of the Muslim community as well as other communities.

In Oct. 2006, the American-Arab Anti-Discrimination Committee (ADC) Communications Director, Laila Al-Qatami, became the first Arab American to be elected to the National Board of Directors of the American Civil Liberties Union (ACLU). Laila Al-Qatami was elected by the ACLU's national electorate to fill one of 30 at-large seats on the ACLU's National Board of Directors. She will serve a three-year term on the National Board, which includes representatives from the 53 ACLU affiliates across the nation, in addition to the at-large seats. Additionally, she was also elected to serve as a member of the Board of Directors for the ACLU National Capital Area (ACLU-NCA) affiliate by the members of the ACLU-NCA. The ACLU, which is nonpartisan and nonprofit, was founded in 1920, and over the years has significantly strengthened and solidified its position as the nation's guardian of liberty. **(9)**

Samina Faheem Sundas, Executive Director of the American Muslim Voice (AMV), was honored to be one of the 100 Diverse Dreamers for "Dream Across America Tour" in June 2007. In eight days via ten cities, the train tour from Los Angeles to Washington brought together one hundred diverse individuals from throughout the country referred to as Dreamers. The Dreams Across America Tour concluded in Washington, D.C. where Dreamers from across the country joined hundreds of immigrant children and their families at an event organized by the Fair Immigration Reform Movement (FIRM). The objective of the "Dream Across America Tour" was to highlight the Immigration issue as the Congress was discussing an

Chapter IX - The Post-9/11 Challenges: The Muslim Response [207]

Immigration bill that was defeated in the Senate on procedural matter on July 2, 2007. **(10)**

The AMV, a prominent Muslim civil rights group, was invited to the "Dream Across America Tour" because of its grassroots outreach to other ethnic and religious communities. Its Executive Director Samina Faheem Sundas was appointed in September 2006 a commissioner to the Human Relations Commission of the Santa Clara County, California. In September 2007,

Samina and her organization was awarded (the Fellowship of Reconciliation) FOR's Martin Luther King, Jr. Peace Prize "for their work to bridge the gap between communities and unite us all under the umbrella of our common humanity."

The American Muslim Voice Outreach Director Syed Zafar Mohsin was given the prestigious "Citizen of the Year" award on in March 2005 from the City of Milpitas, CA. **(11)** Similarly, in May 2007, the AMV President, Khalid Saeed, was honored by the Latino Community. Khalid Saeed of Woodland was acknowledged for his being a "strong voice for the voiceless in Yolo County (CA)." **(12)**

The American Muslim Voice held a solidarity open house in Palo Alto, CA., in April 2005. More than 270 people from all walks of life attended the event aimed at "nurturing the seeds of friendship through personal acquaintance and contacts."

The Illinois-based Council of Islamic Organizations of Greater Chicago (CIOGC) in its interfaith outreach has formed relationships with several faith-based groups, including: the Archdiocese of Chicago; Protestants for the Common Good; the Chicago Board of Rabbis; the Catholic Theological Union; other religious constituencies, including Methodists, Presbyterians, and Unitarians; and faith-based civic groups, such as the National Conference for Community and Justice (NCCJ), and the Council for a Parliament of the World's Religions (CPWR). **(13)**

Consequently, a significant portion of the interfaith dialogue in the Chicago area between Muslims and people of other faiths takes place under the auspices of the Council. The CIOGC constituents organizations and their respective constituents collectively represent about 400,000 strong Chicago area Muslim community. Illinois is home to eight percent of America's Muslims, second only to California and New York.

The CIOGC has successfully collaborated on major cooperative projects with leading Chicago institutions including: the historic "Chicagoans & Islam" gathering in Nov. '02 with United Power for Action & Justice (where, for the first time in the history of America, each of about 2500 American Muslims interacted on a one-to-one basis with fellow Americans from other faiths). The CIOGC also participated in many prominent interfaith events across the region, held independently and with partners like NCCJ, CPWR and the Office of Cardinal George.

The Council also maintains cordial relationships with many Legal & Civic groups such as: Midwest Immigrants and Human Rights Center, Lawyers Committee for Civil Rights Under Law, Federal Defender Program, ACLU, National Conference for Community and Justice, United Power for Action and Justice, Chicago Council on Foreign Relations, Illinois Chamber of Commerce, Rainbow PUSH Coalition, Leadership Council for Metropolitan Open Communities, DuPage Sponsors, and the Illinois Coalition for Immigrant and Refugee Rights.

In February 2007, the Council on American-Islamic Relations, San Francisco Bay Area Chapter (CAIR-SFBA) was joined by the ACLU Immigrants' Rights Project, the ACLU of Northern California, the Asian Law Caucus in filing a lawsuit in federal district court in San Francisco against delay in processing of citizenship applications of the Muslims and Arabs. "This lawsuit deals with the government's recent attempts to evade the law: moving the unreasonable delay earlier to skirt the letter of the law while still violating people's due process rights," said Sin Yen Ling, a staff attorney with the Asian Law Caucus. The Council on American-Islamic Relations' San Francisco Chapter alone had received more than 65 cases, mostly from people of Middle Eastern or South-Asian origin. A similar lawsuit was filed in Los Angeles in August 2006. Filed in U.S. District Court in Los Angeles, the suit also sought class-action status to include all immigrants who have been waiting at least six months for naturalization after filing applications at the U.S. Citizenship and Immigration Service in Los Angeles. **(14)**

In Tampa, Florida, Christians have joined hands in rebuilding the Islamic Education Center that was burned by an arsonist in April 2007. The Rev. Robert Gibbons, pastor of St. Paul's Catholic Church in St. Petersburg, asked his parishioners to contribute shortly after learning about the fire. In Islam & Muslims in the Post-9/11 America the fall, bay area Muslims donated $5,000 to help restore churches in the West Bank and Gaza that were burned by Muslims in the wake of a controversial speech by Pope Benedict XVI. The local Muslims asked Gibbons, who was then vicar general of the Diocese of St. Petersburg, to help ensure their funds made it into the right hands. **(15)**

Worshippers at Bayshore Presbyterian Church also felt compelled to pitch in with a $530 donation and an offer to help clean up fire damage. "Anything that we can do to express our cooperation and encouragement for the Muslims that are meeting here and who are in the minority, we want to do that," said the Rev. Wendy Hare, the church's pastor. "I feel like if our church had a firebomb thrown into it, their community would do the same thing to support us because we're a small church and we would need help rebuilding." **(16)**

Interfaith outreach

The Muslim community has developed more relationships with other faith communities —especially Christian and Jewish — and has found a good deal of support from these communities.

In April 2006, United Methodists and Muslims in Northern Illinois officially created a covenant relationship between the two faith groups. More than 100 leaders of the greater Chicago Islamic community and the United Methodist Northern Illinois Conference celebrated that covenant at an interfaith banquet at the Islamic Foundation in Villa Park. United Methodist Bishop Hee-Soo Jung and Abdul Malik Mujahid, chairman of the Council of Islamic Organizations of Greater Chicago, signed a "Declaration of Relationship" committing the two groups to "a relationship grounded in our mutual love for God and dedication to the ethical core of our faiths." **(17)**

Interestingly, Christian-Muslim dialogue began long before 9/11. In 1995, John Borelli of the Office of Ecumenical and Interreligious Affairs at the United States Conference of Catholic Bishops (USCCB) initiated three regional - West Coast, Midwest and Mid-Atlantic - dialogues with Muslims. These dialogues have taken special significance in the post-9/11 era.

In the words of Dr. Sayyid M. Syeed, former general secretary of the Islamic Society of North America (ISNA) and Muslim co-chairman of the Midwest

Chapter IX - The Post-9/11 Challenges: The Muslim Response [210]

dialogue, Muslim-Catholic understanding in the United States is different from many parts of the world. U.S. Catholics understand the Muslim experiences of discrimination as a religious minority because they had the same experiences two or three generations ago and U.S. Muslims now "are going through a similar experience. ... The cumulative experience of Catholics is a guiding light for us." **(18)** Dr. Sayyid M. Syeed, now heads ISNA's new Office of Interfaith and Community Alliances in Washington, DC after serving as Secretary General at the headquarters since 1994.

The Christian-Muslim dialogues have been addressing a wide range of shared interests from social concerns such as immigration and family life to questions of values, religious freedom, spirituality and scholarly issues.

The first Christian-Muslim (Mid Atlantic) dialogues was held in Indianapolis in I996. The event was cosponsored by the Islamic Circle of North America (ICNA) and the United States Conference of Catholic Bishops (USCCB). In

April 2007, the Mid Atlantic dialogue approved guidelines for pastoral care of couples in interfaith marriages, specifically Catholic-Muslim marriages.

The West Coast dialogue has been focusing on spirituality while Midwest dialogue is concentrating, among other things, on achieving inter-religious cooperation in social issues.

Soon after the tragic events of 9/11, various Islamic centers and mosques were holding open houses to encourage non-Muslims to visit their centers and mosques. The idea was just getting to know one another. Non-Muslims, particularly the Christians visiting a mosque to see how Islam is practiced, or Muslims visiting a local church to get to know the Christians and see what they believe and do.

After the 9/11, off and on Jewish-Muslim dialogues **(19)** also got momentum. A number of new Jewish-Muslim dialogues and events were initiated in several states. For example, the Islamic Masumeen Center in Hopkinton, Mass., and the American Jewish Committee launched a dialogue in 2003. **(20)** In April 2003, the first Muslim-Jewish peace walk was held from synagogue Nahalat Shalom to the Islamic Center of New Mexico in Albuquerque. **(21)**

An unprecedented Jewish-Muslim dialogue took place on May 5, 2007 at a conference on Fear and Trauma: Ruptured Souls; Ruptured Cultures in Washington DC. Two speakers, one Jewish the other Muslim, were addressing the large subject of Fear and Trauma from the perspective of their own backgrounds. A psychoanalyst and scholar of the Holocaust, Dr. Dori Laub, MD and head of American University's Ibn Khaldun Chair of Islamic Studies, Dr. Akbar Ahmed, Ph.D. presented papers and entered into dialogue inviting participation from an esteemed audience of psychoanalysts, mental health professionals, academics, and leaders of organizations interested in Islam and the Holocaust. The conference on Fear and Trauma allowed for the suffering of the Holocaust and the suffering in the world of Islam to be discussed together for the first time. **(22)**

In January 2007, the Los Angeles-based Muslim Public Affairs Council (MPAC) and the Progressive Jewish Alliance (PJA) launched NewGround program to promote Muslim-Jewish relations. "The purpose of NewGround is to create an effective model for Muslim-Jewish interaction that neither ignores nor becomes hostage to the ever-shifting realities in the Middle East. NewGround will create innovative ways to approach the challenges in the Middle East, while acknowledging that each community maintains a diversity of perspectives and level of concern for these issues." **(23)**

MPAC's Executive Director, Dr. Salam Al Marayati and MPAC's senior advisor, Dr. Mahir Hathout have been active in Jewish-Muslim dialogue in Lose Angeles which in December 1999 forged a code of ethics. It bound some 80 signatories to denounce all terrorism and hate crimes, promote civil dialogue, and avoid mutual stereotyping and incitement.

Interestingly, the Zionist Organization of America and the American Jewish Committee launched a nasty smear campaign when the Los Angeles County Human Relations Commission voted in July 2006 to presented their prestigious John Allen Buggs Award for excellence in human relations to Dr. Maher Hathout. Their opposition prompted the commission to reconsider

Chapter IX - The Post-9/11 Challenges: The Muslim Response [212]

and reaffirm its decision in September. Dr. Hathout was given the award in October 2006.

The Jewish-Muslim dialogues and overtures often suffered setback as they cannot escape the impact of events in the Middle East. During the Israeli rampage on Lebanon in August 2006, Dearbon's Jewish and Muslim communities were pulled apart as Rabbi Joseph Klein, in a stunning sermon to his congregation, apologized for working with local Muslim leaders and vowed to boycott interfaith events. **(24)**

Lobbying at the congress

American Muslim political activism was also seen conspicuously during the Israeli rampage on Lebanon in July 2006, when the American Muslim community became very vocal and reached out to elected officials and opinion leaders. As Israel launched intensive attacks on Lebanon, American Jewish groups immediately swung into action, sending lobbyists to Washington, **(25)**

solidarity delegations to Jerusalem and millions of dollars for ambulances and trauma counseling, just as they always have. But this time there was a parallel mobilization by Arab-Americans and Muslim Americans in support of Lebanese and Palestinian victims of the war. They also sent lobbyists to Washington and solidarity delegations to the Middle East.

Both sides also worked to sway public opinion. Jewish groups have held rallies in almost every major American city. Muslim/Arab-American and Lebanese-American groups also organized demonstrations across the nation to protest Israel's killing of civilians and raised funds to support Lebanon.

The Council on American Islamic Relations (CAIR), a major Muslim civil rights group, sponsored news conferences around the country in which Lebanese-Americans and others recount traumatic stories of escaping from Israeli bombardment.

Chapter IX - The Post-9/11 Challenges: The Muslim Response [213]

The pro-Israel lobby has held sway over American policy but that could be changing according to CAIR National Communications Director Ibrahim Hooper. "I don't think it's going to be that American politicians can get away with making speeches pledging allegiance to Israel and nobody's going to challenge them. I think those days are over."

Muslim Day

In reaction to the rise of Islamophobia civil advocacy groups are encouraging Muslims to positively engage their lawmakers, lobbying both for general issues they care about (such as housing and poverty) as well as issues specific to Muslims, like asking their representatives to take a stronger stand against Islamophobia.

On Jan 16, 2012, some 400 Washington State Muslims celebrated the 5th annual Muslim Day at the Capitol and met with dozens of their elected representatives. The event, one of the largest of its kind in the nation, was organized by the Washington state chapter of the Council on American-Islamic Relations (CAIR-WA). The event was also designed to honor the legacy of Dr. Martin Luther King, Jr. and his defense of civil rights through positive civic engagement.

Another similar day was observed on May 7, 2012 in Sacramento, when California Muslims gathered at the Sacramento Convention Center and the State Capitol for the first-ever Muslim Day at the Capitol. The event was organized by the CAIR, to discuss topics ranging from civil rights to immigration with legislators.

On April 5, 2012, Minnesota Muslims gathered at the state Capitol to discuss with legislators issues important to their community. The main topics: Islamophobia, anti-Muslim legislation, photo ID legislation and gun violence. Groups sponsoring the eighth Annual Muslim Day were: Muslim American Society of Minnesota, Al-Amal School, Council on Islamic-American Relations-MN (CAIR-MN), Islamic Center of Minnesota, Islamic Resource Group, Masjid Al-Ihsan Islamic Center, Masjid An-Nur, Masjid At-Taqwa, and Northwest Islamic Community Center.

Chapter IX - The Post-9/11 Challenges: The Muslim Response [214]

Fatwa against terrorism

In a vigorous response to allegations that the American Muslims have not condemned terrorism enough, The Fiqh Council of North America issued a fatwa, or religious edict, in July 2005 saying that Islam condemns terrorism, religious radicalism and the use of violence. The fatwa was later endorsed by more than 200 American Muslim organizations and groups. It was the first time Muslims in North America had issued an anti-terrorism edict, although they had repeatedly condemned such acts of violence. The fatwa had desired result as it was reported widely by mainstream media. The Council on American-Islamic Relations has, meanwhile, launched "Not in the Name of Islam" ad campaign condemning terrorism. However, many in the community were wondering why only Muslims were compelled to issue an edict or ad against terrorism. Neither Christians nor Jews, or people of other faith feel compelled to issue edits declaring their faith's innocence whenever acts of violence and extremism are carried out by individuals or groups who share their faith.

Besides issuing fatwa and ads, the Muslim organizations have launched interfaith dialogue to remove misconceptions about Islam caused by the growing use of anti-Muslim and anti-Islam rhetoric. There has been tremendous response to Muslim outreach as many individuals, communities and civil right groups responded to their plight. American Civil Rights Union and American Lawyers Guild helped the Muslims called for 'voluntary' FBI interviews.

However, despite constant pressure, the American Muslim community remains vibrant with more social and political activism which may be alarming some agenda-driven anti-Muslim groups and individuals. The formation of such groups

In short despite constant pressure the American Muslim community remains vibrant.

Ten years' state of siege has not shaken the confidence of American Muslims in the principles of our founding fathers as enshrined in the Declaration of Independence and Bill of Rights on which our founding fathers aspired to build the new country. They see the scapegoating of the Muslim community as nativism, i.e. a pattern that has emerged during similar crises, when the nation's security becomes threatened, and in times of economic recession, that some sociologists describe as a recurrent tide of Jingoistic racism.

American Muslims have a strong sense of optimism and anticipation that the current wave of anti-Islam and anti-Muslim will recede in due time and they will regain their civic vitality and rejoin the mosaic of other minorities and ethnic groups. The American Muslims will join their predecessors: Japanese Americans, American Jews, Irish Americans and African Americans who also, in times past, endured national intolerance, social prejudice, and legal injustice.

References

(1) A Portrait of Detroit Mosques sponsored by the Institute for Social Policy and Understanding, Michigan, Illinois.
(2) AMP Report - The American Muslim & Arab vote in Election 2004
(3) Democratic National Committee Chairman Howard Dean met with a diverse group of Muslim leaders to talk about the Democratic agenda for change along with efforts to reach out to members of the religious community early on in the election process. Muslim leaders joined Chairman Dean in an informal discussion in which they talked about civil liberties, the Patriot Act, immigration, poverty, engagement of Muslim Americans in the political process, ways the DNC can best reach out to the community and other issues important to Muslim Americans. This meeting was part of a larger outreach by the DNC's Faith in Action Initiative, a mission to involve state parties and religious leaders from around the country in an ongoing dialogue about their shared values within the Democratic Party. (U.S. Newswire - May 17, 2006)
(4) According to the Council on American-Islamic Relations survey of Muslim voters, release on October 24, 2006, 42 percent consider themselves members of the Democratic Party while only 17 per cent are Republican. Another 28 percent do not belong to any party. An informal exit-poll of Muslim voters, conducted by the New Jersey Chapter of the Council on American Islamic Relations (CAIR-NJ), indicated that the vast majority in that state voted for Democrats in the mid-term elections. There are at least 18,000 registered Muslim voters in the state of New Jersey. Seventy-five Muslim voters from Ohio responded to a post-election survey. More than 90 percent of the respondents said they had voted for Democratic Party candidates. (CAIR Bulletin)
(5) AMP Report - American Muslims in 2006 elections
(5a) AMP Report - American Muslims overwhelmingly voted Democratic in 2008
(5b) AMP Report - American Muslims in 2010 election
(6) More Muslims gaining political ground, The Washington Post - November 30, 2006

Chapter IX - The Post-9/11 Challenges: The Muslim Response [216]

(7) More Muslims gaining political ground, The Washington Post - November 30, 2006
(8) More Muslims gaining political ground, The Washington Post - November 30, 2006
(9) ADC Press Release - Oct. 18, 2006)
(10) www.dreamsacrossamericaonline.org
(11) Top citizen is active commissioner, rights advocate - Milpitas Post – March 24, 2005
(12) Civic diversity celebrated at Latino Community dinner - The Democrat Woodland CA – May 21, 2007
(13) http://www.ciogc.org/about_cio.html)
(14) Delay in naturalization process: Civil rights groups file class-action suit against government - AMP Report – February 10, 2007
(15) St. Petersburg Times – July 6, 2007)
(16) St. Petersburg Times – July 6, 2007)
(17) Spero News - April 6, 2006)
(18) Observers say new pope must build on existing outreach to Islam – CNS – April 17, 2005]
(19) By 1987, a Los Angeles Times report estimated that some 60 dialogue groups were operating throughout the United States.
(20) Amid Mideast Conflict, Tense Times for U.S. Interfaith Groups By Omar Sacirbey - Religion News Service
(21) A Muslim-Jewish Initiative by Lynn Gottlieb - Fellowship magazine of Fellowship of Reconciliation (FOR) Nov./Dec. 2003
(22) An Unprecedented Jewish/Muslim Dialogue with Dr. Dori Laub and Dr. Akbar Ahmed http://www.cmjr.org.uk/dialogue.html]
(23) http://www.newgroundproject.org/
(24) Detroit Free Press - Nov. 3, 2006
(25) Reinvigorated by the crisis in the Middle East, Arab Americans across the U.S. met with their members of Congress in their home districts on August 16, 2006 as part of National Arab American Lobby Day. [Arab American Institute - August 16, 2006]

Appendix I

Who are American Muslims? Demographic Facts

According to a report titled,"The American Mosque 2011: Basic Characteristics of the American Mosque, Attitudes of Mosque Leaders:"

- Mosques in the United States in 2011: 2,106
- Mosques in the United States in 2000: 1,209
- Increase in number of mosques since 2000: 75 percent
- American Muslims associated with a mosque: 2.6 million
- Muslims who attend Eid Prayer (the high holiday prayers after Ramadan and Hajj) increased from about 2 million in 2000 to about 2.6 million in 2011. The total Muslim population cannot be determined by this figure, but it does call into question the low estimates of 1.1-2.4 million Muslims in America. If there are 2.6 million Muslims who pray the Eid prayer, then the total Muslim population should be closer to the estimates of up to 7 million.
- The American mosque is a remarkably young institution: over three-fourths (76%) of all existing mosques were established since 1980.
- The vast majority of mosques are located in metropolitan areas but the percentage of mosques in urban areas is decreasing and the percentage of mosques in suburban areas is increasing: in 2000 16% of mosques were located in suburbs and in 2011 28% of mosques are now located in suburbs
- Mosques remain an extremely diverse institution. Only 3% of mosques have only one ethnic group that attends that mosque. South Asians, Arabs, and African Americans remain the dominant groups but significant numbers of newer immigrants have arrived, including Somalis, West Africans and Iraqis.
- Shi'ite mosques are also expanding in numbers, especially since the 1990s. Over 44% of all Shi'ite mosques were established in the decade of the 1990s.

The American Mosque 2011: Basic Characteristics of the American Mosque, Attitudes of Mosque Leaders report was released on February 29, 2012in

Islam & Muslims in the Post-9/11 America

Washington by a coalition of major American Muslim and academic organizations. Other findings of the report said:

- Mosque leaders overwhelmingly endorse Muslim involvement in American society. More than 98 percent of mosque leaders agree that Muslims should be involved in American institutions and 91 percent agree that Muslims should be involved in politics.
- The vast majority of mosque leaders do not feel that American society is hostile to Islam.
- The majority of mosque leaders (56 percent) adopt a flexible approach to interpretation of Quran and Sunnah (the normative practice of Islam's Prophet Muhammad) that takes into account the overall purposes of Islamic law and modern circumstances.
- The vast majority (87 percent) of mosque leaders disagree that "radicalism" is increasing among Muslim youth. Many mosque leaders say the real challenge for them is not radicalism and extremism among the youth, but how to attract and keep them close to the mosque.

Sponsors of the U.S. Mosque Survey 2011 include: The Hartford Institute for Religion Research (Hartford Seminary), the Association of Statisticians of American Religious Bodies (ASARB), the Council on American-Islamic Relations (CAIR), the Islamic Society of North American (ISNA), the Islamic Circle of North America (ICNA), and the International Institute of Islamic Thought (IIIT).

The U.S. Mosque Survey 2011 is part of a larger study of American congregations called Faith Communities Today (FACT), which is a project of Cooperative Congregational Studies Partnership, a multi-faith coalition of denominations and faith groups.To conduct the survey, researchers counted all mosques in America and then conducted telephone interviews with a sample of mosque leaders.

Ihsan Bagby, a professor at the University of Kentucky and lead author of the study, was quoted by AP assaying that the findings show Muslims are carving out a place for themselves despite the backlash. "This is a growing, healthy Muslim community that is well integrated into America," Bagby said. "I think that is the best message we can send to the world and the Muslim world in particular."

Appendix I

The Mosque in America: A National Portrait 2000

Prof. Ihsan Bagby, Associate Professor of Islamic Studies at the University of Kentucky was also the author of "The Mosque in America: A National Portrait," a survey released in April 2001

Mosques in the United States: **1,209**

American Muslims associated with a mosque: **2 million**

Increase in number of mosques since 1994: **25 percent**

Proportion of mosques founded since 1980: **62 percent**

Average number of Muslims associated with each mosque in the United States: **1,625**

U.S. mosque participants who are converts: **30 percent**

American Muslims who "strongly agree" that they should participate in American institutions and the political process: **70 percent**

U.S. mosques attended by a single ethnic group: **7 percent**

U.S. mosques that have some Asian, African-American, and Arab members: **nearly 90 percent**

Ethnic origins of regular participants in U.S. mosques:
South Asian (Pakistani, Indian, Bangladeshi, Afghani) = 33%
African-America = 30 percent
Arab = 25 percent

Sub-Saharan African = 3.4 percent

European (Bosnian, Tartar, Kosovar, etc.) = 2.1 percent

White American = 1.6 percent

Southeast Asian (Malaysian, Indonesian, Filipino) = 1.3%

Caribbean = 1.2 percent

Turkish = 1.1 percent

Iranian = 0.7 percent

Hispanic/Latino = 0.6 percent

- U.S. mosques that feel they strictly follow the Koran and Sunnah: **more than 90 percent**
- U.S. mosques that feel the Koran should be interpreted with consideration of its purposes and modern circumstances: **71 percent**
- U.S. mosques that provide some assistance to the needy: **nearly 70 percent**
- U.S. mosques with a full-time school: **more than 20 percent**

Source: The "Mosque in America: A National Portrait," a survey released in April 2001. It is part of larger study of American congregations called "Faith Communities Today," coordinated by Hartford Seminary's Hartford Institute for Religious Research in Connecticut. Muslim organizations cosponsoring the survey are the Council on American-Islamic Relations, the Islamic Society of North America, the Ministry of Imam W. Deen Muhammed, and the Islamic Circle of North America.

Appendix II

Muslim immigration to the USA

Historically, Muslims have been a part of American society at least since early 17th century when many Muslims journeyed in the first slave ships to Virginia coast. By the eighteenth century there were many thousands of them, working as salves on plantations. These early muslims, cut off from their heritage and families, inevitably lost their Islamic identity as time went by.

The late nineteenth century, however, saw the beginnings of an influx of Arab Muslims, most of whom settled in the major industrial centers where they worshipped in hired rooms. According to Yvonne Y. Haddad the author of A Century of Islam in America, the 20th century witnessed four waves of immigrants from various parts of the Muslim world, most notably Palestine, Lebanon and Pakistan.

In the first wave, from 1875-1912, Syrian, Lebanese and Jordanian laborers migrated and became factory workers and peddlers. The first wave ended with the First World War. In 1924 the door to non-European immigration clanged nearly shut.

The first wave came primarily from what was known as the Greater Syria, which was later divided into Syria, Lebanon, Jordan and Palestine. Most were migrant laborers, uneducated, unskilled, and from peasant backgrounds. Motivated by success stories brought back from Lebanese Christians who had preceded them, they expected to achieve a degree of financial prosperity and then return to their native countries. Historic events periodically interrupted this flow of immigration and changed its character.

During the early 20th century, several hundred thousand Eastern European Muslims immigrated to the United States. The first Albanian mosque was constructed in Maine in 1915, and another followed in 1919 in Connecticut. In 1926 Polish Muslims constructed a mosque in Brooklyn, New York which is still in use today. The Albanian Muslims were also responsible for creating one of the first Islamic associations for Muslims in the United States.

Appendix II: Muslim immigration to the US [222]

By 1920, Arab immigrants worshipped in a rented hall in Cedar Rapids, Iowa and they build a mosque of their own 15 years later. Lebanese-Syrian communities did the same in Ross, North Dakota and later in Detroit, Pittsburgh and Michigan City. Islam had come to America's heartland. The Muslim immigration virtually stopped in 1924, when the Asian Exclusion Act and the Johnson-Reed Immigration Act allowed only a trickle of "Asians," as Arabs were designated, to enter the nation.

In the second wave, from 1930-1938, Arabs from across the Middle East arrive as laborers. The second wave was brought to a halt by the Second World War. During much of this time, immigration laws were blatantly discriminatory. Some hopeful immigrants were turned back at Ellis Island, and in many cases Middle Easterners found it difficult to obtain citizenship. At one point, they were denied citizenship because officials, using the criteria of color and shape of nose could not determine which race they belonged to. Restrictive laws limited the number who were allowed to enter, with preference given to relatives of earlier immigrants.

The third wave from 1947-1960: Palestinians, Egyptians and Eastern European Muslims arrive. Many were well educated. The third wave of immigration, which took place between 1947 and the mid-1960s, affected changing circumstances in Muslim countries. Many who left their homes during this period did so to escape political oppression. Unlike the earlier immigrants, they were often well-educated and from influential families. The largest group consisted of Palestinians displaced by Israel, but there were many from other lands, such as Egyptians whose property had been nationalized by Naser; Iraqis fleeing their country after the 1958 revolution; Syrians of high position who had been excluded from government participation; and East European Muslims from countries like Yugoslavia, Albania and the Soviet Union, escaping from communist rule.

Then, beginning in the 1950's, an influx of Muslim professionals, many of them physicians, finding conditions in their homelands inhospitable, settled in this country after completing their studies. The black movements, the back-to-Africa groups, had come into flower by this time. Great numbers of Muslim students from all parts of the world also began to arrive in this country. This was the period which saw the formation of the early Muslim communities and mosques in such places as Detroit, Ann Arbor, Gary (Indiana), Cedar Rapids (Iowa), Sacramento and the like. Visiting scholars and missionary groups from the Middle East and the Indo-Pakistan subcontinent also began to arrive. Islam began, in a very slow manner, to gain adherents among white Americans. It was this period which also witnessed the formation of national Islamic groups, such as the Muslim Students Association (MSA) of the United States and Canada, later to be replaced by the Islamic Society of North America (ISNA), and their supporting institutions.

The fourth wave from 1967-Present: In 1965 the Johnson Administration introduced many changes in the immigration laws that initiated the third wave of immigration, which continues to the present. Muslims from Asia (primarily the Indian sub-continent), the Arab world and Africa arrive. Most are educated professionals or come as students and remain. The number of Muslims in America was estimated at a quarter million by 1960, but it was only after the liberalization of immigration laws in 1965 that their numbers really increased.

According to the many changes in the immigration laws, the requirements of the U.S. labor market and a potential immigrant's ability to fill established need became major determinants of the would-be immigrants admissibility. Thus, the fourth wave, consists mainly of those who were educated, fluid in English, and Westernized. They came from a wide variety of countries, including many beyond the Middle East. These Muslims have not come to make a fortune and return home, but to settle, to participate in American affluence, and to obtain higher education and advanced technical training for specialized work opportunities. Many were also seeking freedom from what they saw as oppressive ideologies in their places of origin. There are of course some exceptions such as some of the Lebanese Shi'ahs and Palestinians displaced by the conflict in Lebanon, most of whom are illiterate and unskilled. Hence during this period Muslim immigration to America had a direct relationship with the political turmoil in many countries of the Muslim world such as exodus of Palestinians, the 1979 revolution in Iran, the pro-Soviet coup in Afghanistan in 1978 and the Lebanese civil war.

The Muslims from the first two waves were rapidly assimilated, and nothing is left of their presence save a few town names and mosques in scattered places. The third wave built many of the older mosques that are still in use in the great urban centers of the US and Canada. The fourth and final wave has been active in political and social affairs in their communities and in the nation at large. Most of the mosques and Islamic schools on this continent were built as a result of their efforts.

At present, the number of Muslims in the United States is estimated at about 8 million. It is the fastest growing faith in this country. The ten states with the highest concentration of Muslims are California, New York, Illinois, New Jersey, Indiana, Michigan, Virginia, Texas, Ohio and Maryland (listed in order of population). This represents 3.3 million of the Muslim population in the United States.

Most Muslim Americans are first generation immigrants. This new ethnic group, because of modern transportation and communication, has the ability to stay in touch with the "old world" in a way that was not possible for the traditional ethnic groups of America who migrated from Europe. Muslim immigrant groups, then, are living in two worlds. Their children, however, are fast exerting efforts to socialize as Muslim Americans as they grow up, so that they will retain their religious and cultural identity.

Today, American Muslims are very young, with 74% under age 50; highly educated, with 58% holding college degrees; extremely successful, with 50% earning more than $50,000 annually; and involved, in the political process with nearly 80% registered to vote. There are over 1,200 mosques in the United States, and around 2 million Muslims are associated with them. Demonstrating the rapid growth of the Muslim faith in the United States, over 60% of the Mosques were founded after 1980, and 25% since 1994. A recent independent survey conducted by the Hartford Institute for Religious Research showed that almost one-third of U.S. Muslims are converts (30%) and that the mosques are rarely places attended by just one ethnic group. The vast majority of American mosques are places where people of vastly different backgrounds come together, united by their faith.

Appendix III

Evolution of American Muslim institutions and organizations

By Abdus Sattar Ghazali

Early Islamic Centers in the United States

The development of Islamic institutions and centers in the United States came about slowly because the number of Muslims in proportion to the total population has been relatively small (and estimated 30,000 in 1954 and somewhere 100,000 in the early 1970's). Immigrants who came to amass wealth and return to their homelands were not interested were not interested in establishing institutions; their allegiance remained with their families at home, which they helped support financially.

Those Muslims who did decide to settle in this country, however began to think of developing institutions and organizations to preserve and maintain their faith and to instruct their children. Individuals in different areas took the initiative: Abdullah Ingram in Cedar Rapids, Iowa: Muhammad Omar in Quincy, Massachusetts; and J. Howar in Washington, DC.

The earliest recorded group who organized for communal prayer in private homes was in Ross, North Dakota in 1900. By 1920 they had built a mosque. Later they became so integrated into the community that they assumed Christian names, married Christians and in 1948 the mosque was abandoned.

Soon after, in 1919, an Islamic association developed in highland Park, Michigan, to be followed by one in Detroit in 1922, then by the American Muhammedan Society (of Tatar origin) in Brooklyn in 1922, the Young Men's Muslim Association (Arab) in Brooklyn in 1923, and the Arab Banner Society of Quincy in 1930.

Islam & Muslims in the Post 9/11 America

Appendix III: Evolution of Muslim institutions [226]

American Muslim organizations

The end of World War II saw the arrival of large numbers of Muslim students from all parts of the Islamic world, on American university campuses. Initially small Muslim student associations were established on some campuses. A real effort to set up a national organization began in 1963 with the establishment of the Muslim Student Association (MSA). *(1)*

It was at this time that Ayatollah Ruhollah Khomeini was expelled from Iran, Maulana Maudoodi was sentenced to death in Pakistan, Sayed Qutb of the Muslim Brotherhood was jailed and later executed in Egypt, the Masjumi Party was banned in Indonesia and the Algerian revolution was coming to a head. All of these developments had a very strong reaction among the Muslim students in Europe and America. *(2)*

The MSA launched an "action plan," setting up offices across the country with initial headquarters in Gary, Indiana. In 1975, the MSA acquired property in Plainsfield, Indiana and moved there. This also was the period when the North American Islamic Trust (NAIT) was created to hold title to MSA properties such as Islamic centers, the American Trust Publications, the International Graphics Press and the Islamic Book Service. *(3)*

In 1981 the Islamic Society of North America (ISNA) was formed to deal with all aspects of Islamic activity in the country, allowing MSA to concentrate on the campuses. Professional activities are now coordinated through such organizations as the American Muslim Social Scientists (AMSS), the American Muslim Engineers and Scientists (AMES), and the Islamic Medical Association (IMA). (4)

The United Muslims of America (UMA) (UMA) was established in 1982 in the aftermath of Israel's invasion of Lebanon. There was no Muslim political organization at that time. Some Bay Area Muslims realized the need for a Muslim public affairs organization to educate and encourage American Muslims to participate in the political system, and to reach out to the mainstream Americans and build the bridges of understanding between them and the Muslim community. Dr. Islam Siddiqee was the first President and one of the founders of UMA. Others included, Marghoob Qureshi, Dr.

Islam & Muslims in the Post 9/11 America

Appendix III: Evolution of Muslim institutions [227]

Waheed Siddiqee, Mr. Bawani Dr. Joseph DiCaprio, Late Ghafoor Serang, Late Siraj Kadri, Late Sayed Saifullah, Maqsud Al Haq, Javed Ellahie, and Iftekhar Hai.

While there had been attempts to form political action committees, none took hold until the late 1980s and early 1990s when Muslim Americans stepped up their efforts to gain a foothold in the American political system. By that time, many had realized that they risked being socially and politically sidelined or excluded if they didn't get involved. American Muslim political groups lobbied Congress on behalf of Muslim Americans and their issues; educated Muslim American voters; and addressed the political concerns and rights of predominantly immigrant and first-generation American Muslims, whose interests often remained focused abroad. Specifically, four major U.S. Muslim organizations emerged during this time: the Muslim Political Affairs Council (MPAC), the American Muslim Council (AMC), the Council on American-Islamic Relations (CAIR) and the American Muslim Alliance (AMA).

Election year 1988 saw the emergence of various Muslim political action groups foremost among them the Muslim Political Affairs Council "to work for the civil rights of American Muslims and for the integration of Islam into American pluralism."

The American Muslim Council (AMC) was established in 1990 to increase the effective participation of American Muslims in the U.S. political and public policy arenas.

1992 witnessed the establishment of American Muslim Alliance by Dr. Agha Saeed in Hayward, CA. The AMA devoted exclusively to encouraging Muslim participation in political parties and the electoral process.

The Council on American Islamic Relations (CAIR) was established in 1994 by Omar Ahmad and Nihad Awad . The CAIR focuses on defending the civil rights of Muslims, defending Islam against stereotypes and training Muslims in news media relations. Islamic Shura Council of North America was established choosing four of the largest participants of the Bosnia

Appendix III: Evolution of Muslim institutions [228]

Professional organizations

The International Institute of Islamic Thought, an American social sciences organization founded in 1981 is headquartered in Herndon, Virginia, near Washington, D.C. It sponsors research and scholarship, organizes seminars and conferences, and publishes classical and contemporary works including the American Journal of Islamic Social Sciences. The Institute works closely with universities and organizations in North America to help with outreach programs aimed at improving the level of information and education about Islam.

The Islamic Medical Association (IMA) was formed in 1967 to provide a forum for Muslim health professionals to meet and share relevant in formation and services with others of their community as well as benefit the Muslim community. IMA publishes biannually, The Journal of the Islamic Medical Association and holds a national convention annually.

The Association of Muslim Scientists and Engineers (AMSE) was founded in 1969 to help promote scientific research and application of science based upon Islamic principles. It publishes a Newsletter and organizes an annual conference.

The Association of Muslim Social Scientists (AMSS) was formed in 1972 as a professional, academic educational, and cultural body dedicated to the initiation, revitalization, and promotion of Islamic thought. It holds art annual conference and several discipline seminars. AMSS, in cooperation with the International Institute of Islamic Thought (IIIT), publishes a journal American Journal of Islamic Social Sciences (AJISS) and a News bulletin.

References:

1. Muslims in America: The Nation's Fastest Growing Religion *by M.M. Ali* - Washington Report May/June 1996
2. Ibid.
3. Ibid.
4. Ibid.

Appendix IV

The Hidden agenda of the Gallup Poll and the PEW Institute

Opinion polls and surveys are sophisticated propaganda tools while the modus operandi for influencing any opinion and survey is now well established. From its inception a century ago, and in its current construction, the terrain of public opinion polls is far from being a neutral. An opinion poll result can be easily manipulated through:

- the wording of the questions
- the order in which they are asked and
- the number and form of alternative answers

This applies to the recent poll and survey results of Gallup Polls of August 2, 2011 and the PEW Institute survey of August 30, 2011. These surveys were released on the 10th commemoration of the 9/11 terrorist attacks.

The Abu Dhabi-based GALLUP center's poll was reported in the US mainstream media with the such headlines: Muslims in U.S. optimistic about future (Washington Post); Muslims Say They're Loyal Americans (The New York Times); Muslim Americans are most optimistic religious group (CNN); Muslims most optimistic U.S. faith group (San Francisco Chronicle) and Muslims in U.S. upbeat about future (Star Tribune).

However, very little attention was paid to the hidden agenda of the Gallup Center of Abu Dhabi. This agenda is to undermine the major American Muslim civil advocacy and religious organizations. It is a known fact that in the post-p/11 America that a consistent effort has been launched through government policies and anti-Muslim groups to undermine the most visible and active civil advocacy groups like the Council on American-Islamic Relations (CAIR) and the Islamic Society of North America (ISNA).

The Gallup Poll asked few hundred people who took part in this survey: Which national Muslim American organization, if any, do you feel most represents your interests? And the conclusion drawn from the survey was that no national Muslim American organization represents a large percentage of the Muslim community in America. The poll results said that only 12 percent consider CAIR and mere 4 percent consider ISNA as national American organizations.

It is said in the psychology of mass media: "Whoever controls the questions....controls the answers." What was the purpose of this question except to discredit and dislodge American Muslims' most prominent and active civil advocacy and religious organizations.

There has been a two-prong attack on prominent civil advocacy Muslim American organizations in the post-9/11 America. On the one hand there is a vicious attempt to undermine and discredit prominent civil advocacy Muslim American organizations while on the other hand alternate organizations are being encouraged to replace these prominent and well recognized Muslim organizations. An example: At the anti-Muslim hearings in March by Republican Rep. Peter King, CAIR was not invited to testify but a one-man organization – American Islamic Forum on Democracy - established by Arizona doctor Zuhdi Jasser, was invited to represent American Muslims. Dr. Jasser was invited because he is critical of leading Muslim American organizations like the Council on American-Islamic Relations (CAIR) that was target of the hearings. Tellingly Peter King negatively mentioned CAIR more than 50 times during the four-hour session.

The CAIR is the largest vocal Muslim civil liberties organization, modeled on the Jewish Anti-Defamation League (ADL), that has made it a target for criticism. Not surprisingly, it was named as an "unindicted co-conspirator " in the case of the Texas-based Holy Land Foundation (HLF) – one of the largest American Muslim charity that in 2008 was convicted of funding Hamas militant group. In its prosecution of the HLF, the Department of Justice took the extraordinary step of publicly filing a list naming 246 individuals and organizations as "unindicted co-conspirators." Besides CAIR, the list included the Islamic Society of North America (ISNA), America's largest mainstream Muslim community-based organization and the North American Islamic Trust (NAIT), the country's largest holding company of deeds to about 300 mosques, Islamic centers and schools in the U.S.

Appendix IV: The Hidden Agenda of PEW Institute [231]

By branding these individuals and organizations with the "terrorism" label, the government unfairly and irreparably damaged the reputation of mainstream Muslim organizations and many of the named individuals. The prosecution used McCarthyite tactics by implicating mainstream Muslim groups to silence genuine Muslim voices while providing ammunition to the anti-Muslim organizations. This was a brutal attempt to marginalize and disenfranchise mainstream Muslim groups

By asking a question about the national Muslim American organization, the Gallup Poll also attempted to undermine prominent and vocal American Muslim organizations.

The number of Muslims in the U.S.

Now let us see the hidden agenda of the PEW Center surveys.

The most misleading and agenda driven result of the latest PEW survey is regarding the estimate of Muslim population of America. The PEW survey claims that the current population of Muslim Americans is no more than 2.75 million. Not surprisingly, it is basing this calculations on its own 2007 survey that estimated the Muslim American population at 2.4 million which was closer to the estimates announced by the American Jewish Committee in October 2001.

The AJC study – titled Estimating the Muslim Population in the United States – claimed that the best estimate of Muslims in the United States is 2.8 million at most, compared to the 6 or 7 million figure used by many researchers and Muslim organizations.

The PEW surveys, just like the AJC report, seem to undercut the influence of American Muslims. It looks another desperate attempt to discount the role of American Muslims.

The PEW survey of 2007, titled "Muslim Americans: Middle Class and Mostly Mainstream," claimed to be the most extensive, covers the views of 1,050 Muslims interviewed in English, Arabic, Urdu, and Farsi. According to Luis Lugo, director of the Pew Forum, the Washington-based organization spent $1 million on the poll. It paid $50 to each of the 1,050 Muslims surveyed.

Islam & Muslims in the Post 9/11 America

Appendix IV: The Hidden Agenda of PEW Institute [232]

The PEW survey of 2011, titled, "Muslim Americans: No Signs of Growth in Alienation or Support for Extremism," is based on the interviews with 1,033 Muslim American. Interviews were conducted by telephone between April 14 and July 22, 2011 by the research firm of Abt SRBI. Interviews were conducted in English, Arabic, Farsi and Urdu.

Associated Press reporting the survey result said the findings offer an uncommon portrait of the Muslim American community, which Pew estimates at roughly 2.75 million, or nearly 1 percent of the U.S. population.

The PEW's misleading demographic figures of American Muslims already made an entry into the Wikipedia encyclopedia's article on American Muslim population estimates. Pew numbers are now quoted as authentic reference when estimate of American Muslims is given.

Religious denominations, like all interest groups, can gain or lose political clout based on perceptions of their size, according to J. Gordon Melton, director of the Institute for the Study of American Religion in Santa Barbara, Calif. In the case of the U.S. Muslim community, Melton says, its efforts to influence policy in the Middle East would get a boost if it were viewed as being larger than the country's Jewish population, which is estimated at 6 million. "It's a political question: How does it sway votes?" he argued.

The American Jewish Committee's executive director David Harris has warned that the increasingly visible American Muslim lobby posed a challenge to U.S.-Israel relations. In an article published by the Jerusalem Report in May 2001, Harris urged American Jewry to unite with Israel to battle against the growing Arab and Muslim lobbies here and the challenge they present to long-standing U.S. support for Israel. Harris cited the "myth" of high Muslim population figures as one tactic Muslims are using to advance their position.

The American Jewish Committee and other groups estimate the number of Jews in this country is about 6 million. "Six million has a special resonance," Harris wrote in the Jerusalem Report magazine. "It would mean that Muslims outnumber Jews in the U.S. and it would buttress calls for a redefinition of America's heritage as 'Judeo-Christian-Muslim,' a stated goal of some Muslim leaders."

Islam & Muslims in the Post 9/11 America

Appendix IV: The Hidden Agenda of PEW Institute [233]

The American Jewish Committee survey of Muslim population was conducted by Tom W. Smith of the National Opinion Research Center in Chicago who questioned the study, "The Mosque in America: A National Portrait," released in April 2001 by the Council on American-Islamic Relations.

The CAIR study reported that the number of mosques rose by about 25 percent, to more than 1,200, from 1994 to 2000. Based on reports of attendance at some mosques, researchers estimated the number of American Muslims at 6 million to 7 million. The project surveyed individual mosques, finding that 340 adults and children participated at the average mosque and that another 1,629 were "associated in any way" with the average mosque's activities, yielding a figure of 2 million Muslims. The authors then adjusted the estimate to 6 million to 7 million overall to take into account family members and unaffiliated Muslims.

Based in part on that report, most media organizations, as well as the White House and the State Department, have said that there are at least 6 million Muslims in the country.

CAIR's 2001 study findings were reaffirmed by another major survey of the Mosques in the United States. On February 29, 2012 a comprehensive study of the mosques - "The American Mosque 2011: Basic Characteristics of the American Mosque, Attitudes of Mosque Leaders" - was released.

Sponsors of the U.S. Mosque Survey 2011 include: The Hartford Institute for Religion Research (Hartford Seminary), the Association of Statisticians of American Religious Bodies (ASARB), the Council on American-Islamic Relations (CAIR), the Islamic Society of North American (ISNA), the Islamic Circle of North America (ICNA), and the International Institute of Islamic Thought (IIIT). The U.S. Mosque Survey 2011 is part of a larger study of American congregations called Faith Communities Today (FACT), which is a project of Cooperative Congregational Studies Partnership, a multi-faith coalition of denominations and faith groups.

One of the major finding of the study is related to the estimated population of American Muslims. The study finds: "Muslims who attend Eid Prayer (the high holiday prayers after Ramadan and Hajj) increased from about 2 million

Appendix IV: The Hidden Agenda of PEW Institute [234]

in 2000 to about 2.6 million in 2011. The total Muslim population cannot be determined by this figure, but it does call into question the low estimates of 1.1-2.4 million Muslims in America. If there are 2.6 million Muslims who pray the Eid prayer, then the total Muslim population should be closer to the estimates of up to 7 million."

It may be recalled that the former Congressman, Paul Findley, in his book Silent No More: Confronting America's False Images of Islam, estimates that about 3.2 million Muslims turned out for vote and 65 percent voted for President Bush in November 2000 elections. According to Mr. Findley "Best estimates put the national Muslim population at seven million, 70 as the percentage of those eligible to vote, and 65 as the percentage of those eligible who actually voted. This means that the national turnout of Muslims on Nov.7, 2000 came to 3.2 million."

It is important not to overlook the positive aspects of the Gallup and PEW surveys which clearly showed that American Muslims are mainstream, highly educated, middle-class people who believe that hard work pays off. It also confirmed that, overall, American Muslims have a positive view of the larger society. They are overwhelmingly satisfied with their lives in the United States, and most say their communities are excellent or good places to live.

Not surprisingly, the Associated Press, reporting about the latest American Mosques study tried to give credence to the biased PEW estimates about the population of American Muslims while undermined the estimates of the latest Mosque study. The AP report said: "the estimates of the total American Muslim population have become a contentious issue as Muslims seek to have a voice in public life. The U.S. Census does not ask about religion. Pew conducted a survey last year that estimated the American Muslim community encompassed 2.75 million people, or nearly 1 percent of the U.S. population, a finding similar to that of other recent surveys. Bagby's 2000 report had estimated the U.S. Muslim population to be as high as 7 million, a number widely criticized as inflated. In this latest report, Bagby did not report a definitive population number, but stood by his earlier assertion that the United States could be home to as many 7 million Muslims."
[American Muslim Perspective Comment – September 18, 2011/updated March 1, 2012]

Islam & Muslims in the Post 9/11 America

Appendix V

American Muslims in politics

1 - American Muslim political activism

Although the population of Muslims in America increased substantially by the1970s because of massive immigration from the Middle East and South Asia but the new Muslim immigrants showed little interest in domestic issues. Instead, their focus remained on their homelands and U.S. foreign policy issues affecting the Islamic world such as the Palestine-Israel conflict; U.S. sanctions against Iraq; and conflicts in Kashmir and Chechnya. Their community activities were confined to the building of mosques and Islamic centers.

African American Muslims, on the other hand, generally tend to focus on domestic issues, such as urban development, education, and economic and racial justice. Given their disparate interests and priorities, formulating a united political platform between the two Muslim groups was not easy.

In the 1980s, as the Muslim Americans began to take the initial steps toward political participation, some questioned whether Islam even permitted them to participate in the political life of a non-Muslim country. That concern all but disappeared starting in the 1990s. Today this debate has taken a backseat as the majority of Muslim-Americans face the political reality that nonparticipation could lead to exclusion and denial of rights. (1)

For the first time, Muslim Americans flexed their political muscles in different constituencies in 1990s. In New York, Pakistani taxi drivers organized an alignment and campaigned to defeat Congressman Stephen J. Solarz. The nine-term congressman was the most vocal leader of the Indian lobby in Congress. He lost his congressional seat to some determined Pakistani activists who were still learning the ropes of politics in the Big Apple. Although his campaign fund was greater than the aggregate of all five opponents, he was defeated. Pakistanis' campaign against him paid off in favor of one of the Spanish candidates in a newly constituted seat. That was

Appendix V: American Muslims in politics [236]

1992. The first time, probably, when any Muslim group made a successful effort in any US election. (2)

In 1996 Bill Clinton (at least as compared with Bob Dole) had earned the vote of U.S. Muslims because he had gone further than any other president in U.S. history to give Islam some standing as an integral part of American society. But this was Clinton not as a Democrat but as a pro-Muslim initiator. He had started the process of going beyond the political convention of treating the United States as a Judeo-Christian community only. In personal behavior Clinton fell below Islamic standards of family values, but in official behavior he was a particularly ecumenical President of the United States. (3)

Under his watch, President Clinton recognized a major Islamic institution within the U.S. - the fast of Ramadan. He sent an open letter to believers wishing them a blessed fast. Under the Clinton watch, the White House for the first time ever celebrated Eid el Fitr to mark the end of Ramadan at which the first lady recognized the increasing expansion of the Muslim community within the United States and wished Muslims well. (4)

Under Clinton's watch the first Muslim chaplains of the U.S. military were appointed - with the major participation of the American Muslim Council. Under Clinton's watch Arab and Muslim Americans met with the President of the United States and discussed issues of Arab and Muslim concern. Under Clinton's watch Muslim representatives were received by Anthony Lake of the National Security Council and explored with him the implications of U.S. policy towards Bosnia. (5)

However, the Clinton-Gore administration did not come the rescue of Salam Al-Marayati, an American Muslim whose appointment to the National Commission on Terrorism was reversed due to Zionist pressure on Democratic Congressman Richard Gephardt? (6)

While in foreign policy Clinton was no less friendly to Israel than any other U.S. president, in domestic policy he was more Muslim-friendly than any other president in the history of the United States. Those Muslims who voted

Appendix V: American Muslims in politics [237]

for him in 1996 instead of for Bob Dole might have taken some of such factors into account. (7)

In 1996 also, Muslims in New Jersey endorsed Richard Zimmer, a Republican candidate in an open Senate seat. But concerned about Jewish votes, Zimmer announced that he did not ask for the Muslim community's endorsement. Upon hearing this, Muslims withdrew their endorsement and put their support behind the Democratic candidate, Robert Torricelli. This candidate won the elections with a slight margin and publicly acknowledged that his success was due to the support of the Muslim community. (8)

Muslims in New Jersey, in 1990s, continued to make good electoral choices through their bloc votes. While doing that they have effectively created a counter voter bloc on which candidates can rely upon. Governor Christine Todd Whitman of New Jersey is a regular guest at Muslim events in New Jersey, of course with a scarf covered head. New Jersey was the first state in which Halal food laws were passed. (9)

"Muslims beginning to embrace politics" was the title of an article written by Mary Otto in Free Press Washington on October 31, 1998. He wrote: "America's millions of Muslims -- adherents to possibly the nation's fastest-growing religion -- are gradually learning to embrace politics. The change can be seen in the hopeful politicians who flock to meet voters in Detroit-area mosques and in California Islamic centers. At Muslim gatherings across the country, thousands of people have registered to vote. And, in a departure from the past, some Muslims are entering politics themselves, and the professionals among them are learning to exercise their financial clout."

In May 1998, four major American Muslim political organizations – American Muslim Alliance, American Muslim Council, the Council on American-Islamic Affairs and Muslim Public Affairs Council – formed the American Muslim Political Coordination Council (AMPCC) to coordinate their policies. And on January 23, 1999, a joint meeting of Council of Presidents of Arab Organizations and the American Muslim Political Coordination Council, in Washington, DC, brought together nine major political organizations which

Appendix V: American Muslims in politics [238]

included: the Arab American Institute (AAI.), the Association of Arab American University Graduates (AAUG), the American Arab Anti-Discrimination Committee (ADC), the American Muslim Alliance (AMA), the American Muslim Council (AMC), the Council on American Islamic Relations (CAIR), the Coalition for Good Government (CFGG), the Muslim Pubic Affairs Council (MPAC), and the National Association of Arab Americans, (NAAA). They identified 4 areas of coordination and cooperation: The future of Jerusalem; Civil and human rights; Arab and Muslim participation in the electoral process; and Access and inclusion in political structures.

The coalition of the nine American Muslim and Arab-American groups, in 1999, launched an effort to register Muslim voters in anticipation of the year-2000 election. The American Muslim Council has assembled a voter registration kit to facilitate the registration process. The American Muslim Alliance devoted its second annual leadership conference in Detroit to political education and to raising awareness in the minds of elected legislators of the presence of the Muslim community in America. They covered skills related to campaigning, critical evaluation of local politics, comparison of the political programs of the major parties and coalition building. (10)

But how should the Muslims vote?

According to a John Zogby poll of 2000, 46 percent of Muslims said they are Democrats, compared with 39 percent of all Americans, and 16 percent said they are Republicans, compared to 34 percent of all Americans. The number of independent Muslims, at 26 percent was almost exactly the same as among all Americans. The liberal, moderate, conservative and very conservative numbers, as well, mirrored the general American population.

Research shows that prior to 1990, Muslims voted overwhelmingly for the Republican Party and the American Muslims continue to display conservative tendencies on a range of economic and social issues. A 1996 survey commissioned by the American Muslim Council and the Middle East Broadcasting Company showed that just over 50 percent of those polled supported recently enacted welfare reforms while only 26 percent opposed the legislation. At the same time Muslims tend to be strongly pro-family, fiscally conservative, anti-abortion and do not oppose the death penalty. (11)

During the last six years, however, a significant shift has taken place in the voting habits of American Muslims. In 1996, most of the roughly one million who are registered have set aside their conservative inclinations to vote for Bill Clinton by a margin of two-to-one (in some polls the ratio was three-to-one). This dramatic shift should not be overstated, however Clinton's relative success among Muslims despite their natural antipathy towards his policies and values is the result of a vigorous campaign on the part of the White House combined with a sense of alienation by the Republicans. Muslim have, by and large, felt unwelcome in the Republican Party in recent years as a result of widespread, stereotypical and xenophobic attitudes towards Islam and Muslims at all levels of the Party. (12)

Dr. Ali Mazrui argues that the Muslims should avoid the mistake which African Americans have made for much of the twentieth century - that of being predictably for one political party and having nowhere else to go. In recent decades African-American votes have been too predictably identified with the Democratic Party - with the result that neither party has tried very hard to court their vote. They have simply tried not to alienate them completely. Muslim voters should behave differently. They should use the vote as a leverage to reward those who take Muslim concerns seriously and to punish those who ignore those concerns. In some years more Democrats may deserve Muslim support than Republicans; in other years the Republicans may turn out to be the more Muslim-friendly. (13)

Muslims, in keeping with traditional Islamic teachings, are usually conservative on moral issues. Muslims in America tend to oppose abortion and homosexual rights and espouse some version of the "family values" so often touted by American conservatives. However, many Muslims feel caught between the two major political parties. According to Sulayman Nyang, an African studies professor at Howard University and a frequent

Appendix V: American Muslims in politics [240]

commentator on Muslim issues, "Muslims are Republicans on family values, but Democrats on social welfare." (14)

American politics is, at once, simple as well as very complex. The domination by the Democratic and Republican parties simplifies the ideological spectrum. If you are on the right, you go with the Grand Old Party (GOP), and if you are on the left, you go with the Democrats. As Muslims, we can be on both sides of the spectrum. Remember Amir Muawiyyah (RAH) - he was very much on the right. And remember Abu Dharr (RAH) - he was very much on the left. However, the freedom that politicians enjoy to vote their conscience, while making the matter interesting, brings complexity and unpredictability to the system. To navigate through this unpredictability, we must not only closely follow the issues; we must follow the records of politicians too. (15)

The good news is that the deliberation over policy issues has become more and more publicized and inclusive. Candidates participate in literally hundreds of town meetings to present their views and hear from the public. We as Muslims must go to these meetings and participate. Let the candidates hear our concerns. Most importantly, we must let them know that we are there and that we are as powerful as any other American. We must exercise our political rights and demand that they accommodate our needs and interests. (16)

In the 2000 presidential elections, Muslim Americans made history when, at the advice of their leadership, voted in bloc for George Bush. At the present moment, some Muslims support the social justice agenda of traditional Democrats while others support the Republicans' conservatism on social issues. Still others find that Green Party has the best policies, an excellent record and provides them with the protest vote option. However, if Muslims' voting choice is based solely on policy issues then their votes are bound to be divided. On the other hand, if the goal is to empower Muslims as one voting bloc, then Muslims will have to look at which vote will get them recognition as political players. A bloc vote does not mean 100 percent of Muslim votes. If Muslims are able to deliver 60 to 70 percent of their votes to

Appendix V: American Muslims in politics [241]

any candidate, that will be a milestone in the process of empowerment of Muslims in America, whether that candidate wins or not. (17)

Encouraged by the 2000 bloc vote, the American Muslim organizations charted an ambitious plan to launch a massive registration campaign to register Muslim voters and contest at least 200 seats in 2002 mid term elections. However, after the 9/11 tragic attacks the Muslim community found itself besieged by profiling, official discrimination, negative media campaign and hate crimes. Consequently, the number of Muslim candidates in November 2002 elections was much smaller as compared to the 2000 elections. In 2000, 152 candidates for various public offices were elected out of about 700 candidates. In 2002, only ten candidates out of about 70 were elected to various public offices which include one State Senator and three State Assemblymen and one judge of the Superior Court. (18)

Gaining political influence requires three main steps: fundraising, recruiting candidates and voting. The American Muslim community's performance on fundraising for candidates and recruiting candidates to contest various offices was not appreciable in 2004 Election. However, the community was more active politically. This is the silver lining to 9/11, the Patriot Act and the mass detentions. It has pushed us to be proactive and take a stand, to be part of the political process. Now the Muslims are realizing that America's politics is about numbers: dollars you donate to your favorite candidates, or votes you can generate for them. Although their campaign fundraisers produced meager results but they were able to mobilize the community to get out and vote. Disenchanted by President Bush's policies, Muslims voted for Democratic candidate John Kerry. (19)

The seven-million-strong American Muslim community got a big political push when the Minnesota Democrat Keith Ellison was elected as the nation's first Muslim member to the US Congress in November 7, 2006 elections. Ellison's election was accompanied by a massive turnout of the American Muslim voters to make their voices heard. (20)

Appendix V: American Muslims in politics [242]

Throughout most of their American experience, members of the Muslim community have refrained from fully engaging in civic society. This is now changing. American Muslims are moving from the margins to the mainstream. At the beginning of 2008, we see that the American Muslims have overcome many formidable obstacles in their struggle for political enfranchisement. However, the journey is far from over.

Appendix V: American Muslims in politics [243]

References

1. Media Guide to Islam, San Francisco State University
2. How a bloc vote will empower Muslims in America? by Abdul Malik Mujahid - Palestine Times - November 2000
3. On Being An American and a Muslim: Dilemmas of Politics and Culture By Ali A. Mazrui
4. Ibid.
5. Ibid.
6. Our Community Has Never Been More Powerful! *By A. Omar Turbi* Washington Report on Mideast - October/November 2000
7. Mazrui
8. Mujahid
9. Ibid.
10. American Muslim engagement in politics By Imad-ad-Dean Ahmad of Minaret of Freedom Institute
11. Islamic Institute
12. Ibid.
13. Mazrui
14. Ira Rifkin, "Muslims and the Ballot Box: Party Ties Nothing Sacred for Believers in America," *Dallas Morning News* 17 August 1996
15. How Can Muslims Impact American Politics? By Muqtedar Khan – Islamonline.com - April 11, 2000
16. Ibid.
17. Mujahid.
18. AMP Report
19. Ibid.
20. Ibid.

Appendix V: American Muslims in politics [244]

2 - American Muslim bloc vote in 2000 elections

American Muslims made history in 2000 presidential elections when they voted en bloc for George Bush. The American Muslim Political Coordinating Council Political Action Committee (AMPCC-PAC), a coalition of four major American Muslim organizations, only two weeks before the election announced its endorsement of George W. Bush for president, citing his outreach to the Muslim community and his stand on the issue of secret evidence.

In a post-election survey of American Muslim voters conducted by the Washington, DC-based Council on American-Islamic Relations (CAIR), one of the nation's largest grassroots Muslim advocacy and civil rights groups, nearly three-quarters of respondents indicated that they had voted for Texas Governor Bush. Of these, 85 percent noted that the endorsement of Bush by the American Muslim Political Coordinating Committee Political Action Committee (AMPCC-PAC) was a factor in their vote. In this survey of 1,774 voters, 72 percent of Muslim respondents said they voted for Bush, 19 percent supported Green Party candidate Ralph Nader, and only 8 percent favored Vice President Al Gore. Muslims, therefore, became the only bloc vote for Bush.

The former Congressman, Paul Findley, in his book Silent No More: Confronting America's False Images of Islam, estimates that about 3.2 million Muslims turned out for vote and 65 percent voted for President Bush. Mr. Findley said: The importance of Muslim bloc voting arises from its magnitude as well as its focus. Best estimates put the national Muslim population at seven million, 70 as the percentage of those eligible to vote, and 65 as the percentage of those eligible who actually voted. This means that the national turnout of Muslims on Nov.7 came to 3.2 million.

Here is an excerpt from Paul Findley's analysis of Muslim bloc vote:

Appendix V: American Muslims in politics [245]

George W. Bush should thank Florida Muslims for opening his way to the White House. Responding to a national campaign, they discarded normal Democratic Party allegiance and voted as a block for the Republican from Texas, providing him with a statewide net gain in Florida of more than 64,000 Muslim votes.

Had they not voted as a bloc, Vice President Al Gore would have emerged as the clear winner shortly after the polls closed on Nov. 7 (2000). There would have been no recounts, no long, divisive wrangling in state and federal courts. Even with dimpled ballots left uncounted, Gore's Florida total would have substantially topped the Texas governor's, giving the vice president the majority of the nation's electoral votes and quick certification as president-elect.

A June poll showed a slight national Muslim preference for Gore, but an intensive campaign that began on Sept. 3 transformed Muslim sympathies into a nine-to-one landslide for Bush when votes were counted. In Florida, the state that proved pivotal in the ultimate certification of the president-elect, Bush's Muslim margin was even greater.

The importance of Muslim bloc voting arises from its magnitude as well as its focus. Best estimates put the national Muslim population at seven million, 70 as the percentage of those eligible to vote, and 65 as the percentage of those eligible who actually voted. This means that the national turnout of Muslims on Nov.7 came to 3.2 million.

According to an exit poll of 1,774 Muslims, 72 percent voted for Bush and 8 per cent for Gore. This means an estimated 2.3 million Muslims voted for Bush and only 2576,000 voted for Gore, a national net gain for Bush in excess of two million.

The Muslim impact in Florida was even more impressive. Accepting the assumptions used in the national analysis and 200,000 as the Muslim population in Florida, 140,000 Muslims were eligible and 91,000 actually voted. If 80 percent - a conservative estimate - supported Bush, this means he received 72,000 Muslim votes. If 8 percent - a generous estimate - voted for Gore, his total vote came to 7,238. In Florida, the net Muslim vote for Bush topped 64,000. Of the total Muslim vote, 26,000 were from first-time voters. The national exit poll of Muslims showed that 36 percent cast ballots for the first time.

A December 1999 survey of Muslim voters showed only 25 percent for Bush

Muslims entered the presidential arena in earnest because they were troubled by challenges to their civil rights at home and to their interests in the Holy Land - especially Jerusalem. They responded to these issues rather than to party or personality. Early in the year, polls showed the Democratic Party more popular among Muslims than the Republican Party. Their hearts, however, belonged to Green Party candidate Ralph Nader, who condemned Israel for excessive force against Palestinian protesters and was the first Arab American to run for President.

Although sympathetic to a number of Gore's domestic positions, Muslims were upset over his attachment to Israel, particularly his unequivocal acceptance of Jerusalem as its exclusive capital, and what they perceived as his lack of concern for the plight of Palestinians. Muslims see Israel's control of East Jerusalem as a continuing threat to Haram al-Sharif, one of Islam's holiest shrines.

On election day, Muslims pinned their hopes for improved Middle East policies on Bush and were pleased when he promised to halt the use of secret evidence in deportation hearings, a policy Muslims considered especially offensive because they viewed it as directed mainly at their community.

The most important factor that led Muslims to vote as a bloc for Bush was the unity and perseverance of the leaders of four principal public policy

Appendix V: American Muslims in politics [247]

organizations: the American Muslim Alliance (AMA), the Council of American-Islamic Relations (CAIR), the American Muslim Council (AMC), and the Muslim Public Affairs Council (MPAC). In participating, two of the leaders - Dr. Agha Saeed, founder and chairman of AMA and the chief enginer of Muslim bloc voting, and Salman Al Marayati, national director of MPAC - departed from their customary allegiance to the Democratic Party. CAIR was represented by Oman Ahmad and Nihad Awad and AMC by Yahya Basha, M.D.

Banding together at the American Muslim Political Coordination Council (AMPACC), they organized voter-education and registration drives early in the spring primary campaigns. In the late spring and summer of 2000, they sponsored workshops in major cities for candidates campaign volunteers and prospective voters.

Over Labor Day weekend at Chicago's O'Hare Airport, they won enthusiastic support for bloc voting for president from an audience of more than 10,000 Muslims. Hoping for personal interviews with both Bush and Gore, they delayed their recommendation for president until two weeks before Election Day.

Their decision followed an interview with Bush in Detroit on Oct. 5, during which he promised to listen to their policy concerns. Gore canceled a scheduled interview. News of their endorsement was circulated through e-mails, notices in mosques and Islamic centers, and sermons by imams during congregational prayers on the Friday before the election….

152 Muslims elected to local & state offices in 2000

According to American Muslim Alliance, about 700 Muslim Americans ran for various local, state and federal offices in the 2000 elections. At least 152 of them were elected to local and state offices. These individuals were elected as members of precinct committees, delegates to Democratic and

Appendix V: American Muslims in politics [248]

Republican party conventions, city councils, state assemblies, state senates, and judgeships. Ninety-two of these were elected from Texas.

Mr. Saghir Tahir, President of the New Hampshire Chapter of the American Muslim Alliance – one of the leading American Muslim organization, was elected to the State Assembly from the 38 District. Mr. Larry Shaw, the highest-ranking elected Muslim in America, was re-elected unopposed in North Carolina. Judge David Shakoor was also re-elected to his judicial post. AMA New Jersey Activist Hassan Fahmy was elected to Prospect Park City Council. American Muslim voter turn out exceeded the national average and, at least, 40% of the Muslims who voted in the year 2000 presidential election did so for the first time. As estimated through AMA's post-election telephone survey, more than 80% of the Muslim Americans cast their votes for George W. Bush. About 10% voted for Ralph Nader.

3 - Few Muslim candidates in November 2002 elections

Encouraged by the 2000 bloc vote, the American Muslim organizations charted an ambitious plan to launch a massive registration campaign to register Muslim voters and contest at least 200 seats in 2002 mid term elections. However, after the 9/11 tragic attacks the Muslim community found itself besieged by profiling, official discrimination, negative media campaign and hate crimes.

Consequently, the number of Muslim candidates in November 2002 elections was much smaller as compared to the 2000 elections. In 2000, 152 candidates for various public offices were elected out of about 700 candidates. In 2002, ten candidates out of about 70 elected to various public offices which included one State Senator and three State Assemblymen and one judge of the Superior Court.

According to the American Muslim Alliance, the 2002 candidates which included:

Appendix V: American Muslims in politics [249]

1. Three candidates for US Congress – Mr. Syed Mahmood (13th District CA), Mr. Maad Abu Ghazalah (12th District CA), Mr. Ekram Yusri (5th District, New Jersey
2. Three candidates for State Assemblies, three for State Senates
3. One for Governor (Washington State), Dr. Mohammad Saeed
4. One for Judgeship, David Shaheed - Indiana
5. One for County Commissioner, Nasim Ansari (Michigan)
6. 10 for city and township councils

The following candidates were elected:

Mr. Larry Shaw, State Senate, North Carolina

Ms. Yaphett El-Amin, State Assembly Missouri

Mr. Rodney Hubbard, State Assembly Missouri

Mr. Saghir Tahir, State Assembly, New Hampshire

Judge David Shaeed, Judge Superior Court Indiana

Mr. Wayne Smith, Mayor of Irvington, New Jersey

Mr. Nasim Ansari, County Commissioner, Michigan

Mr. Abdul Akbar, City Council Member, Georgia

Mr. Hassan Fahmy, City Council Member, New Jersey

Dr. Muhammad Ali Chaudhry, Member Township Council, New Jersey

4 - The tale of the American Muslim vote in 2004 Election

Gaining political influence requires three main steps: fundraising, recruiting candidates and voting. The American Muslim community's performance on fundraising for candidates and recruiting candidates to contest various offices was not appreciable in 2004 Election. However, the community was

Appendix V: American Muslims in politics [250]

more active politically. This is the silver lining to 9/11, the Patriot Act and the mass detentions. It has pushed us to be proactive and take a stand, to be part of the political process. Now the Muslims are realizing that America's politics is about numbers: dollars you donate to your favorite candidates, or votes you can generate for them. Although their campaign fundraisers produced meager results but they were able to mobilize the community to get out and vote.

Evidently, whether intended or not, Muslims voted en bloc on November 2, 2004 presidential election, a behavior that is undoubtedly the outcome of personal and collective experiences, not a political strategy per se. The only reason for en mass Muslim and Arab vote for Senator Kerry was the civil rights issue as they endured much of the brunt of the Bush administration's transgression on the country's rights, and particularity their civil liberties.

At the same time, the Muslim community showed its eagerness to participate in the political process. This was confirmed by various studies and hundreds of media reports. A study, which surveyed Muslims in and around Detroit, Michigan -- an area that has the largest concentration of Muslims in the country -- demonstrated the growing perception that Muslim communities, which in the past have been viewed as isolated and inward-looking, are now seeking greater political involvement in the U.S. Over 60 percent of those polled cited civil rights issues as their top public policy concern, according to the study by Michigan-based the Institute of Social Policy and Understanding released in April 2004.

The mainstream media played an important role in highlighting the concerns Arabs and Muslims, particularly abridgment of their civil rights, the during 2004 election campaign. The media helped in motivating them to participate in the political process by registering as voters. It reported extensively about the voter registration campaigns by various local Muslim and Arab community organizations as well as Islamic centers and mosques throughout the nation.

Appendix V: American Muslims in politics [251]

A study of more than 100 media reports shows that the media stressed that civil rights was the defining issue for the Muslims and Arabs after the 9/11. For example, according to Seattle Post-Intelligencer (2/4/2004), Muslims in cities across the nation voiced concern over an anti-Muslim backlash after the 2001 terror attacks, and what they call the subsequent assault on civil liberties by the Bush administration. Of the more than 1,200 detainees caught up in the post-Sept. 11 dragnet, most were Muslims or people from Arab or southern Asian nations. An Agence France Presse report (2/6/2004) said: The three million Arab-Americans, who have felt ostracized since September 11, 2001, want to show they can be a mighty political force in this year's presidential election.

Civil rights was the major issue in 2000 presidential election when the American Muslim community voted virtually en bloc for George Bush. Ironically, four years later, civil rights remained the most significant issue for the Muslims who this time voted overwhelmingly for Senator John Kerry. An exit poll, on Nov. 2, by the Council on American-Islamic Relations (CAIR) indicated that 93 percent of Muslim voters were casting their ballots for John Kerry. In a democratic system vote is the best instrument to express one's opinion. And Muslims joined millions of citizens to express their opinion about the Bush administration policies.

Muslim vote for a Democratic candidate is not new. In 1996, they voted for Democratic President Bill Clinton. According to Zogby Polls, more than 50 percent of Muslims were voting for Democratic Party in nineties with only 16 percent committed to Republican Party. The first time Muslims tried to use bloc vote at the national level was in 2000. Traditionally, Arab-Americans and U.S. Muslims vote in large numbers. An estimated 79 percent are registered, and 85 percent of those say they vote, according to a 2001 poll taken on behalf of Georgetown University in Washington, D.C.

As the American Muslim community grows, it is becoming increasingly aware of its social and political potential. American Muslims have distinct views on issues such as abortion, prayer in public schools, welfare reform, immigration, and civil rights. They seek to promote family values, prevent

Appendix V: American Muslims in politics [252]

crime, combat drug abuse, and encourage other worthwhile social goals but it will not be an exaggeration to say that abridgement of civil rights was the single issue that galvanized the Muslim and Arab community. A barrage of post 9/11 discriminatory policies impacted them. This is not to say that the Muslims and Arabs were not concerned with other election issues. But obviously all communities are motivated by the issues that affect them most. A Democratic Presidential hopeful, Dennis Kucinich best reflected their sentiments when he said during a visit to a Florida Mosque: "The defining issue for Muslims is the restriction of civil liberties."

However, in this election, the American Muslim organizations apparently did not play any significant role in motivating the voters who from the very beginning of the election campaign were seen to concentrate mainly on the civil rights issue because they were affected by the biased policies of the Bush administration in the aftermath of 9/11.

Foreign policy issues remained the driving force of American Muslim politics. Except in the area of foreign policy, Muslims look at presidential candidates in the same way that non-Muslim Americans do. According to the Zogby International/Arab American Institute study, the administration's Middle East policy is a major reason for Bush's loss of support among Arab-Americans. In fact, two-thirds of them stated that the administration's Middle East policy was very important in determining their vote. When asked to evaluate Bush's handling of the Middle East, only 18% expressed approval – 78% expressed disapproval. And according to more than 50% of the Arab-Americans surveyed in the ZI/AAI poll, the administration's civil rights and civil liberties policies are also among their top concerns. The stated reason for this is their widespread concern with the administration's behavior. The civil rights issue even overshadowed the Middle East problem and the Muslims and Arabs supported Senator Kerry despite their reservations about his support toward Israel.

In the past, Muslims and Arabs have voted along social and ethnic lines, according to James Zogby, president of the Washington-based Arab American Institute. Many business-owning Arabs, for example, are

Appendix V: American Muslims in politics [253]

Republicans, but African-American Muslims vote for Democrats, he said. "There is incredible diversity within ... the ethnic and racial groups of Islam and the religious community doesn't yet operate as a political constituency," Zogby said. This time, however, Zogby and others predict racial and conservative beliefs may take a backseat. The erosion of civil liberties, the unresolved Iraqi War and Israeli-Palestinian conflict will be front and center, according to the New York Daily News, August 9, 2004.

Besides becoming the most important election issue, the abridgment of the civil rights proved an important factor in motivating the American Muslims and Arabs for political activism. American Muslims have increased their participation in political and social activities since 9/11, according to a poll released on Sept. 10, 2003 by the Council of American-Islamic Relations. The poll said that roughly half of American Muslims surveyed say they have increased their social (58 percent), political (45 percent), inter-faith (52 percent) and public relations activities (59 percent) since the 9/11 terror attacks.

During the last one year, the Muslim and Arab political activism was extensively reported by the mainstream media with such headlines (few examples): Arab vote poses a challenge for Bush - Civil liberties concerns, foreign policy have cut support from 2000. *(The Dallas Morning News - October 18, 2003;)* Muslim-American Activism: Enhanced Muslim Interest in American Politics. (*Washington Report on Middle East Affairs – October 2003); Arab-Americans organize to influence elections. (News Day - December 13, 2003);* Muslim vote may be shifting: Bush enjoyed support from Islamic community - before Sept. 11, terrorist attacks and wars. *(Dallas News – January 9, 2004);* New Jersey Muslims stressing political participation. (News Day - January 5, 2004); Muslim vote may shift to Democrats. (*Deseret Morning News - February 09, 2004); Arab-American group fights bias, rallies voters.* (South Florida Sun-Sentinel - February 7, 2004): - U.S. Muslims seek greater electoral clout.(*Seattle Post-Intelligencer - February 4, 2004.*

Appendix V: American Muslims in politics [254]

While media reported Muslim and Arab political activism, opinion polls gauged the presidential candidates' preferences.

Preliminary results of an exit poll, on Nov. 2, by Council on American-Islamic Relations (CAIR) indicated that more than 90 percent of Muslim voters are casting their ballots for John Kerry in today's election. In that early survey of 537 Muslim voters, 93 percent of respondents said they voted for Kerry, 5 percent favored Ralph Nader and less than 1 percent said they supported President Bush. In the key battleground state of Florida, a CAIR sampling of 335 Muslims who cast their votes on Nov. 2 or in early polling shows that 95 percent voted for Kerry and just 3 percent voted for President Bush. Ralph Nader received under 2 percent of Muslim votes. In Ohio, a similar sampling of 222 Muslim voters showed 86 percent voting for Kerry, 4 percent for Bush and 10 percent for "other" or a third party.

"We are seeing an unprecedented level of voter mobilization by the American Muslim community in this election," said CAIR Executive Director Nihad Awad. "I believe Muslim voters have come of age and will be a factor in all future elections." Muslims from almost every state responded to the exit poll, with the most responses coming from California, Virginia, Texas, Maryland, Illinois, New York, Florida, and Ohio. Surveys were faxed and e-mailed to Muslim individuals and organizations nationwide.

The last poll of the Council on American-Islamic Relations (CAIR), released just 11 days before the election on Oct 22, finds that 80 percent of likely American Muslim voters said they plan to vote for Sen. John Kerry on November 2. The poll, conducted following the third presidential debate, also indicated that just two percent said they will vote to re-elect President Bush and 11 percent of Muslim voters favor Ralph Nader. Only four percent of the Muslim voters said they are still undecided.

At least a dozen polls since April this year showed that American Muslims and Arabs are leaning towards John Kerry despite some reservations about his policies on the Middle East. Taking queue from the opinion polls many American Muslim and Arabs groups had formally endorsed the Kerry-

Appendix V: American Muslims in politics [255]

Edward ticket in October 2004, just less than one month before the election. The Muslim and Arab organizations that have formally endorsed Senator Kerry included:

The Muslim-American Political Action Committee, an affiliate of Muslim American Society Freedom Foundation; the Arab American Political Action Committee (AAPAC), a major Arab American group that has supported George Bush in 2000, endorsed John Kerry; Muslims for a Better North Carolina and Najee Ali, director of Project Islamic Hope in Los Angeles, which represents African-American Muslims. The American Muslim Taskforce on Civil Rights and Elections (AMT), a coalition of ten Muslim organizations announced its belated qualified endorsement for Senator Kerry on Oct. 21, 2004.

However, endorsements of the Muslim organizations in October came too late to impact the decision of the Muslim voters who had made up their minds long before as was confirmed by various polls, studies and media reports. Apparently, it was the mood of the community that forced these organizations to endorse Senator Kerry. Michael Meehan, a Kerry campaign spokesman, has made this point very clear when he said endorsements were helpful, but "at this late point in the election cycle, we are trying to turn supporters into voters and recent polling shows we have support among American Muslims 10-to-1."

President Bush still had some support within the Muslim community. Muhammad Ali Hasan, co-founder of a group called "Muslims for Bush," said that Muslims can support Bush for bringing liberation and democracy to the Islamic world. Non-endorsement of any presidential candidate by the Muslim Public Affairs Council (MPAC) was also interpreted by many as an implied endorsement for Bush because the Muslim community was going to vote for Kerry.

American Muslim voters went to poll with a deep conviction that their vote is the best guarantee to safeguard their rights. During the last one year the Muslims and Arabs have shown great political maturity and enthusiasm to

Appendix V: American Muslims in politics [256]

participate in the national political process. Their political activism was also reflected in dozens of voter registration campaigns during the last one year. The Muslim organizations had set a goal to register one million new voters.

However, the Muslims must realize that voting is not the end of the road, but the beginning of a long struggle that requires commitment, skill and resolve. In the next election round they have to be more active in elections at all levels, particularly local elections and campaigns. Also make alliances with other communities for outreach. Otherwise, after the election, their success will be confined to self-congratulating press releases by their organizations, filled with false victories and espousing equally false hopes.

In the final analysis, like the 2000 election, there is no reliable exit poll data about the Muslim vote in 2004. Only one exit poll was issued by CAIR on Nov. 2 which is touted as 93 percent Muslim vote for Kerry. Like 2000, the void is being filled by leaders claiming to have delivered a bloc vote which may not be convincing to many as the Muslim leaders claimed as much as 72 percent vote to Bush. But independent analysts gave a estimate - based on pre-and post-election surveys - that in 2000 Bush received about 50 percent of the Muslim vote, Gore about 25 percent, and Ralph Nader 10 percent. Muslim organizations bear the responsibility to make credible post-election surveys and studies about the Muslim vote and the Muslim candidates.

The Arab American Institute (AAI) has issued its final post-elections poll results which showed that John Kerry received 63% of the Arab American vote, while President Bush won 28%. An AAI report indicates that forty-four Arab American candidates were on the ballot this year-from Ralph Nader's controversial independent bid for President to Mohammad Khairallah's successful bid to be reelected as city councilman in Prospect Park, NJ. Overall, 24 won and 20 lost. Five Arab American candidates in Michigan won, including two Democratic state representatives and one Republican sheriff. Mitch Daniels, a Republican from Indiana won his bid to become Governor of that state.

Appendix V: American Muslims in politics [257]

Ralf Nader factor: When Ralph Nader announced his candidacy in February 2004 as an independent candidate, there was a general perception among many Muslims and Arabs that he may again prove a spoiler in 2004 as he was in the 2000 presidential election. Arab American Institute President Dr. James Zogby's comments best reflected their views: "We must deal with reality. I have great respect for Ralph Nader. His service is legendary and his principled challenge is inspirational. But this election is not about Ralph Nader. The real choice in 2004 is between George Bush and John Kerry. For me, it's clear."

Democrats woo Muslim and Arab voters
Democratic convention 2004

The number of Muslim and Arab delegates to the July 2004 Democratic National Convention had grown by 60 percent. Forty three Muslim and Arab delegates were representing 20 states at the 2004 convention, up from 25 Muslims at the Democratic convention four years ago.

The American Muslim Task Force, formed by a number of Muslim organizations in February 2004, held a hospitality suite during the Democratic convention in Boston. More than 200 delegates attended the AMT Hospitality Suite. It was great opportunity to secure their support in urging the Democratic Party to improve its position on civil rights and inclusion.

The AMT-initiated petition urging the DNC to insert the following language in the party platform as an addendum was signed by more than 200 delegate including the entire Hawaii delegation and most of the Texas delegation. The key part of the petition read:

"The Democratic Party reaffirms its commitment to due process, equal justice, freedom of religion, speech, assembly and privacy, protection from unreasonable searches and seizures, the presumption of innocence, access to counsel in judicial proceedings, and fair, speedy and public trial. We oppose ex post facto laws, secret proceeding and use of secret evidence,

Appendix V: American Muslims in politics [258]

and we also seek repeal of those sections of the USA PARTIOT ACT deemed manifestly unconstitutional and un-American.

Democrats hold conference call with AMT leaders

On Oct. 14, 2004, representatives of the American Muslim Task force held a conference call with Senator Ted Kennedy, Steve Elmendorf, Kerry - Edwards Deputy Campaign Manager, and Mona Pasquil, Director of Communities. Dr. Maher Hathout, Senior Advisor to the Muslim Public Affairs Council, and Dr. Agha Saeed, Executive Director of the American Muslim Alliance, shared the issues that could determine the Muslim vote. A statement issued by the Kerry campaign said: "As Senator Kennedy stated, civil liberties and inclusion of American Muslims exist in the heart and soul of John Kerry and are issues that they both have fought for in the Senate. In response to Dr. Hathout's question Senator Kennedy mentioned that expanding the Cultural Bridges Program was one step or example of inclusion of talented and brilliant Muslims. Steve Elmendorf, Deputy Campaign Manager reiterated that a Kerry - Edwards administration will engage and involve Muslim Americans. Lastly, in response to Mr. Kareem, Sen. Kennedy stressed that we are in an ongoing dialogue to build trust within a community that has been trampled on for the past three years." George Kivork National Director of Ethnic Outreach

The American Muslim Taskforce on Civil Rights and Elections included: American Muslim Alliance (AMA), Council on American-Islamic Relations (CAIR), Islamic Circle of North America (ICNA), Islamic Society of North America (ISNA), Muslim Alliance of North America (MANA), Muslim American Society (MAS), Muslim Public Affairs Council (MPAC), Muslim Student Association - National (MSA-N), Project Islamic Hope (PIH) and United Muslims of America (UMA).

Letter to Arab Americans

In Oct. 2004, in a letter to Arab Americans, senior Kerry adviser Rand Beers committed that a Kerry administration would do as much. Beers wrote:

Appendix V: American Muslims in politics [259]

John Kerry and John Edwards believe that bringing security and stability to the Middle East is vital to American national security, to the security of Israel and other countries in the region, and to the aspirations of the Palestinian people for a viable Palestinian state. In a Kerry-Edwards administration, the Israeli-Palestinian conflict will not be an afterthought. . . .[Kerry and Edwards] will work tirelessly to achieve a stable, lasting peace with security in the Middle East and ensure that American leadership is a source of hope in the region. Beers went on to say that a Kerry administration would take steps to end and prevent racial profiling. The Ashcroft Justice Department has unfairly targeted Muslim and Arab-Americans and has selectively enforced the immigration laws against these communities. John Kerry and John Edwards will uphold constitutional rights and protections, and civil rights laws.

MPAC hosts American Muslim Activists and Kerry-Edwards Campaign meeting

In response to a request from the Kerry-Edwards campaign, the Muslim Public Affairs Council (MPAC), on Sept. 16, 2004, hosted a meeting between former Governor Jean Shaheen (D-CT), Chairperson of the Kerry Campaign, and American Muslim activists throughout the country. Participants represented Muslims in the key battleground states of Ohio, Pennsylvania, Arizona, Iowa, and Florida as well as New York, California, Michigan, Texas, Virginia, and Washington, DC.

Dr. Maher Hathout, Senior Advisor to MPAC, articulated the following most urgent concerns of American Muslims on behalf of the attending leaders to campaign officials, according to a MPAC press release.

1. American Muslims expect of a future Kerry-Edwards administration to examine the Patriot Act in light of the Constitution and the general tenor of law enforcement in the past 50 years. We should maintain only those provisions of the Act which enhance our government's ability to defend the country, while strictly respecting the Constitution and freedoms available through other laws. Many elected officials allege that the Patriot Act was not

Appendix V: American Muslims in politics [260]

fully debated. In a Kerry-Edwards administration, there must be such debate and America Muslims should be participants. American Muslims have the requisite expertise and willingness to offer intelligent insight on the course of our nation in this post-9/11 era.

2. American Muslims expect to be included in a future Kerry-Edwards Administration. Visits that lack substance and group pictures are insufficient. American Muslims expect to be offered policy-making positions dealing with issues in which they can offer expertise, with regard to Counterterrorism policy, Health, and Education in such agencies as the Department of Justice, the State Department, the Department of Housing and Urban Development, FBI, the Department of Homeland Security and others. American Muslims are not asking for preferential treatment, we are only asking to be represented in positions that offer opportunities to make positive change.

3. A Kerry Administration must be determined to ensure the First Amendment rights of American Muslims to freely practice their religion. Exercise of the fifth pillar of Islam, Charity, is a Constitutional right of all Americans. American Muslims should have the right to offer money to any group of people around the world and within the US who use that money for a charitable purpose within the bounds of the law. Access to transparently legitimate institutions which can disperse such funds is the responsibility of the government, whether through a certification process or otherwise. Any certification process should not be burdensome or impossible to comply with.

According to MPAC, this meeting demonstrated a desire on the part of the Kerry-Edwards campaign to understand the needs of American Muslim communities, and clarify their position on issues critical to the voters. "MPAC encourage the Bush-Cheney campaign to extend similar opportunities for Muslims to voice their opinions and offer an expert, authentic voice on issues affecting America" the MPAC press release concluded. **(MPAC press release Sept. 16, 2004)**

Pelosi, Democratic leaders hold roundtable discussion with Muslim American leaders

On July 14, 2004, House Democratic Leader Nancy Pelosi (D-CA), Congressman John D. Dingell (D-MI), Congressman John Conyers (D-MI), Congressman Charles Rangel (D-NY), and other Congressional Democrats were joined by national leaders of the Muslim American community in a roundtable discussion on issues of mutual concern to Democrats and Muslim Americans. The discussion centered on working together to defend civil rights and to restore civil liberties, a press release from Pelosi's office said.

"This discussion is only the first in an ongoing dialogue between Congressional Democrats and Muslim Americans," Pelosi said. "We share a fundamental principle - the belief that diversity is the backbone of our communities. Generations of Muslims have made positive contributions in every aspect of American life. We must now work even more closely to navigate through the challenges we face as a nation."

"Since September 11th, many Muslim Americans have been subjected to searches at airports and other locations based upon their religion and national origin, without any credible information linking individuals to criminal conduct," Pelosi continued. "Racial and religious profiling is fundamentally un-American and we must make it illegal.

"When the Patriot Act was enacted, it was intended to be accompanied by strong Congressional oversight to prevent abuses of our civil liberties. That oversight has not occurred, particularly with the mass detention campaign ordered by Attorney General Ashcroft, which to date has led to more than 5,000 foreign nationals being detained since September 11th. Moreover, individuals' assets have been frozen on the basis of secret evidence that they have no opportunity to confront or rebut, and such processes are a fundamental denial of due process. We must correct the Patriot Act to prevent abuses of our civil liberties."

Appendix V: American Muslims in politics [262]

Working with Conyers, the Ranking Democrat on the House Judiciary Committee, Democrats have introduced legislation to end racial profiling, limit the reach of the Patriot Act, and make immigration safe and accessible. Leader Pelosi is a proud cosponsor of the End Racial Profiling Act, the Security and Freedom Ensured Act (SAFE), and the Safe, Orderly, and Legal Visas Enforcement Act (SOLVE).

"These measures are long overdue, and we call on the Republican leadership in Congress to bring them to a vote now," Pelosi said. "As we protect and defend the American people, we must protect and defend the Constitution and the civil rights that define our democracy. Ours is a country of great diversity and we must stand together as one America."

The following Democrats also participated in the discussion: former Democratic Whip David Bonior (D-MI), Congressman Gregory Meeks (D-NY), and Congressman Nick Joe Rahall (D-WV).

The American Muslim groups represented at the meeting included the Council on American-Islamic Relations, the Islamic Society of North America, Indian Muslim Council, Muslim Public Affairs Council, Muslim American Society, Association of Pakistani Physicians of North America, Muslim Bar Association, National Association of Muslim Lawyers, and the Universal Muslim Association of America. **(Press Release from Pelosi's office, July 14, 2004.)**

MPAC Convention

During the two day (Dec. 20-21, 2003) convention of the Muslim Public Affairs Council (MPAC) presidential hopefuls provided representatives, sent video presentations and called, by special phone connection, into plenary sessions to speak to Muslim attendees and their issues. In addition, a White House representative participated in a packed plenary session entitled "Iraq Beyond Saddam Hussein."

Appendix V: American Muslims in politics [263]

Candidates Howard Dean, Dennis Kucinich, and John Kerry all made special efforts to speak to American Muslims during plenary sessions from their campaign travels in the mid-west. "The efforts on behalf of the White House and Democrat presidential candidates to court the Muslim vote is a clear sign that they recognize and understand our issues and that they are taking us seriously," stated Salam Al-Marayati, executive director of MPAC.

During their phone calls candidates shared their perspectives on a range of American Muslim issues including the injustices of the Patriot Act, the Administration's unilateral decision-making regarding Iraq, the misguided immigration registration program, and their plans to advance a peaceful solution to the war in Iraq and the conflict between Palestinians and Israelis.

"I think that this November will see American Muslims coming to the polls in unsurpassed numbers to cast their vote. American Muslims feel empowered and more then ever included and engaged in the political process of our nation," commented Al-Marayati. "This is due," he continued, "to actions our elected leaders took in response to 9-11 as well as the dramatic increase in voter registration drives and the large number of American Muslim youth who have become eligible to vote since the last presidential election."

Muslims launch website supporting Kerry

On August 10, 2004, a private group officially launched a new website encouraging Muslim Americans to vote for John Kerry in the November presidential election. The site http://www.muslimsforkerry.com featured news, articles, testimonials, forums, voter registration links and a blog. "Muslims voters in this election are a crucial demographic for the campaigns, because of their concentration in battleground states like Michigan and Ohio," said Shahed Amanullah, one of the founders of MuslimsForKerry.com. "In this election Muslim voters will come out in large numbers and vote for the candidate that offers this country the brightest future. That candidate is clearly John Kerry, and we believe that as Muslims weigh the various options in the months ahead, they will come to the conclusion that Kerry

Appendix V: American Muslims in politics [264]

American Muslim Task Force's role in 2004 election

On February 17, 2004, in Washington, a number of American Muslim organizations announced the formation of the American Muslim Taskforce on Civil Rights and Elections (AMT), to concentrate on helping Muslims become "full partners in the development and prosperity of our homeland," defending the civil rights of all Americans and developing alliances "on a wide variety of social, political, economic, and moral issues."

Task force organizers said they will put forward a "civil rights plus" agenda for the 2004 election cycle in which civil rights is the most important issue, but not the only issue. The AMT election plan states: "We remain equally committed to (the issues of) education, homelessness, economic recovery, environmental and ecological safety, electoral reform, crime, and global peace and justice."

The AMT, after eight months of deliberations, met in Washington on Oct. 19, 2004 to discuss endorsement of a presidential candidate. However, nine-hour marathon meeting failed to bring any results that led to speculations that the AMT will not endorse any candidate. After days of confusion, a split in its ranks and an intensive pressure from the Muslim community, the American Muslim Taskforce on Civil Rights and Elections - Political Action Committee (AMT-PAC) on Oct. 21, 2004 called on Muslims nationwide to vote for Sen. John Kerry. However it called its move as a 'protest vote' to safeguard civil rights of the Muslim community. An AMT-PAC statement issued in Washington stressed that "because pluralism is based on partial agreements, support for Sen. Kerry is premised on our overall effort to help restore liberty and justice for all."

The AMT pointed out that despite disagreements with Sen. Kerry on some domestic and international issues, including the war in Iraq, it is willing to work with him to help restore due process and equal justice in accordance with the U.S. Constitution. However, the AMT acknowledged the considerable outreach to the Muslim community by Sen. Kerry's campaign, particularly by his campaign co-chair Sen. Edward Kennedy and appreciated

Appendix V: American Muslims in politics [265]

the ongoing dialogue with Muslim leaders about problems posed by the USA PATRIOT Act.

The AMT's belated endorsement was a welcome development because it responded to the aspirations of the Muslim community. However, the question remained, how the qualified endorsement of AMT influenced the Muslim voters, majority of whom had already made up their mind to support Kerry? Michael Meehan, a Kerry campaign spokesman, has made this point very clear when he said endorsements were helpful, but "at this late point in the election cycle, we are trying to turn supporters into voters and recent polling shows we have support among American Muslims 10-to-1."

The AMT endorsement came after a major split in its ranks when the Muslim Public Affairs Council (MPAC) a major component of the AMT quit the coalition quietly after it refused to support endorsement to any presidential candidate. MPAC was one of the three organizations that envisaged, at the ISNA convention of 2003, the establishment of AMT as a successor to the American Muslim Political Coordination Council (AMPCC) that announced its support to Bush in 2000 elections. The other two groups were American Muslim Alliance (AMA) and Council on American-Islamic Relations (CAIR).

Apparently, a unanimous AMT decision was not possible in the presence of MPAC, hence it was forced to leave the coalition. Only one day before the AMT endorsement, the MPAC issued a long statement about its decision of not endorsing any presidential candidate saying: "An endorsement is far too important to give away without delivering solid promises to the community that their interests will be of paramount importance to the next President. Leaders of other religious and ethnic communities throughout our country do not endorse unless they receive such promises. We should not be any different."

Alluding to the many opinion polls and persistent media reports, the MAPC statement acknowledged that it trusts the political judgment and maturity of American Muslim voters and added: "In this election, Muslim voters must vote their conscience based on what is best for themselves, their

Appendix V: American Muslims in politics [266]

communities and their country. Our decision not to endorse a candidate in the 2004 Presidential election must not be viewed as a directive for American Muslims to reconsider their decision. Rather it is a reminder that although candidates are willing to take our votes, they are not yet willing to announce such to the country."

Despite MPAC's departure, the AMT still maintained 10 members as a marginal group, Muslim Ummah of North America (MUNA), was quietly inducted to fill the MAPC slot. AMT includes: American Muslim Alliance (AMA), Council on American-Islamic Relations (CAIR), Islamic Circle of North America (ICNA), Islamic Society of North America (ISNA), Muslim Alliance in North America (MANA), Muslim American Society (MAS), Muslim Ummah of North America (MUNA), Muslim Student Association-National (MSA-N), Project Islamic Hope (PIH), and United Muslims of America (UMA).

The qualified endorsement of Kerry by the AMT stirred the Muslim community and drew sharp reaction from many intellectuals and writers. One analysis said: American Muslim Taskforce Insults John Kerry and Alienates George Bush. While another comment was entitled: Flip Flopping AMT (Alluding to the earlier reports that the AMT was unlikely to support any candidate.)

The AMT leadership, following the qualified endorsement, spent all its energies in defending its decision and claiming that there was no rift among its ranks, despite disassociation of the MPAC, one of its major component. The AMT chairman Dr. Agha Saeed described the community reaction as a marginal matter. (The AMT is the successor to American Muslim Political Coordination Council (AMPCC) that supported Bush in 2000 election. However, the AMPCC ignored the Muslim community's opinion when it refused to endorse Syed Rifat Mahmood, a Republican Congressional candidate from California, apparently because he was not electable against the Democrat incumbent Pete Stark.)

Appendix V: American Muslims in politics [267]

The post-decision developments did not augur well for the AMT. The Islamic Society of North America (ISNA), a well-respected organization that included in the list of AMT components posted the following announcement on its website: "ISNA firmly stands by and reiterates its standing policy, in its capacity as a religious, not-for-profit, 501(c)(3) tax-exempt organization, to (1) not support, endorse or oppose the candidacy of any persons seeking election to public office, and (2) not permit any organization to support, endorse or oppose any political candidate in its name."

On the election eve, The Council on American-Islamic Relations (CAIR) urged every eligible Muslim voters to got to the polls and vote for the candidates of their choice. The CAIR statement issued in Washington, did not refer to the AMT endorsement of Senator Kerry. Apparently at the last moment the CAIR objective was to bring out maximum Muslim vote. Many Muslim organizations and Muslim intellectuals and analysts have been urging the community that the most important thing is participation in the political process. What counts, is your vote.

The politics of bloc vote

This discussion leads us to the issue of bloc vote politics. Many Muslim Americans are opposed to the politics of bloc voting which they believe will be harmful for the American Muslim community. But Many American Muslim leaders believe that the American Muslim community does not enjoy the same financial clout that is enjoyed by the American Jews. Therefore, the only alternative left for the Muslims to have an effective voice in the presidential elections is to vote in bloc. In 2000, African American Muslims, who are generally Democrat, were particularly upset that American Muslim organizations, instituted by the immigrant majority, had endorsed the Republican candidate without regard to their opinion and interests. In 2004, the AMT tried to address African American Muslims complaint and brought Muslim American Society into its fold.

On August 11, 2004, theChicago-based Institute for Social Policy and Understanding issued a paper the entitled: Presidential elections 2004:

Appendix V: American Muslims in politics [268]

What Should American Muslims Do? The paper was written by Dr. Muqtedar Khan, the Director of International Studies at Adrian College in Michigan and a Non-Resident Fellow at Brookings Institution in Washington DC.

The paper pointed out that the African American Muslims have special relations with the Democratic Party. "The community must help and encourage them to develop and nourish this relationship further. Muslim organizations had developed links with the Republicans during the 2000 campaign. The community must renew and strengthen those links. It should avoid ridiculing or condemning those Muslims who may choose to work with the Bush campaign or the Republican Party."

The ISPU paper provided an insight into the pros and cons of a bloc vote and the role of Muslim political organizations and groups in the election. It enumerated the following advantages of a bloc vote:

(1) In a close election, a community can play a decisive role in determining the outcome.

(2) In close elections, voting blocs can actually coerce political parties to change their electoral platforms.

(3) If the politics of bloc voting were correctly applied, it could help unite the community.

(4) Bloc voting gives American Muslim Organizations and leaders greater influence and access in mainstream politics. Politicians and the media will seek them if they think these leaders are capable of manipulating and delivering the "Muslim Vote."

(5) One symbolic advantage of bloc voting is the recognition of the community as a whole being an important political player. It gives recognition and awareness to their leaders, organizations and issues. Sometimes, the media attention to these issues can be dangerous, while on

other occasions, it can be salutary. American Muslims achieved this in 2000; its necessity in 2004 is debatable.

The ISPU paper pointed out that while the advantages of bloc voting have been pervasively discussed within the community, especially given its prominence as an issue in the 2000 elections, the negative aspects of bloc voting are less studied and comprehended. According to ISPU, "the risks and dangers" of a bloc vote are likely to be:

(1) The biggest danger of bloc voting is the likelihood of endorsing the eventual loser. In American elections the probability of doing so is 50%. By officially endorsing a single party or candidate, the community effectively alienates itself from the other party/candidate and in a way declares its opposition openly. In the eventuality of the defeat of the endorsed candidate, the community will then be vulnerable to reprisals or isolation from government access. If, for example, American Muslims officially endorse John Kerry, vote for him in huge percentages (92-93% as CAIR's membership survey indicates) and George W. Bush still wins, the community could face further difficulty, given current administration attitudes toward American Muslims.

(2) The community must learn to develop long-term and meaningful relationships with the two parties. Recent months have seen two parallel developments: American Muslim leaders' rhetoric about the existence of a Muslim vote bloc and its use to vote against George W. Bush...Since American Muslims are not going to support the Bush-Cheney ticket, the Republicans may as well solicit - or manipulate - the American Jewish vote by appearing to be extremely pro-Israel. It is tragic that the Palestine issue divides the Muslim and Jewish communities into adversaries even though the two communities have identical interests on most domestic issues, such as defending America's secular ethos by protecting it from the rise of Christian fundamentalism, strengthening the welfare state and the civil rights environment.

Appendix V: American Muslims in politics [270]

(3) An additional risk for American Muslims if their leadership insists on bloc vote politics is the possibility of (a) exposing the absence of political unity within the community and (b) actually exciting existing minor fissures into becoming major cleavages. The marginalization of the African American Muslims through the endorsement of George W. Bush in 2000 likely led to the establishment of Muslim Alliance of North America (MANA), an organization that seeks to represent indigenous Muslim interests. The creation of MANA serves as an expression of a vote of no-confidence by indigenous Muslims in the legitimacy of the national organizations established and managed by immigrant Muslims.

(4) American Muslims must recognize that the overall philosophies and political agendas of the two parties are pretty stable and enduring. Republicans stand for reducing taxes for the rich, pushing religiously motivated political goals – such as abortion; whereas Democrats seek to pursue social liberalization and strengthen the welfare state. If American Muslim values are stable then they too must have a long-term relationship with one party. Or there must be Muslim factions aligned with each party.

(5) Excessive pontification about the power and impact of the Muslim voting bloc on American politics and policies may cause more anger, resentment and distrust within the general American population.

(6) The issue of endorsement also presupposes the ability of the so-called national organizations to set the agenda of all American Muslims. Many American Muslims are very distrustful of the national leadership.

(7) Bloc voting is a reflection of a superficial, instrumental understanding of, and attitude toward, democracy. Participation in democratic processes should not be viewed as a partisan engagement in a zero-sum game.

Muslim Americans elected to office in 2004

Appendix V: American Muslims in politics [271]

Many American Muslims have been elected to public offices in 2004 despite the wave of Islamophobic attacks and stereotyping of Muslims. Muslim candidates ran for a number of offices at local, state and federal levels.

No comprehensive data is available about the elected Muslim officials but fragmented media reports provide some information. According to Pakistan Times the following four American Muslims were re-elected in November 2004 elections:

Mr. Larry Shaw (Democrat), State Senate, North Carolina; Ms. Yaphett El-Amin (Democrat), State Assembly Missouri; Mr. Rodney Hubbard (Democrat), State Assembly Missouri, and Mr. Saghir Tahir (Republican), State Assembly, New Hampshire.

The successful candidates were voted in by a minimum of 60 per cent, which underlines the considerable support they enjoyed within their constituency.

Dr. Mohammad Ali Chaudhry was elected Mayor Bernards Township, New Jersey.

Two Muslim candidates, Akhtar Sadiq (Democrat-Georgia) and Abul Akbar (Democrat-Georgia), ran for state senate but did not make it this year. Ferial Masry, (Democrat-California), a Muslim woman for CA State Assembly also failed to make in November 2004.

Arif Khan (Libertarian-Wisconsin) and Dr. Mohammad H. Said (Democrat-Washington State) ran for US Senate. Mr. Khan lost in the general election while Dr. Said lost the primary. **(Source Pakistan Link December 3, 2004)**

5 - American Muslims in 2006 Elections

The seven-million-strong American Muslim community got a big political push when the Minnesota Democrat Keith Ellison was elected as the nation's first Muslim member to the US Congress in November 7, 2006 elections. Ellison's election was accompanied by a massive turnout of the American Muslim voters to make their voices heard.

"Tonight, we made history," Mr Ellison said in a victory speech to supporters. "We won a key election, but we did much more than that. We showed that a candidate can run a 100% positive campaign and prevail, even against tough opposition."

Throughout his campaign Ellison, a criminal defense attorney who converted to Islam as a college student, focused on issues that resonate in his electoral District in Minneapolis. Ellison won 56 percent of the vote, defeating Republican Alan Fine and the Independence Party's Tammy Lee, both of whom garnered 21 percent of the vote.

Another Muslim, Ahmad Hassan, failed in his congressional bid on Republican ticket. In Texas District 18, Ahmad Hassan, an Egyptian American, lost to Democrat Sheila Jackson Lee who was re-elected with a massive 80 percent of the vote.

Before Ellison's election to the House, Larry Shaw, a Democrat State Senator of North Carolina, was the highest Muslim elected official in the United States. Larry Shaw, a corporate executive, was re-elected to the State senate on November 7.

It is not clear how many Muslim Americans contested in the 2006 elections but there are fragmented reports that dozens were candidate for various offices from US Congress, State Senate and assemblies to local bodies.

Appendix V: American Muslims in politics [273]

In New Hampshire, Saghir "Saggy" Tahir was re-elected for a third term of the State House of Representatives in Nov. 7 elections.

The number of Muslim candidates for various offices across the nation hit an all-time high of about 700 in 2000 but then declined dramatically, to about 70 in 2002 and about 100 in 2004, according to the American Muslim Alliance, a national organization.

In 2002, Maad Abu-Ghazalah, an Arab-American and Syed Rifat Mahmood, a Pakistani-American, made unsuccessful congressional bids from California. In 2004, Ferial Masry, a Saudi-born woman lost her bid for congress in California while, Maad Abu-Ghazalah also made another abortive bid.

The midterm elections witnessed an intensive voter registration and get-out-to-vote campaigns by the American Muslim groups. Consequently, in key elections throughout the country, candidates were beginning to realize the impact of the Muslim electorate which is the result of the increasing interaction of Muslim communities with elected officials and candidates.

The Muslim community demonstrated its importance in this election particularly in the states where it has large concentration of population. In states like Virginia which has substantial concentration of Muslim population, the Muslim vote became the critical vote in tipping the balance on control of the US Senate. In Virginia Incumbent senator George Allen was defeated by his Democratic opponent, Jim Webb, giving Democrats control of the Senate with 51-members.

There are approximately 60,000 Muslim voters in Virginia, with 85% of them living in Northern Virginia. According to the Muslim American Society Center for Electoral Empowerment Director (MASCEE) Mukit Hossain, it is estimated that 47,700 Muslims voted for Jim Webb, which positively contributed to his narrow victory over Senator George Allen. The MASCEE

Appendix V: American Muslims in politics [274]

also helped support a larger Muslim voter turnout in Virginia by recruiting 230 volunteers for some 200 election sites.

An informal poll of Muslim voters, conducted by the New Jersey Chapter of the Council on American Islamic Relations (CAIR-NJ), indicated that the vast majority in that state voted for Democrats in the mid-term elections. There are at least 18,000 registered Muslim voters in the state of New Jersey.

CAIR-NJ contacted 100 Muslim voters from various districts to ask how they had voted. Of 100 Muslim voters contacted, 77 said they had voted for the Democratic Party candidates. This result was in line with a recent CAIR poll of Muslim voters nationwide indicating that American Muslims lean toward the Democratic Party.

An informal poll of Muslim voters, conducted by the CAIR Columbus office indicated that the overwhelming majority of Muslim voters in that state voted for Democrats in the mid-term elections. Seventy-five Muslim voters from Ohio responded to a post-election survey. More than 90 percent of the respondents said they had voted for Democratic Party candidates.

A pre-election CAIR survey revealed that 42 percent Muslim voters consider themselves members of the Democratic Party while only 17 per cent are Republican. Another 28 percent do not belong to any party.

The survey also pointed out that 49 percent of the registered voters in the survey said that they voted regularly. Previous surveys also indicate that the American Muslim community has the highest turnout of voters in elections.

Similarly, another poll by the Arab American Institute (AAI) pointed out that strong majorities of Arab-American voters in four key states — Michigan, Ohio, Pennsylvania and Florida — intend to vote for the Democratic candidates for senate. It may be pointed out that about 40 percent of the 3.5 million-strong American Arab community is Muslim and the rest is Christian.

Appendix V: American Muslims in politics [275]

Like Muslim Americans, Arab Christians have also been complaining of discrimination in the post-9/11 era.

Arab American Institute said 2006 historic elections will have a significant impact on the Arab American community. Eighty-two percent of the candidates supported by the state and local Arab American community leaders in fifteen states were victorious. Of the 39 Arab American candidates vying in the election, 24 won their races.

The Muslim groups had launched a vote registration campaign and also get-out-to-vote campaign. They particularly targeted 12 states with a high concentration of Muslim population: California, 20 percent; Illinois, 8.9 percent; New York, 8.6 percent; Texas, 7 percent; New Jersey, 6.8 percent; Michigan, 6.7 percent; Florida, 6.4 percent; Virginia, 6.3 percent; Maryland, 3.1 percent; Ohio, 3 percent; Pennsylvania, 2.9 percent; and Minnesota, 2.8 percent.

The Muslim American Society, which had set up voter registration booths in mosques across the country, has added 30,000 new voters to the rolls just weeks before the election.

In Illinois, another state with a heavy concentration of Muslims, the Council of Islamic Organizations of Greater Chicago had been working to register more of the area's approximately 400,000 Muslims to vote.

The Muslim Public Affairs Council (MPAC) held four Election Forums in Virginia, Kansas and California, providing an opportunity for more than a dozen candidates to meet with the American Muslim community to share their perspectives on pressing current issues.

In several states the American Muslim Alliance (AMA) issued an election advisory suggesting its preference for the candidates who supported the Muslims on the issue of civil rights which remains the top Muslim concern in elections since 2000.

Appendix V: American Muslims in politics [276]

Interestingly, an important impact of Muslim political activism was that the candidates who were vocal supporters of profiling the Muslims and Arabs lost elections in Illinois, Pennsylvania and Wisconsin.

Republican candidate for Illinois' 17th Congressional District Andrea Zinga said: "Profiling doesn't bother me if we are profiling the people who. . .have caused the outrages against our nation and caused the deaths of American citizens. . .We're talking about Mideastern men."

In Pennsylvania, Sen. Rick Santorum lost his seat in the Senate after targeting so-called "Islamic fascism" during his campaign. Santorum even linked the Islamic concept of Jihad to Nazism when he said: "Mein Kampf means struggle; jihad means struggle."

In Wisconsin, 3rd Congressional District GOP candidate Paul Nelson suggested looking for anyone who is "wearing a turban and his name is Muhammad" when he was questioned about his call for profiling of Muslims.

And in Florida, both gubernatorial candidates repudiated anti-Muslim remarks made by supporters during the campaign.

While it is unclear if Muslim American voters have the numbers to tip any tight elections, many political observers believe that they have achieved unprecedented levels of political organization and electoral enthusiasm.

At least two million Muslims are registered voters. A 2001 poll by Zogby International found that 79 percent of the country's Muslims are registered to vote.

CAIR/MAS report on 2006 election efforts

On Nov. 14, 2006, the Council on American-Islamic Relations (CAIR) offered a report to the Muslim community on its efforts to promote political participation in the recent mid-term elections.

Appendix V: American Muslims in politics [277]

CAIR Chapters in 11 states participated in non-partisan election efforts. States with "get out the vote" and other activities included: Arizona, California, Connecticut, Florida, Illinois, Michigan, Missouri, New Jersey, Ohio, Pennsylvania, and Texas.

Other highlights of CAIR's non-partisan election activities included:

* National: The creation of a database of some 400,000 American Muslim voters developed by matching state records of registered voters with an extensive list of Muslim first and last names.
* Arizona: 11,000 automated get out the vote calls were made.
* Florida: 10,000 voter guides were distributed at state mosques.
* Illinois: More than 1000 Muslims were registered to vote in the Third Congressional District. Two hundred Muslim volunteers also got out the vote on election day in the Chicago area by knocking on doors and making phone calls.
* Ohio: 1,200 get out the vote calls were made in the Columbus area.
* Texas: More than 3,500 Muslims in the Dallas area were contacted and urged to vote. More than 800 Muslims were contacted in the San Antonio area.
* California: 500 posters were distributed to mosques and businesses around the state urging Muslims to register to vote. CAIR-CA also distributed a congressional scorecard and held a voter education forum with candidates and representatives for and against propositions on the ballot.

Results of informal exit polls in Ohio and New Jersey indicate that more than 75 percent of Muslim voters in those states cast their ballots for Democrats in the mid-term election.

Democrats' wins hinged on Muslims – Washington Times

The Washington Times reported on November 14, 2006 that Muslim voters, an electoral ally of President Bush as recently as 2000, played a key role in turning over control of the Senate to Democrats.

Appendix V: American Muslims in politics [278]

"Although the-get-out-the-vote campaign was nonpartisan, there is no doubt that our strategy to support a large Muslim voter turnout in areas with potentially close election races was a correct one," said Mahdi Bray, director of the Muslim American Society (MAS) Freedom Foundation. "We looked at the states with close races and matched them up with states that had a large concentration of Muslims."

MAS also targeted races in Florida, Georgia, Michigan, North Carolina, Ohio and Pennsylvania.

In the U.S. Senate race in Virginia, more than 50,000 self-identified Muslim voters went to the polls, MAS said. A commanding majority of them, 92 percent, or 47,092, voted for the Democratic challenger, James H. Webb Jr. Mr. Webb won his race against Sen. George Allen, the Republican incumbent, by 9,326 votes.

"If Muslims had decided to put their weight behind Allen, Republicans would have had at least a tie in the Senate," said Mukit Hossain of MAS, which conducted the survey.

Muslim turnout of registered voters was exceptionally high in Virginia, at 86 percent, MAS reported. About 13 percent, or 7,822, of them were first-time voters.

Muslims also celebrated the victory of Keith Ellison, the first Muslim elected to Congress. The Democrat won his race with 56 percent of the vote in Minnesota's traditionally liberal 5th District. Mr. Ellison, who describes himself as a moderate Muslim, won the backing of the National Jewish Democratic Council, even though his opponent, Republican Alan Fine, was Jewish.

Muslim voters have not always turned against Republican candidates. A survey by the Center for American Islamic Relations found that 78 percent of Muslims supported Mr. Bush during his first presidential election in 2000.

Appendix V: American Muslims in politics [279]

CAIR found that Muslims were drawn to Mr. Bush's conservative stances on social issues and their hope that he would overturn provisions of a 1996 law, backed by the Clinton administration, that allowed for "secret evidence" in the deportation of immigrants with suspected terrorist ties.

Some estimates show that 60,000 Muslims voted for Mr. Bush in Florida. Those numbers nearly flipped in 2004, with most surveys showing Mr. Bush receiving about 7 percent of Muslim support against his opponent, Sen. John Kerry, Massachusetts Democrat.

Mr. Hossain is president of the Virginia Muslim Political Action Committee, a group that endorsed Mr. Webb's candidacy. However, Mr. Hossain says neither the Virginia PAC nor MAS has a partisan affiliation. He said the PAC endorsed Mr. Webb and other Democratic candidates because of their positions on civil liberties, immigration and health care. Mr. Hossain did not hide his personal preference for Mr. Webb and his enthusiasm for Democratic victories a week ago, appearing at a press conference yesterday wearing a Webb campaign button on his jacket.

Appendix V: American Muslims in politics [280]

6. American Muslims overwhelmingly voted Democratic in 2008

According to the American Muslim Task Force on Civil Rights and Elections, a coalition of Muslim civil advocacy groups, American Muslims overwhelmingly voted for Democratic Presidential candidate Senator Barrak Obama in the 2008 election.

On November 6, 2008, the American Muslim Task Force released a poll of over 600 Muslims from more than 10 states, including Florida and Pennsylvania, and it revealed that 89 percent of respondents voted for Obama, while only 2 percent voted for McCain. It also indicated that 95 percent of Muslims polled cast a ballot in this year's presidential election—the highest turnout in a U.S. election ever—and 14 percent of those were first-time voters.

The Newsweek reported a Gallup Center for Muslim Studies survey as saying that U.S. Muslims favored Obama in greater numbers than did Hispanics (67 percent of whom voted for Obama) and nearly matched that of African-Americans, 93 percent of whom voted for Obama. More than two thirds who were polled said the economy was the most important issue affecting their decision on Nov. 4th, while 16 percent said the wars in Iraq and Afghanistan informed their vote—numbers that put Muslims roughly on a par with the general population.

In this election, Muslim Americans changed their party affiliation from Republican to Democratic – a stark change from the strong Muslim support for George Bush in 2000 when they voted for Bush in an en bloc vote. The major shift occurred as many Muslim Americans became subject to wiretapping, mishandling of civil liberties, religious, ethnic, and racial profiling.

According to the Newsweek, in 2008, many more Muslims were drawn into the Democratic party by Obama himself since Muslims across the country were captivated by the senator's promise of unity and hope. On the Muslim-Americans for Obama Web site (Mafo2008.com), their mission statement includes the following: "That we support Barack Obama because, among

Appendix V: American Muslims in politics [281]

other reasons, he rejects the politics of fear, challenging our nation to embrace its collective identity, where each American has a stake in the success and well-being of every American."

But many Muslims kept their presidential preference a secret in the months leading up to Super Tuesday, fearing that an endorsement from them might in fact work against Obama, the Newsweek said addin: After all, this was an election year in which the word "Muslim" was used as shorthand to connote anti-American leanings and a hidden love of terrorism.

Extensive campaigns to motivate the Muslim voters

The seven million-strong American Muslim community had a rough time during the 2008 election campaign with smear against Islam, bigotry and stereotyping. Tellingly, despite the messages of inclusiveness and tolerance from both major parties, neither campaign has been overly anxious to court the Muslim vote. To their disappointment, neither presidential candidate has visited a mosque, yet both have made multiple visits to churches and synagogues.

This is the reason that no major American Muslim organization - such as AMT, CAIR and MPAC -has formally endorsed Obama although they remain heavily tilted towards him because of their grievances against the Bush's anti-Muslim policies. However, the Muslim organizations have launched extensive campaigns to motivate the Muslim voters to go out and vote.

The American-Arab Anti-Discrimination Committee (ADC) has dedicated major resources to protect the Arab and Muslim American votes through the ADC Voter Protection Unit (ADC VPU). The ADC VPU is a special unit composed of a full-time lobbyist, three attorneys in Washington, DC, and one attorney in Dearborn, Michigan. This unit of professionals is dedicated to protecting the Arab and Muslim American communities from voter intimidation and other attempts at chilling the communities' right to vote.

The Arab American Institute has launched the Yalla Vote campaign, "Our Voice. Our Future. Yalla Vote '08." It is organizing Arab Americans across the country to motivate the Arab voters. More than 50 Arab American

Appendix V: American Muslims in politics [282]

organizations from around the country have signed on to Yalla Vote '08 campaign.

The American Muslim Taskforce had designated Friday, Oct. 31st as 'National Muslim Voter Education Day USA' and Nov 1-2 as 'National Voter Mobilization Weekend.'

The American Muslim Voice has urged the Muslims to participate in the national political process to make their voice effective.

The Council on American-Islamic Relations (CAIR) called on American Muslim voters to turn out in large numbers at the polls on November 4th as a positive response to Islamophobic bias and stereotyping in political campaigns.

In October 2008, the Muslim Public Affairs Council held seven election town hall forums in Ohio and Pennsylvania in an effort to educate Muslim American voters on key issues and provide an opportunity for interaction with candidates for local, state and federal offices.

What Are Muslim Voters Like?

Muslims in the U.S. have proved to be a highly-educated, family-oriented, and diverse group of voters. The results of a 2008 national survey, commissioned by the Washington-based Council on American-Islamic Relations (CAIR), show that most Muslim voters identify themselves as either Democrat or Independent.

The CAIR survey indicates that the Muslim voters are:

Young: More than three-fourths (78 percent) of respondents said they are between the ages of 30 and 54.

Highly Educated: A majority (65 percent) said they have a bachelor's degree or higher.

Appendix V: American Muslims in politics [283]

Middle Class: Almost half of respondents (43 percent) said they have a household income of $50,000 or higher.

Family Oriented: More than three-fourths of (77 percent) said they are married.

Religiously Diverse: More than half (52 percent) of respondents said they attend a mosque at least once a month, but than one-fifth (21 percent) said they seldom or never attend a mosque. While 46 percent of the respondents said they consider themselves "Sunni," 38 percent said they view themselves as "just Muslims." Ten percent said they are "Shia," while two percent said they are "Sufi," a more mystical interpretation of the faith.

Involved in Civic Life: The vast majority of Muslim respondents (87 percent) said they regularly go to the polls on Election Day and almost half (45 percent) said they volunteer for an institution serving the public.

Democratic or Independent: Forty-nine percent of respondents said they consider themselves Democrats and 36 percent said they are politically independent. Only 8 percent of respondents said they are Republicans. When asked about their preferred presidential candidate, almost half of respondents (45 percent) said they "don't know or haven't decided."

According to the Muslim American Society Center for Electoral Empowerment, more than 2.2 million Muslims are eligible to vote in November. That number accounts for a fraction of the voting population but these voters could swing any number of races from local to national. There are approximately 6-7 million Muslims in the U.S. with large and affluent populations in the battle states of Virginia, Florida, Michigan, Minnesota, Missouri, Nevada, Wisconsin, Ohio and Pennsylvania. This population is divided almost evenly between African Americans (24%), Arab Americans (26%), Asian Americans (26%) and others (24%).

Bigotry in action: Islamophobia in 2008 presidential race

Closing months of 2007 witnessed an alarming increase in Islamophobia by the Republican political leaders who exploited the anti-Islam and anti-Muslim atmosphere prevailed in the post-9/11 America thanks to the government's

Appendix V: American Muslims in politics [284]

internal and external policies as well as some political and religious leaders and agenda-driven media.

Republican presidential candidate Congressman Tom Tancredo reiterates considering "taking out Muslim holy sites" if another terror attack were to take place on American soil. Another Republican Presidential hopeful Senator John McCain says that the United States is a Christian nation and that his Christian faith is of better spiritual guidance than Islam. Yet another Republican presidential candidate Mitt Romney rules out a cabinet position for a Muslim because of their small population.

At the same time, Republican Congressman Peter King, political advisor of another presidential hopeful, Rudy Giuliani, says that there are too many mosques in the United States and adds that the Muslims should be placed under FBI surveillance. New York Congressman King is a ranking Republican on the House Homeland Security Committee. Surprisingly, the front runner hopeful Giuliani endorsed his advisor's statement as Giuliani refused to ask King to retract his statement.

Less than a week after Senator John McCain clinched Republican nomination for November presidential election, Steve King, a leading Republican Congressman launched a bitter racist and Islamophobic attack against Senator Barak Obama, a leading Democratic presidential hopeful.

On an Iowa radio station on March 8, 2008, Congressman Steve King said, "if [Obama] is elected president, then the radical Islamists and their supporters will be dancing in the streets in greater numbers than they did on September 11 because they will declare victory in this War on Terror."

Echoing Cincinnati radio talk show, Bill Cunningham, who warmed up McCain crowd by chanting Barack Hussain Obama, King said: "[Obama's] middle name [Hussain] does matter...because they read a meaning into that in the rest of the world...They will be dancing in the streets because of his middle name [and] because of who his father was and because of his posture that says: pull out of the Middle East and pull out of this conflict."

Congressman King, who is the ranking Republican member of the House Judiciary Subcommittee on Immigration, Citizenship, Refugees, Border

Appendix V: American Muslims in politics [285]

Security and International Law, reiterated his comments on March 10 in an interview with the Associated Press saying, "[Obama will] certainly be viewed as a savior for them," King told The Associated Press, "That's why you will see them supporting him, encouraging him."

Such bigoted and ignorant comments from a rightwing Republican are not unexpected. They echo outrageous comments that have become commonplace among right-wing commentators and radio talk show hosts. Alarmingly, King's fear promoting comments are part of an increasingly vicious pattern as malicious forms of anti-Muslim and anti-Arab bigotry are becoming more prevalent in mainstream discourse.

Disappointedly, Hillary Clinton, in her negatively campaigning, was also playing the religious bigotry card. When Hillary Clinton lost 11 primaries in a row, and saw her life long dream slipping away, she in effect in words and pictures told the American people, "Barack Obama is a clucking Muslim trigger!" When asked if Barack Obama was a Muslim she said, "I don't know." Hillary Clinton's comment came as her campaign staff sent a picture of Barack Obama dressed like an African Muslim to the Drudge Report. Her negative campaign worked and helped in giving her victory in Texas and Ohio primaries.

Obama's picture episode

In February 2008, a furor has erupted as a photo of Barack Obama in a white turban spread across the Web, drawing accusations of fear-mongering and racism from the Obama campaign. The photo was taken on a 2006 trip Sen. Obama made to Kenya. The picture first appeared on the Drudge Report website which said it was circulated by Clinton's staffers and quoted one saying: "Wouldn't we be seeing this on the cover of every magazine if it were [Clinton]?"

The photo came in the wake of e-mail campaigns claiming Obama was raised a Muslim. Tellingly there was no hint of a denial by Clinton campaign. Asked if the Clinton campaign has been circulating the picture, it has effectively responded: "There's nothing wrong with the picture." The row came as the rivals campaign for two crucial primaries on March 4. Hillary

Appendix V: American Muslims in politics [286]

Clinton needed strong victories in both Ohio and Texas to keep her White House campaign alive.

The photo episode, a cheap shot from Clinton campaign, climaxes the smear campaign against Obama. In December, two Clinton Iowa volunteers resigned after forwarding a hoax e-mail that falsely said Obama is a Muslim possibly intent on destroying the United States. Obama is a member of the United Church of Christ and repeatedly clarified that he has never been a Muslim, but false rumors about Islamic ties keep circulating on the Internet.

The photograph, which showed Obama wearing a turban and swaddled in white fabric, was taken in 2006, when the Illinois senator was on a tour of Africa. Obviously, the photograph was intended to suggest that Obama has hidden Islamic sympathies.

The photos were an obvious intent to trigger a mental picture of Obama's alleged Muslim roots to undermine his campaign and take votes away from his promising presidential campaign run.

Even more troubling was the fact that the mere attempt to argue that a candidate who may have any "Muslim-ness" in his family background should be automatically disqualified from the Presidency.

Those who hatched the Muslim Obama rumors would not have bothered had it not been for a political and cultural environment in which demonizing Muslims and their faith.

While religion should not be a factor in selecting a presidential candidate, distortions of faith -- which has included emails absurdly claiming Obama is a "secret Muslim" -- have become a prime example of negative campaigning.

The picture episode was a deplorable new low in negative campaigning during this election season and the broader issue we face is: What does this attempt to smear Obama say about our society?

Muslim voters detect a snub from Obama

Appendix V: American Muslims in politics [287]

When Mr. Obama began his presidential campaign, Muslim Americans from California to Virginia responded with enthusiasm, seeing him as a long-awaited champion of civil liberties, religious tolerance and diplomacy in foreign affairs, the New York Times reported in June 2008, adding: But more than a year later, many say, he has not returned their embrace.

The New York Times pointed out that while the senator has visited churches and synagogues, he has yet to appear at a single mosque. Muslim and Arab-American organizations have tried repeatedly to arrange meetings with Mr. Obama, but officials with those groups say their invitations — unlike those of their Jewish and Christian counterparts — have been ignored.

Aides to Mr. Obama denied that he had kept his Muslim supporters at arm's length. They cited statements in which he had spoken inclusively about American Islam and a radio advertisement he recorded for the recent campaign of Representative Andre Carson, Democrat of Indiana, who this spring became the second Muslim elected to Congress.

In May 2008, Mr. Obama also had a brief, private meeting with the leader of a mosque in Dearborn, Mich., home to the country's largest concentration of Arab-Americans. And this month, a senior campaign aide met with Arab-American leaders in Dearborn, most of whom are Muslim.

According to the New York Times when Senator Barak Obama courted voters in Iowa in December 2007, Representative Keith Ellison, the country's first Muslim congressman, stepped forward eagerly to help. Mr. Ellison believed that Mr. Obama's message of unity resonated deeply with American Muslims the paper said adding: He volunteered to speak on Mr. Obama's behalf at a mosque in Cedar Rapids, one of the nation's oldest Muslim enclaves. But before the rally could take place, aides to Mr. Obama asked Mr. Ellison to cancel the trip because it might stir controversy. Another aide appeared at Mr. Ellison's Washington office to explain. "I will never forget the quote," Mr. Ellison said, leaning forward in his chair as he recalled the aide's words. "He said, 'We have a very tightly wrapped message.' "

Detroit episode

Appendix V: American Muslims in politics [288]

In June 2008, two Muslim women wearing head scarves were barred by campaign volunteers from appearing behind Mr. Obama at a rally in Detroit.

After the episode in Detroit, Mr. Obama telephoned the two Muslim women to apologize. "I take deepest offense to and will continue to fight against discrimination against people of any religious group or background," he said in a statement.

Such gestures have fallen short in the eyes of many Muslim leaders, who say the Detroit incident and others illustrate a disconnect between Mr. Obama's message of unity and his campaign strategy. "The community feels betrayed," said Safiya Ghori, the government relations director in the Washington office of the Muslim Public Affairs Council.

Even some of Mr. Obama's strongest Muslim supporters say they are uncomfortable with the forceful denials he has made in response to rumors that he is secretly a Muslim. (Ten percent of registered voters believe the rumor, according to a poll by the Pew Research Center.) In an interview with "60 Minutes," Mr. Obama said the rumors were offensive to American Muslims because they played into "fearmongering." But on a new section of his Web site, he classifies the claim that he is Muslim as a "smear."

The Muslim smear campaign brought desired results. Public opinion surveys carried out beginning in 2008 showed that a number of Americans (predominately Republicans), believe that Obama is either a Muslim, is the Antichrist or both. In March 2008, a survey conducted by Pew Research Center found that 10% of respondents believed that he is a Muslim. Those who were more likely to believe he is a Muslim included political conservatives (both Republicans and Democrats), people who had not attended college, people who lived in the Midwest or the South, and people in rural areas. [Wikipedia]

A University of Georgia study found that the percentage of Americans who believed that Obama is a Muslim remained constant at approximately 20% in September, October, and November 2008, despite frequent attempts by the media to correct this misperception. [Wikipedia]

Appendix V: American Muslims in politics [289]

Fear-mongering in 2008 presidential election

In a replay of the 2004 and 2006 elections the desperate Republican Party was playing its typical tactic, Scare America. With little to fall on nearly eight years of President Bush's misrule that landed the nation in the worst economic crisis since the Great Depression, the desperate Republican Party has ratcheted up its campaign with half-truths and fear mongering which has been the hallmark of the Bush Administration.

To borrow Arianna Huffington, fear is a frighteningly effective sales pitch -- one that has worked like a charm for Republicans since the days of the Cold War Red Scares, and especially since 9/11.

The most blatant use of fear mongering came on the final day of the Republican National Convention when John McCain delivered his GOP nomination acceptance speech and Rudy Giuliani and Mitt Romney hyped the threat of the so-called "Islamic terrorism."

The Republican presidential nominee Senator John McCain declined to stop using the adjective "Islamic" to describe terrorists and extremist enemies of the United States. Steve Schmidt, a former Bush White House aide who is now a McCain media strategist, told The Washington Times that the use of the word is appropriate and that the candidate will continue to define the enemy that way.

Mr. McCain often uses the term "Islamic" to describe terrorist enemies. The two remaining Democrats in the presidential field, Sen. Barack Obama of Illinois and Sen. Hillary Rodham Clinton of New York, generally shun such word usage. Mr. McCain, an ex-Navy fighter pilot and leading hawk on the Iraq war, regularly uses the term "Islamic" in major foreign-policy speeches and in news conferences.

In a speech in May 2008 to the Los Angeles World Affairs Council, Mr. McCain said the formation of an international coalition "will strengthen us to confront the transcendent challenge of our time: the threat of radical Islamic terrorism." In a Republican debate in January, Mr. McCain turned to then-rival Mitt Romney and said, "I raised it many times, as to whether you have

Appendix V: American Muslims in politics [290]

the experience and the judgment to lead this country in the war against radical Islamic extremism."

In a July speech to Christians United for Israel, Mr. McCain said, "Violent Islamic extremists would have us believe that there is only one acceptable religious practice, and that those who diverge from it are not entitled to life or liberty. They are wrong; very, very wrong."

When it comes to Muslims, the divisive rhetoric coming out of this year's elections ranges from the exclusionary to the just plain bigotry.

Republican front runner John McCain has said he would prefer a Christian president and that the Constitution established America as a "Christian nation." Before dropping out of the presidential race, Mitt Romney conceded that he would not appoint an American Muslim to a cabinet position because Muslims are a low percentage of the population.

One of Mike Huckabee's campaign advisers, Jim Pinkerton, recently advocated putting a "cop in front of every mosque" in America "just for safekeeping."

John Deady, co-chairman of the New Hampshire Veterans for Rudy Giuliani, told the British newspaper The Guardian in late December: "We need to chase [Muslims] back to their caves or, in other words, get rid of them."

Calif. Muslim candidate receives death threat

With a desperate Republican campaign playing fear-mongering card to prop up John McCain, the bigotry and Islamophobia was filtering down to local politics. A Muslim candidate, Todd Gallinger, for Irvine City Council (California) reported receiving a phoned death threat after being smeared by a council member's Islamophobic remarks.

Attorney Todd Gallinger, a Muslim convert, told the Los Angeles Time that a man called his office, about three weeks after Councilman Steven Choi spoke at a forum and urged voters not to support him because he worked for

Appendix V: American Muslims in politics [291]

the Council on American-Islamic Relations (CAIR), a leading Muslim civil rights group.

The CAIR, which has 35 offices in the United States and Canada, is "a dangerous Islamic organization," Choi told 150 business leaders. The LA Times said that although Choi did not name Gallinger, the comment was clearly aimed at the 29-year-old lawyer, who has done legal work for the CAIR's Southern California chapter in Anaheim.

Hate-provoking DVD

In a pathetic attempt to scare people into voting for John McCain, 28 million copies of a right-wing, terror propaganda DVD produced in Israel - "Obsession: Radical Islam's War Against the West" – was mailed and bundled in newspaper deliveries to voters in swing states.

The New York Times in September 2008 inserted 145,000 DVDs in its papers delivered in the following markets: Denver, Miami/Palm Beach, Tampa, Orlando, Detroit, Kansas City, St Louis, Cincinnati, Philadelphia, Pittsburgh, Milwaukee/Madison. These are all in swing states. Next, it was being distributed in many newspapers in the electoral battleground states of Ohio, Michigan, Florida, Pennsylvania and Colorado, in addition to North Carolina.

The Clarion Fund, founded by Israeli-Canadian Rabbi Raphael Shore, paid millions of dollars to get the DVD out. Not surprisingly, the shadowy Clarion Fund has refused to disclose its board of directors or donors.

The noxious propaganda movie, also distributed at the Democratic and Republican parties nomination conventions by Watch Obsession Organization, has been relegated to the university film circuit where right-wing and pro-Israel campus groups have organized screenings.

Jewish and Republican students groups have sponsored scores of screenings of the propaganda film amid protests and rising student tensions on many campuses. A screening at the Pace University in New York was canceled last year and rescheduled only months later after administrators pressured the Jewish Student organization, Hillel's leaders into calling off

Appendix V: American Muslims in politics [292]

their event. Not surprisingly Georgia Tech screening sponsored by the College Republicans required extra security as part of the so-called Islamophobic week dubbed as "Islamofascism Awareness Day" in 2007. Tellingly, a screening at New York University, distributors of the film required viewers to register at IsraelActivism.com, the Web site of Aish HaTorah's Hasbara Fellowships.

"The threat of Radical Islam is the most important issue facing us today. But it's a topic that neither the presidential candidates nor the media are discussing openly. It's our responsibility to ensure we can all make an informed vote in November," reads the sleeve of the DVD.

The movie attempts to equate Islam with Nazism, with showcases scenes of Muslim children being encouraged to become suicide bombers, interspersed with shots of Nazi rallies with narration by commentators such as Islamophobist Daniel Pipes.

Other anti-Muslim and anti-Islam luminaries featuring the film are: Alan M. Dershowitz, Steven Emerson, Brigitte Gabriel, Martin Gilbert, Caroline Glick, Alfons Heck, Glen Jenvey,John Loftus, Itamar Marcus, Walid Shoebat andProf. Robert Wistrich.

The arrival of the controversial DVD on the eve of the election was clearly intended to scare voters into supporting McCain, turning them against the candidate whose middle name happens to be "Hussein." "It was intended to be a way of linking Obama to Islam, but it backfired when a lot of people began saying wait, what's going on?" the Newsweek quoted Jen'nan Read, a professor of sociology at Duke University as saying. "It not only mobilized many Muslim-American voters, but brought out other undecided voters in support of Obama rather than McCain."

7. American Muslims in 2010 election

Since 9/11, there has been a steady rise in Islamophobia, however during mid-term election campaign there was an exponential rise of anti-Islam and anti-Muslim bigotry. Many Religious Right leaders and opportunist politicians asserted repeatedly that Islam is not a religion at all but a political cult, that Muslims cannot be good Americans and that mosques are fronts for extremist 'jihadis.' There was a substantial increase in the number of political candidates using Islamophobic tactics in an effort to leverage votes, and use such tactics as a platform to enhance their political visibility.

Consequently, Muslims rejected the Republican Party at the polls in 2008 and 2010. According to the American Muslim Taskforce on Civil Rights and Elections, just 2.2 percent of Muslims voted for Sen. John McCain in 2008.

As Stephan Salisbury reported, during the 2010 midterm election campaign, virtually every hard-charging candidate on the far right took a moment to trash a Muslim, a mosque, or Islamic pieties. In the wake of those elections, with 85 new Republican House members and a surging Tea Party movement, the political virtues of anti-Muslim rhetoric as a means of rousing voters and alarming the general electorate have gone largely unchallenged. It has become an article of faith that a successful 2010 candidate on the right should treat Islam with revulsion, drawing a line between America the Beautiful and the destructive impurities of Islamic cultists and radicals.

Throughout the 2010 election campaign the seven-million strong American Muslim community and their faith were dehumanized as the Republican Party once again used Islamophobia as a political tool. The anti-Islam and anti-Muslim rhetoric depicting Islam as enemy got steam from the Quran-burning publicity stunts by a minor church in Florida. Two more elements were added to this anti-Muslim hysteria in this election campaign. Controversy over the 51Park project popularly known as Ground Zero mosque and conspiracies that Sharia law will displace the US constitution.

To borrow Kelley B. Vlahos: In fact, anti-Muslim rage in today's national discourse is populism's low-hanging fruit, and many Republicans hungrily

Appendix V: American Muslims in politics [294]

grabbed at it with both fists and were duly rewarded this campaign season. Sure, not every one of the Sarah Palin/Tea Party-endorsed candidates won on Nov. 2, but those who did, won in part because of their willingness to indulge in the Islamophobia coursing through the Republican base today, not despite it. The same Republican base that helped the party torpedo the Democrats last Tuesday, taking back the House, six senate seats, six governorships, and 680 slots in state legislatures.

Never in any U.S. elections before so many campaign ads were aired mongering fear against Islam or Muslims. This year, Republicans have crossed all limits. They are openly bashing Muslims and Islam to get more votes in elections.

In August 2010, Republicans amplified their rhetoric to turn the so-called "Ground Zero Mosque" into a campaign issue.

The American Society for Muslim Advancement and the Cordoba Initiative received tentative approval in May 2010 for construction of the $100 million Islamic center in lower Manhattan. New York City's Landmarks Preservation Commission voted unanimously August 3, 2010 to allow the demolition of a building on Park Place that would be replaced by a mosque.

The developer, Sharif el-Gamal, a real estate investor born in New York, has said the center would include meeting rooms, a prayer space, a 500-seat auditorium and a pool. Two mosques, founded in 1970 and 1985, are already within several blocks of the proposed center. They are so busy and crowded that a search was begun for more space.

Republican gubernatorial candidate Rick Lazio voiced concern over the project in early July 2010, calling on N.Y. Attorney General Andrew Cuomo, who was also the Democratic gubernatorial candidate, to investigate the center's funding. Cuomo rejected the call for an investigation and responded to Lazio in a letter, asking, "What are we about, if not religious freedom?"

Leading Republican figures like Newt Gingrich, a former speaker of the House, and former Alaska governor Sarah Palin, the party's 2008 vice-presidential nominee, had been voicing opposition to the Islamic center.

Appendix V: American Muslims in politics [295]

At an iftar dinner for Ramadan held at the White House on Aug. 13, 2010, President Barrack Obama supported the right of Muslims throughout the U.S. – including in lower Manhattan – to build new mosques and community centers, saying, "as a citizen, and as president, I believe that Muslims have the same right to practice their religion as anyone else in this country."

After his remarks were widely interpreted as an endorsement of the New York City Islamic center, he clarified the next day that his comments were meant to address the issue of religious freedom rather than "the wisdom of making the decision to put a mosque" near the ground zero site.

Inflammatory rhetoric surrounding Park51 project stirred hatred

The inflammatory rhetoric surrounding the project has stirred hatred toward Muslims in America. There has been so much fear-mongering and so much misinformation in the debate peddled by bigots and rightwing politicians. The constant vilification of Islam and Muslims over the air on radio talk shows, in newspapers and the Internet was contributing to the rise in anti-Muslim sentiment across the country.

Not surprisingly, a poll on August 29 by the extreme right San Diego, California 760 KFMB AM talk radio station indicated that 70% of those polled are in favor of forced registration for American Muslims in a national database.

The same day a poll conducted by Chris Matthews show at the MSNBC revealed that more than half of Republicans polled say they have a negative attitude toward Islam, this compared to only 27% of Democrats.

A PEW Institute poll result released on August 24 corroborated the findings of Chris Mathews show. By more than two-to-one (54% to 21%), Republicans expressed an unfavorable opinion of Islam and by more than four-to-one (74% to 17%), Republicans say they agree more with those who object to the building of the Ground Zero Mosque. By contrast, more Democrats agree with the center's supporters than its opponents (by 47% to 39%).

Appendix V: American Muslims in politics [296]

According to a new TIME poll, 61% of respondents opposed the construction of the Park51 project, compared with 26% who support it. Yet the survey also revealed that many Americans harbor lingering animosity toward Muslims.

Twenty-eight percent of voters do not believe Muslims should be eligible to sit on the U.S. Supreme Court. Nearly one-third of the country thinks adherents of Islam should be barred from running for President — a slightly higher percentage than the 24% who mistakenly believe the current occupant of the Oval Office is himself a Muslim.

The Arab American Institute poll

The Arab American Institute on Nov. 1, announced its poll results indicating that 66 percent of Republican voters now hold an unfavorable view of Arabs; 85 percent hold an unfavorable view of Muslims. Compare that to 28 percent who hold a favorable view of Arabs, and 12 percent who hold a favorable view of Muslims.

According to the poll, most Arab Americans favor Democrats over conservative Republicans despite their belief that US President Barack Obama has done a poor job in the Middle East. They believe Republicans have been exploiting ignorance about Islam and the media-induced fear of US Muslims in efforts to gain votes, especially among the conservative Evangelical Christians, in the November mid-term elections.

The poll indicated that many Americans regard their fellow Muslim citizens in a negative light, while most Muslim Americans believe that Islamophobia has never been so high in the United States.

James Zogby, director of the Arab American Institute, said: "The GOP has become captive of several groups that now dominate the party's base and have transformed its thinking. The 'religious right' and its 'end of days' preachers like Pat Robertson, William Hagee and Gary Bauer, presently constitute almost 40% of Republican voters. This group's emphasis on the divinely ordained battle between the forces of 'good' (i.e. the Christian West and Israel) and the forces of 'evil' (Islam and the Arabs) has logically given rise to anti-Muslim prejudice.

"Then there are the Christian right's ideological cousins, the neo-conservatives, who share an identical Manichean and apocalyptic world view, though with a secular twist. And into the mix must be thrown Islamophobic right-wing radio and TV commentators like [Bill] O'Reilly, [Glenn] Beck, [Rush] Limbaugh, [Michael] Savage and company, who daily spew their poison across the airwaves.

"The combination produces a lethal brew that is dangerous not only for the intolerance it has created, but the sense of certitude and self-righteousness it projects."

Park51 controversy leads to political engagement

Motivated by the anti-Islam fervor generated by Park51 Arab and Muslim American organizations and individuals used different methods and tactics were to engage their communities. Leading civil advocacy groups like the Council on Islamic-American Relations (CAIR) and the Muslim Public Affairs Council (MPAC) were acquainting American Muslims with the voting process. The CAIR released voting guides for 23 states that explain when polls open, how to register to vote, what identification is needed and voters' rights.

Leading American Muslim civil advocacy organizations reached out to American Muslims through a series of workshops conducted across the country.

And it's not just in the lead-up to the midterm elections that American Muslims were engaging in the political process. Organizations such as the Council of Islamic Organizations of Greater Chicago helped organize Muslim Action Day in April 2010, when community representatives met legislators at the state capitol to discuss voter issues.

Project Mobilize Chicago

Appendix V: American Muslims in politics [298]

In Chicago, with more than 400,000 Muslim population, organizations like Project Mobilize, Mosque Foundation, CIOGC and CAIR-Chicago and have been active in voter registration. In the city's southwest suburbs, in the 10 precincts surrounding one of largest mosques in the country, 20% of the registered voters are Muslim.

Project Mobilize is a nonprofit organization with the mission of developing the political potential of the Muslim community in Chicago's southwest suburbs. Launched in 2009, it is the first professional political action organization that focuses on the grass-roots political empowerment and engagement of American Muslims through local politics.

Election Day saw the Muslim community in full force doing everything in their civic repertoire from canvassing the houses of people who have yet to vote to making phone calls to registered voters to standing outside polling sites with postcards listing Muslim endorsements of candidates.

The twist this year came in the form of colorful, clearly printed endorsement postcards listing 6 candidates who committed themselves to working on behalf of their Muslim constituents should they be elected to office. Project Mobilize mailed over 1500 of these postcards ahead of Election Day to Muslim voters throughout the Stickney, Palos, Lyons, and Worth townships. On Election Day, almost 20 volunteers spread their efforts across 8 polling sites to make sure Muslim voters had these postcards in hand when they cast their votes.

The Muslim community came out in record numbers to vote during an election season many other communities decided to sit out. The hallmark example of this comes from precinct 44 in Bridgeview, IL. The Muslim community makes up almost 80 percent of the registered voters in this precinct alone and therefore serves as a trend indicator for the Muslim American electorate. Exit polls from precinct 44 revealed that the candidates specific to those voters – candidates Project M endorsed – won in that precinct.

Reema Ahmad, the Director of the Project Mobilize, says that the goal of her group is fielding Muslim American candidates for office. "This is really the next logical step towards us fulfilling our political aspirations. It's about developing that potential, ensuring that people who have aspirations to hold public office know how to get into those positions and garner the support they need," Ahmad said.

The AMT's 2010 Election Plan

On June 13, 2010, the American Muslim Taskforce on Civil Rights and Elections, a nonpartisan umbrella organization, held a town hall meeting at the Dar Al Hijrah Islamic Center in Falls Church, VA to define objectives, issues, strategies; sets forth a bottom-up, community- based decision-making process.

The meeting provided the community with the opportunity to discuss important political matters such as civil liberties and American foreign policy. Muslim leaders were also working to rally the community for heavy involvement in the coming midterm election.

The AMT also released its Vision, Mission and 2010 Election Plan.

Mission and Objectives: Our four main objectives are to: 1) become full partners in the defense, development and prosperity of our homeland, the United States, 2) defend civil and human rights of all, 3) mainstream the American Muslim community, and 4) develop alliances with like-minded fellow Americans on a wide variety of social, political, economic and moral issues.

Issues: Election efforts will focus on a "Civil Rights Plus" agenda. By this we mean that 'the civil rights for all' is the main issue but not the only issue. We remain equally committed to education, homelessness, economic recovery, environmental and ecological safety, electoral reform, crime, and global peace and justice. Our 'civil rights plus agenda' is broadly organized under three categories: a) civil and human rights, b) domestic issues of public good and general welfare, c) global peace with justice, prevention of war, and US relations with the Muslim world.

Appendix V: American Muslims in politics [300]

Strategy: Our overall strategy is premised on the belief that "Our vote is the best guarantee of our civil rights and the best expression of our citizenship". The AMT will organize strategic mobilization of the American Muslim voters at local, state and federal levels, with primary focus on key states and key races. Voter Registration and Voter Education Viewing elections as an opportunity for both self-empowerment and direct participation in discussions about all issues including America's sense of direction and destiny, the AMT shall expend its maximum energy in educating, organizing and mobilizing the American Muslim voters.

The American Muslim Taskforce on Civil Rights and Elections (AMT), includes 11 Muslim Advocacy groups: American Muslim Alliance (AMA), American Muslims for Palestine (AMP), Council on American-Islamic Relations (CAIR), Islamic Circle of North America (ICNA), Muslim Alliance of North America (MANA), Muslim American Society - Freedom (MAS-F), Muslim Legal Fund of America (MLFA), Muslim Ummah of North America (MUNA), Muslim Student Association - National (MSA-N), North American Imams Federation (NAIF), and United Muslims of America (UMA).

Burning of the Quran stunt

The 2010 election season witnessed another method of anti-Muslim bigotry – desecration of the Quran. Anti-Islam and anti-Muslim Pastor Terry Jones of a tiny Florida Church, known as the Dove World Outreach Center, planned to commemorate 9/11 by burning copies of the Quran. He abandoned the Quran burning stunt when US Secretary of Defense phoned him saying that his provocative act would inflame the Muslim world and jeopardize the lives of American troops now deployed in many Muslim countries.

The Miami Herald quoted Pentagon spokesman Geoff Morrell as saying that Gates had weighed concerns that making such a call could encourage copycats who want attention, but felt that "if that phone call could save the life of one man or woman in uniform, that call was worth placing."

Pastor of the 50-member Pentecostal church, Jones, made the stunt abandoning announcement at a press conference while standing alongside Imam Muhammad Musri, the president of the Islamic Society of

Appendix V: American Muslims in politics [301]

Central Florida. He claimed that his decision to scrap the burning of Muslims' holy book was tied to his understanding that the New York Islamic cultural center project officially named as Park51 but popularly known as the Ground Zero mosque, would be scrapped or relocated.

However, Imam Feisal Abdul Rauf has not agreed to such a deal. Park51 posted a Twitter feed after Jones spoke. It said that "it is untrue that Park51 is being moved. The project is moving ahead as planned." Tellingly, Jones had never invoked the New York mosque controversy as a reason for his planned protest. He cited his belief that "the Quran is evil" because it espouses something other than biblical truth and incites radical, violent behavior among Muslims.

Tellingly, Jones message was not lost to many. Torn pages of the Quran were found on Sept 10 at the front of the Islamic Center of East Lansing, Michigan. Some of the pages appeared to be smeared with feces.

Amid heightened hate speech and fear-mongering mosques in California, Tennessee, New York, Illinois, Wisconsin, Kentucky, Texas, and Florida have faced vocal opposition or have been targeted by hate incidents. In one incident, on the 9/11 eve, vandals spray-painted "9-11" on windows and countertops at the Muslim owned Jaffa Market in Columbus, Ohio. Some cash and a laptop computer were stolen, while several display cases were vandalized. On Sept 8, back wall of the Hudson Islamic Center in New York was pained with slur "sand n**gers" and an obscenity. In early September, a Phoenix under construction mosque was vandalized. Paint was spilled on the floor and several tall, arched glass windows were broken by what appeared to be gunshots. There was also anti-Muslim graffiti. The same mosque was vandalized in the February.

The presence of mosques and the building of new mosques have become a divisive issue in several communities across the country in recent years. A church may be a church, and a temple a temple, but through the prism of emotion that grips many Americans, almost a decade after 9/11, a mosque can apparently represent a lot of things.

Oklahoma anti-Shariah measure

Appendix V: American Muslims in politics [302]

Islam-bashing for political gain was a chilling feature of this year's election campaign and demagogues misled Oklahomans to pass an anti-Muslim ballot measure. The Oklahoma anti-Islam measure is one of the best examples of politicians duping the public through fear mongering. It is demonizing the Muslims in order to mobilize votes. The voters of Oklahoma were badly misled by demagogues into passing a profoundly un-American measure.

Demagoguery is defined as: "the practice of a leader who obtains power by means of impassioned appeals to the emotions and prejudices of the populace." Oklahoma Rep. Rex Duncan's proposed the anti-Islam ballot measure, known as SQ 755, is a great example of this practice. When it was proposed, Sen. Anthony Sykes, a co-author, dubbed it the "Save Our State," amendment saying, "Sharia law coming to the U.S. is a scary concept."

The anti-Muslim frenzy strengthened by a media blitz by Muslim-basher Act! For America in support of the measure brought the desired results.

While, nearly 70 percent of voters in the state cast ballots approving the measure, it also helped in posting historic gains for the Republicans in Oklahoma House and Senate after several Democratic incumbents were knocked out of office.

Perhaps every Republican now imagines to have discovered the winning formula to either get reelected or unseat their Democratic opponent in the coming elections.

A campaign called Act! For America, had launched a "media blitz" in the state of Oklahoma. The campaign included a radio ad and opinion articles in state newspapers. Muslim-basher President of ACT, Brigitte Gabriel, stated, "We want to make sure that the people in Oklahoma are educated about what Shariah law is all about and its ramifications. We're not taking any chances with this initiative passing marginally. We hope it passes with great victory."

Former House Speaker Newt Gingrich is one of the top voices spreading concern that Islamic law may creep into American courts, although he has not provided proof that such fears are justified.

Appendix V: American Muslims in politics [303]

Gingrich attracted national headlines in September at the Values Voter Summit in Washington when he declared, "I am opposed to any efforts to impose Sharia in the United States." "We should have a federal law that says under no circumstances in any jurisdiction in the United States will Sharia [law] be used in any court to apply to any judgment made about American law," Gingrich said.

The anti-Sharia bills symbolize the anti-Islam and anti-Muslim campaigns which increase bias among the public by endorsing the idea that Muslims are second-class citizens. They encourage and accelerate both the acceptability of negative views of Muslims and the expression of those negative views by the public and government agencies like the police.

Judge bars certification of Oklahoma measure

In a strongly-worded ruling a federal judge in Oklahoma on November 29, 2010 granted an injunction that bars certification of an anti-Islam state ballot measure (SQ 755) passed in the November 2 election.

Muneer Awad, executive director of the Council on American-Islamic Relations in Oklahoma, quickly challenged the amendment, saying it demonizes his faith. The judge on Nov. 8 agreed to a temporary restraining order barring the state Election Board from certifying the SQ 755 results. Her order on Nov 29 means the Election Board is barred indefinitely from certifying the results.

If it had been certified, SQ 755 would have amended that state's constitution to forbid judges from considering Islamic principles or international law when deciding a case.

The ruling by Chief Judge Vicki Miles-LaGrange of the United States District Court for the Western District of Oklahoma ordered a preliminary injunction to block the certification of the amendment by the Oklahoma State Board of Elections until a final determination is made based on the merits of a lawsuit against SQ 755 filed by Muneer Awad, executive director of CAIR's Oklahoma chapter (CAIR-OK). In her ruling in support of Awad's legal arguments, Judge Miles-LaGrange wrote:

Appendix V: American Muslims in politics [304]

"This order addresses issues that go to the very foundation of our country, our (U.S.) Constitution, and particularly, the Bill of Rights. Throughout the course of our country's history, the will of the 'majority' has on occasion conflicted with the constitutional rights of individuals, an occurrence which our founders foresaw and provided for through the Bill of Rights."

Federal court deals blow to "anti-Muslim" bigots

In a major blow to the anti-Islam and anti-Muslim bigots taking refuge behind the so-called anti-Sharia legislation, a federal appeals court on January 10, 2012 agreed with a lower court that blocked an Oklahoma law that would have barred state courts from considering or using the so-called Shariah law.

The judge for the 10th U.S. Circuit Court of Appeals in Denver, Colo., agreed with the lower court and upheld the injunction — rejecting an appeal by the state of Oklahoma. "Because the amendment discriminates among religions, it is 'suspect,'" the higher court ruled, "and 'we apply strict scrutiny in adjudging its constitutionality.'"

"While the public has an interest in the will of the voters being carried out ... the public has a more profound and long-term interest in upholding an individual's constitutional rights," the 10th U.S. Court of Appeals said.

The Denver-based court ruled 3-0 that the rights of an Oklahoma City Muslim, Muneer Awad, likely would be violated if the ban on Shariah law takes effect. "When the law that voters wish to enact is likely unconstitutional, their interests do not outweigh Mr. Awad's in having his constitutional rights protected," the judges wrote in a 37-page decision.

Appendix V: American Muslims in politics [305]

The Muslim swing vote in 2012 election

As the 2012 presidential election season moved into full swing, the American Muslim minority community has become a more important player on the political landscape, especially in key swing states, says a report titled Engaging American Muslims: Political Trends and Attitudes released by the Institute for Social Policy and Understanding on April 3, 2012.

According to Farid Senzai, author of the report, although it is true that American Muslims constitute a small percentage of the national population, they are concentrated in key swing states such as Michigan, Ohio, Virginia, Pennsylvania and Florida. "Despite being very diverse and far from monolithic, this constituency is growing faster than any other religious community and has become increasingly visible and sophisticated in its political engagement. Republicans who found the Muslim community an easy target in the primaries may find themselves in trouble in the states that may determine the winner of the election."

The report examined a decade's worth of data on American Muslim political attitudes and includes a case study of Florida, which remains a perennial tossup. In addition to the razor-thin margin in 2000, the state's 2004 and 2008 elections were settled by less than 2% of the vote. In 2000, a few hundred votes decided the election; an estimated 60,000 Muslims in Florida voted for Bush. Florida's Muslim population, which has been growing since the 1980s, is now estimated by some to include 124,000 registered voters. No campaigner can afford to disregard them.

The report primarily draws upon surveys conducted by the Muslims in the American Public Square (MAPS) project in 2001 and 2004, the Pew Research Center's national surveys on the American Muslim Community in 2007 and 2011, and the Muslim American Public Opinion Survey (MAPOS) conducted between 2006 and 2008.

Key findings of the report

American Muslims were at a political and social crossroad after September 11, 2001. Soon after 9/11, the majority of Muslims engaged in a massive

Appendix V: American Muslims in politics [306]

political shift away from the Republican Party. Arab-American and South Asian-American Muslims who initially supported Governor George W. Bush (R-TX) in the 2000 presidential election gave their support to Senator John Kerry (D-MA) in 2004. This political realignment was a result of several factors, among them the passing of laws such as the PATRIOT Act and the Bush administration's decision to invade Afghanistan and Iraq. Between 2001 and 2004, the percentage of American Muslims who were dissatisfied with the country's direction soared from 38 percent to 63 percent.

The shift toward the Democratic Party was further strengthened when the community voted overwhelmingly for Senator Barack Obama (D-IL) in 2008. Despite some disappointments, the community strongly supported him during his first term in office. In 2011, Obama continued to maintain a higher approval rating among American Muslims than the general public.

Since 9/11, American Muslims have faced increased discrimination, profiling, and hate crimes. The MAPS study suggests that they have experienced a dramatic increase in all types of discrimination since that tragic incident. In 2009, 58 percent of Americans expressed the belief that Muslims face "a lot" of discrimination. The increased animosity toward them, coupled with the rise of Islamophobia, has motivated the community to mobilize and become more politically active.

Research has shown that American Muslims are well informed about politics and pay attention to what is happening both at home and abroad. The vast majority of them want to be politically involved, with 95 percent stating that American Muslims should participate in the political process. Voter registration in the community, however, continues to trail that of the general public. The Pew survey suggests that 66 percent of the community's were registered to vote in 2011. This percentage would likely be much higher if one were to count only those who are citizens and therefore eligible to vote.

Contrary to growing public opinion, most American Muslims do not see a conflict between their faith and being American or living in a modern society. The majority of them feel that American Muslims, a large number of whom are immigrants or children of immigrants, should adopt American culture and become part of the mainstream. Furthermore, studies support the idea that mosques, like churches and synagogues, are associated with a higher level of civic engagement. American Muslims who were engaged in their mosques were found to be 53 percent more involved in civic activities (e.g., charity organizations, school and/or youth programs) than those who were not connected or involved with a mosque.

American Muslims are more concerned with domestic than foreign policy

Surveys have also examined the community's opinions on a number of policy issues. The data suggest that American Muslims, much like the American public in general, are more concerned with domestic than foreign policy and with the economy in particular. They generally demonstrate a high level of support for immigration and support the view that immigrants strengthen, rather than burden, the country. However, there are important racial distinctions on this issue, as African-American Muslims have a much less favorable view of immigrants. During the past decade, American Muslims have also become more accepting of homosexuality.

When it comes to American policy in the Middle East and the "war on terror," American Muslims have been largely unsupportive of the wars in Afghanistan and Iraq, with the lowest amount of support being found among African-American Muslims. There has been, however, a decreasing skepticism about the sincerity of the "war against terror" over the decade. Most community members believe that the best way to combat terror is to change American policy in the Middle East and to address the region's social, economic, and political issues. The majority of them continue to believe that Israel and Palestine can coexist and that a solution to the conflict is possible.

The Florida case study suggests that the American Muslim voter community is increasingly engaged, in part due to the mobilization efforts of Emerge USA and similar organizations. In a swing state, the community has the potential to impact the election's outcome. Similarly, American Muslims in Michigan were found to be very active and politically engaged.

Muslim bashing by Republicans

In an OpEd in New York Times, Farid Senzai, pointed out that as the 2012 presidential election picks up steam, Republican candidates find it tempting and beneficial to bash Muslims as a way to attract voters. He went on to say:

"In the wake of the 2010 midterm elections, "Americans are learning what Europeans have known for years: Islam-bashing wins votes," the journalist Michael Scott Moore wrote that November. At the time, many of the 85 new Republican House members buoyed by the surging Tea Party movement found the political virtues of anti-Muslim rhetoric an easy way to prove their mettle to the surging conservative base.

"Since then, the animosity against Muslims has only intensified. Republican presidential hopefuls Herman Cain and Newt Gingrich frequently warned that Muslims were attempting to take over the government and impose Shariah law, using "stealth Jihad," as Gingrich put it in a speech at the American Enterprise Institute late last year.

"The problem for the United States, the former speaker of the house argued, is not primarily terrorism; it is Shariah — "the heart of the enemy movement from which the terrorists spring forth." Rick Santorum, not one to shy away from the subject, continues to conflate Muslims with radical Islamists. He has often warned audiences of the dangers of losing the war to "radical Islam," even suggesting in a 2007 speech at the National Academic Freedom Conference that the American response to the threat should be to "educate, engage, evangelize and eradicate."

Farid Senzai believes that this type of anti-Muslim rhetoric is deployed by some candidates in an apparent attempt to tap into hostility among the voters who make up the base of the party. In a sense, this approach is validated by recent polls suggesting that Republicans are more likely to have anti-Muslim sentiments. The political scientists Michael Tesler and David Sears wrote in their 2010 book, "Obama's Race," that feelings about Muslims are a strong predictor about feelings about Obama. They found that

Appendix V: American Muslims in politics [309]

"general election vote choice in 2008 was more heavily influenced by feelings about Muslims than it was in either 2004 voting or in McCain-Clinton trial heats." As we get closer to the November election, the most likely Republican nominee, Mitt Romney, will have to balance between pandering to voters on the far right of his party, some of whom are already wary of him, and more moderate voters.

While an anti-Muslim strategy may have worked in the past, it is risky because many agree that the outcome of the 2012 presidential election will probably be determined in no more than twelve states, Senzai warned and added that these are the same states where minority groups, including American Muslims, are likely to play a decisive role.

The Report Recommendations

1) Provide Resources to Further Mobilize the Community: Empirical evidence suggests that American Muslims are increasingly active and civically engaged citizens. Although their level of political incorporation and mobilization has increased over the past decade, the community as a whole is still not as engaged as it could be. For example, some levels of involvement trail behind those of the general public, including the percentage of those who are active members of a political party or contribute to political campaigns. Community organizers must provide the information and resources needed to help motivate and mobilize the community further.

2) Tap into the Community's Active Segments: Nationally, African-American Muslims were found to be most active in almost all categories of political participation, compared to immigrant Muslims. In addition, state level data in Michigan showed high political engagement by women and young people. Community organizers and political strategists should tap into these highly active subgroups to lead their communities.

3) Engage with Mosque Communities: Evidence suggests that higher levels of religiosity and mosque attendance lead to higher levels of political participation. This can be seen in mosque participants' higher voting levels, increased awareness of the issues, writing to their representatives, engaging

Appendix V: American Muslims in politics [310]

peacefully in political protest, and other indicators of political activity. Candidates, political leaders, and community organizers trying to reach out to Muslim voters should reach out to the mosque leadership and active members.

4) Speak to the Issues That Concern American Muslims: The American Muslim community can be cultivated for either a Republican or a Democratic candidate, particularly in such swing states as Michigan, Ohio, Pennsylvania, and Florida. This report highlights evidence that candidates can build better relations with the community by demonstrating awareness of those issues that are of most concern to community members.

Farid Senzai is assistant professor of political science at Santa Clara University and director of research at the Institute for Social Policy and Understanding.

Appendix VI

2001-2011: A decade of civil liberties' erosion in America

The people can always be brought to the bidding of the leaders. Tell them they are being attacked, and denounce the peace-makers for lack of patriotism and for exposing the country to danger. [Nazi leader Herman Goering]

By Abdus Sattar Ghazali

Prof. Gary Orfield of the UCLA Civil Rights Project wrote in May 2003: "The loss of civil rights often begins with the reduction of rights in a time of crisis, for a minority that has become the scapegoat for a problem facing the nation. The situation can become particularly explosive in a time of national tragedy or war. But when civil rights for one group of Americans are threatened and the disappearance of those rights is accepted, it becomes a potential threat to many others." [1]

Prof. Orfield wrote this while commenting on the plight of Arabs and Muslims who were the immediate target of Patriot Act provisions and other legislations in the aftermath of 9/11. However his prediction proved correct about the erosion of civil rights of all citizens. In the last ten years we have seen a steady erosion of the fundamental rights and civil liberties, all in the name of national security.

The gradual erosion of our civil liberties came in the shape of Warrantless Wiretapping, abuse of the USA PATRIOT Act, the National Security Entry/Exit Registration System (NSEERS), the Real ID Act, the Military Commissions Act, No Fly and Selectee Lists, Abuse of Material Witness Statute, Attacks on Academic Freedom and monitoring peaceful groups.

Appendix VI: A decade of civil liberties erosion [310]

The so-called War on Terror has seriously compromised the First, Fourth, Fifth and Sixth Amendment rights of citizens and non-citizens alike. From the USA PATRIOT Act's over-broad definition of domestic terrorism, to the FBI's new powers of search and surveillance, to the indefinite detention of both citizens and non-citizens without formal charges, the principles of free speech, due process, and equal protection under the law have been seriously undermined.

As Glenn Greenwald pointed out, the most disgraceful episodes in American history have been about exempting classes of Americans from core rights, and that is exactly what these recent, terrorism-justified proposals do as well. Anyone who believes that these sorts of abusive powers will be exercised only in narrow and magnanimous ways should just read a little bit of history, or just look at what has happened with the always-expanding police powers vested in the name of the never-ending War on Drugs, the precursor to the never-ending War on Terrorism in so many ways. [2]

To quote Glenn Greenwald again: "A primary reason Bush and Cheney succeeded in their radical erosion of core liberties is because they focused their assault on non-citizens with foreign-sounding names, casting the appearance that none of what they were doing would ever affect the average American. There were several exceptions to that tactic -- the due-process-free imprisonment of Americans Yaser Hamdi and Jose Padilla, the abuse of the "material witness" statute to detain American Muslims, the eavesdropping on Americans' communications without warrants -- but the vast bulk of the abuses were aimed at non-citizens. That is now clearly changing.

"The most recent liberty-abridging, Terrorism-justified controversies have focused on diluting the legal rights of American citizens (in part because the rights of non-citizens are largely gone already and there are none left to attack). A bipartisan group from Congress sponsors legislation to strip Americans of their citizenship based on Terrorism accusations. Barack Obama claims the right to assassinate Americans far from any battlefield and with no due process of any kind.

Appendix VI: A decade of civil liberties erosion [311]

The Obama administration begins covertly abandoning long-standing Miranda protections for American suspects by vastly expanding what had long been a very narrow "public safety" exception, and now Eric Holder explicitly advocates legislation to codify that erosion.

"John McCain and Joe Lieberman introduce legislation to bar all Terrorism suspects, including Americans arrested on U.S. soil, from being tried in civilian courts, and former Bush officials Bill Burck and Dana Perino -- while noting (correctly) that Holder's Miranda proposal constitutes a concession to the right-wing claim that Miranda is too restrictive -- today demand that U.S. citizens accused of Terrorism and arrested on U.S. soil be treated as enemy combatants and thus denied even the most basic legal protections (including the right to be charged and have access to a lawyer). This shift in focus from non-citizens to citizens is as glaring as it is dangerous." [3]

With the victory of Democrats and election of Obama in 2008, it was hoped that the Bush era of warrantless wiretapping, indefinite detention, torture and police statism would recede. Obama was voted into office on promises that included undoing abuses carried out under the Bush administration - promises to protect privacy, to end government-sanctioned torture and rendition programs and to end the use of military commissions for non-enemy combatants – but his administration has toed the Bush era policies.

According to July 2011 ACLU report "Establishing the New Normal," the current White House has not just failed to meaningfully follow through on its promises, but has also taken abusive policies, and, as shown in the case of targeted and interminable detentions, eroded civil rights to unprecedented levels. The ACLU enumerates the following top ten abuses of power since 9/11: [4]

1. Warrantless Wiretapping — Soon after the September 11 terrorist attacks, President Bush issued an executive order that authorized the infamous National Security Agency (NSA) warrantless wiretapping program. This secret eavesdropping program allowed the surveillance of certain telephone calls placed between a party in the United States and a party in a foreign country without obtaining a warrant through the Foreign Intelligence Surveillance Court.

Appendix VI: A decade of civil liberties erosion [312]

In December 2005, the New York Times reported the National Security Agency was tapping into telephone calls of Americans without a warrant, in violation of federal statutes and the Constitution. Furthermore, the agency had also gained direct *access* to the telecommunications infrastructure through some of America's largest companies. The program was confirmed by President Bush and other officials, who boldly insisted, in the face of all precedent and the common understanding of the law, that the program was legal.

During the presidential campaign season, Obama's campaign promised that he would vote to filibuster any bill that gave amnesty to telecom companies that had cooperated with Bush's illegal NSA warrantless wiretapping program. But then Obama voted to legalize the program, to give immunity to the government and its connected telecoms. He voted for cloture — against filibuster. And now this issue is not even being debated. We have a Bushian surveillance state approved by both political parties. It is a bipartisan feature of leviathan, much like Social Security or the war on drugs.

2. Torture, Kidnapping and Detention — In the years since 9/11, our government has illegally kidnapped, detained and tortured numerous prisoners. The government continues to claim that it has the power to designate anyone, including Americans as "enemy combatants" without charge. Since 2002, some "enemy combatants," have been held at Guantanamo Bay and elsewhere, in some cases without access by the Red Cross. Investigations into other military detention centers have revealed severe human rights abuses and violations of international law, such as the Geneva Conventions. The government has also engaged in the practice of rendition: secretly kidnapping people and moving them to foreign countries where they are tortured and abused. It has been reported the CIA maintains secret prison camps in Eastern Europe to conduct operations that may also violate international standards. Congress made matters worse by enacting the Military Commissions Act, which strips detainees of their habeas rights, guts the enforceability of the Geneva Conventions' protections against abuse, and even allows persons to be prosecuted based on evidence beaten out of a witness.

Appendix VI: A decade of civil liberties erosion [313]

3. The Growing Surveillance Society — In perhaps the greatest assault on the privacy of ordinary Americans, the country is undergoing a rapid expansion of data collection, storage, tracking, and mining. Today the government is spying on Americans in ways the founders of our country never could have imagined. The FBI, federal intelligence agencies, the military, state and local police, private companies, and even firemen and emergency medical technicians are gathering incredible amounts of personal information about ordinary Americans that can be used to construct vast dossiers that can be widely shared with a simple mouse-click through new institutions like Joint Terrorism Task Forces, fusion centers, and public-private partnerships. The fear of terrorism has led to a new era of overzealous police intelligence activity directed, as in the past, against political activists, racial and religious minorities, and immigrants.

This surveillance activity is not directed solely at suspected terrorists and criminals. It's directed at all of us. Increasingly, the government is engaged in suspicionless surveillance that vacuums up and tracks sensitive information about innocent people. Even more disturbingly, as the government's surveillance powers have grown more intrusive and more powerful, the restrictions on many of those powers have been weakened or eliminated. And this surveillance often takes place in secret, with little or no oversight by the courts, by legislatures, or by the public.

4. Abuse of the Patriot Act — In 2001, just 45 days after 9/11, Congress passed the USA PATRIOT Act severely limiting the constitutional rights of immigrants and US citizens. The Act permitted non-citizens to be jailed based on mere suspicion without charges and detained indefinitely. It broadened the definition of activities considered "deportable offenses," including defining soliciting funds for an organization that the government labels as terrorist as "engaging in terrorist activity". The PATRIOT Act also subjected lawful advocacy groups to surveillance, wiretapping, harassment, and criminal action for legal political advocacy, expanded the ability of law enforcement to conduct secret searches and engage in phone and internet surveillance, and gave law enforcement access to personal medical and financial records. Related executive orders barred press and the public from immigration hearings of those detained after September 11th, allowed the government to monitor communications between federal detainees and their

Appendix VI: A decade of civil liberties erosion [314]

lawyers, and ordered military commissions to be set up to try suspected terrorists who are not citizens.

On May 26, 2011, Congress, rejecting demands for additional safeguards of civil liberties, approved a four-year extension to key provisions of the Bush era Patriot Act that will allow federal investigators to continue to use aggressive surveillance tactics in connection with suspected terrorists. One of the sections of the Patriot Act extended by Congress (Section 206) is the "roving wiretap" power, which allows federal authorities to listen in on conversations of foreign suspects even when they change phones or locations. Another provision, Section 215 of the Patriot Act, gives the government access to the personal records of terrorism suspects; it's often called the "library provision" because of the wide range of personal material that can be investigated. The third provision extended for four year is Section 6001 of the Intelligence Reform and Terrorist Prevention Act. In 2004, Congress amended the Foreign Intelligence Surveillance Act to authorize intelligence gathering on individuals not affiliated with any known terrorist organization, with a sunset date to correspond with the Patriot Act provisions.

5. Government Secrecy — The Bush administration has been one of the most secretive and nontransparent in our history. The Freedom of Information Act has been weakened , the administration has led a campaign of reclassification and increased secrecy by federal agencies (including the expansion of a catch-all category of "sensitive but unclassified"), and has made sweeping claims of "state secrets" to stymie judicial review of many of its policies that infringe on civil liberties.

The July 2011 report by the American Civil Liberties Union, "Drastic Measures Required," illustrates the vast and systemic use of secrecy, including secret agencies, secret committees in Congress, a secret court and even secret laws, to keep government activities away from public scrutiny. "Our government has reached unparalleled levels of secrecy," said Laura W. Murphy, director of the ACLU Washington Legislative Office. "Though this administration's attempts to be transparent are laudable, the reality has been that it is just as secretive as its predecessor. Congress has

Appendix VI: A decade of civil liberties erosion [315]

the tools to curb this excessive secrecy but it must be more aggressive in using them. It's time to drastically overhaul the way our government classifies information.

6. Real ID — The 2005 Real ID Act, rammed through Congress by being attached to a unrelated, "must pass" bill, lays the foundation for a national ID card and makes it more difficult for persecuted people to seek asylum. Under the law, states are required to standardize their driver's licenses (according to a still undetermined standard) and link to databases to be shared with every federal, state and local government official in every other state

Real ID requires people to verify legal residence in the US in order to get a driver's license, permits secret deportation hearings and trials, reduces judicial review of deportation orders and makes non-citizens (including long-time permanent residents) deportable for past lawful speech or associations.

7. No Fly and Selectee Lists — The No-Fly list was established to keep track of people the government prohibits from traveling because they have been labeled as security risks. Since 9/11 the number of similar watch lists has mushroomed to about 720,000 names, all with mysterious or ill-defined criteria for how names are placed on the lists, and with little recourse for innocent travelers seeking to be taken off them. The lists are so erroneous several members of Congress, including Senator Ted Kennedy (D-MA), have been flagged.

8. Political Spying — Government agencies — including the FBI and the Department of Defense — have conducted their own spying on innocent and law-abiding Americans. Through the Freedom of Information Act, the ACLU learned the FBI had been consistently monitoring peaceful groups such Quakers, People for the Ethical Treatment of Animals, Greenpeace, the Arab American Anti-Defamation Committee and, indeed, the ACLU itself.

9. Abuse of Material Witness Statute — In the days and weeks after 9/11, the government gathered and detained many people — mostly Muslims in the US — through the abuse of a narrow federal technicality that permits the arrest and brief detention of "material witnesses," or those who have important information about a crime. Most of those detained as material

Appendix VI: A decade of civil liberties erosion [316]

witnesses were never treated as witnesses to the crimes of 9/11, and though they were detained so that their testimony could be secured, in many cases, no effort was made to secure their testimony.

The government has found alternative ways to hold people indefinitely without charge, sometimes simply because they believe the person might do something in the future. They have used immigration detention to target certain groups based on racial or religious profiling, abused federal grand jury conspiracy charges, and held activists on the vague charge of "material support." [The Center for Constitutional Rights]

10. Attacks on Academic Freedom — The Bush administration has used a provision in the Patriot Act to engage in a policy of "censorship at the border" to keep scholars with perceived political views the administration does not like out of the United States. The government has moved to over classify information and has engaged in outright censorship and prescreening of scientific articles before publication.

The following two measures may be added to this list of abuse of power:

1. In August of 2002 the Department of Justice initiated **the National Security Entry/Exit Registration System (NSEERS)** "special registration" program requiring nearly 85,000 men from 24 Muslim countries and North Korea to voluntarily report to INS facilities for "special registration" which entailed fingerprinting, photographing, and questioning about their immigration status. The men were required to appear for annual interviews if they stayed in the US for more than one year and to register with immigration officials when they leave the country.

While no terrorist has been found through the program 13,000 of the men who voluntarily reported ended up in deportation proceedings due to their immigration status. In December 2003, the NSEERS program was supplemented by US-VISIT, a program that takes biometric measurements of people entering the US from certain countries including fingerprints and face scans.

Appendix VI: A decade of civil liberties erosion [317]

On April 27, 2011, The Department of Homeland Security (DHS) announced the end of the National Security Entry-Exit Registration System (NSEERS). This special registration process is no longer required.

2. In October of 2006 **The Military Commissions Act** (MCA) was signed into law, effectively creating a separate system of justice for non-citizens. The act denies non-citizens the right to challenge their detention in court, allows any non-citizen to be tried by military commission and permits indefinite detention of non-citizens. The act will also allow non-citizens to be convicted on the basis of coerced testimony, hearsay evidence and warrantless searches, and sanction interrogation practices that amount to torture. This law effectively abolished habeas corpus for individuals declared "enemy combatants" by the U.S. government.

The American Civil Liberties Union (ACLU) reports that "the Military Commissions Act gives the president absolute power to decide who is an enemy of our country and to imprison people indefinitely without charging them with a crime." According to ACLU's MCA fact sheet: "This law removes the Constitutional due process right of habeas corpus for persons the president designates as unlawful enemy combatants. It allows our government to continue to hold hundreds of prisoners more than four years without charges, with no end in sight."

Senator Obama voted against the Military Commissions Act of 2006, which stripped the federal judiciary over habeas corpus review power over aliens detained abroad. Obama gave a speech that September on the Senate floor pleading his colleagues to amend the bill and restore habeas corpus. He criticized the Detainee Treatment Act and lamented the procedural inadequacy of the Combatant Status Review Tribunals. He pointed out the irony of the multi-tiered judicial processes used to process so-called enemy combatants. [5]

Obama appealed to habeas corpus many times in public, casting his lot with these principles that were part of the "Anglo-American legal system for over 700 years." "The great traditions of our legal system and our way of life" were at stake, he boldly said. He repeatedly said we must close down

Appendix VI: A decade of civil liberties erosion [318]

Guantanamo, and he would do so. He cheered on the *Boumediene v. Bush* decision in 2008 that overturned the military commissions act's worst elements and extended habeas to Guantanamo. He pointed out that the commissions were not even yielding many convictions, and consistently decried the "legal black hole" of having a system unchecked by habeas corpus, prisoner of war protections or the Geneva Convention. [6]

Obama reverted to Bush detention policy in virtually every way

After week one in the White House, Obama reverted to Bush detention policy in virtually every way. One of the first major disgraces concerned detainees at Bagram, the prison camp in Afghanistan, where Bush began shipping more detainees after Guantanamo was no longer his lawless playground, and where Obama has increased funding and the prison population. Four men sued for habeas relief. Justice John Bates, a federal judge appointed by Bush found that habeas should apply, in limited capacity, to Bagram, given that the Supreme Court ruled that it extended to Guantanamo. Obama's administration appealed this ruling, using Bushian reasoning down the line. [7]

Bagram is even worse than Guantanamo, where at least the CRST process existed, and the military commissions have freed hundreds of people. Bagram is simply a dungeon beyond the law, and Obama has basked in it with only a little criticism from the left. As for Guantanamo, Obama had promised to close it by January 2010. It is not closed and current plans indicate it will be closed, perhaps around the end of Obama's first term. There is talk of bringing Gitmo to the mid-west, which raises other concerns of setting the precedent that you don't need to go to Cuba to find an American legal black hole. A cry for justice in the spirit of "Yes We Can" has morphed into a totalitarian-style five-year plan. And the abuses there have only gotten worse. [8]

Raymond Azar, Obama's first rendition victim, was not even an alleged terrorist or belligerent. He was accused of a white-collar crime that shouldn't even be a crime — failing to come forward regarding very minor corruption in defense contracting. But for an alleged white-collar non-crime, this Lebanese man working at Sima International was arrested in Afghanistan

Appendix VI: A decade of civil liberties erosion [319]

and, according to his testimony, taken to Bagram, deprived of sleep, stripped naked, subjected to extreme temperatures and stress positions, deprived of food, confined in a metal box and railroaded into a plea bargain lest he never see his family again. **[9]**

Judge blocks enforcement of National Defense Authorization Act

On December 31, 2011, President Obama signed the National Defense Authorization Act (NDAA), codifying indefinite military detention without charge or trial into law for the first time in American history. The NDAA's dangerous detention provisions would authorize the president — and all future presidents — to order the military to pick up and indefinitely imprison people captured anywhere in the world, far from any battlefield.

Section 1021 of the NDAA vaguely endorses the claimed presidential authority to indefinitely detain Americans as enemy combatants under "existing law," i.e. the Authorization to Use Military Force Act.

Section 1021 of the NDAA explicitly allows for the indefinite detention of Americans captured abroad, as well as foreigners.

Section 1022 of the NDAA authorizes the indefinite military detention of Americans. While this section does not require the military to detain U.S. citizens, the authority or option to do so remains.*

The power to indefinitely detain individuals under the NDAA remains "until the end of hostilities" – an indefinite and undetermined length of time.

According to American Civil Liberties Union (ACLU)

- The law is an historic threat because it codifies indefinite military detention without charge or trial into law for the first time in American history. It could permit the president – and all future presidents – to order the military to imprison indefinitely civilians captured far from any battlefield without charge or trial.
- This kind of sweeping detention power is completely at odds with our American values, violates the Constitution, and corrodes our

Appendix VI: A decade of civil liberties erosion [320]

Nation's commitment to the rule of law, which generations have fought to preserve.
- The breadth of the NDAA's worldwide detention authority violates the Constitution and international law because it is not limited to people captured in an actual armed conflict, as required by the laws of war.
- Under the Bush administration, claims of worldwide detention authority were used to hold even a U.S. citizen captured on U.S. soil in military custody, and many in Congress assert that the NDAA should be used in the same way. The ACLU does not believe that the NDAA authorizes military detention of American citizens or anyone else in the United States. Any president's claim of domestic military detention authority under the NDAA would be unconstitutional and illegal.
- Nevertheless, there is substantial public debate and uncertainty around whether Sections 1021 and 1022 of the NDAA could be read even to repeal the Posse Comitatus Act and authorize indefinite military detention without charge or trial within the United States.
- The law does not require even an allegation that a detained person caused any harm or threat of harm to the United States or to any U.S. interest. Mere allegation of membership in, or support of, an alleged terrorist group could be the basis for indefinite detention. Under the American justice system, we don't just lock people up indefinitely based on suspicion.
- More than ten years after the 9/11 attacks, with the United States withdrawing from Iraq and Afghanistan, the United States should not be asserting new worldwide authority for the military to imprison persons seized in any country.
- We have seen how disregard for the rule of law has disastrous results for America's standing in the world. It is time for a return to the rule of law. It is time to turn that page.

Judge Blocks Controversial NDAA

On May 16, 2012, Judge Katherine B. Forrest of the Southern District of New York blocked the Section 1021of National Defense Authorization Act (NDAA) that purported to "reaffirm" the 2001 authorization to use military force against Al Qaeda. A group of activists and journalists had argued that the vague wording of the law could subject them to indefinite military detention because their work brings them into contact with people whom the US considers to be terrorists, and in doing so violated their First Amendment rights.

Forrest agreed with the plaintiffs that the relevant section of the law was "not merely an 'affirmation'" of the 2001 authorization for use of military force (AUMF). "Basic principles of legislative interpretation," she wrote, "require Congressional enactments to be given independent meaning"—judges can't simply assume a law does nothing. None of this brings the war on terror to a halt, mind you, because Forrest says there are "a variety of other statutes which can be utilized to detain those engaged in various levels of support of terrorists," so her injunction "does not divest the Government of its many other tools."

Judge Forrest's decision, however, has to be read in the context of what happened in court: When Forrest asked the government lawyer charged with defending the statute whether the journalists, who said their work has brought them into contact with groups like Hamas or the Taliban, could be indefinitely detained, the government's lawyer wouldn't say:

JUDGE: Assume you were just an American citizen and you're reading the statute and you wanted to make sure you do not run afoul of it because you are a diligent U.S. citizen wanting to stay on the right side of [the law], and you read the phrase 'directly supported'. What does that mean to you?

GOVERNMENT: Again it has to be taken in the context of armed conflict informed by the laws of war.

JUDGE: That's fine. Tell me what that means?

GOVERNMENT: I cannot offer a specific example. I don't have a specific example.

When asked again whether one of the journalists' activities would qualify as "substantial" support for a terrorist group, the government attorney said, "I don't know what she has been up to."

Appendix VI: A decade of civil liberties erosion [322]

This ruling came as part of a lawsuit brought by seven dissident plaintiffs — including Chris Hedges, Dan Ellsberg, Noam Chomsky, and Birgitta Jonsdottir — alleging that the NDAA violates "both their free speech and associational rights guaranteed by the First Amendment as well as due process rights guaranteed by the Fifth Amendment of the United States Constitution."

The ruling was a sweeping victory for the plaintiffs, as it rejected each of the Obama DOJ's three arguments: **(1)** because none of the plaintiffs has yet been indefinitely detained, they lack "standing" to challenge the statute; **(2)** even if they have standing, the lack of imminent nforcement against them renders injunctive relief unnecessary; and **(3)** the NDAA creates no new detention powers beyond what the 2001 AUMF already provides.

Chris Hedges wrote: "It was a stunning and monumental victory. With her ruling she returned us to a country where—as it was before Obama signed this act into law Dec. 31—the government cannot strip a U.S. citizen of due process or use the military to arrest him or her and then hold him or her in military prison indefinitely. She categorically rejected the government's claims that the plaintiffs did not have the standing to bring the case to trial because none of us had been indefinitely detained, that lack of imminent enforcement against us meant there was no need for an injunction and that the NDAA simply codified what had previously been set down in the 2001 Authorization to Use Military Force Act."

Maybe the ruling won't last, Hedges said adding: "Maybe it will be overturned. But we and other Americans are freer today than we were a week ago. And there is something in this."

Weeks after Obama signed the law, Pulitzer Prize-winning journalist Chris Hedges filed a lawsuit against its so-called "Homeland Battlefield" provisions. Several prominent activists, scholars and politicians subsequently joined the suit, including Pentagon Papers whistle-blower Daniel Ellsberg; Massachusetts Institute of Technology professor Noam Chomsky; Icelandic parliamentarian Birgitta Jonsdottir; Kai Wargalla, an organizer from Occupy London; and Alexa O'Brien, an organizer for the New

Appendix VI: A decade of civil liberties erosion [323]

York-based activist group U.S. Day of Rage. They call themselves the Freedom Seven.

Criminalizing Whistleblowing

As Tom Burghardt, the San Francisco Bay Area-based activist reports [10]: The National Security State's assault on our right to privacy comes hard on the heels on moves in Congress, spearheaded by troglodytic Republicans (with "liberal" Democrats running a close second) to criminalize whistleblowing altogether.

In February 2011, the Muslim-hating Rep. Peter King (R-NY) introduced the SHIELD Act in the House, a pernicious piece of legislative flotsam that would amend the Espionage Act and make publishing classified information, and investigative journalism, a criminal offense.

Also in February, legislation was introduced in the Senate that "would broadly criminalize leaks of classified information," Secrecy News reported.

Sponsored by Senator Benjamin Cardin (D-MD), the bill (S. 355) "would make it a felony for a government employee or contractor who has authorized access to classified information to disclose such information to an unauthorized person in violation of his or her nondisclosure agreement," Secrecy News disclosed.

In an Orwellian twist, Cardin, who received some $385,000 in campaign swag from free speech advocates such as Constellation Energy, Goldman Sachs and Patton Boggs (Mubarak's chief lobbyist in Washington) according to OpenSecrets.org, said that the bill would "promote Federal whistleblower protection statutes and regulations"!

As *Secrecy News* points out, the bill "does not provide for a 'public interest' defense, i.e. an argument that any damage to national security was outweighed by a benefit to the nation." In other words, you don't need to know about government high crimes and misdemeanors. Why? *Because we say so.*

Appendix VI: A decade of civil liberties erosion [324]

In November 2010, shortly after WikiLeaks began publishing Cablegate files, King fired off a letter to Secretary of State Hillary Clinton and Attorney General Eric Holder demanding that WikiLeaks be declared a "foreign terrorist organization" and the group's founder declared a "terrorist ringleader." We know the fate reserved for "terrorists," don't we?

Obama Wants to Read Your Email [11]

The Obama U.S. Department of Justice (DoJ) also wants another new law too. This one would require Internet companies to retain data and records of user activity online. In doing so, the Obama administration is supporting measures advocated by the Bush administration that pose a grave threat to free speech and the freedom of the Internet. The sweeping legislation would cover cell phone service, Internet records, and email.

Data retention legislation would jeopardize the privacy of millions of Americans who use the Internet. The Electronic Frontier Foundation (EFF) notes, "A legal obligation to log users' Internet use, paired with weak federal privacy laws that allow the government to easily obtain those records, would dangerously expand the government's ability to surveil its citizens, damage privacy, and chill freedom of expression." Once again, congressional Republicans are more than happy to cooperate in passing such a dangerous law; anything to go after those awful terrorists — even if it shreds the U.S. Constitution.

Laptops Galore [12]

Although they can cite no legal basis for their high-handed actions, the U.S. Department of Homeland Security claims that its agents have the right to look though the contents of a international traveler's electronic devices, including laptops, cameras and cell phones, and to keep the devices or copy the contents in order to continue searching them once the traveler has been allowed to enter the U.S., regardless of whether the traveler is suspected of any wrongdoing.

Documents obtained by the ACLU in response to a Freedom of Information Act (FOIA) lawsuit for records related to the DHS policy reveal that more than 6,600 travelers, nearly half of whom are American citizens, were subjected to electronic device searches at the border between October 1, 2008 and June 2, 2010.

No law authorizes this power nor is there any judicial or congressional body overseeing or regulating what DHS is doing. And the citizens to whom this is done have no recourse — not even to have their property returned to them.

FBI agents encouraged to search your trash, public databases just to sniff around for crime

The Federal Bureau of Investigation plans to issue new rules for its agents saying, essentially, that they can and should dig through our trash and search databases if people who aren't suspects but who are simply being assessed or looked at. The new FBI trash-digging policy will be a part of the agency's updated Domestic Investigations and Operations Guide, a source tells the New York Times. The changes apply not to criminal investigations but, apparently, to agents' ability simply to sniff around "proactively," according to the Times. The paper states that some agents wanted the trash-sifting powers so they could use evidence found among refuse to pressure people to snitch on others.

The F.B.I. recently briefed several privacy advocates about the coming changes. Among them, Michael German, a former F.B.I. agent who is now a lawyer for the American Civil Liberties Union, argued that it was unwise to further ease restrictions on agents' power to use potentially intrusive techniques, especially if they lacked a firm reason to suspect someone of wrongdoing. "Claiming additional authorities to investigate people only further raises the potential for abuse," Mr. German said, pointing to complaints about the bureau's surveillance of domestic political advocacy groups and mosques and to an inspector general's findings in 2007 that the F.B.I. had frequently misused "national security letters," which allow agents to obtain information like phone records without a court order. [13]

Some of the most notable changes apply to the lowest category of investigations, called an "assessment." The category, created in December 2008, allows agents to look into people and organizations "proactively" and without firm evidence for suspecting criminal or terrorist activity. Under

Appendix VI: A decade of civil liberties erosion [326]

current rules, agents must open such an inquiry before they can search for information about a person in a commercial or law enforcement database. Under the new rules, agents will be allowed to search such databases without making a record about their decision. Mr. German said the change would make it harder to detect and deter inappropriate use of databases for personal purposes. [14]

The new rules will also relax a restriction on administering lie-detector tests and searching people's trash. Under current rules, agents cannot use such techniques until they open a "preliminary investigation," which — unlike an assessment — requires a factual basis for suspecting someone of wrongdoing. But soon agents will be allowed to use those techniques for one kind of assessment, too: when they are evaluating a target as a potential informant. Agents have asked for that power in part because they want the ability to use information found in a subject's trash to put pressure on that person to assist the government in the investigation of others. [15]

Freedom of Speech Curbs [16]

As Geoffrey R. Stone, a professor of law at the University of Chicago and the chairman of the board of the American Constitution Society, wrote in the New York Times on January 3, 2011:

The so-called Shield bill, now introduced in both houses of Congress in response to the WikiLeaks disclosures, would amend the Espionage Act of 1917 to make it a crime for any person knowingly and willfully to disseminate, "in any manner prejudicial to the safety or interest of the United States," any classified information "concerning the human intelligence activities of the United States."

Although this proposed law may be constitutional as applied to government employees who unlawfully leak such material to people who are unauthorized to receive it, it would plainly violate the First Amendment to punish anyone who might publish or otherwise circulate the information after it has been leaked. At the very least, the act should be expressly limited to situations in which the spread of the classified information poses a clear and imminent danger of grave harm to the nation.

And finally, a central principle of the First Amendment is that the suppression of free speech must be the government's last rather than its first resort in addressing a problem. The most obvious way for the government to prevent the danger posed by the circulation of classified material is by ensuring that information that must be kept secret is not leaked in the first place.

If we grant the government too much power to punish those who disseminate information, then we risk too great a sacrifice of public deliberation; if we grant the government too little power to control confidentiality at the source, then we risk too great a sacrifice of secrecy. The answer is thus to reconcile the irreconcilable values of secrecy and accountability by guaranteeing *both* a strong authority of the government to prohibit leaks *and* an expansive right of others to disseminate information to the public.

Criminalizing peacemaking

In June 2010, the Supreme Court exposed Americans to jail sentences of up to 15 years just for giving advice to groups the U.S. government considers untouchable. In the course of arguing the Holder v Humanitarian Law Project case in the Supreme Court, Georgetown Law Professor David Cole warned that the federal law against providing "material support" to U.S.-designated terrorist groups could be used to improperly target and prosecute a whole range of humanitarian, human rights and peace advocacy groups based on protected exercise of speech and other First Amendment rights.

The Patriot Act has broadened the "material support" concept to encompass "expert advice and assistance" to "foreign terrorist organizations" as designated by the Secretary of State. As journalist Courtney Martin noted, "The definition of material support includes everything from providing aid to distributing literature to political advocacy."

Appendix VI: A decade of civil liberties erosion [328]

During arguments in February 2010, Solicitor General Elena Kagan, defended the law and urged a broad interpretation that would allow prosecution of a U.S. citizen who filed a legal brief on behalf of a terrorist organization. "What Congress decided," Kagan told the court, "is that when you help Hezbollah build homes, you are also helping Hezbollah build bombs."

In Holder v. Humanitarian Law Project, the court ruled that the USA Patriot Act's expanded definition of "material support" for "foreign terrorist organizations" passes Constitutional muster. The broad wording of the statute not only makes it a crime to support violent activities, but also prohibits Americans from offering "services" or "training, expert advice or assistance" to any entity designated as a terrorist group.

In a 6-3 opinion written by Chief Justice John G. Roberts Jr., the court essentially dismissed a challenge to the material support law brought by the Humanitarian Law Project. The project wanted to advise the Kurdistan Workers' Party (PKK) -- which for years has been on the U.S. terrorist list -- on filing human rights complaints with the United Nations and conducting peace negotiations with the Turkish government.

Justice Breyer, who was joined in dissent by Justices Ruth Bader Ginsburg and Sonia Sotomayor, proposed a narrower interpretation of the material support law: Individuals should not be subject to prosecution unless they knowingly provided a service they had reason to believe would be used to further violence.

The Supreme Court decision essentially makes advocacy of peace and humanitarian issues illegal with respect to the 40 or so designated groups. To borrow Joshua Holland, the material support law essentially criminalizes promoting dialogue in conflict zones and undermines efforts to provide nonviolent solutions to previously violent groups, equating such actions with trafficking weapons.

All kinds of missionaries, fair-election proponents and humanitarian workers could be placed in jeopardy. People like Three Cups of Tea author Greg Mortenson could be in trouble since he has had to meet with a variety of

Appendix VI: A decade of civil liberties erosion [329]

foreign country nationals in war zones to successfully formulate consensus to build schools for girls in Pakistan and Afghanistan. So could former President Jimmy Carter who engages in pro-democracy efforts to monitor election fraud in many places in the world.

Civil liberties advocates said they also feared repercussions for U.S.-based critics of the Israeli government, who might be charged with aiding Hamas, which Washington has designated as a terrorist group. One such critic is former President Jimmy Carter, whose private Mideast diplomatic efforts have included contact with Hamas.

The ruling "threatens our work and the work of many other peacemaking organizations that must interact directly with groups that have engaged in violence," said Carter, whose organization filed arguments with the court.

Since 2001, Islamic charities have struggled to deal with the uncertainty caused by the material support provision. According to the Bill of Rights Defense Committee, "Muslims fulfilling their obligation to contribute to [charity]…risk inadvertently supporting a current or future [Foreign Terrorist Organization]. In 2004, in order to avoid this, Muslim leaders asked the DOJ for a list of acceptable charities. The DOJ responded that their request was 'impossible to fulfill' and that it was 'not in a position to put out lists of any kind, particularly of any organizations that are good or bad.'" Several people have already been jailed in the United States for their charitable activities in the Islamic world. [17]

FBI now investigating domestic peace activists

In the early morning of Sept. 24, 2010, the FBI agents raided homes of peace activists in Chicago and Minneapolis, issued subpoenas to 14 activists, and tried to question others around the country, including prominent antiwar organizers in North Carolina and California.

Appendix VI: A decade of civil liberties erosion [330]

The raids were conducted under the pretext of investigating potential "material support" and "terrorism" charges. The targeted individuals included leaders of the Arab American Action Network, the Colombia Action Network, and the Twin-Cities Anti-War Committee. The FBI has said no arrests have been made, and there was there no "imminent danger" to the public. Instead it has claimed it is currently looking for evidence in an ongoing investigation for possible "material support" for terrorism.

Authorities haven't revealed the targets of the investigation or its exact nature, other than to say it involves activities concerning the material support of terrorism. However, The FBI documents were found on April 30 at the Minneapolis home of longtime anti-war activist Mick Kelly whose home was among those raided by the FBI in September. Huffington Post quoted the FBI spokesman Steve Warfield as saying that most of the papers appeared to be legitimate FBI documents and were left behind by mistake.

The documents, which are not labeled as classified, suggest that activists' involvement with people in Colombia sparked the investigation.

"The captioned case was initially predicated on the activities of Meredith Aby and Jessica Rae Sundin in support of the Revolutionary Armed Forces of Colombia (FARC), a U.S. State Department designated foreign terrorist organization (FTO), to include their previous travel to FARC-controlled territory," one document says. "Since opening the original investigations, an additional 16 Subjects in six FBI Field Divisions have been identified."

The document goes on to say that people in the Minneapolis, Chicago, Phoenix, Detroit, Los Angeles and Charlotte, N.C., divisions have "provided and/or conspired to provide material support to the FARC and/or the Popular Front for the Liberation of Palestine, also a U.S. State Department designated FTO."

The documents given to the AP also include a strategic plan for the FBI's raid, a subpoena, and a list of questions that agents would presumably use in an interview. The subpoena, which was made public previously, orders Kelly to appear before a grand jury and bring information relating to any trips to Colombia, the Palestinian territories, Jordan, Syria or Israel. It also commands him to bring records relating to the Middle East and Colombia.

Appendix VI: A decade of civil liberties erosion [331]

The documents include a list of over 100 questions. The top of the list says the questions "pertain to a terrorism investigation." Many deal with activities of the Freedom Road Socialist Organization, to which Kelly and Sundin both belong.

Former Reagan official Paul Craig Roberts believes that the US government by raiding the homes of anti-war activists is establishing in the mind of the public that anyone who criticizes the War on Terror is aligned with terrorists. He further argues that under the rubric of terror the government has stripped Americans of their civil liberties.

To borrow Kristen Boyd Johnson, there are two sides of the terror coin, after all: the people who want to kill you and the people who dislike the United States being at war all the time. Keep tabs on them both. Hell, just keep tabs on everyone. Everyone is now a terrorist.

NATO protesters in Chicago held on terrorism charges

On May 16, 2012, three young men, arrested for protesting against NATO summit in Chicago, were charged on terrorism-related offences. Police claimed that the charges of conspiracy to commit terrorism, providing material support for terrorism and possession of an explosive or incendiary device, are the result of a month-long investigation into a group they believe was making Molotov cocktails. Attorneys representing the men say the charges are fabricated and aimed at intimidating activists. Sarah Gelsomino of the Peoples Law Office said: "Clearly in an attempt to continue this intimidation campaign on activists. Charging these people who are here to peacefully protest against Nato for terrorism, when in reality the police have been terrorizing activists in Chicago, is absolutely outrageous." **[The Guardian - May 18, 2012]**

Dave Lindorff, an investigative reporter and Counter Punch writer, wrote: "It seems pretty clear by now that the three young "domestic terrorists" arrested by Chicago police in a warrantless house invasion reminiscent of what US military forces are doing on a daily basis in Afghanistan, are the victims of planted evidence -- part of the police-state-style crackdown on anti-NATO protesters in Chicago last week."

Appendix VI: A decade of civil liberties erosion [332]

Writing under the title, Planting evidence to sow fear, Lindorff said: "The Chicago Police clearly realized that it would be hard to convince a jury that the homemade beer-making equipment in the house was some dreaded bio-terror weapon, so for good measure they apparently dropped off some glass jars with gas in them and tried to make out that the kids were preparing molotov cocktails. That's the word from National Lawyers Guild attorneys representing the men. They say their clients and others like them coming into Chicago from out of town to join in protests against the NATO summit were "befriended" by police informants and undercover Chicago Police, who then offered to obtain gasoline or explosive materials like toy rocket motors, and who proposed actions like firebombing police stations."

Lindorff warned that this kind of entrapment and official deceit by police should alarm every American. "It's bad enough when police plant evidence and lie about evidence in order to win convictions, since it means innocent people will be sent to prison or worse. But with the new post 9-11 terrorism laws, like the state terrorism statutes in Illinois being applied in these cases, it becomes far more difficult for a victim of such police and prosecutorial misconduct to challenge the case against her or him. In terror cases, the government can claim "national security" to hide the evidence and even the identity of the witnesses from the defendants and the courts, the jury and the public, and can avoid ever being questioned about it publicly. In a worst case, the federal government doesn't even need to bring the case to trial. If the victim is accused of being a terrorist, under the latest National Defense Authorization Act (NDAA) and various executive orders, that person can be locked away indefinitely without trial -- exactly the kind of abuse that led American colonists to rise up against their British colonial overlords 237 years ago." [**Information Clearing House – May 24, 2012**]

Top Secret America

On July 19, 2010, the Washington Post published the first installment of its Top Secret America project, a two-year investigation into the national

Appendix VI: A decade of civil liberties erosion [333]

security buildup in the United States that followed the Sept. 11, 2001, terrorist attacks.

"The top-secret world the government created in response to the terrorist attacks of Sept. 11, 2001, has become so large, so unwieldy and so secretive that no one knows how much money it costs, how many people it employs, how many programs exist within it or exactly how many agencies do the same work" the Post's Dana Priest and William Arkin write. "After nine years of unprecedented spending and growth, the result is that the system put in place to keep the United States safe is so massive that its effectiveness is impossible to determine."

Here are just a few of the investigation's findings included in the online report:

* "Some 1,271 government organizations and 1,931 private companies work on programs related to counterterrorism, homeland security and intelligence in about 10,000 locations across the United States."

* "An estimated 854,000 people, nearly 1.5 times as many people as live in Washington, D.C., hold top-secret security clearances."

* "In Washington and the surrounding area, 33 building complexes for top-secret intelligence work are under construction or have been built since September 2001. Together they occupy the equivalent of almost three Pentagons or 22 U.S. Capitol buildings — about 17 million square feet of space."

Moreover, the Post writes, "51 federal organizations and military commands, operating in 15 U.S. cities, track the flow of money to and from terrorist networks," and "Analysts who make sense of documents and conversations obtained by foreign and domestic spying share their judgment by publishing 50,000 intelligence reports each year — a volume so large that many are routinely ignored." Since 9/11 no fewer than 263 intelligence and counterterrorism organizations have been "created or reorganized."

The Violent Radicalization and Homegrown Terrorism Prevention Act 2007

Appendix VI: A decade of civil liberties erosion [334]

Perhaps more disturbing still is "The Violent Radicalization and Homegrown Terrorism Prevention Act of 2007" (read Thought Control Act). The bill was passed on Oct 23, 2007 by a margin of 404-6 where as the Senate version of the bill is still awaiting action.

Under cover of studying "violent radicalization," the bill would broaden the already-fluid definition of "terrorism" to encompass political activity and protest by dissident groups, effectively criminalizing civil disobedience and non-violent direct action by developing policies for "prevention, disruption and mitigation."

Despite the fact that the legislation has not been signed into law, the Department of Homeland Security is moving towards implementing a provision of the Violent Radicalization and Homegrown Terrorism Prevention Act of 2007. One of the bill's provisions gives the Department of Homeland Security the authority to fund a University based Center of Excellence to study ways to thwart what the government believes are extremist belief systems and radical ideologies of individual Americans.

The "Violent Radicalization and Homegrown Terrorism Prevention Act of 2007" creates a ten member new commission which will study how to prohibit ". . . . .the process of adopting or promoting an extremist belief system . . . . .to advance political, religious, or social change.. . . ." Spreading these beliefs to "advance political, religious, or social change" is defined as "radicalization." If you are trying to educate your fellow countrymen, to democratically influence popular opinion, then you may find yourself accused of "facilitating ideologically-based violence."

It also establishes a Center of Excellence for the Prevention of Radicalization and Home Grown Terrorism that will study the social, criminal, political, psychological and economic roots of the problem to provide further suggestions for action to address these dangers.

The DHS is already funding a Center of Excellence to study thought criminals in the United States at the University of Maryland.

Under cover of studying "violent radicalization," both bills would broaden the already-fluid definition of "terrorism" to encompass political activity and

Appendix VI: A decade of civil liberties erosion [335]

protest by dissident groups, effectively criminalizing civil disobedience and non-violent direct action by developing policies for "prevention, disruption and mitigation," Tom Burghardt argues and calls it COINTELPRO 2.0.

The bill's language hides its true intent

The bill's vague and open-ended language hides its true intent as to what "violent radicalization" and "homegrown terrorism" are? It will be whatever the administration says they are. Violent radicalization is defined as "adopting or promoting an extremist belief system (to facilitate) ideologically based violence to advance political, religious or social change." [18]

Homegrown terrorism is used to mean "the use, planned use, or threatened use, of force or violence by a group or individual born, raised, or based and operating primarily with the United States or any (US) possession to intimidate or coerce the (US) government, the civilian population....or any segment thereof (to further) political or social objectives." [19]

Along with other repressive laws enacted after 9/11, the new law may be used against any individual or group with unpopular views - those that differ from established state policies. Prosecutors henceforth will be able to target believers in Islam, anti-war protesters, web editors, internet bloggers and radio and TV show hosts and commentators with views the bill calls "terrorist-related propaganda." [20]

Many observers fear that the proposed law will be used against U.S.-based groups engaged in legal but unpopular political activism, ranging from political Islamists to animal-rights and environmental campaigners to radical right-wing organizations. There is concern, too, that the bill will undermine academic integrity and is the latest salvo in a decade-long government grab for power at the expense of civil liberties. [21]

American Muslims alarmed at CIA-NYPD covert surveillance

The seven-million strong Muslim American community was alarmed at the revelation that the New York City Police Department have carried out covert surveillance on Muslims with the help of the CIA. An Associated Press (AP)

Appendix VI: A decade of civil liberties erosion [336]

report recently published by the Washington Post [22] exposed the NYPD spy program, which is allegedly being conducted with the assistance of individuals linked to the CIA.

Following a month-long investigation, the AP reported that the NYPD is using covert surveillance techniques "that would run afoul of civil liberties rules if practiced by the federal government" and "does so with unprecedented help from the CIA in a partnership that has blurred the bright line between foreign and domestic spying."

The AP report follows a recent Mother Jones [23] revelation that after years of emphasizing informant recruiting as a key task for its agents, the FBI now maintains a roster of 15,000 spies — many of them tasked with infiltrating Muslim communities in the United States. "In addition, for every informant officially listed in the bureau's records, there are as many as three unofficial ones, according to one former high-level FBI official, known in bureau parlance as "hip pockets."

The informants could be doctors, clerks, imams. Some might not even consider themselves informants. But the FBI regularly taps all of them as part of a domestic intelligence apparatus whose only historical peer might be COINTELPRO, the program the bureau ran from the '50s to the '70s to discredit and marginalize organizations ranging from the Ku Klux Klan to civil-rights and protest groups."

The AP investigative report revealed that the NYDP has dispatched teams of undercover officers, known as 'rakers,' into minority neighborhoods as part of a human mapping program. The report said: The NYDP have monitored daily life in bookstores, bars, cafes and nightclubs. Police have also used informants, known as 'mosque crawlers,' to monitor sermons, even when there's no evidence of wrongdoing.

The NYPD officials have scrutinized imams and gathered intelligence on cab drivers and food cart vendors, jobs often done by Muslims. Many of these operations were built with help from the CIA, which is prohibited from spying on Americans but was instrumental in transforming the NYPD's intelligence unit, the AP report added.

Indiana Supreme Court rules against Fourth Amendment

Indiana's highest court has turned against our rights and the Constitution of the United States. The Supreme Court of Indiana decided on May 12, 2010 that the Fourth Amendment of the U.S. Constitution does not apply to the citizens of Indiana.

The Fourth Amendment to the United States Constitution, vacated by the Indiana Supreme Court, says: The right of the people to be secure in their persons, houses, papers, and effects, against unreasonable searches and seizures, shall not be violated, and no Warrants shall issue, but upon probable cause, supported by Oath or affirmation, and particularly describing the place to be searched, and the persons or things to be seized.

The Indiana Supreme Court, in a 3-2 decision, ruled that cops can force their way into your home without a search warrant. Overturning a common law dating back to the English Magna Carta of 1215, the Indiana Supreme Court ruled that Hoosiers have no right to resist unlawful police entry into their homes.

Justice Steven David writing for the court said if a police officer wants to enter a home for any reason or no reason at all; a homeowner cannot do anything to block the officer's entry.

The court's decision stems from a Vanderburgh County case in which police were called to investigate a husband and wife arguing outside their apartment. When the couple went back inside their apartment, the husband told police they were not needed and blocked the doorway so they could not enter. When an officer entered anyway, the husband shoved the officer against a wall. A second officer then used a stun gun on the husband and arrested him.

Disastrous fallout of the ruling: Radio host Mike Church has reported on his website that Newton County Sheriff Department head, Don Hartman Sr., contends the ruling means that random house to house searches are

Appendix VI: A decade of civil liberties erosion [338]

now possible. "According to Newton County Sheriff, Don Hartman Sr., random house to house searches are now possible and could be helpful following the Barnes v. STATE of INDIANA Supreme Court ruling issued on May 12th, 2011. When asked three separate times due to the astounding callousness as it relates to trampling the inherent natural rights of Americans, he emphatically indicated that he would use random house to house checks, adding he felt people will welcome random searches if it means capturing a criminal."

In other words, the Fourth Amendment is dead, at least for the time being, in Indiana – and at least one "law officer" is ready to start searching houses at random. All he needs now is an excuse.

At the original trial, Barnes wanted the jury to be apprised of the Fourth Amendment's limitations on police conduct regarding unlawful entry into his home. His tender instructions to the jury: "When an arrest is attempted by means of a forceful and unlawful entry into a citizen's home, such entry represents the use of excessive force, and the arrest cannot be considered peaceable. Therefore, a citizen has the right to reasonably resist the unlawful entry." The court refused to allow the reading, and Barnes was convicted of battery on a police officer, resisting law enforcement, and disorderly conduct.

Justice Robert Rucker and Justice Brent Dickson, dissented from the ruling, saying the court's decision runs afoul of the Fourth Amendment of the U.S. Constitution." In my view the majority sweeps with far too broad a brush by essentially telling Indiana citizens that government agents may now enter their homes illegally — that is, without the necessity of a warrant, consent or exigent circumstances," Rucker said. "I disagree."

Conclusion: Defending Our Civil Liberties

Rights can never be taken for granted, Prof. Gary Orfield [24] argues by adding: In a nation that rightly proclaims its commitment to freedom across the world, our freedoms at home are our most precious asset and any threat to them undermines our credibility everywhere in an age of instant global communication. Prof. Orfield

Appendix VI: A decade of civil liberties erosion [339]

reminds us that the history of the United States is that rights are not given, they are won and they must always be defended.

The core challenge during the Obama era to civil liberties is to rollback the repressive policies of the Bush regime, while fighting any further erosion of constitutional rights. Many Americans resisted the attacks on civil liberties during the Bush administration. Over 400 local governments and several states passed resolutions supporting the Bill of Rights and objecting to parts of the Patriot Act and other post-9/11 laws, executive orders, and policy changes. Some cities passed ordinances directing police to facilitate, not impede, peaceful demonstrations.

Attacks on civil liberties are not minor infringements on the rights of a few extremists. Today they affect a vast cross-section of Americans. It will not be too much to say that the chilling effect of denials of our democratic freedoms curtails political debate within the U.S.

To borrow Paul Craig Roberts, an Assistant Secretary of the Treasury in the Reagan Administration, [25] today Americans are unsafe, not because of terrorists and domestic extremists, but because they have lost their civil liberties and have no protection from unaccountable government power. One would think that how this came about would be worthy of public debate and congressional hearings.

References

[1] One Nation Indivisible, under God, with Liberty and Justice for All: Civil Rights for Arabs, Muslims, and South Asians by Prof. Gary Orfield - May 2003

[2] New target of rights erosions: U.S. citizens By Glenn Greenwald - May 13, 2010]

[3] Ibid.

[4] [Top Ten Abuses of Power Since 9/11 [http://www.aclu.org/keep-america-safe-free/top-ten-abuses-power-911]]

[5] Civil Liberties in Obama's America by Anthony Gregory - March 20, 2010.

[6] Ibid.

Appendix VI: A decade of civil liberties erosion [340]

[7] Ibid.

[8] Ibid.

[9] Ibid.

[10] The Obama Administration's War on Civil Liberties by Tom Burghardt - Feb 21, 2011

[11] Civil Liberties We Are a Police State Bob Bauman - March 23, 2011

[12] Ibid.

[13] F.B.I. agents get leeway to push privacy bounds, New York Times – June 12, 2011]

[14] Ibid.

[15] Ibid.

[16] New York Times - January 3, 2011

[17] How Easy Is It for Peaceful People to Violate the Patriot Act? By Joshua Holland

[18] American Muslim Perspective
http://www.ghazali.net/archives2007/html/radicalization_act.html

[19] Ibid.

[20] Ibid.

[21] Is America Already a Police State? by Nathan Coe - March 20, 2009

[22] With CIA help, NYPD built secret effort to monitor mosques, daily life of Muslim neighborhoods by Matt Apuzzo and Adam Goldman - Washington Post – August 24, 2011

[23] The Informants by Trevor Aaronson – Mother Jones - September/October 2011 Issue

[24] Prof. Gary Orfield, Op. cit.

[25] 9/11 After A Decade: Have We Learned Anything?   By Global Research -- August 24, 2011

Appendix VI: A decade of civil liberties erosion [341]

www.ingramcontent.com/pod-product-compliance
Lightning Source LLC
Chambersburg PA
CBHW071300110426
42743CB00042B/1120